T0325070

HUMAN MEMORY
MODELED WITH STANDARD
ANALOG AND DIGITAL CIRCUITS

HUMAN MEMORY MODELED WITH STANDARD ANALOG AND DIGITAL CIRCUITS
Inspiration for Man-made Computers

JOHN ROBERT BURGER

WILEY

A JOHN WILEY & SONS, INC., PUBLICATION

For general information on our other products and services or for technical support, please contact our Customer Care Department within the United States at 877-762-2974, outside the United States at 317-572-3993 or fax 317-572-4002.

Wiley also publishes its books in a variety of electronic formats. Some content that appears in print may not be available in electronic formats. For more information about Wiley products, visit our web site at www.wiley.com.

Library of Congress Cataloging-in-Publication Data:

Burger, John Robert, 1940-
  Human memory modeled with standard analog and digital circuits: inspiration for man-made computers / John Robert Burger.
      p. cm.
  Includes index.
  ISBN 978-0-470-42435-3 (cloth)
  1. Memory–Computer simulation. 2. Artificial intelligence. I. Title.
  QP406. B87 2009
  612.8′23312–dc22

                                        2008047051

Printed in the United States of America

10 9 8 7 6 5 4 3 2 1

This book is dedicated to my children, Terry and Heather

The author thanks his lovely spouse, Leone Lucille Burger,
for her helpful encouragement

CONTENTS

PREFACE

The models created for this book introduce human memory and basic cognition in logical terms. These models use standard analog and digital circuits, which in contrast to models that include nonphysical components, may be applied directly to the goal of constructing a machine with artificial intelligence: ultimately, a self-contained robot with the ability to learn. Writing from a circuits and systems perspective, the book extends across specialized disciplines, including neuroscience, psychology, and physics, to achieve uncommon breadth and generally valuable models.

The book is a valuable reference for those who need to know about the logic of human memory and for computer scientists and engineers interested in artificial intelligence and cognitive machines. Students everywhere are encouraged to read this book for their own general education and because someday they may be called upon to apply the futuristic concepts expressed in this book. When time is short, it is possible to take a shortcut through the book as mapped by the solid-line path in Figure P-1. The material skipped ought, of course, to be read at a later date. After the motivating introduction in Chapter 1, a busy reader may wish to go directly to neural memory toward the end of Chapter 3. Chapter 4 is interesting and worth studying, especially the system diagram for human memory and cognition.

In Chapter 5 we explain neurons as logic devices and propose a model for all-digital learning, a topic of immense importance. Chapter 6 is optional, since artificial neurons differ significantly from biological neurons. In Chapter 7 we introduce an important topic, energy per bit of information and the need for reversible logic. The first half of Chapter 8 is intended primarily for electrical engineers who might someday accomplish adiabatic circuit design, but the

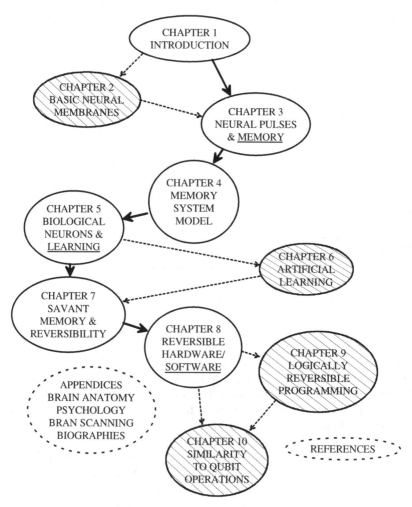

FIGURE P-1 Chapter flowchart.

second half of Chapter 8, on reversible addition and subtraction, may benefit everyone. Chapters 9 and 10 contain extra material on reversible programming for those with a real interest in electrically and logically reversible systems.

Optional uses for the book include teaching logically reversible computers, as presented in Chapters 4, 7, 8, and 9, with Chapter 10 optional. Readers with narrow interests in the design of integrated circuits might focus on Chapters 4, 5, 7, and 8. Those with interests chiefly in biology or general neuroscience might focus on the logical neuron as presented in Chapters 2, 3, 4, and 5. The exercises at the end of chapters vary considerably in difficulty, so it is recommended that only two or three of the easiest ones be formally assigned to undergraduates at a given time. Others may be reserved for extra credit.

Finally, readers are encouraged to realize that modeling is neither research nor a quest for new knowledge. Modeling applies old knowledge in a creative process to synthesize a circuit or system that is capable of simulating such knowledge. Basic knowledge comes partly from the list of further reading at the end of the book, and chiefly from various scientists, mostly deceased now, but mentioned throughout. Partly to honor them, but mainly to enlighten students about the trials and tribulations of the past, short biographies of a few workers important to this book are provided as an appendix. There are also appendixes on human brain anatomy, the psychology of memory, and brain scanning.

Many thanks to Barbara Gleason (BGleason Design & Illustration, Eugene, Oregon) for the drawings of biological objects in this text. Special thanks to Leone Burger for compiling data for the biographies of Appendix D.

JOHN ROBERT BURGER

CHAPTER 1

BRAIN BEHAVIOR POINTS THE WAY

INTRODUCTION

The mysterious brain, underneath its understated facade, is just another computer, only with unimaginable parallelism and efficiency. It is a memory-based associative computer that works not with addresses, such as street numbers, but with features such as shape and shade. The end result is a sequence of mental pictures to light our way through life.

This book takes a fresh new look at artificial intelligence from the perspective of modeling human memory as a system, an all-digital system based on current knowledge about memory and cognition. At the bottom, neurons and their membranes are modeled with analog circuits to create arbitrary Boolean logic. At the top, memory system operations, including memorization, memory search, cognition, and learning, are modeled using digital circuits. The process of modeling is grounded in basic physics as expressed using standard analog and digital circuits. Standard analog and digital circuits offer a special advantage over the more abstract forms of modeling. Circuits may be integrated into silicon or simulated in software for systems that require some degree of artificial intelligence. Equally significant, brain models are a wellspring for new ideas and inventions.

For example, presented later in this book is a novel computer taken from brain memory models. As in neural circuits, signals switch in the kilohertz

Human Memory Modeled with Standard Analog and Digital Circuits:
Inspiration for Man-made Computers, By John Robert Burger
Copyright © 2009 John Wiley & Sons, Inc.

range, which is relatively slow, but logic is massively parallel, and therefore the end result is actually more efficient than a modern dissipative machine. Once started, the logic requires practically no power, a feature suggested by the neural models in this book, and hence this novel design may rightly be claimed to be an adiabatic computer. An adiabatic computer is one whose heat dissipation approaches zero while executing programs, permitting a package smaller than would otherwise be possible.

It is hoped that this book will inspire applications, not just in computer design, but in related fields such as medicine, logic devices, robotics, artificial intelligence, neuroscience, and last but not least, education. Modeling is important to any science, but it is especially important to neuroscience, because these areas have a vast and exponentially growing quantity of data, the taking of which has immeasurably outpaced the development of models to explain and digest this explosion of information. Without adequate models, scientific progress would be difficult to impossible.

MODELING

It is amazing to realize that the performance of integrated circuits continues to increase exponentially, seemingly without bound. For example, the capacity of memory chips continues to double approximately every two years, thanks to the focused work of thousands of dedicated but nameless engineers and technicians. These people are involved in technology, which is really quite different from science. The two should never be confused. *Science* creates models in an attempt to understand nature; *technology* creates practical inventions to make life easier.

Simple accurate models are an indication of scientific maturity. For example, physics has a quantum model to explain observed behavior of particles. Unfortunately, this model is more mathematical than physical, but it accurately explains physical data. In the words of Werner Heisenberg (1901–1976), a founder of quantum mechanics, "the laws of nature which we formulate mathematically in quantum theory deal no longer with the particles themselves but with our knowledge of elementary particles."

Electrical science has James Clerk Maxwell (1831–1879), whose equations predict the behavior of electrical signals conducted through wires and radiated through space. It is perhaps obvious that electromagnetic waves are incorporeal, although they interact with matter in familiar ways. In modern physics, when describing waves and particles it may be concluded that for the most part, only the model is tangible; what is being modeled is not. Waves and particles, of course, make up everything that is possible in the physical world.

In the words of Herbert Alexander Simon (1916–2001), computer science is a science of the "artificial," that is, machines designed by engineers. Engineered computers are much simpler than brains evolved in nature. Modeling as pursued in this book is an attempt to create an emergent model of an evolved biological system that is concealed, well protected, and pretty much impenetrable. As long as human knowledge is finite no model in any field should be taken as a final measure of absolute truth. An important goal in working with all scientific models is that they may be changed and upgraded.

Modeling Goals of the Past

Models with standard analog and digital circuits have an advantage: They translate readily into engineering practice. In contrast, fashionable brain models usually do not have engineering practice as a goal. Consider three historical goals:

1. To study the sensitivities of a particular neural network to its parameters. For example, the output of a small rhythmic circuit in response to the timing of synaptic signals: Understanding can be increased this way, which in itself is considered worthwhile.
2. To discover some yet unknown relationship between a neural structure and its function. For example, why does the cerebral cortex have exactly six layers of neural gray matter? Modeling and simulation might reveal an answer to this question.
3. To discover which direction experimental investigation ought to take. Quite often, neural data are incomplete or nonexistent. For example, when a person makes a decision, there is some evidence that the brain makes the decision before the person is aware of the decision. Could it be that the brain tells you what to do, and not the other way around? This might be an interesting area of research.

Molecular biologists have strived to model neural systems molecule by molecule in what might be termed *bottom-up modeling*. Unfortunately, molecular models are very far removed from a brain system. Results can be pointless when building from the bottom up, with no master plan. Complex systems, both biological and artificial, necessitate not only bottom-up but also top-down modeling. *Top-down modeling* strives to synthesize known behaviors into a model, one that supports, or at least does not contradict, what we think we know.

Like computer systems, human memory systems necessitate both bottom-up and top-down modeling; standard analog and digital elements are an excellent choice for human memory. In this type of modeling it is useful to employ analog circuits to model the behavior of neurons, and digital circuits to model memory systems and cognition. Higher-level blocks in this text, in contrast to alternative models, are intended ideally to represent a particular interconnection of neurons, not just a floating abstraction defined by tables and calculus.

Brain modeling often involves higher levels of abstraction as supported by such simulators as the Genesis neural simulator and by the publicly available Neural Simulation Language. Unfortunately, as higher functions are modeled, the block properties of the components used in the simulation can depart from reality. For example, a block labeled "amygdala" might have no realistic structure at all, having instead a set of equations with no physical basis. On the other hand, if a "realistic" model based on individual molecules and ion channels is employed, computational complexity increases beyond reason, if not today's technology. Modeling like this is opposite the positive philosophy pursued herein: to illuminate a topic, not obscure it.

Standard circuit elements were never intended for modeling the paths of individual ions or electrons. An individual neuron can be modeled quite satisfactorily by assigning collective properties to electrical flow: for example, average current per unit time through a cross section of area. Whenever possible in this book, electrical models are derived from physical models. A simplified physical model, for example, may involve the average properties of thermally excited particles at temperatures known to exist biologically.

All models are, of course, based on a given body of knowledge. This implies that some information is excluded either deliberately or unintentionally. For example, the stochastic properties of ion channels are excluded as not being particularly useful in the model of a system. Modeling in this book is based primarily on the knowledge expressed in the appendixes and in the publications recommended for further study.

Uses of Models

Models involving circuits can be employed to reach historical goals, but models do more than this: They affect thinking. For example, it has been proposed that explicit long-term memory within the brain depends on synaptic growth. The problem is that growth takes time, whereas explicit long-term memories form rapidly, practically instantly, as can be demonstrated by those gifted with photographic memory. This fact brings the synaptic growth model into question, because it does not agree with what is seen in special cases.

In this book we present a model of long-term memory that does not require biological growth. Under this model, impressions may be captured by neural latches. Neural latches are not an enhanced form of short-term memory that eventually "time" out, but are completely different, latching instantly and holding indefinitely.

As another instance of models affecting thinking, it has been proposed that an action potential for cognition is coded not as a single bit, but with additional information. But a single bit from a single axon is sufficient for memory system logic, as demonstrated herein. So whatever burst duration, frequency, and amplitude may mean, they are not really needed for brain logic.

Natural philosophers, including Socrates (470–399 B.C.) have suggested that nature acts by the most economical means. Maupertuis (1698–1759) garnered attention with his *principle of least action* by observing that "Nature is thrifty in all its actions." This principle is apt for evolved systems, including neurons and brains. Under this principle, from the point of view of efficiency some models are better than others.

Relating to the synaptic growth model is the *one-neuron model*, in which a single large neuron is proposed to hold a given long-term memory. The problem is that no efficient circuit exists to send the contents of a single neuron into conscious short-term memory, which apparently is an integration of a great many features for a single image and a great many neural connections. This is an example of how the lack of an efficient circuit raises questions.

As another instance of the lack of an efficient circuit, consider a word of long-term memory. A word in this context is not a component of a language, but a collection of memory cells linked together by interneurons so that a memory can be recalled as a single image. It has been proposed that memories are added contiguously, implying that memory words keep expanding to some randomly long length. But the resulting model leads to an inefficient circuit with technical problems for searching, recall, and memorization, not to mention excessive duplication of feature-detecting neurons as common features are used over and over. Far more efficient for circuit-modeling purposes are words of approximately the same length, each with parallel connections to a common set of features. Thus, the lack of an efficient circuit model brings into question the idea of ever-expanding, randomly long memory words.

To summarize, simple models are important to simulation and prediction of behavior, and to general education. Models affect thinking in at least three ways:

1. Credibility increases when there is a model that predicts known facts.
2. Theories with simple models tend to be favored over those with complex models, all else being the same.
3. Some models are better than others from the point of view of circuit efficiency.

WHY THINKING DISSIPATES SO FEW CALORIES

Why does thinking use so few calories? Standard data suggest that a brain consumes roughly 10% of the net energy expenditure of the body and that it does so essentially without regard to level of mental effort. As evidence that brain neurons take precious little energy compared to muscles, consider the kilocalories dissipated for various activities, as shown in Figure 1-1. Note that these are "large" or "food" calories. One kilocalorie equals 4.184 kj of energy.

Averages in the data were taken over gender, age, ethnicity, and weight. The category of "reading" would include calories for eye movement and page turning, so the values above are for the entire body, not just for the brain and not just for thinking. Clearly, ordinary mental activities such as reading are nearly as efficient as sleeping. The brain rests very little, if any, even during

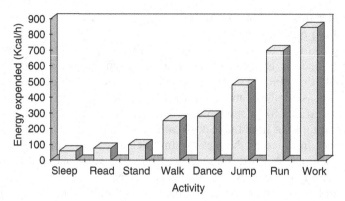

FIGURE 1-1   Typical calories expended. (Data from http://www.tooelehealth.org/ Community_Health/CVD/Calories_Burned.html.)

sleep, as evidenced in part by dreams. Apparently, brain neurons, like those for breathing and heartbeats, need no rest.

An hourly use of 50 kcal/h translates into about 60 W of power. Applying the 10% rule, that leaves 6 W, more or less, for the entire brain. All joking aside, maintenance and all other brain activity absorbs less power than is expended be a dim light. If overhead energy is discounted, subtracting the calories used for maintenance, growth, and health in every cell of the body, few remain for the logical operations of neurons. There are nearly a trillion neurons in which virtually no energy is needed per neuron for ordinary mental activities, too few calories to measure easily.

It is remarkable that thinking uses so few calories, given that billions and billions of neurons are involved. Relatively simple man-made computers with only a miniscule fraction of the brain's computing elements, perhaps only a million gates, dissipate hundreds of watts and run very hot indeed. To convince yourself, simply touch a working computer chip. As a result, computers need heat sinks and cooling fans, and chips must be slow enough to minimize heat generation. Temperature poses a serious engineering limitation for computers.

Functional magnetic resonance imaging (fMRI) is an example of a modern tool (described in Appendix C) that appears to produce an image of the energy, or calories, consumed by different parts of the brain for given human actions. fMRI aims to observe oxygenated hemoglobin, related to calories consumed by neurons, but requires averages taken over several seconds to image signals that are extremely weak. The fact that fMRI signals are very weak is indirect evidence that calories expended in thinking are few.

fMRI probably does not image the extremely small energies dissipated for action potentials but may show a secondary effect related directly to action potentials. During an action potential one expects a brief reduction in heating within the neural membrane, the heating that occurs constantly for maintenance, growth, and health in any human cell. There normally is about

−70 mV across the membrane, which has a small conductance and so dissipates a small amount of energy. During an action potential the *average* voltage across a neural membrane is slightly lower because membrane voltage alternates between about −70 and + 40 mV. This reduces dissipation in the membrane and probably changes the amount of oxygenated hemoglobin being processed, as fMRI purports to observe.

Common sense tells us that mental exercise is not a way to lose weight. Mental activity does not cause one to work up a sweat, nor does it get the heart racing. It appears that no energy at all is required for ordinary mental activity, including such items as recall, memorization, reasoning, reading, and listening. Mental activity is way down on the kilocalorie scale, not counting energy for cellular maintenance, growth, and health. Learning in the memory system model falls into a different category since energy is expected to be required for synaptic growth.

The lack of energy dissipation for ordinary mental activity is more than an interesting topic for dinner table conversation, because it points to the adiabatic model of neurons as logic devices, those that operate with little or no dissipation of energy. Aside from the adiabatic neuron, other adiabatic models for computation may be found in the theory of quantum mechanics.

Computer engineers may be interested to know that adiabatic logic is theoretically possible using common solid-state circuits. Once charged with electrical energy, such circuits transfer charge back and forth without loss, eventually returning all charge and its associated energy back to the power supplies from whence it came. With careful design, adiabatic logic leads to adiabatic computers for packaging into very small volumes. Small volumes are feasible because adiabatic logic runs cool. If the brain is any inspiration, we need to greatly expand our use of adiabatic logic for everyday life.

THE MIRACLE OF PARALLEL PROCESSING

The human brain is unique in nature in that it supports millions and millions of channels computing simultaneously. They are serviced by a large number of sensory inputs and deliver a large number of motor nerve outputs, all in parallel. The strength of a system like this is easily overlooked, since it operates effortlessly. How does one comprehend millions of little computers in parallel? We humans are lucky to juggle two or three things at once.

Mental activity is generally sequential: that is, one thing at a time. But memory searches are not sequential. Effectively, a human being can poll all memories in parallel and recall a particular episode from millions of events experienced long ago. This is a type of parallel processing. A style of man-made parallel processing known as *associative memory* works along these lines but on a much smaller scale. Associative memory finds items not by addresses, but by attributes such as patterns in the data. Modern computers employ associative memory only to an extremely limited extent: for example, to quickly find the most recent addresses

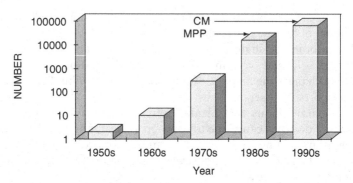

FIGURE 1-2 Brief history of massively parallel (associative) processing (CM = connection machine; MPP = massively parallel processor).

used by the microprocessor. To emulate brains for use in robots and artificial intelligence, we need to greatly expand our use of associative memory.

The possibilities for problem solving increase dramatically if millions of basic computations can be carried out simultaneously. Unfortunately, many people fail to see the possibilities of massive parallelism, because it requires a different type of thinking. As an example of a new way of thinking, consider finding prime factors. If a given large number is copied many times, and concurrently, if each copy is divided by a different prime number, the prime factors of that large number can be identified instantly. Simply flag those results whose remainder is zero.

Autistic savants perform amazing mental feats, including the immediate recognition of a prime number (one that cannot be divided evenly except by itself and unity). We do not know how they do it, exactly. One theory is that they simply memorize. However, given all that a savant can do, simple memorization is unlikely. Parallel processing must be occurring.

It may be noted that parallel processing is not limited to arithmetic. Finding the shortest path through a given maze, for example, is possible using a massively parallel processor, but only if the maze is not too large. Although not yet involved in everyday applications, the idea of massively parallel processing is certainly not new. Figure 1-2 is a snapshot of historical efforts at parallel processing.

The size of parallel processors tends to be increasing, yet parallel processing remains a topic of research and has run into serious problems. People generally prefer sequential procedures, which brings us back to the statement that parallel programming requires thinking in unaccustomed ways.

SINGULARITY

Machine intelligence approaching the human level is expected to produce a step in the economic growth rate of the past, as nicely exposed in an article by Robin Hanson (1959–). According to Hanson (*IEEE Spectrum*, June 2008, pp. 44–50)

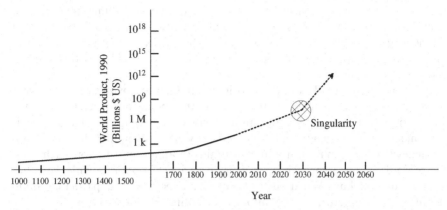

FIGURE 1-3 Idealized economic growth, including a singularity.

and others, a societal discontinuity is imminent, brought about by robots with artificial intelligence, similar to the original industrial revolution. The date of this new robotic revolution is uncertain, but it is known as the *singularity*. This word comes from an idealization of economic output as shown in Figure 1-3. Mathematically, the rate of change of economic growth, the slope of the curve, will experience an abrupt step. Going even further mathematically, the rate of change of the "rate of change" will be singular, that is, go to infinity at this magical point.

The original industrial revolution has been going on for quite some time, since about 1750, a general result of the pervasive application of machines. Since then the world economy has doubled roughly every 15 years or so. The switch from an agricultural society to an industrial society resulted in a speedup of roughly 100. Assuming a similar speedup as a result of the singularity, the economy would double not in 15 years, but in a month or two, assuming no setbacks due to war, plague, or cosmic disaster.

We see the original industrial revolution, but do we understand it? Machines are partially responsible. Machines like the steam engine, were possible because of advances across a broad front in metallurgy, metalworking, and engineering knowledge. No single spectacular gain in one area is responsible, since a complex machine has thousands of parts, each of which might depend on dozens of technologies. A gain in one technology causes only a slight improvement overall. This is the *law of diminishing returns*. To have an economic revolution there must be exponential growth.

Exponential growth was provided in the eighteenth century by capitalism, in which incremental improvements and novel applications were accomplished by countless hands-on builders. The original industrial revolution continues today sustained with higher-capacity memory chips, improved computers, and the World Wide Web, as promoted by thousands of innovative capitalists.

What is there today sufficiently broad-based as to induce a singularity? We know that improvement in just one sector of technology is insufficient, owing to the law of diminishing returns. But what if there were something that corrected a chronic shortage in all sectors: human attention and intelligence. Most financial gain in rich countries today goes for direct and indirect costs of labor. An innovation that drastically reduces this cost could very well start an economic revolution.

Machine were involved in the original industrial revolution; intelligent machines may be involved in the second, this being a cornerstone of the singularity hypothesis. But how can a machine be intelligent? One answer is that machine intelligence will follow shortly after computer hardware approaches the performance of a human brain. In an attempt to approach what the brain does, one approach is to "reverse engineer" the brain with the aid of scans and modeling. When such processes are perfected, a particular brain might be manufactured. The duplicated brain, of course, can always be unplugged, unless it is adiabatic and requires no external power.

Modeling efforts are currently under way. Project BlueBrain is a joint effort by IBM (International Business Machines) and École Polytechnique Fédérale de Lausanne in Switzerland to reverse-engineer a brain, but not a human brain. Their goal is mapping and modeling the roughly 10,000 neurons and 30 million synapses in a rat's neocortical column. The real goal, by the way, is a human brain. If the mental powers of a human could be approached, it would be more than a scientific curiosity. The chief factor of economic production that has been chronically scarce throughout history, human intelligence, would suddenly become widely available with mass production.

Imagine that machines approach human cognition and are able to perform most human jobs. With a growing workforce of intelligent computers created more quickly than it takes to breed, raise, and educate humans, the economy would explode. The cost of producing such a workforce will drop at an accelerating rate. Intelligent computers may even learn to design and manufacture other computers, all of which suggests a step in economic growth rate.

What does the future hold? To quote Robin Hanson: "Stuffed into skyscrapers by the billion, brainy bugbots will be the knowledge workers of the future." Operating at machine subsistence levels, their main cost will be rent for their miniature volumes, occasional parts for repair, and hopefully, no airconditioning bills. The singularity is a plausible view of the not-too-distant future—and it is not all bad. Humans would labor less for income while gaining by renting real estate for intelligent machines and by investing in the maintenance of computers. They would have ample time to labor for pressing matters such as exploring the universe.

THE BENEFITS OF READING THIS BOOK

This book is written primarily for those with interests in artificial intelligence, computer science, neuroscience, robotics, and peripheral fields such as artificial neural networks, psychology, and medicine. The book views the brain from a circuits and systems perspective, circuits and systems being the author's major at the University of California–Los Angeles in the 1970s. Knowledge in the aforementioned fields is enhanced by models of human memory using standard analog and digital circuits. Beyond formal knowledge, there is much in this book to help a reader personally. For example, when trying to spark the retrieval of something that has been forgotten, it is helpful to think of a wide variety of cues. When attempting to recall a person's name, we use such clues as the name of his or her spouse or the type of car the person drives. Sometimes, for example, a forgotten name pops forth immediately upon seeing the person from whom you first heard the name.

Nearly everyone has tried to remember something, but cannot; hours later the desired memory emerges, usually at an unexpected moment. This is because long-term memories are routinely searched in the background, subliminally. Humans are not particularly aware of this phenomenon of *delayed recall*, but once they are, they may take advantage of an everyday process in their own brains, the process of subliminal memory search. To recall facts, make decisions, or solve problems, it is wise to allow the unconscious to work for you, giving it time to do so for a day or two.

Dreams, daydreaming, or brainstorming are common experiences. In dreaming, a person becomes aware of random episodes from long-term memory, quite often relating to the solution of a difficult problem. The brain never quits, it seems, trying to solve a difficult problem, perhaps a problem with emotional impact that has no logical solution. Such common experiences as dreaming and delayed recall show that memory searches proceed randomly, unnoticed. When a sought-after memory is found that matches all available cues, it pops immediately into your conscious short-term memory with a certain modest excitmemt.

Once it is decided that something will be placed into unconscious long-term memory, it also helps to memorize cues for retrieving that information. Also, one must rehearse in a regular way both information and cues for memory; rehearsing in a random or irregular way is not expected to be as effective in the model of this book. Regular rehearsal is necessary to trigger a memorization enable signal, after which information in short-term memory goes automatically into the next available location in subconscious long-term memory.

Learning is facilitated by understanding the learning models discussed in this book. Placing information from the senses or from long-term memory into short-term memory on a regular basis is detected internally as a "need to learn." Regular practice is important at first because this enables the brain to generate a need to learn.

Upon receipt of a need-to-learn signal, there is a decoding of the contents of short-term memory to spur the growth of neurons and synaptic connections where they are needed. Over a period of time, this growth fosters new abilities, such as learning to recognize a new feature without analysis, or learning to follow a complex procedure automatically in a mindless way. At first, new synapses are small and could dissolve in a couple of weeks because of thermal and chemical activity. Therefore, it is helpful for a person to engage in overlearning and relearning to resist forgetting. Relearning is usually easier than the initial learning; it is encouraging to realize this progress.

A person can "learn how to learn." This is largely a matter of organizing the material to be learned into a more efficient form. For examples, numbers to be learned can be imagined as sporting event scores; audio tones and visual textures can be given names; a message to be learned can be broken into phrases that rhyme; the steps of a procedure to be learned can be numbered to facilitate learning.

Of course, one must always keep in mind that learning involves synaptic growth and is totally different from memorizing, which involves a latching of neural memory cells. Memorizing is intended for recall through the apparatus of short-term memory. Learning can essentially bypass short-term memory so that what is learned can be realized automatically without thinking.

Rehearsal aids learning; if a person wants to learn a skill, he or she must practice. Synaptic development requires time; so if nothing else, a person must patiently practice what was learned and to allocate sufficient time to reinforce what was learned.

Last but not least, neural circuit models might provide a professional benefit to medical practitioners. By understanding neural circuits, a brain malfunction might be related to circuit faults, which gives a practitioner the language to describe the probable cause of a malfunction. Subsequent circuit simulation might suggest corrective actions and might someday even predict the outcome of proposed surgery prior to an operation. Better medicine and better engineering are examples of real physical benefits that many are pursuing.

OVERVIEW OF THE BOOK

Standard circuit models are provided throughout to avoid the usual vagueness when it comes to describing brain operations verbally. Maupertuis gave us a principle of least action, interpreted to mean that systems evolve to be efficient. This principle has been applied to the modeling of neurons as logic devices all the way up to system models for associative memory. This principle leads us to a model of the brain as an adiabatic, massively parallel computer that does not lose information. Just the thought of an adiabatic, massively parallel computer is enough to suggest revolutionary new ideas in the minds of inventive engineers. Next we describe how the book evolves.

Chapter 1: Brain Behavior Points the Way In this chapter we introduce neurons in parallel that require virtually no energy for signals. Their signals are modeled to exist above the calories dissipated for common maintenance, growth, and health, common to all cells in a mammalian body. This adiabatic model creates new possibilities for explaining brain behavior. For example, an adiabatic model like this, in which action potentials come and go without dissipation, creates the possibility of long-term memory based on a simple circuit.

Chapter 2: Neural Membranes and Animal Electricity A voltage differential is developed because of charge transfer through a thin neural membrane, and this differential places it under significant electrical stress. To model a neural pulse electrically, sensitive regions of a membrane are modeled as ferroelectric: that is, as sensitive to an electric field. Reducing the electric field triggers a charge transfer that is driven by thermal energy. The resulting pulse is regulated by the ferroelectric particles within the membrane in that as internal voltage accumulates, a reversed electric field forces a reversal of the sensitive particles within the membrane. This reversal initiates a decrease in internal voltage. As voltage drops below its original equilibrium value, the pulse is forced to terminate because ferroelectric particles are driven back into their original positions. The sensitive particles of interest within the membrane are reset, and this enables a return to rest conditions. The model is such that an unlimited number of additional pulses can be triggered in a continuous manner if necessary.

Chapter 3: Neural Pulses and Neural Memory In this chapter we employ a simple physical model involving thermally active ions to derive by hand the waveform of a neural pulse. Underlying this model is the probability that thermally excited ions and stray electrons can tunnel into the sensitive regions of a membrane. Tunneling explains the magnitudes of the charge transfers commonly observed.

To model short-term memory neurons, ionic concentrations are modified to create and then hold positive charge within dendrites that have been exposed to excitatory neurotransmitter ions. This causes continuous triggering of the soma and axon with enhanced frequency but reduced amplitude lasting for a few hundreds of milliseconds. Connecting neurons respond to this signal. Explicit long term memory, in contrast, is modeled as a latching that occurs when the output neurotransmitters of an adiabatic neuron are fed back to dendritic receivers. Once latched, memory cells hold their features indefinitely without significant energy dissipation.

Chapter 4: Circuits and Systems for Memorization and Recall An all-digital model of the memory system is synthesized with an eye toward explaining the brain technically. Central to this model, which is a rudimentary cognitive architecture, is short-term memory organized as a long word of features. Short-term memory, that of which a person is conscious, is connected to millions of similar words forming a large associative memory which is assumed to hold all relevant information, including past problem solutions and decisions. This memory is searched by random selection from short-term memory, cues that are applied to recall long-term memory words up to tens per second. Such recalls, alternated with sensory images, are flashed subliminally to an interface circuit associated with short-term memory. Here, an encoder, such as a priority encoder, calculates an *index of importance* as an ongoing process. If the index for an image is higher than the current index for short-term memory, that image is gated immediately into short-term memory. This establishes a *direction of attention*, essentially a moving picture in conscious short-term memory as supported by a model based on standard digital logic.

Chapter 5: Dendritic Processing and Human Learning   Dendritic pulses created by excitatory neurotransmitter ions are recognized to be electrical solitons that propagate away from their point of creation without dispersion or attenuation. Simulations indicate that solitons are easily reflected at the soma, and when they collide with oncoming solitons, they annihilate each other, thus reducing the number of solitons triggering the soma. It is shown that solitons are capable of arbitrary Boolean logic. AND–OR logic is possible, as solitons charge soma capacitance to trigger a neural pulse. Neurons with digital properties are shown to support an all-digital learning model for humans. Two types of learning are identified: (1) combinational learning, to recognize a new feature in sensory data without having to stop and think about it, and (2) state machine learning, for new procedures that are executed without concentration, such as dancing or reciting a poem. Circuit models are suggested in support of all-digital learning for both new features and new procedures. Both types of learning avoid passing information through short-term memory for evaluation, thus increasing efficiency as necessary for species survival. Standard digital logic is modeled in support of the ideal of an intelligent robot that can actually learn beyond mere memorization.

Chapter 6: Artificial Learning in Artificial Neural Networks   In this chapter we present learning as defined for artificial neural networks. Artificial neural networks use analog weighting factors and analog summation, so differ from the all-digital ideal. Learning in an artificial neural network is equivalent to designing weighting factors, often a tedious iterative process. Overall, the tremendous success of artificial neural networks demonstrates the importance of learning in machines.

Chapter 7: The Asset of Reversibility in Humans and Machines   After considering the abilities of gifted savants, we speculate that their advanced abilities are the result of parallel processing within long-term memory, a type of processing in which no energy is dissipated. It is shown that no energy is lost in a system that is *electrically reversible*, that is, in which a given amount of charge is applied, all of which is recovered. To be electrically reversible, a computer must lose no information and so may be logically reversible, although a logically reversible machine need not be adiabatic. A reversible programming concept is introduced based on a "wiring" diagram as envisioned for the savant brain.

Chapter 8: Electrically Reversible Nanoprocessors In this chapter we present a case study for the original design of an adiabatic parallel computer using solid-state technology. Brain-inspired, the design avoids data buses during a computation—a major bottleneck and a source of heat dissipation in conventional computers. Central to the design are nanoprocessors, words of memory with conditional toggling capability within each word. An array of nanoprocessors constitutes an associative processor that can be designed to be electrically and logically reversible. Example programs in a wiring diagram are provided for vector addition and subtraction.

Chapter 9: Multiplications, Divisions, and Hamiltonian Circuits In this chapter we demonstrate a variety of programs possible for an electrically reversible parallel computer, including multiplication and division based on add-shift and subtract-shift algorithms. Solutions to SAT or NP-complete problems using a reversible parallel computer are introduced. The problem of finding all Hamiltonian circuits in a small graph is discussed, particularly the easy part: checking to determine if a given cycle is indeed Hamiltonian. Electrically and logically reversible computers are limited in practice by the number of nanoprocessors that can be brought to bear on a problem. Molecular-sized nanobrains, if they become available, will significantly increase the number of nanoprocessors, although perhaps not enough to solve SAT problems with thousands of variables. Qubits can be smaller than nanobrains and show promise for solving large problems.

Chapter 10: Quantum Versus Classical Computing The goal of this final chapter is to introduce quantum computers and to identify what the various biological, electrical, and quantum computing systems have in common. All such systems may use wiring diagrams, for example, so the transforms implied by reversible gates such as UN, SCN, DCN, and MCN are held in common. Wiring diagrams are used to explain savant brains as well as to program adiabatic parallel computers and quantum algorithms and to manipulate qubits, these being physically reversible. Such systems have in common that no information is lost and that basic computations are adiabatic, not counting energy overhead to maintain a workable environment.

The following appendixes may prove useful for general information.

Appendix A: Human Brain Anatomy This is a summary of basic brain information, some of which is used by the book's memory model.

Appendix B: The Psychological Science of Memory This is a summary of basic memory psychology, some of which is used by the book's memory model.

Appendix C: Brain Scanning This is a summary of fundamental imaging and scanning methods used to study the brain.

Appendix D: Biographies of Persons of Scientific Interest   This is a short collection of biographies of interesting and occasionally unpleasant characters who contributed to topics discussed in this book.

For Further Study   Finally, there is a brief list of published material for further study.

APPLICATIONS OF THE MODELS IN THE BOOK

Unlike models with abstract symbols, those expressed as standard analog and digital circuits can be simulated with ordinary software, constructed with everyday technology, tested by standard methods, and applied in various ways. The models described in this book bring to mind applications that today's students will undoubtedly come across in the course of their careers.

Artificial Membranes

One goal in the field of artificial membranes is to build a membrane that is as close as possible to a biological membrane using nanotechnology and genetic engineering. Toward this end, the models in this book provide an interesting perspective. Here we model membranes as containing sensitive regions with ferroelectric properties such that membrane particles are held together tightly by an electric field, but relaxed in a lower field. When relaxed, or triggered, it is possible to have charge transfers that constitute a neural pulse.

An artificial membrane ideally would behave like this, although such a membrane has yet to be manufactured. Interestingly, purple membrane films have been found to display ferroelectric behavior (termed *bioferroelectricity* in the literature). Purple membranes, characteristically hexagonal in shape are two-dimensional structures consisting of a transmembrane protein surrounded by 10 lipid molecules. They are relatives of man-made liquid crystals (a 5 billion market) based on ferroelectric properties.

Practical membranes have important applications, such as microfiltration, reverse osmosis, pervaporation (separation of liquids by vaporization), gas separation, dialysis, and chromatography. This translates into water purification, removal of microorganisms in dairy products, water desalination, dehydrogenation of natural gas, hemodialysis, and fuel cell components.

For the most part, artificial membranes with ferroelectric properties are not yet available, although many proposals have been made. For example, one proposal is to engineer membranes in the form of cells with internal bipolar charges within the voids, to mimic ferroelectrics. Another interesting proposal is to build a silicon chip with patches of artificial membrane so that filtration might be regulated using standard complementary metal–oxide semiconductor (CMOS) electronics. The neural model in this book is one way to gauge artificial membranes. Such membranes may be characterized by the pulses they generate when immersed in ionic solutions and adjustable electric fields.

If an artificial membrane approached the behavior of a neural membrane, it would facilitate molecular-sized elements known as *nanodevices*. Currently, a variety of these have been proposed to assist with cancer detection, diagnosis, and treatment. What is needed are general-purpose nanodevices: not just as nanobots for medicine, but for general applications to computers and communications.

Imitation Neurons

Imitation neurons approximate biological neurons both physically and electrically and are unrelated to *artificial neurons* for artificial neural networks. Artificial neurons are merely electronic amplifiers or computer subroutines to simulate amplifiers. Imitation neurons are modeled after biological neurons and might someday be fabricated using the methods of *nanotechnology*: engineering on a molecular scale, normally 1 to 100 nm, and to the fabrication of devices within that size range.

As decades roll by, analog and digital amplifiers are shrinking in size and increasing in efficiency, slowly approaching the efficiency of the everyday neuron. Beginning with vacuum tubes early in the twentieth century, amplifying technology evolved to the transistor in midcentury. Today's transistors are much smaller and more efficient in terms of heat dissipation, with temperature increases well below the melting point of silicon thus permitting very large scale integrations that were impossible a short time ago.

We have now entered an age of nanotechnology that promises further decreases in device size. Nanotechnology has arrived because of the recent availability of such novel tools as the atomic force microscope and the scanning tunneling microscope. Combined with refined processes such as electron beam lithography and molecular beam epitaxy, the deliberate manipulation of nanostructures has become possible. The birth of nanotechnology is generally assumed to be in 1989 when IBM scientist Don Eigler wrote out the company's logo using 35 individual xenon atoms arranged on a nickel plate at low temperature and high vacuum.

Imitation neurons are a goal, and once perfected, would be a superior choice for nanoprocessors of the future. Imitation neurons are expected to be small and flexible, like biological neurons. Currently, flexible circuits are in great demand for devices such as connectors, liquid-crystal displays, and digital cameras. A minuscule neuron, in principle, can generate any large-scale Boolean function or any large-scale analog-to-digital conversion for an astonishingly large number of inputs. Most important, properly constructed imitation neurons would merely borrow energy from the ionic solutions in which they are immersed, like the biological models of this book. They would produce a burst of pulses internally, dissipating neither energy nor power.

As a sign of progress in nanotechnology, IBM scientists recently announced that they have created an embryonic nanoprocessor using a single carbon-nanotube molecule and a standard semiconductor processes. The circuit, called a *ring oscillator*, consists of 12 field-effect transistors laid along a carbon nanotube 18 μm long, which is about one-fifth the width of a human hair. Clearly, it is far from molecular sized, but remember, this is only the beginning. The direction being pursued is to make circuits faster and compatible with regular silicon technology for everyday integrated circuits.

At the molecular level, random thermal activity would be quite rough on rigid technology, so flexible wet technology must be considered. In the context of watery technology, it is conceivable that imitation neurons might someday replace damaged biological nerve connections. This is not a surprising concept in view of successes in brain–machine interfacing. Neuroscientists have significantly advanced brain–machine interface technology, to the point where severely handicapped people who cannot contract even one leg or arm muscle can now compose and send e-mails independently and operate a television set. They are using only their thoughts to execute these actions. One day these and other handicapped persons may be able to feed themselves with a robotic hand that moves according to their mental commands. The hope is that imitation neurons might enable the muscles of the paralyzed to be useful again.

Artificial Neural Networks

Artificial neural networks are based on artificial neurons, each of which is composed of a weighted sum and a comparator, giving a true or a false output. An artificial neural network can be taught to recognize important patterns in a large field of data using an iterative algorithm to design the weights. The fact that a machine can learn this way is quite amazing.

Applications of artificial neural networks include system identification and control (vehicle control, process control), game playing and decision making (backgammon, chess, racing), pattern recognition (radar systems, face identification, object recognition), sequence recognition (gesture, speech, handwritten text recognition), medical diagnosis (tumor recognition), financial applications (recognition of trends in the prices of stocks), data mining (knowledge discovery in databases), visualization, and e-mail spam filtering. Artificial neural networks are undoubtedly an engineering success.

Artificial neural networks employ analog weighting factors and linear summation and thus depart from the all-digital ideal. Digital circuits are ideal since they are small, inexpensive, and tolerate noise. The all-digital system model in this book assumes thousands of neurons uniquely detecting thousands of features, with each neuron essentially an arbitrary digital circuit with many inputs. Many billions more constitute an associative memory with processing ability, an associative processor.

Learning is exceedingly important to the illusion of intelligence. Learning in the book's model begins with a need-to-learn signal that permits the directed insertion of new digital circuits where they are needed, somewhat as in a field-programmable gate array.

Beyond artificial neural networks, pattern recognition can be done in other ways, assuming the availability of parallel nanoprocessors. For example, if analog information has been converted into a sea of digital data in no particular order, the data can be searched with ease. Words with a given pattern can be located instantly by parallel nanoprocessors efficiently solving "needle in a haystack" problems, provided that the haystack is not too large. Inspired by models of human memory processing, designs for electrically and logically reversible parallel nanoprocessors are given later in the book.

Computer Design

Norbert Wiener (1894–1964) defined the original meaning of the term *cybernetics* to be the study of control and communications in humans and machines. There seems to be no doubt that the study of control and communications in people and machines has been an inspiration over the years for various computer designs. The amazing brain has always been an inspiration for computer design, beginning with the fact that both brains and computers are memory based. Louis Couffignal (1902–1966), another pioneer of cybernetics, characterizes cybernetics as "the art of ensuring the efficacy of action." This characterization brings to mind the guiding principle of modeling with standard analog and digital circuits: Maupertuis's principle of least action.

Historically, brain models were not all that accurate, but they still served the field of computer design. Models help inventers in mysterious ways. For example, neurons and neural systems are modeled as electrically reversible, implying that no information or energy is lost as a result of cognitive activity. This interesting model applies readily to computer design. Once an engineer knows enough to conserve charge, computers are easily designed to be adiabatic with no power or heat dissipation, as presented in this book, using CMOS as an example technology. When little or no heat is dissipated, engineers gain an option to design computers into much smaller packages without concern for temperature increases resulting from heating.

To compensate for the slowness of adiabatic logic, massive parallelism is desirable, as in human memory. This implies billions of little nanoprocessors all operating at once, analogous to words of biological memory, synchronized by signals from peripheral registers, analogous to short-term memory. Data buses, essential to conventional random-access and read-only memory (RAM and ROM), are avoided, since they create bottlenecks and waste energy. Once developed, massively parallel adiabatic computers will find uses in areas of space exploration, medical implants, databases, human guides, and computations that are impossible in any other way. As molecular-sized nanoprocessors materialize, their numbers will increase beyond belief, helping to solve difficult problems that have thousands of variables.

Robotics

Although the appearance and capabilities of robots vary vastly, all robots relate to a movable mechanical structure under some form of autonomous control. A sophisticated robot has some degree of artificial intelligence, or ability to make choices based on the environment, often using a preprogrammed sequence. This conveys the sense that a robot has intent or agency of its own. Robots that are more or less intelligent are currently being used in manufacturing, lifting and moving in distribution centers, household chores, military operations, and perhaps most important, in toys.

Cognition models may be visualized for robots to enhance their autonomy. For instance, for good performance, sensory inputs and motor outputs should operate in parallel. The human memory model in this book uses a word of short-term memory in conjunction with a very large number of long-term memory words, equally wide. This structure facilitates associative processing based on images in short-term memory. Microprocessor serial processing, still in use for most practical robots, is poorly suited to a multidimensional environment.

Ideally, sensory information would go into short-term memory as it does in a human brain. As in the cognitive model presented in this book, cues for an ongoing memory search may be taken from short-term memory. Pseudorandom combinations of cues may be employed to recall memorized images to a subliminal level at rates of perhaps tens per second. Each recall may be analyzed for importance according to specified criteria, where importance is a digital encoding function. Sensory images are analyzed similarly. When an index of importance surpasses that of the current contents of short-term memory, which is fading away, a new short-term memory enters. This creates a moving picture or a direction of attention in short-term memory.

If a robot is to appear intelligent in a minimal way, it must be able to make helpful decisions. When a decision is needed in a system of the digital variety, a memory search recalls similar problems to locate a ready-made decision. If a problem cannot be solved logically in this way, attempted solutions, taken randomly, will make a robot seem all too human. A robot that identifies a problem and recalls a procedure to solve the problem certainly has a degree of artificial intelligence, but this is minimal intelligence. It is necessary to learn to behave better. The next step in the evolution of robots is to enable them to "learn" procedures without having to bring every step of a solution into short-term memory. Humans routinely perform procedures to solve problems without full evaluation in short-term memory; this is possible because of a process of learning in which *neural state-machine learning* develops within long-term memory. Neural state-machine learning permits us to walk, brush our teeth, or memorize a long poem without an excessive amount of pondering. The ideal robot could do this, too.

Humans also learn to recognize special combinations of sensory inputs without having to ponder a number of related combinations. For example, a human can learn to recognize a special color such as chartreuse, a mixture of yellow and green. Humans need not tie up their short-term memory cells with items relating to yellow and to green, and they do not necessarily need to recall a dictionary of color names. They can learn to recognize chartreuse *immediately*, termed *combinational learning* in this book. The day is coming when robots, in the interests of efficiency, will have the capability for combinational learning.

Using the all-digital model described in this book, a *need-to-learn signal* is first created by digital filters associated with short-term memory. Learning is accomplished with decoders that connect to where additional logic circuits are required. Unlike the field-programmable gate array, human learning does not need a download from an outside computer. Learning is self-contained. Suffice it to say that without learning, robots will always be awkward, and except for the simplest behaviors will black-out as their memories are tied up unnecessarily with mundane computations.

Artificial Intelligence

Artificial intelligence is a branch of computer science usually involving software for mainframe computers, to perceive important aspects of the environment and display a reasoned, humanlike response. Among the topics of interest in artificial intelligence are reasoning, knowledge, learning, and the ability to communicate. A high level of artificial intelligence has not yet been achieved and is considered a goal for the future.

Artificial intelligence has been approached as a programming problem. A traditional measure of artificial intelligence is to send questions to a computer via a keyboard and to judge by the answers whether or not there is a human at the other end. This is the *Turing test*. As an example of what has been considered artificial intelligence, Deep Blue was the first computing machine to win a chess match against a reigning world champion, Garry Kasparov. Other examples of artificial intelligence are the ability to understand sights, such as faces, and to understand sounds, such as spoken commands.

The field of artificial intelligence could benefit from the model of human memory and cognition presented in this book, especially artificial intelligence as it applies to self-contained robots. Brain circuits operate in parallel, as opposed to the high-speed serial processing that computer manufacturers prefer to sell us. Engineers are well paid to increase clock speeds in order to run long programs of serial instructions. Ironically, the result is a machine that is sometimes slower than older models, because software always grows faster than hardware. The point is that parallel processing will be required to match what humans do routinely.

Of all the aspects of artificial intelligence, the ability to learn is a most convincing sign of intelligence. One aspect of learning involves the development of neural state machines directly embedded in associative memory, with the capability to execute procedures without evaluation in short-term memory, as noted above for robots. It would be nice if a machine could learn to fetch a ball, like a dog does. Better yet, perhaps a machine could, without a lot of additional programming, learn to walk across a garden while pouring a glass of wine.

Intelligent machines need to recognize sights and sounds without saturating a central processor. For example, it would be nice if a machine could learn to recognize a new face that appears often, such as that of a household pet. The learning involved is called *combinational learning*, another form of all-digital learning explored in this book.

Neuroscience

Neuroscience is the scientific study of the structure, function, and development of the nervous system, so traditionally, it is a branch of biology. Neuroscience expanded significantly in the second half of the twentieth century and now includes branches in molecular biology, artificial neural networks, and computational neuroscience. Here we emphasize electrical models, so apparently "electrical neuroscience," although seldom mentioned, is another branch of neuroscience.

The neuron in this book is modeled as an analog circuit. These analog underpinnings suggest that in its own way, a neuron can calculate arbitrary Boolean functions. Using many such gates, a memory system can be modeled to provide neuroscientists with a new perspective. In this book, problem solving and decision making as well as information retrieval are considered to be memory related.

Modeling with digital circuits clarifies the actions taken by a memory system when cues are inadequate or when cues are ambiguous. Modeling offers a novel point of view for most traditional issues in memory theory, such as strong memories versus weak memories, accuracy of memory, and threshold-of-effort for memorization and the meaning of recognition. All of these central issues are touched upon by the book's human memory system model based on standard analog and digital circuits.

The Beginnings of a Cognitive Architecture

Random searches are useful in computers, so here is an idea from computer science that might be useful in practice. As modeled in this book, but now with a little more detail, to recall something, a name, for example, cues in short-term memory are made available. But when a name cannot be remembered, a memory search proceeds in the background, subliminally, and may continue for hours. This search has an element of the unpredictable, given that all logical deductions of the forgotten name have failed. Later, unexpectedly, the correct name often pops forth.

The possibility of subliminal searches for forgotten facts is significant. Instead of a forgotten name, one may just as well search for solutions to problems, or decisions based on past experiences. Searches with random variables occur all the time during dreaming and brainstorming. After some time, potential solutions often emerge for a person who persists in trying to find a solution. Difficult illogical problems are sometimes solved in this way, although certain problems have no solutions.

The memory model in this book attempts to calculate a *direction of attention*, a topic of immense interest not only to neuroscientists, but also to psychologists. A memory search begins with a gating of cues taken from among the features held in short-term memory. Cue subsets are selected pseudorandomly to address a variety of associated images in long-term memory. Recalled briefly and subliminally are a great many associated memories, tens per second. Such recalls alternate with impressions from sensory encoders to minimize sensory input dead time.

Each impression is flashed unnoticed against interface neurons, where a digital encoder creates an index of importance for each image. The index of importance depends on attributes in short-term memory, including bright features and strong emotions. If a subliminal recall has sufficient importance compared to what is currently in short-term memory, it is enabled by gates to become the next impression in short-term memory. This new image constitutes a direction of attention in conscious short-term memory. Direction of attention is thus achieved with a self-contained digital circuit model.

What is presented is a model of the human memory system build up from neurons. Along the way are memory searches, memorizing, and an index of importance in deciding on the direction of attention. Since the model is cast in standard analog and digital circuits, a physical structure is implied, not just an input–output formula. The result is budding cognitive architecture that may be of value for the development of artificial intelligence and intelligent robots.

General Education

This book is in its own way quite cross-curricular and strives to promote general education. General education is extremely important because it raises exponentially the number of people who are able to appreciate basic knowledge about the human memory system, thus increasing the level of support for basic research. Models are a powerful educational tool that make a subject interesting and understandable. In contrast, volumes of random, disconnected clinical facts, however academically correct, are often confusing and boring. As a way to keep students awake, the appeal of simple models cannot be denied.

CONCLUSIONS

Today, tens of thousands of researchers routinely publish what amounts to hundreds of thousands of papers every year. Seldom are these bits and pieces of knowledge reduced to a useful model. Frequently, data are published based on no model at all. The publication is justified as just another brick in a huge, overwhelming data structure. Our work here should not be considered as traditional research because it runs in a totally different direction, a direction in which existing knowledge is distilled in order to create simple models. Simple models aid education and spur interest, but they do much more.

Simple models are useful for:

1. Calculating the sensitivities of a particular neural network to its parameters
2. The discovery of some yet unknown relationship between a neural structure and its function
3. The discovery of a direction that experimental investigation ought to take

Models affect thinking

- Theories need models that are in agreement with observed facts.
- Theories with simple accurate models tend to replace theories that lack such models.
- Some theories are better than others from the point of view of model efficiency.

In this book we describe novel models of neurons, memory systems, and cognitive architectures justified in part because they point to interesting engineering applications. Modeling human memory with standard analog and digital circuits inspires computer design in two major ways:

1. A neuron may be modeled as adiabatic as far as neural signals go. This implies that the brain is an adiabatic computer: not counting calories for growth and maintenance. Energy for neural pulses is modeled as being merely borrowed; subsequently, it is returned to where it came from, the ionic solutions of the body. Adiabatic models open new possibilities for the inventive mind. For example, long-term memory circuits can be understood as neural latches with circulating signals that do not burn energy. Models like this also suggest man-made computers, electrically and logically reversible using carefully designed CMOS logic.
2. The brain is modeled as massively parallel. If everyday computers had this sort of parallelism, the world would be a very different place. Computer images would appear instantly, for example. Better yet, Web searches would be instant and accurate, actually responding only to the subject of a search. Parallelism is essential to an adiabatic computer. Indeed, without it, a CMOS adiabatic computer would be hopelessly slow.

Modeling in this book is governed in part by a principle of least action. This principle suggests that things in nature tend to operate efficiently, the underlying reason being that efficiency is necessary for species survival. Adiabatic neurons are an important aspect of efficiency. The brain, for example, performs recalls approaching tens of images per second, yet dissipates practically no detectable energy in doing so. As a tribute to the efficiency of parallel processing within the brain, millions of subconscious words of memory are instantly searched and analyzed subliminally to deliver a recall. With an eye to efficiency, we now begin to model the workings of the wonderful brain—inscrutable, but an amazement of nature with complexity beyond comprehension.

EXERCISES

1-1 A computer may be modeled in two ways: top-down, beginning with what needs to be accomplished, and bottom-up, beginning with components available for the hardware.

(a) As an example of a top-down model, sketch a block diagram of a word processor.

(b) As an example of a bottom-up model, identify hardware components to capture analog signals at the microphone input.

1-2 Compare the human brain to a man-made computer.

(a) List something for which the brain is better than the computer.

(b) List something for which the brain is not as good as the computer.

1-3 Energy and power are closely related, as a little research soon reveals.

(a) Provide an equation that relates energy to power. Define all variables and units.

(b) Provide an equation that relates power to energy. Define all variables and units.

(c) Provide conversions into joules for the following units: kilocalories, calories, electron volts, watthours, and British thermal units.

1-4 Describe an everyday situation in which parallel processing speeds up a task.

1-5 Consider grade-school arithmetic.

(a) When adding a column of integers, how can parallel operations be used? Provide a numerical example.

(b) When multiplying, how can parallel operations be used? Provide a numerical example.

(c) When dividing a smaller integer into a larger integer, can parallel operations be used? Provide a numerical example.

1-6 Based on information provided in this chapter, list the names of massively parallel associative computers from the past. Do research to describe then technically.

1-7 Name ways in which brain theory affects computer design.

1-8 Based on information provided in this chapter, sketch a block diagram of a memory system that will provide a direction of attention.

1-9 How does an imitation neuron differ from an artificial neuron as used in an artificial neural network?

1-10 List potential applications of imitation neurons.

1-11 List practical applications of artificial learning intelligence in robots.

1-12 What are the benefits of human memory system modeling?

1-13 Create, through research, a list of the hopes and fears associated with a singularity.

CHAPTER 2

NEURAL MEMBRANES AND ANIMAL ELECTRICITY

INTRODUCTION

Here, we introduce the reader to the underlying physics of neurons and their signals and to the long-term goal of modeling human memory systems from the bottom up. Neurons are famous for their electricity, as has been known since the days of Luigi Galvani in the late eighteenth century. His publications included the observation that an electrical charge causes the dissected leg of a frog to twitch. Accurate sketches of neurons were originally presented in the late nineteenth and early twentieth centuries by such medical doctors as Johannes Evangelista Purkinje and Santiago Ramón y Cajal, showing that neurons have a treelike structure that is suggestive of electrical circuitry. Eventually, in the mid-twentieth century, much progress took place in showing that neurons are electrically active devices and that, indeed, they form complex circuits.

It is now thought that neural membranes are responsible for the electricity that transverses neurons. A thin membrane serves to separate positive and negative charge to create a steady voltage of a few millivolts. Although this dc voltage is low, it results in a significant electrical field since the membrane is very thin, only a few nanometers thick. This electric field, if it were in air, would create a bolt of electricity. Fortunately, a membrane does not pass electrical

Human Memory Modeled with Standard Analog and Digital Circuits:
Inspiration for Man-made Computers, By John Robert Burger
Copyright © 2009 John Wiley & Sons, Inc.

charge via spark, otherwise known as *dielectric breakdown*, thanks to the high dielectric strength of a membrane compared to air.

At rest, an electric field aligns ferroelectric particles in sensitive regions of a membrane so as to reduce charge transfer to a relatively low level. Under these conditions, there occurs an internal equilibrium or rest voltage that is negative to about − 70 mV inside the neuron. A suitable trigger creates conditions for ion channels, each with components and forces still being studied. Triggering is caused by showers of excitatory neurotransmitter ions on dendritic receivers, and these result in electrical surges to trigger other regions of dendrites and, depending on the logic being generated, the soma.

A trigger is essentially a reduction in the electric field in the membrane, causing a relaxation of ferroelectric particles in a sensitive region of the membrane. These ferroelectric particles serve to regulate a transfer of charge via ion channels. This charge flows through ion channels as created by thermal activity in the ionic solutions about the membrane. Channels are possible nearly everywhere except in regions protected by myelination, the white matter of axons, or in dendritic regions under the influence of inhibitory neurotransmitter ions.

Ion channels permit charge transfer and a corresponding increase in internal neural voltage relative to the outside. Subsequently, the inside voltage moves from a negative equilibrium value of roughly − 70 mV to a positive value of about + 40 mV as membrane capacitance is charged. Since voltage went from negative to positive, there is a reversal of the electric field through the membrane.

The reversed electric field forces sensitive ferroelectric particles to rotate to a new polarity in the membrane. This stops current flow into the neuron but does not stop current flow out of the neuron as initiated by internal ions. Internal voltage is thus discharged back toward equilibrium. Before a pulse can terminate properly, however, the voltage must drop slightly below its equilibrium value. This forces the ferroelectric particles in the sensitive region to snap back into their original orientation. When they do, they close the ion channels so that internal voltage returns to rest at about − 70 mV. The neuron is now ready to be triggered again to produce a full-sized neural pulse. The entire process takes only a few milliseconds per pulse.

In this chapter we discuss physical neurons and their membranes, reserving for Chapter 3 a simplified derivation of a neural pulse. Physical information as presented below is essential to understanding neural electricity for anyone interested in education relating to neural networks or neuroscience. Let us study, therefore, the basic neuron and its magical electricity, paying particular attention to its behavior as an active device.

THE PHYSICAL NEURON

Most neurons can be explained using the simplified schematic shown in Figure 2-1. Neurons are not two-dimensional as shown but rather, are three-dimensional,

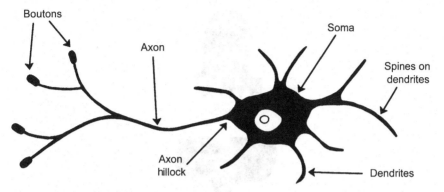

FIGURE 2-1 Neural parts (not drawn to scale).

with branches reaching in all directions. Surrounding the neuron are cells termed *glial cells* (not shown), which provide chemical balance and appropriate support for regeneration. It is estimated that a neuron rebuilds itself every three months, molecule by molecule. An outgrowth of glial cells is called *myelination*, which is *white matter* that forms about axons to insulate them electrically, thus speeding the propagation of pulses.

An overview of the various parts of a neuron is given below.

- The cell body, termed the *soma*, is about 25 μm in diameter and not much larger than the cell nucleus contained within. The nucleus contains DNA (*deoxyribonucleic acid*), a tiny ladderlike twisted and folded molecule that is packed with information. Sections of the DNA molecule are known as *genes;* these are essentially building plans to construct appropriate molecules when they are needed. The entire complement of human genes, termed the *genome*, contains about 30,000 genes.

- *Spines* are little protrusions on the dendrites for the reception of signals as conveyed by neurotransmitters. Neurotransmitters trigger dendritic pulses to activate a neuron electrically. These receivers are roughly analogous to input ports for digital logic. Various types of spines are depicted in Figure 2-2.

- Dendrites, or *gray matter*, can have many more branches than shown. Dendrites propagate a pulse now recognized to be an electrical soliton, with the ability to trigger the soma. Dendrites in conjunction with the soma can accomplish any Boolean logic.

- The *axon hillock* is where the axon emerges from the soma. It and the soma generate neural pulses that propagate down the axon, away from the soma.

- The *axon* is a fine cablelike projection that can range in length from a few millimeters to many centimeters. Axons typically have myelination, white matter that insulates them from the surrounding environment. Each

Stubby

Mushroom

Thin

FIGURE 2-2   Spines are $\approx 1\,\mu m$ tall; bulb diameters are $\approx 0.5\,\mu m$.

neuron has exactly one axon, but this axon can undergo extensive branching along its path. In equilibrium, there is negative voltage of about $-70\,mV$ relative to the outside medium. If triggered, positive pulses with peaks of roughly $+40\,mV$ propagate from the soma along the axon. Pulses usually occur in short bursts, the presence of which may be modeled to be binary 1; the absence of pulses may be modeled to be binary 0.

- Buttons or *boutons* form at the tips of the axon branches. From the boutons are emitted neurotransmitters for signaling other neurons. Boutons are roughly analogous to output ports in digital logic.

- The *synapse*, or synaptic cleft, is the small gap between a bouton and a receptor. It is about 20 nm, $(20 \times 10^{-9}\,m)$ wide, across which neurotransmitter ions drift and diffuse. Although the gap is extremely small, boutons and receptors never touch each other. Figure 2-3 is an artist's concept of a synapse.

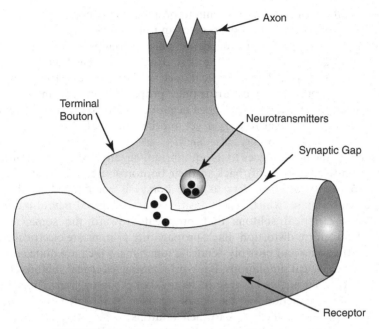

FIGURE 2-3   Idealized synapse (not drawn to scale).

The human brain has a gigantic number of synapses, as many as 1000 trillion in a 3-year-old child, declining with age to about 500 trillion by adulthood (1 trillion = 10^{12}). Synapses are central to neural logic. An automatic ability to understand new features in sensory data and an automatic ability to execute new procedures can be learned as unused neurons develop new synaptic connections. The ability to develop new synaptic contacts in new locations has been termed *synaptic plasticity*.

Neurotransmitters

Neurotransmitters for logic purposes move in the narrow gap between the bouton and the dendritic receptor. In the simplest of physical models, positive neurotransmitter ions are repelled by positive pulses that arrive at the bouton of the axon. Neurotransmitters then drift, and possibly diffuse away from their presynaptic source. Neurotransmitter ions subsequently shower a postsynaptic receiver. Neurotransmitter ions may cling briefly to the receiver because the receiver holds negative voltage when in equilibrium. In the simplest of models, negative charge attracts positive ions. Staying with a simple model, the presence of positive neurotransmitter ions close to a receiver serves to trigger a dendritic pulse (assuming a suitable combination of receiver and excitory neurotransmitter ion). In other locations closer to the soma, positive ions surrounding a small segment of a branch can attenuate propagating dendritic pulses (in the case of a suitable combination of receiver and inhibitory ion).

Soon after a positive-going dendritic pulse develops, neurotransmitters, those that triggered the pulse in the first place, are repelled away from the receiver. They are repelled, in a simple model, by the positive charge in the very pulse they triggered. But as a dendritic pulse propagates away from the vicinity of its triggering, dendritic voltage goes negative again. Neurotransmitters are pulled back to the receiver to trigger yet another pulse, and so on for a short sequence of pulses known as a *pulse burst*.

Eventually, the bouton goes to its equilibrium negative voltage, encouraging neurotransmitter ions to drift back to their bouton source for eventual reuse. The return of neurotransmitters to their homes is encouraged by the just-triggered neural pulse, which repels positive ions. Triggered neural pulses are identified as electrical solitons that propagate toward the soma without significant waveform distortion. Back-propagating solitons are electrical reflections from the soma and possibly dendritic junctions, which are quite common according to electrical simulations. Back-propagating electrical solitons contain positive charge that further ensures the removal of excitatory ions. Thus, in this model the logical action of the given neuron is disabled as *excitatory neurotransmitters* are pulled back to their boutons.

Neurotransmitters can be either excitatory or inhibitory. *Inhibitory neurotransmitters* are modeled as clinging to their receivers for a longer time, reliably preventing any dendritic pulses from being actively propagated through their domain. Inhibitory neurotransmitters are set free to a small extent by the pulses they repel but mainly by thermal activity in the ionic solution surrounding the neuron. If the dendrites of a given neuron are activated again before the previous inhibitory neurotransmitters are freed completely, the neuron will tend to display similar Boolean logic. Neurons are dedicated to specific nonreconfigurable logic in a human memory model, so reconfiguration is insignificant. Once freed, neurotransmitters return to their homes.

Neurotransmitters may be amino acids: *glutamate* and *aspartate* (excitatory), *gamma-aminobutyric acid* and *glycine* (inhibitory). Glycine is a major neurotransmitter in the brain stem and spinal cord. Between 10 and 30 atoms join to form about 20 types of amino acids, which are the building blocks for neurotransmitters, as well as proteins and hormones. There are more than 50 neurotransmitters, far more than necessary for logic signals.

Modified amino acids that act more slowly are termed *monoamines*. Perhaps the reader has heard of them: *acetylcholine, dopamine, histamine, noradrenalin, epinephrine*, and *serotonin*. The monoamines modulate (or regulate) the actions of the amino acid neurotransmitters. Serotonin, for example, is involved in synaptic development. Dopamine is said to be released by cigarette smoking, producing a good feeling (at the expense of health).

The most complex neurotransmitters are the peptides, such as *oxytocin* and *endorphin*. Peptides are chains of amino acids that are found everywhere in the nervous system, going everywhere by way of the circulatory system. Peptides have been found to modulate postsynaptic receptivity. Experimentally, it is found that peptides loosely control the range of pleasure and pain. *Endorphin* is endogenous (naturally produced) morphine. The peptide endorphin can reduce pain or increase euphoria. Peptides affect decisions. A peptide called *angiotensin* affects one's perception of thirst. Alcohol has effects that are similar to those of peptides, to excite or sedate, depending on one's mood.

Drugs and alcohol can affect the production or destruction of the neurotransmitters involved in neural triggering. The infamous nerve gas sarin can kill because it affects neurotransmitters responsible for muscular control and thus prevents control over the muscles needed to sustain life. This book is concerned mainly with the logical properties of neurotransmitters, which are simplified to be either excitatory or inhibitory.

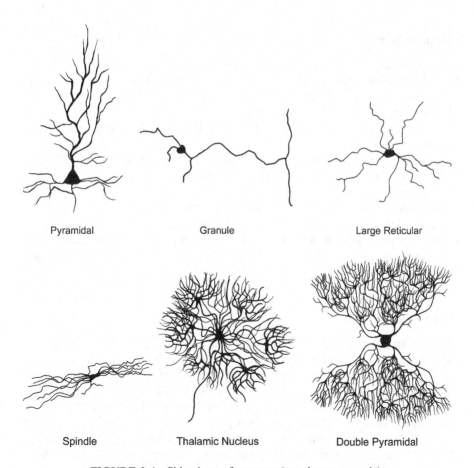

| Pyramidal | Granule | Large Reticular |

| Spindle | Thalamic Nucleus | Double Pyramidal |

FIGURE 2-4   Side views of neurons (not drawn to scale).

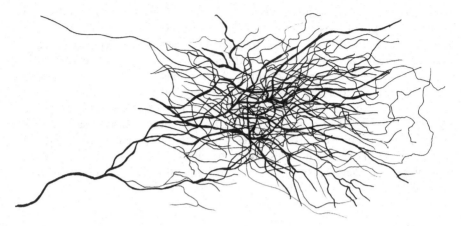

FIGURE 2-5   Two intersecting neurons.

Physical Shapes

Santiago Ramón y Cajal (1852–1934) published drawings of nerve cells in the later nineteenth century. He showed that neurons differ considerably in appearance, as suggested by the artist's sketches of nerve cells in Figure 2-4. Shapes other than these are also known.

Neural circuits can be complex. Figure 2-5 illustrates the intersection of two neurons.

It is estimated that adult humans have up to 100 billion neurons (that is, 10^{11}). This is far more than the average number of hairs on a head, 10^4. Thus, the average number of hairs, roughly, in greater Los Angeles, with its population of 10 million, is the same as the number of neurons in a single brain. In contrast, the nematode worm has only 302 neurons. Theoretically, a neuron can interact with millions of other neurons practically instantaneously. An interesting analogy is a cell phone, which can reach millions of other telephones in the world.

Neural Membranes

Common to all neurons is a thin membrane or bilayer of phospholipids (lipids); membranes are approximately 1 to 5 nm in thickness. In comparison, a human hair is about 25,000 nm in diameter (1 nm = 10^{-9} m). A neural membrane is extremely thin and quite porous and therefore has interesting properties. Proteins of various shapes and sizes are either attached to, or embedded in the membrane, so the surface is quite rough (see Figure 2-6). Not shown in the diagram is the fact that each particle, molecule, and atom is under significant stress and will be polarized because of an intense, near-breakdown electric field across the membrane.

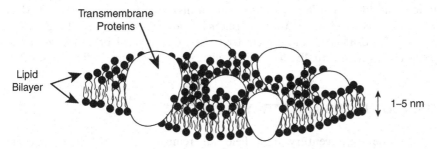

FIGURE 2-6   A neural membrane, illustrating the phospholipid bilayer.

Before discussing the electrical properties of membranes, it is worthwhile to note the history of neural electricity. Descartes developed a theory of animal electricity as a substance that flows through nerves and activates muscles (René Descartes, 1596–1650). Luigi Galvani (1737–1798) and an assistant discovered

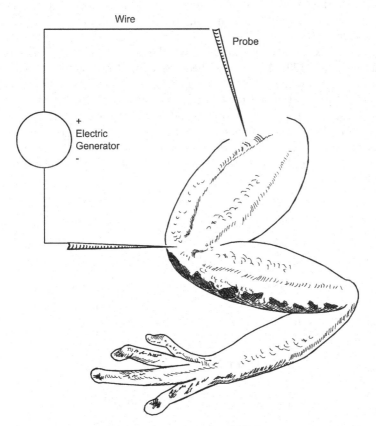

FIGURE 2-7   Galvani's frog leg.

quite by accident in 1780 that the legs of a dissected frog would twitch when the nerve was touched with a steel scalpel (one with an electric charge, as in Figure 2-7). Studies of animal electricity led to chemical batteries, electrical generators, and eventually, to modern electrical engineering and neuroscience.

IONIC SOLUTIONS AND STRAY ELECTRONS

In the nineteenth century in a field far removed from medicine, Svante Arrhenius (1859–1927) first suggested what we call an ionic solution. He proposed that when a salt such as table salt, sodium chloride (NaCl), is dissolved in water, it tends to split into electrically charged ions, Na^+ and Cl^-. Splitting is facilitated by water (H_2O) molecules, which are nonsymmetrical in shape and therefore naturally polar; that is, they are little electrical dipoles.

Ions and electrons might recombine into atoms, given that positive and negative charges attract, but atoms are soon ionized again by the polar H_2O; charged particles will drift under the influence of an electric field, as suggested in Figure 2-8. If a chloride ion hits a positive terminal, chlorine atoms result. If a sodium ion hits a negative terminal, sodium atoms result. This process is termed *electrolysis*.

In electrolysis, electrodes can become plated with metals. Years before, Michael Faraday (1791–1867) published a law for electroplating based on the definition of a given amount of electronic charge, the *coulomb,* which is about 6.25×10^{18} electrons (named for Charles de Coulomb, 1736–1806). Faraday's law (for electroplating) states that $96,500\,C$ ideally electroplate one *gram equivalent weight*. A gram equivalent weight is the atomic weight of an element in units of grams. For example, 1 gram equivalent weight of silver would be $107.8\,g$, since the atomic weight of silver is 107.8. The valance of a silver atom is 1 (one loosely bound electron).

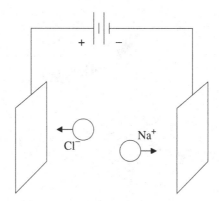

FIGURE 2-8 Ions in an electric field.

One *ampere* is equivalent to 1 C per second through a circuit. This equals 3600 C in 1 hour. What theoretically is electroplated in 1 h, ideally, is $107.8 \times (3600/96,500) \approx 4.02$ g of silver. Faraday's law assumes an electroplating environment in which current density (amperes per unit area) is low (so plenty of ions are available) and voltage is low (so that bound electrons are not pulled free). Having a low current density implies that the cross-sectional area of the ionic solution is large.

We now consider what happens at higher current densities as measured in amperes per square meter. Figure 2-9 shows typical electroplating current efficiency, although current efficiencies vary considerably, depending on temperature and chemicals in the solution. The *efficiency* is the actual plating weight divided by the expected plating weight as predicted by Faraday's law. Current density is expressed in units of A/m^2 or $pA/\mu m^2$ ($1\,pA = 10^{-12}\,A$); a micrometer (μm) is a millionth of a meter ($1\,\mu m^2 = 10^{-12}\,m^2$). There is a substantial decrease in efficiency above about $0.5\,pA/\mu m^2$, indicating charge transport by carriers other than ions. Apparently, electrons become involved. Figure 2-9 suggests that charge transfer from electrons is about 50% at $4\,pA/\mu m^2$. An estimate of current density in an axon of diameter $2\,\mu m$ is $4\,pA/\mu m^2$, which implies that about 50% is due to electrons. Axons are narrower than this, implying a percentage of charge transfer due to electrons. Clearly, electrons are available if needed.

Stray electrons are available for brief times because of thermal energy. Water has an interesting assortment of electrons and ions that may be involved in charge transfer. For example, pure neutral water dissociates to some extent into H^+ and OH^-, and such ions may carry some charge, with concentrations of OH^- ions each ready to lend an electron. Beyond this, due to thermal energy, there is a possibility of stray free electrons not only from OH^- but from H_2O itself. Oxygen can be modeled with four electron hybrid orbitals, as illustrated in Figure 2-10. Two atoms of hydrogen, each with one orbital electron, attach to two of the four sp^3 orbitals, leaving two lone pairs. To some extent, other molecules of H_2O are expected to form *hydrogen bonds* with the lone pairs in liquid water. On the other hand, orbitals are occasionally exposed to the open.

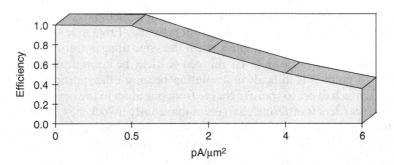

FIGURE 2-9   Ions involved in electrical conduction in an ionic solution.

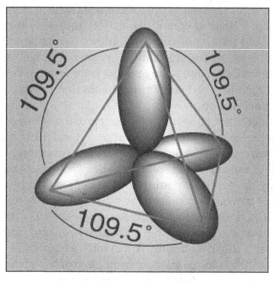

FIGURE 2-10 Hybrid sp³ orbitals. (From http://commons.wikimedia.org/wiki/Image:Sp3-Orbital.png.)

In a chaotic situation, electrons may be freed for a short time because of sharp collisions. Once freed, they may quickly accelerate in an electric field and avalanche, and thus multiply.

As a source of stray electrons, consider *Brownian motion* (Robert Brown, 1773–1858), which is chaotic thermal aggitation involving atoms, ions, and electrons as well. Stray electrons, knocked free by thermal aggitation, are not quite as plentiful as ions, but electrons are extremely mobile and very spread out in space. They are free only for a brief time between particle collisions, which is why they are termed stray electrons and not free electrons. Not available for long, but with great mobility, stray electrons may have a role to play when explaining some of the mysteries of neural electricity as explored in this chapter.

Ions carry positive charge; but positive charge is equivalent to removing electrons from a region. So there are two ways to model charge: as an excess of ions or as a shortfall of electrons; the result is similar. From a signaling point of view, ions and electrons accomplish much the same thing, a transfer of charge. The physical transport of a given charged particle, be it ion or electron, from point A to point B is difficult in a solution because other particles block the path. It is much easier to transfer charge from one atom to the next closest, with all charge carriers transfering charge simultaneously in lock step, resulting in a fast transfer of charge. In theory, Maxwell's equations apply (James Clerk Maxwell, 1831–1879). Neural electromagnetic waves do not, of course, travel at the speed of light, about 30 cm/ns in free space. In the axon of a neuron, electromagnetic speeds are closer to 30 nm/ns, because of the low current densities from ionic current sources and the high capacitance per unit area of a membrane.

NERNST VOLTAGE

Inspired by Arrhenius's theory of ionic solutions, Walther Nernst (1864–1941) was able to predict the static voltage across a thin membrane with different concentrations of the same type of ionic solution on each side. This prediction, termed *Nernst voltage* or *Nernst potential*, has proved useful in explaining biological membranes. Nernst voltage is important to the stability and health of a neuron.

To understand Nernst voltage, it is helpful to consider the behavior of ions. There are two main scientific alternatives to modeling Nernst voltage, each resulting in a similar calculation of the magnitude of the voltage:

1. The membrane is permeable to particles such as sodium and potassium ions, which can diffuse through completely.
2. Ions cannot pass through the membrane, but electrons can tunnel into the membrane with a significant probability of passing through.

These alternatives are introduced below and are elaborated later in the chapter.

Conditions for an analysis can be established by assuming that a higher concentration of ions of a given type are on the left of a membrane and a lower concentration of the same type are on the right, as shown in Figure 2-11a. Assume, further, that negative ions can be ignored because they are larger and because the membrane is not permeable to them.

All particles are assumed to move about vigorously, bounce off each other, and collide with the membrane. Alternative theory 1 is that ions diffuse completely through the membrane to the right side. *Diffusion* is a transport process relating to thermal activity in which particles from a higher concentration, as on the left, tend to move to a lower concentration, as on the right side of the figure. An analysis of the effects of diffusion is left as an end-of-chapter exercise.

If ions pass completely through the membrane to the right side, the concentrations on the right side will increase physically because of diffusion. As small currents are expected to leak through the membrane, there will be a steady flow of current that slowly brings additional ions to the right side of the membrane to maintain a given voltage across the membrane capacitance. The number of ions entering this way is significant and increases steadily with time. When a small volume on the right is considered, it is soon discovered, at least theoretically, that ion concentrations change significantly in a few hours, depending on the volume assumed. A quantitative estimation of contaminating ion concentrations is given later for the much larger current densities through

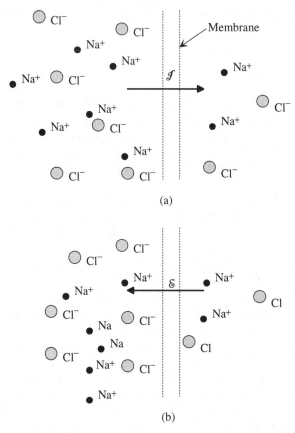

FIGURE 2-11   Charge transport by electron capture: (a) initial cindition; (b) positive change on the right.

ion channels in a neural pulse, using the estimated volume of a neuron. There are few reports of this upward creep in ionic concentrations, which would not be noticed except in a small volume. The concentrations are usually assumed to be absolutely fixed for diffusion analysis, suggesting that no ions actually pass through the membrane. In point of fact, to maintain fixed concentrations, ions must not pass through.

The ionic diffusion model seems to be a variation on the *osmosis model*. In this model a membrane does not permit ions to pass through at all. Instead, water molecules transverse a membrane that is permeable to water but not permeable to the solute. It may be observed that water moves from lower concentrations to higher concentrations so as to reduce the differences in the concentrations. We know that the osmosis membrane in question is permeable to water and that water indeed moves through the membrane. In the case of cellular osmosis, pressure increases with time, eventually stopping the osmosis process.

Alternative theory 2 assumes that a membrane is not particularly permeable to ions, similar to the membrane in the osmosis model that is not permeable to ions. This alternative theory leads to a model that is of interest later in the chapter, where ion channels are analyzed in detail. At this point, only a qualitative description of theory 2 is provided. Sharp collisions between particles set electrons free for brief periods of time. When thermally energetic stray electrons hit on the right, they tunnel into the membrane.* They may be captured by ions hitting the membrane on the left. Capture probability explains voltages typically observed across a membrane.

To calculate voltage buildup, we assume that concentrations on the left are higher than these on the right. Then an increased number will hit from the left, simply because there are more ions on the left. Charge movement in the sense of *electrical current* is denoted by a script I ($\mathscr{I}$) in Figure 2-11. Electrical current, otherwise known as *Ben Franklin current*, is defined to move positive charge, thanks to a guess by Benjamin Franklin (1706–1790). Electron current moves in a direction opposite to electrical current. Membrane charge builds up because of the transfer of negative charge to the left (or alternatively, positive charges entering to the right); an electric field, denoted by a script $\mathscr{E}$, thus goes from positive to negative to define a line of force. The transport process is slowed because of the electric force caused by the positive charge building up on the right. This charge will repel positive ions away from the membrane. Eventually, equilibrium is achieved as portrayed in the lower part of the figure. Note in the figure an increased quantity of positive charge on the right caused by a shortfall of electrons on the right. The result is the voltage termed Nernst voltage.

When the concentrations of ions are fixed, it is fairly easy to compute the Nernst voltage across the membrane. Transport of charge from a higher concentration of sodium, N_1, through a membrane, to a lower concentration of sodium, N_2 is modeled as on the left of Figure 2-12, where $\mathscr{I}$ represents Ben Franklin current from N_1 to N_2 and a script E ($\mathscr{E}$) is an electric field that resists this tendency. In the Figure 1 mM/cm^3 means that the total number of particles in a cubic centimeter is about 6.02×10^{20}. Typical concentrations of ions in a neuron are indicated on the right of the figure. To derive the voltage component across the membrane because of a particular ion, it is possible to model the membrane as a potential barrier assuming a potential ΔV that repels ions attempting to move from N_1 to N_2. Thus, only ions with higher speeds in the thermal distribution can enter the membrane and capture an electron. The probability of charge transfer due to ions on the left is proportional to N_2; the probability of charge transfer due to ions on the right is proportional to N_1. Ludwig Boltzmann (1844–1906), famous for analyzing thermal energy, derived

---

* The probability of quantum penetration of electrons with energy 2 eV going through 1 nm of barrier presenting a potential barrier of 5 eV is about 10^{-10}. This is shown in Chapter 5 to be more than enough to build up the amounts of charge being discussed. Ions penetrate far less, but deep enough to capture stray electrons.

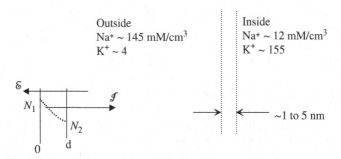

FIGURE 2-12   Model of ion transport showing concentrations in ions/cm³.

a relationship between the ratio of these probabilities and the height of an assumed potential barrier:

$$\frac{N_2}{N_1} = e^{-\Delta V/(kT/q)}$$

The quantity kT/q is known as the *fundamental constant of electronics*; it is about 25.8 mV at room temperature (300 K or 27°C). Rearranging the equation above becomes a form of the Nernst result:

$$\Delta V = + \frac{kT}{q} \ln \frac{N_1}{N_2}$$

Here k is Boltzmann's constant, T is temperature in Kelvin, and q is the charge of an electron in coulomb. Following are the approximate Nernst potentials from inside to outside (right to left) of a membrane at human body temperature (37°C or 310 K):

$$Na^+ : \quad +66\,mV$$
$$K^+ \;\; : \quad -97\,mV$$

The sign depends on which side has the higher concentration. Sodium (Na^+) has a higher concentration on the outside (left). Potassium (K^+) has a higher concentration on the inside (right). Other ions (not shown) are also present in an actual neuron and affect the neural potential.

The Neuron as a Pulse Generator

Voltage is relative, of course, and requires a reference point. As an arbitrary reference point, the voltage to the outside (left) of a membrane is assumed to be zero. By considering a linear combination of all voltages expected in a neuron, it is found that there is a voltage of about $-70\,\text{mV}$ inside a neuron relative to the outside. This is defined to be the *equilibrium* or *rest voltage*. Clearly, there is a difference between $-70\,\text{mV}$ and the sum of the values listed above ($-31\,\text{mV}$), showing that the actual mix of ions differs from those in the example.

At some point in time, a triggering event in the form of a positive electric field in the membrane initiates a voltage pulse. Ideal and laboratory versions of a neural pulse taken from *wikimedia commons* are shown in Figure 2-13. The "real" pulse may be distorted by imperfections in experimental equipment. Clearly evident is a relatively symmetric peak, after which undershoot occurs. Following undershoot in the experimental pulse, there appears to be another

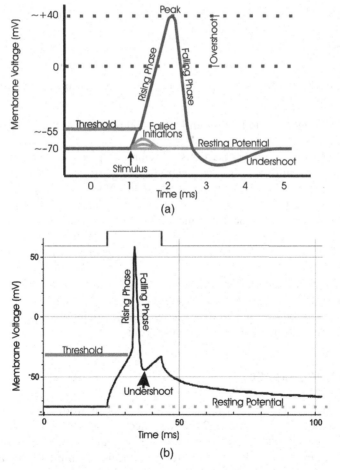

FIGURE 2-13   (a) schematic and (b) real action potential pulses. (from http://en.wikipedia.org/wiki/Action_potential.)

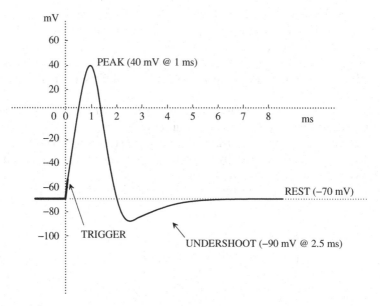

FIGURE 2-14 Reference pulse and internal voltage relative to the outside.

attempt at triggering that apparently fails, allowing the pulse to return to equilibrium.

Patterned after these publications, a reference pulse was constructed for use in this book and is presented beginning at $t = 0$, as in Figure 2-14. The lab model pulse reaches a maximum of about 40 mV within 1 ms and then drops to a minimum of about -90 mV, the *undershoot voltage*, at about 2.5 ms. The rise time is faster than the fall time. Subsequently, the waveform recovers fairly quickly, within a couple of milliseconds, to its equilibrium voltage of about -70 mV. Typically, there is a burst of several identical pulses (not shown).

A brief low-voltage trigger with lower energy is able to initiate a relatively longer and higher-voltage pulse with a higher energy content. For this reason, the neuron may be referred to as an *active circuit* analogous to a monostable multivibrator or "one-shot" in digital electronics.

ION-CHANNEL MODEL

A model was offered by British medical doctors Alan Hodgkin (1914–) and Andrew Huxley (1917–) in 1952 that was nicely supported with data taken by electrically probing the giant axon in a squid. Data were taken roughly as shown in Figure 2-15. Voltage across the membrane is sampled using amplifier 1 in a negative feedback loop; a triggering voltage is applied via Δv_{trig} at amplifier 2. This circuit is called a *voltage clamp* because the goal in this circuit,

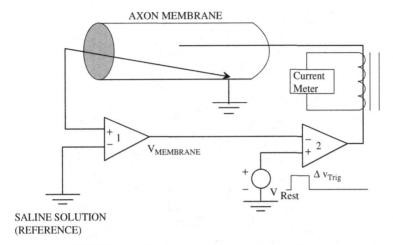

FIGURE 2-15   Voltage clamp for a giant squid axon.

after responding to time delays in the probes as well as in the amplifiers, is to maintain constant voltage across the membrane using negative feedback. The current in amperes (coulombs per second) flowing out of amplifier 2 is measured with a sensitive galvanometer. The current so observed is related directly to membrane current. The current surge may be used to reconstruct the voltage pulse expected across the membrane capacitance. A smaller, more accurate version of the voltage clamp is called a *patch clamp*.

Patch Clamp

Modern technology led to the invention of the *patch clamp* by Erwin Neher (1944–) and Bert Sakmann (1942–) in the early 1980s (see Figure 2-16). The patch clamp is a glass pipette with a tip diameter of only about 1 μm which is pressed gently against a membrane. Slight suction is then applied to seal a "patch" of the membrane. It is said to be possible to insulate the internal solution electrically from the surrounding ionic solution with a resistance in the thousands of megohms (1 MΩ = $10^6 \, \Omega$).

Probes like this rely on applying a given voltage and observing a current (or applying a given current and observing the voltage). They can observe the volt–ampere characteristics of the membrane patch being tested. When testing a membrane, short bursts of current have been observed (Figure 2-17) which are said to be the result of individual ion channels opening (conducting) and closing (nonconducting) randomly within the area of the patch.

What is interesting is that these data look like dielectric breakdown. In equilibrium, a membrane is indeed close to dielectric breakdown. Assuming a voltage of 70 mV and a thickness of 1 nm, the electric field in the membrane is

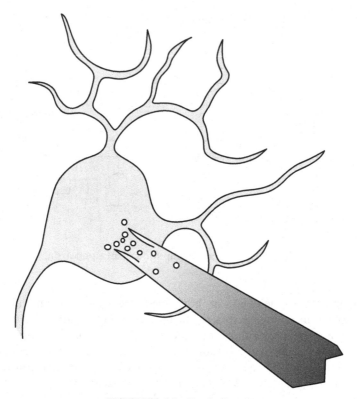

FIGURE 2-16 Patch clamp.

70 mV/nm or 700 kV/cm. This is more than 23 times what it takes to create lightning in the atmosphere given that 30 kV/cm is an approximate threshold for breakdown in air. Breakdown is usually initiated by a random event such as a stray electron knocked loose by thermal agitation. In a high electric field, an electron within a membrane easily accelerates, collides, and in the case of an electron, will avalanche along with countless other electrons. *Avalanching* consists of electrons becoming accelerated in the electric field, knocking additional

FIGURE 2-17 Recording electrical current from a patch clamp.

electrons free and resulting in a pulse of current. The purported random ion channels shown in Figure 2-17 look very much like dielectric breakdown.

Geiger counters for radiation detection work on the avalanche principle. Energetic electrons multiply into many other electrons as they rush through the gas tube. Geiger counters are triggered specifically by photons of radiation. Assuming the ion-channel model, sodium ions enter through *sodium ion channels* in the membrane, where they charge membrane capacitance. Soon after, potassium ions leave in different channels, called *potassium channels*, and thus discharge membrane capacitance. The resulting ionic imbalance is subsequently restored by a process called *ion pumping*, in which sodium and potassium levels are restored to their initial concentrations. To relate ion channels to observed waveforms, ion channels have to switch on and off in a timely way. Figure 2-18 is an artist's rendition of the ion-channel model as commonly visualized.

Initially, both sodium and potassium channels are closed. Then a trigger opens the sodium channel. Sodium ions (black dots) move inside the soma (the inside is on the bottom), producing a positive voltage. At this point, the sodium channel closes (the little flap on the bottom); the potassium channel opens. Potassium ions (gray dots) move outside the soma (the outside is on the top). Finally, both channels close, restoring equilibrium. Thousands of these two types of ion channels, and possibly other types of ion channels, are assumed to open randomly, resulting in enough average current to create a neural action potential.

Shortcomings of the Ion-Channel Model

The ion-channel model presented above raises the following seven questions:

1. Does a neuron eventually become damaged because too many polluting sodium ions enter?
2. Does a neuron become damaged because too many essential potassium ions leave?
3. What keeps foreign particles out of the neuron while an ion channel is open?
4. How does an ion-selective channel work?
5. What is the physical structure of the valves?
6. What moves them physically?
7. What triggers ion channels?

Question 1 can be explored using a model of the soma. Consider sodium ions passing into a soma model that is $D = 25\,\mu m$ in diameter so that $R = 12.5\,\mu m$. The volume inside is $\frac{4}{3}\pi R^3 = 8.16 \times 10^{-15}\,m^3$. But the nucleus might have a radius of $10\,\mu m$ and a volume of $4.18 \times 10^{-15}\,m^3$. Net ionic fluid volume is thus roughly $3.98 \times 10^{-15}\,m^3$. Using a sodium concentration of $12\,mM/cm^3$, and Avogadro's number (6.0221×10^{23}) as the number of atoms in a mole, there are

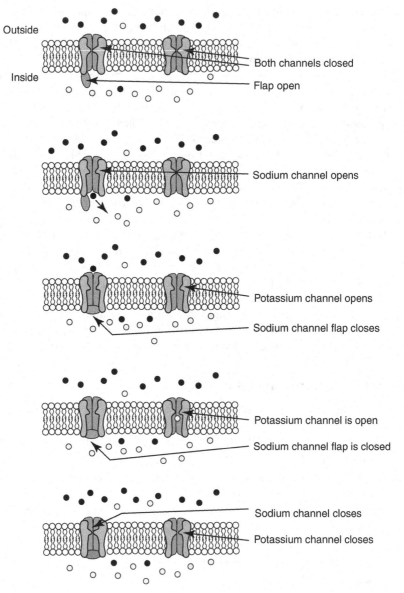

FIGURE 2-18   Sodium and potassium channels (black dots, sodium ions; gray dots, potassium ions).

about 7.2×10^{21} ions/cm^3, or 7.2×10^{27} ions/m^3. This results in a total of about $7.2 \times 10^{27} \times 3.98 \times 10^{-15} \approx 2.86 \times 10^{13}$ ions that reside inside the soma. This may be rounded to be a reference point:

$$\approx 3 \times 10^{13} \text{ ions/soma}$$

To achieve a proper neural pulse, it will be seen (in Chapter 3) that sodium current density could be as high as $0.3\,\text{mA/cm}^2$. Current may be converted into ion flow by dividing by electronic charge $q \approx 1.6 \times 10^{-19}$. The soma surface area is $\pi D^2 \approx 1963\,\mu\text{m}^2$. Thus, the number of ions entering can be calculated to be $0.3 \times 10^{-3}\,\text{A/cm}^2 \times (1\,\text{cm}/10^4\mu\text{m})^2 \times 1963\,\mu\text{m}^2/1.6 \times 10^{-19}\,\text{C} \approx 3.7 \times 10^{10}$ ions per second entering. This is another reference point:

$$\approx 3.7 \times 10^{10}\text{s}^{-1}/\text{soma}$$

A simple model has sodium surges for about 2 ms and then potassium surges for about 4 ms; sodium enters each 2 ms of every 6 ms. If a neuron is being used continuously, the time for sodium contamination to equal the sodium count within the soma is

$$\frac{3 \times 10^{13}}{\frac{2}{6} \times 3.7 \times 10^{10}} = 2432\,\text{s} \approx 40.53\,\text{min}$$

In this scenario the entering sodium ions outnumber the internal sodium ions after about 40 minutes of mental activity. At this rate, action potentials are eventually stopped by the fact that the sodium ions entering and leaving through an open ion channel are equal. In the case being considered, it must be assumed that ion pumping can force out sodium ions in excess of about $3.7 \times 10^{10}\,\text{s}^{-1}$.

When a pulse is completed and charge neutrality is achieved again, the quantity of potassium lost must equal the quantity of sodium gained. The loss of potassium ions from inside the neuron is equally problematic. In the worst case being considered, it must be assumed that potassium ions are manufactured at a rate exceeding $3.7 \times 10^{10}\,\text{s}^{-1}$. From another point of view, an action potential might complete in 30 ms, resulting in about $3.7 \times 10^{10} \times 30 \times 10^{-3} \approx 10^9$ ions per action potential burst. Thus, a neuron might permit $3 \times 10^{13}/10^9 \approx$ 30,000 action potentials before it fails due to ion poisoning. In terms of dollars, for exemple, this is a lot, but in terms of what is required of a neuron, it is nothing. We would hate to think, for exemple, that one's heart would fail after only 30,000 beats.

Not only question 1, but all seven questions have easy answers if one is willing to consider an electron capture model in which ions never have to transverse a membrane to create neural signals. Think of positive ions as tunneling very slightly into a membrane but not necessarily entering the soma. Instead, they capture stray electrons that have tunneled briefly into the membrane from inside the soma, the other direction. The end result is the same, giving a similar action potential. But now the questions can be answered quite easily:

1. Sodium ions never enter!
2. Potassium ions never leave!

3. The cell is never open to foreign particles!
4. Electrically, there is no need for ion-selective channels!
5. Ion channel valves and flaps are the result of standard piezoelectric and ferroelectric properties in sensitive regions of the membrane!
6. Electric fields drive ferroelectric particles!
7. Ion channels do not open by themselves; rather, they are opened by random impacts of thermally energetic ions!

Ion Channels as Energetic Particles Hitting Ferroelectric Membranes

Consider a region on the surface of a neural membrane as depicted in Figure 2-19. The diameter of the region is left as a variable (d). Also unspecified in what follows are the molecules that reside within the ion-channel region. The resting electric field is very high in a membrane (the electric field is about 70 mV/nm or 700 kV/cm). Molecules in a membrane will be polarized into dipoles capable of locking onto other molecules. At equilibrium, particles in the subject locality are modeled as being locked together, as illustrated in Figure 2-20.

Ions and electrons in the ionic solution are in thermal equilibrium, so each particle in the ionic solution is active; ions are slow and large; electrons are fast and small. Na^+ and K^+ ions do not penetrate significantly into the dielectric membrane, only enough to cause a Nernst voltage, since it is assumed held firm,

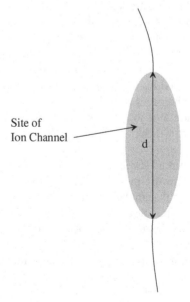

Site of
Ion Channel

d

FIGURE 2-19   Ion channel on the surface of a neural membrane.

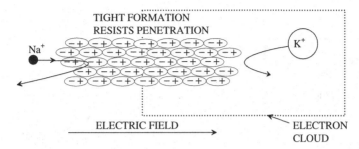

FIGURE 2-20 Membrane under conditions of equilibrium.

that is, held mechanically tight by the aligned polarized particles.* In other words, there are virtually no openings in the membrane fabric; dipoles cling together. When a material's mechanical properties are affected by an electric field as in this model, the material is characterized as *piezoelectric*.

If there is a triggering event that substantially reduces the electric field, the dielectric particles lose their tight polarization, becoming looser, more porous, and more elastic. Under these conditions, Na$^+$ ions with significant thermal energy (speed) can push slightly into the membrane (but not necessarily through), thus initiating an ion channel. Figure 2-21 is an artist's concept of what happens when membrane particles relax because of a triggering event. Na$^+$ ions penetrate the dielectric but soon bounce back, since it is improbable quantum mechanically that a large sodium ion will tunnel completely through a membrane. While embedded within the membrane, however, a sodium ion has a probability of capturing a stray electron from the interior of the cell that has tunneled into the membrane from the other side. Electrons are visualized, quantum mechanically, to be a cloud that penetrates throughout a certain volume. The *Heisenberg uncertainty principle* prevents knowledge of the locations and speeds of electrons.

Even a rather high barrier offers a reasonable chance of electron capture, as tunneling calculations tend to support. There are many energetic ions and plenty of random electrons, and fortunately, only a small probability of capture, since only a small probability is needed in a neuron. The probability of capture must be quite small because only a fraction of a milliampere of electrical current per square centimeter is required for a neural pulse. Probabilities of capture are employed in Chapter 3.

In the ferroelectric model of a membrane, the membrane's electrically sensitive particles control the transfer of charge. Because of electron capture (and perhaps to a lesser extent, sodium punch-through), negative charge is taken from inside the soma (the right side in Figure 2-21). Consequently, a positive voltage builds up inside. Potassium ions actively penetrate the

---

* Iron filings in a magnetic field behave similarly, clinging together to stop a rolling lead ball bearing (BB). Reducing the magnetic field lets a rolling BB pass into the filings.

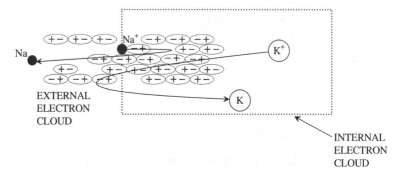

FIGURE 2-21 Penetration of ions and electrons when particles relax because of electric field reduction.

membrane from the inside, but they are larger than sodium and slower to capture outside electrons. This is fortunate, since they must not overpower the positive voltage accumulating across the membrane inside the neuron.

As the interior voltage increases, the electric field becomes strongly reversed. At some point the sensitive ferroelectric particles will adjust into a new orientation (Figure 2-22). Membrane particles will not be quite as tight, because the reversed electric field is not quite as strong as the equilibrium field. This new orientation will hold until it is reset by a negative undershoot of soma voltage. The new orientation effectively resists sodium-induced currents, partly because the formation is tight again and partly because of changes in the local electric field at the surfaces of the membrane.

The local field at the outside surface of the membrane now has a positive value and thus will repel positive ions. The positive space charge within the cell will also repel sodium ions, although this charge is farther away and does not hold steady as do the molecular orientations. Concurrently, the local electric field on the inside of the membrane, where stray electrons roam, will repel electrons. Sodium current is thus greatly reduced, a condition that holds until the membrane particles are able to snap back into their rest position.

As the electric field subsides, potassium ions continue to be attracted by the local electric field at the inside surface of the membrane and thus are accelerated into the membrane; similarly, random free electrons are propelled into the membrane from the outside by the electric field at the outside surface. This is facilitated in part because sensitive particles in the membrane are not as tightly aligned as they were in equilibrium, given that the electric field is not quite as high in the reverse direction. Overall, potassium ions continue to create channels and capture electrons back into the cell; in effect, they remove positive charge from the inside. Potassium current eventually forces the interior positive voltage to drop below the rest potential (about $-70\,\mathrm{mV}$).

When internal voltage reaches a certain negative threshold, somewhere below about $-70\,\mathrm{mV}$, all the membrane's polar particles will snap back into alignment

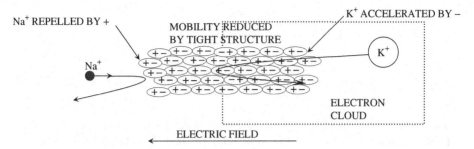

FIGURE 2-22   Reverse polarization greatly reduces Na⁺ penetration.

as they were initially in equilibrium, mechanically tight to resist both sodium and potassium current. Subsequently, low-level transport mechanisms serve to restore a Nernst potential or equilibrium voltage within the soma.

Under this model, membrane particles can snap back and forth between two orientations. In materials science, hysteresis is quite common in the electrostatic characteristics of materials. Hysteresis means that a given value of electric field supports two possible values of permittivity, resulting in two possible values of displacement **D** as shown in Figure 2-23. Displacement **D** is related to electric field **E** by the equation: $\mathbf{D} = \varepsilon\mathbf{E}$ where ε is permittivity, a variable. Materials with this characteristic are termed *ferroelectric* even though they contain no iron, since they behave in analogy to a ferromagnetic material such as iron.

Undershoot is required to move the operating point from point 1 to point 2 in Figure 2-23. In other words, the sensitive parts of the membrane should be reset; undershoot pulls the particles into a tight formation for equilibrium. The hysteresis loop explains undershoot in a neural pulse. Neural pulses with

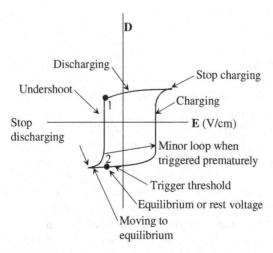

FIGURE 2-23   Ferroelectric (hysteric) characteristic.

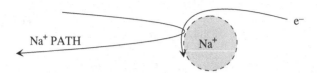

FIGURE 2-24   Artist's rendition of an electron being captured.

diminished amplitude are assumed possible as soon as a few membrane particles snap into their original positions, for neural voltages in the approximate vicinity of point 1 in the figure. Normally, a membrane is triggered at some point after undershoot to give a full pulse. It may be triggered an infinity of times, giving virtually the same waveform, as is necessary in an efficient neural system.

To recap, ions and electrons undergo chaotic thermal activity. Energetic electrons are small, light, and very mobile; in an ionic solution, some are momentarily free to tunnel into the membrane. If an energetic positive ion from the outside happens to move into the membrane at the right moment, an electron from the inside may be captured. An artist's rendition of capture is shown in Figure 2-24. As the ion bounces elastically back away from the membrane, the captured electron is pulled to the outside of the neuron. Electron capture leaves a positive charge within the soma that contributes to a neural pulse.

To have significant voltage buildup inside a neuron, a great many such captures must occur. Even so, the probability of capture has to be very small to result in the small neural pulses observed. Internal charge can be created by the actual punching through of a positive ion into a neuron, although this means that a relatively large object has to push through a relatively thick barrier, an accomplishment that is improbable in the world of physics. Then, once inside, it must somehow get out.

APPLICATIONS

A type of manufactured purple membrane (bacteriorhodopsin) film has been reported to be ferroelectric, and this is taken as encouragement for the model above (http://pubs.acs.org/cgi-bin/abstract.cgi/jpcbfk/2001/105/i14/abs/jp001054y.html). Purple membranes are a two-dimensional "crystal" consisting of a transmembrane protein surrounded by 10 lipid molecules within a basic hexagonal geometry. They are akin to man-made liquid-crystal displays, which, incidentally, depend on ferroelectric properties. Liquid-crystal displays are a $15 billion industry. Liquid crystals are composed of moderate-sized organic molecules that tend to be elongated like a cigar, although other exotic shapes are possible as well. In an electric field the molecules can line up to modify the polarization of light being transmitted through the crystal structure, thus creating a basis for screens and displays for laptops and other electronics.

Ferroelectric behavior is an interesting and promising property of certain materials, including organic compounds, silicon dioxide (quartz), and ceramics (such as barium titanate, $BaTiO_3$). Ferroelectrics come under a class of materials known as *electrets*, materials that display a permanent electric charge. Applications of ferroelectrics are numerous. Some of these materials have a very high dielectric constant (permittivity) and thus are suitable for very tiny surface-mount capacitors. The hysteresis inherent in such capacitors is suitable for nonvolatile computer memory, known as *ferroelectric RAM*. It has an advantage over flash memory in applications such as radio-frequency identification technology, since ferroelectric RAM can tolerate an increased number of read–write cycles.

Closely related to ferroelectric capacitors are piezoelectric capacitors. These form the heart of medical ultrasound imaging machines in which the capacitors generate an ultrasound "ping" and then listen to the returning signal reflected from internal objects. Related applications are vibration sensors, sound detection, and high-voltage pulses for flash cameras. Other applications of ferroelectric capacitors are as pyroelectric capacitors, capable of detecting very small temperature differences, used for fire sensors and infrared imaging. Last but not least is the ferroelectric tunnel diode, built with a nanometer-sized ferroelectric film between metal electrodes. By applying an appropriate voltage, electrons are able to tunnel through the film to produce a transfer of charge through the device for precision oscillator and trigger circuits.

Artificial membranes do some, but are not intended to do all, of what a biological membrane does. Experiments have produced silicon chips with patches of artificial membrane on the surface, for example, and self-supporting artificial membranes are currently under investigation. One goal of artificial membranes is to replace biological membranes for purposes such as hemodialysis.

The models in this chapter might provide clues to the manufacture of thin, strong membranes. Strength might be affected by a strong electric field, for example. It has been found that membranes engineered in the form of cells with internal charges in the voids are able to mimic ferroelectrics. The manufacture of ferroelectric membranes, perhaps using genetic engineering and nanotechnology, could mean the beginning of real progress toward manufacturing *imitation membranes*. The aim is to manufacture an imitation membrane that does all that a biological membrane does. Ideally, the result will be a flexible and efficient membrane that generates a pulse similar to a neural pulse, possibly leading to an imitation neuron. A device that imitates a neuron and works as efficiently as a neuron would be most useful for computations and communications. The membrane model given above may serve as a guide not just for understanding the neuron, but for constructing imitation neurons for use in active circuits.

CONCLUSIONS

The physical properties of neural particles and ferroelectric membranes have been introduced in this chapter in preparation for a derivation of a neural pulse waveform in Chapter 3. Sensitive regions of a neural membrane are modeled with ferroelectric particles that normally are held tight by the electric field in the membrane. But given a triggering event, the membrane particles relax. Sodium ions randomly hitting from the outside can now penetrate the membrane. In the diffusion model they pass completely through, but in this model several additional operations must be assumed to restore the neuron to its initial ionic composition.

In the electron capture model, positive ions capture stray electrons from within the membrane that have tunneled from the other side, thus building up a positive internal voltage across the membrane capacitance. In this model, ion-selective channels are unnecessary, mainly because the physical properties of sodium are naturally very different from those of potassium. The electron capture model is efficient in that neurons avoid contamination and have the capability to operate without rest, nonstop.

Internal voltage accumulates after a trigger, which reverses the electric field and forces the ferroelectric particles into a reversed orientation. This greatly reduces the sodium penetration, in part because membrane molecules become locked together again, but in the opposite way. Another factor is the reversed local electric field at the surface of the membrane, which repels sodium. The reversed orientation is held until particles in the membrane are forced to snap back into their equilibrium positions by undershoot.

Meanwhile, potassium ions inside the soma are assumed to capture electrons from the outside. Potassium ions are encouraged by the local electric fields, but they are larger and work more slowly than sodium ions. As sodium currents come to a stop, the local electric fields at the surface of the membrane actually encourage potassium penetration. Potassium discharges the internal positive charge, and eventually, the internal voltage undershoots its equilibrium value. This forces ferroelectric particles in the sensitive regions of a membrane to snap back into their original tight formation. Both sodium and potassium currents are greatly reduced at this point, so that low-level charge transport mechanisms can take over to restore rest voltage.

In a ferroelectric material, the resulting displacement (**D**) versus electric field (**E**) curve follows a typical hysteretic loop in which there are double values of **D** for any given **E**. Hysteresis explains undershoot in a neural pulse. Undershoot is desirable to reset the membrane so that another full-sized neural pulse can be triggered.

Manufactured purple membrane films have been found to display ferroelectric behavior, and this may be viewed as a milestone in the push to manufacture an imitation neuron. This may happen someday using the tools of genetic engineering and nanotechnology, perhaps even repairing nerve damage. Aside from medical applications, imitation neurons suggest a new type of amplifying device of major importance to computers and communications, essentially a wet technology that supports a very large number of inputs, reasonably small, flexible, and efficient.

EXERCISES

2-1 The neuron is a basic building block in the brain.

(a) Sketch an idealized neuron and label all parts correctly. Include typical dimensions.

(b) Sketch the way in which one neuron communicates with another, labeling all parts. Include typical dimensions.

2-2 Describe the structure of liquid water using sketches of atoms and electrons.

2-3 Describe physically the differences between sodium ions, potassium ions, and calcium ions. List weights, sizes, and valances. Provide sketches of your vision of how these ions might look.

2-4 Consider $1\,cm^3$ of a solution whose temperature is 37°C or 310 K. Each particle in the solution is said to have thermal energy. In fact, the average thermal energy is about 6.4×10^{-21} J per particle. What, in your own words, is thermal energy? Relate thermal energy to the kinetic energy $\frac{1}{2}mv^2$ of the particles.

2-5 Apply the Nernst equation to calculate the net Nernst potential assuming that Na^+ has 150 mM on the left and 10 mM on the right, and that K^+ has 130 mM on the right and 20 mM on the left.

2-6 Important concepts follow from Faraday's law. One gram equivalent weight of silver is 107.8, since the atomic weight of silver is 107.8; the valance of silver is 1 (one loosely bound electron). One gram equivalent weight is sometimes termed a *mole*, which is known to contain about 6.022×10^{23} atoms. Apply Faraday's law to calculate the following:

(a) How many grams of silver can be plated using 1 A for 2 h? Note that 1 A is equivalent to 1 C/s; 1 C is about 6.25×10^{18} electrons.

(b) Assume that the electrolyte through which the 1 A flows is held by a tank that is $10 \times 10 \times 50$ cm. Electrodes of size 10×10 cm are assumed on each end. What is the current density in amperes per square centimeter when 1 A is applied?

(c) What will happen if the electrical current density in amperes per square centimeter is forced to exceed the density of silver ions in number per square centimeter?

2-7 It is important to understand the units of electrical resistance. Mobility μ is a constant of proportionality between drift velocity v_d of a charged particle in cm/s and electric field $\mathscr{E}$ in V/cm. This can be expressed as the mobility equation

$$v_d = \mu \mathcal{E}$$

Assume that the charged particles are electrons. The mobility equation can be shown to be a form of Ohm's law, with I in amperes, V in volts, and R in ohms of resistance, usually expressed as

$$I = \frac{V}{R}$$

(a) Using the equations above, derive an equation for resistance in terms of electron mobility, electron concentration n in electrons per cubic centimeter, electronic charge q, and conductor length L using units of centimeters. Note that electrical current equals the number of electrons (nAL) multiplied by the charge per electron (q), divided by the time (L/v_d) to travel the distance L. Electrical resistance (R) in the answer will be proportional to L/A. The constant of proportionality in a given material is *resistivity* $\rho = 1/qn\mu$.

(b) A typical value of resistivity for salt water is $\rho = 34.5\,\Omega \cdot \text{cm}$, where resistivity is $\rho = 1/qn\mu$. Assuming this, calculate the resistance R_s in ohms for a segment of axon 2 μm in diameter and 1 mm long.

(c) The G_L through a neural membrane can be assumed to be 0.4 mS/cm^2. Note that a siemans is a unit of conductance, or I/V, the reciprocal of resistance. Given G_L, what is the resistance of a square centimeter of neural membrane?

(d) Assuming a membrane 5 nm thick, determine the resistivity of the above membrane in units of $\Omega \cdot \text{cm}$.

2-8 The Nernst equation has many applications in the study of thin membranes. The Nernst equation can be interpreted as a balance between (1) drift in an electric field that pulls positive ions from right to left, and (2) diffusion, from high concentrations N_1 on the left, to low concentrations N_2 on the right. The electrical current density (A/cm^2) as a result of diffusion is

$$J_D = -qD\frac{dN}{dx}$$

where q is 1.6×10^{-19} C, the electronic charge on a positive ion, D is a diffusion constant; n is a variable denoting ionic concentration in ions per cubic centimeter; and x is the distance from left to right into the membrane. The current density through a given material due to an electric field is

$$J_E = qnu\mathbf{E}$$

where u is mobility and $\mathbf{E}$ is the electric field (V/m) going from positive charge to negative charge, defined to be $\mathbf{E} = -dV/dx$; V is voltage.

(a) Let $J_D = J_E$, integrate, and derive an equation for the Nernst potential ΔV in terms of D, μ, and the concentrations N_1 and N_2 across a membrane.

(b) Compare with the equation in the text; identify a relation between D, μ, and kT/q. This is known as the *Einstein relation*.

2-9 A positive electric field through a membrane can be modeled to be a vector that goes from a positive charge on the right to a negative charge on the left.

(a) Using the neural pulse provided in this chapter, calculate the maximum and the minimum electric field in V/m in a neural membrane that is 5 nm thick.

(b) Look up the breakdown field for air in V/m at room temperature and pressure.

(c) Look up the breakdown field for Teflon in V/m at room temperature and pressure; compare it to air.

2-10 The concept of hysteresis is important. Line receivers in connections between computer components such as printers typically employ Schmitt triggers. Schmitt triggers have hysteresis to resist false triggers because of noise pickup by the interconnections.

(a) Graph a typical hysteresis loop for the output versus input voltages of a CMOS Schmitt trigger using the following information. Assume a noninverting Schmitt trigger whose output jumps from 0 to 3 V if the input exceeds 2.5 V; the output returns from 3 V to 0 if the input drops below 0.5 V.

(b) Sketch a pulse that moves linearly between 0 and 3 V and then back to 0. Assume that the pulse has a full width at half maximum equal to 4 ms.

(c) Apply this pulse to the input of the Schmitt trigger. Graph the output of the Schmitt trigger as a function of time. Note that when the Schmitt trigger changes state, this is analogous to ferroelectric particles snapping into a new orientation.

CHAPTER 3

NEURAL PULSES AND
NEURAL MEMORY

INTRODUCTION

In this chapter we provide a physical model for a single pulse of an action potential, the derivation of which is considered essential for students in artificial intelligence and neuroscience. Action potentials are voltage pulses that are generated by triggering the sensitive areas of a membrane, which is possible in dendrites, soma, and axon. The sensitive regions of a ferroelectric membrane are triggered by any event that reduces the electric field through the membrane. Sensitive particles within the membrane are then able to relax, effectively permitting a transfer of negative charge from the inside surface of the membrane, equivalent to leaving a positive charge inside. Transfers of charge are initiated by random ions hitting the membrane and capturing stray electrons, assumed to tunnel deeply into the membrane.

Positive voltage accumulates up to about $+40\,mV$. This causes a reversed electric field within the ferroelectric membrane that forces molecules within a sensitive membrane to reverse their orientation. This reversal, in turn, slows dramatically the accumulation of positive charge inside the neuron. In fact, it encourages a transfer of negative charge back *into* the neuron because of internal potassium ions that continue to be effective for charge transfer. These

Human Memory Modeled with Standard Analog and Digital Circuits:
Inspiration for Man-made Computers, By John Robert Burger
Copyright © 2009 John Wiley & Sons, Inc.

charges are integrated by the capacitance on the inside surface of the membrane, so internal positive voltage begins to drop.

Internal voltage moves through zero and goes negative, hence effecting a restoration of the ferroelectric molecules to equilibrium within the membrane. Eventually, the voltage across the membrane undershoots its equilibrium value of about $-70\,$mV inside the neuron relative to the outside. Undershoot assures that virtually all sensitive particles within the membrane are snapped into their equilibrium orientations, thus terminating the main part of a neural pulse. Subsequently, the voltage across the membrane returns to an equilibrium level by the same mechanisms that resulted in a Nernst voltage, ready to be triggered repeatedly.

Telegraphist's Equations

Usually, pulse propagation analysis in dendrites and axons involves numerical solutions to the *telegraphist's equations*.* However, within a neural path, inductance is insignificant, whereas current sourcing, distributed according to where the membrane is sensitive, is a major factor. Therefore, the telegraphist's equations simplify considerably, permitting a useful amount of manual analysis to predict physical behavior. In Chapter 5 we examine a computer analysis of the propagation and the logical activities of pulses in dendrites.

Conscious short-term memory, not to be confused with subconscious long-term memory, is extremely important to human cognition and is intimately related to the neural pulse model. Short-term memory beyond a few milliseconds is hypothesized to be the result of a minor modification to the neural pulse model, a modification that effectively slows the transfer of positive charge out of the dendrites. In this way the dendritic pulse is stretched out in time and may trigger an extended burst of axonal pulses for relatively long durations, hundreds of milliseconds. According to results in psychology, short-term memory can be retained for as long as a few seconds and may serve for moment-to-moment living. An extended burst is considered special not only because it lasts long, but because it has a slightly reduced amplitude using the model in this book. Short-term memory is modeled in Chapter 4 as being able to accept images from the senses or information from long-term memory.

---

* Standard equations for signals in a line relative to a ground plane:

$$\frac{\partial v}{\partial x} = -Ri - L\frac{\partial i}{\partial t}$$

$$\frac{\partial i}{\partial x} = -Gv - C\frac{\partial v}{\partial t} + I_S(x, t)$$

R is the series resistance, L the series inductance, G the shunt conductance, C the shunt capacitance; x the distance along the line, $v = v(x, t) =$ voltage on the line, $i = i(x, t) =$ current in the line, and $I_S(x, t)$ a distributed current source due to membrane activity.

Those gifted with photographic memory are living examples of subconscious long-term memory at its best, recording impressions with virtually no time expended for memorization. Long-term memories last indefinitely, especially if recalled occasionally and refreshed. Such memories cannot be erased, but they eventually fade away due to lack of use. The output neurotransmitters in long-term memory neurons have a neural path back to their dendritic receivers. This creates an indefinitely long cycling of neural pulses within the neuron. Long-term cycling is physically possible because neural signals use practically no energy or calories. Neural signals are considered separate from cellular maintenance and growth.

Long- and short-term memory systems are referred to as *explicit memory*. Memory systems for learning and for reflexes, responses that bypass the brain, are referred to as *implicit memory*. Implicit memory is established over time by a process of synaptic growth, so must not be confused with explicit memory, which is created instantly in the model used in this book. Synaptic growth and human learning are discussed in Chapter 5.

DERIVATION OF A NEURAL PULSE USING BASIC PHYSICS

The goal of this section is to present a physical model from which the waveform of a neural pulse can be derived.

Charge Transfer Analysis

To derive a neural pulse in a simple way, a membrane is going to be modeled as a potential barrier. Prior to triggering, the membrane is in equilibrium and is assumed to have an infinitely high barrier to charge transfer. After triggering there will be an assumed fixed barrier for sodium ions and an assumed fixed barrier for potassium ions. The heights of the barriers are expressed as fixed probabilities for charge transfer through the barrier. The probabilities for charge transfer are going to be chosen arbitrarily so that the result calculated closely approximates an experimentally measured pulse. This implies that there is an arbitrary multiplicative factor on the derived sodium current and on the derived potassium current.

In an ionic solution at body temperature, 37°C or 310 K, all particles, atoms, ions, and electrons are in motion because of thermal energy. But when a membrane is triggered, only the most energetic particles will have significant ability to push into the membrane. To proceed with a simple model based on basic physics, consider the concentrations of sodium and potassium about a neural membrane shown in Figure 3-1. Note that $1\,\text{mM/cm}^3$ means that the total number of particles in a cubic centimeter is about 6.02×10^{20} (Avogadro's number divided by 1000). Only positively charged ions (cations) are shown; an equal number of negatively charged ions (anions) are not shown because they are not used in this model; negative ions cannot easily capture negative charge from within the soma, nor can they build up a positive charge within the soma.

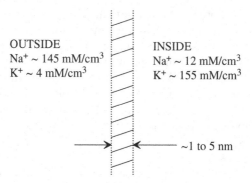

OUTSIDE
Na$^+$ ~ 145 mM/cm^3
K$^+$ ~ 4 mM/cm^3

INSIDE
Na$^+$ ~ 12 mM/cm^3
K$^+$ ~ 155 mM/cm^3

~1 to 5 nm

FIGURE 3-1 Na$^+$ and K$^+$ concentrations about a neural membrane.

In thermal equilibrium all particles are in motion with a speed distribution akin to that of a Maxwell–Boltzmann probability distribution. The speed of given elements affects the count per second hitting a potential barrier, all else being equal. At a given average energy, the average speed of sodium is faster than that of potassium because the atomic weight of sodium is about 23, compared to 39 for potassium. Average speed at body temperature (about 37°C or 310 K) can be calculated using the definitions of kinetic energy and average thermal energy per particle:

$$E = \tfrac{1}{2}mv^2 = \tfrac{3}{2}kT \approx 6.4 \times 10^{-21}\,\text{J} \approx 40\,\text{meV}$$

Note that Boltzmann's constant (k) and absolute temperature (T) in kelvin combine to specify average energy ($\tfrac{3}{2}kT$) measured in millielectron volts (meV). Named in honor of Lorenzo Avogadro (1776–1856), *Avogadro's number* (6.0221367×10^{23}) equals the approximate number of atoms in a mole, defined to be a gram atomic weight of an element (atomic weight expressed in grams). This allows an approximation of the weight proportional to the mass of an ion of sodium:

$$m = \frac{23\,\text{g}}{6 \times 10^{23}}\frac{1\,\text{kg}}{10^3\,\text{g}} = 3.83 \times 10^{-26}\,\text{kg/ion}$$

The resulting average speed, derived from $E = \tfrac{1}{2}mv^2$, is therefore about 578 m/s. In other words, sodium requires 17.3 µs to move 1 cm. A similar calculation for potassium (atomic weight 39, mass 6.5×10^{-26} kg, speed 443 m/s) yields 22.5 µs/cm, showing that potassium takes significantly longer to go the same distance because at a given energy it is more massive and thus slower.

An estimate of the number of ions per square centimeter per second pushing into a membrane may be found by considering a cubic centimeter of ions, as in Figure 3-2. Let C_i be ionic concentration. Consider a reference C_i of 1 mM,

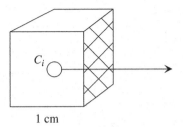

FIGURE 3-2   Model for ionic calculations.

about 6.02×10^{20} ions/cm^3. All ions are assumed to have a uniform distribution of directions in three dimensions and a distribution of speeds. In a first-order model, one-sixth of the ions begin from one wall of a cube and move to the other wall with a certain average speed. As an estimate, the number of ions per second per square centimeter hitting the right-side wall of the membrane is $\frac{1}{6}$ mM, divided by average speed:

$$N_{Na} \approx \frac{(1/6)6.02 \times 10^{20}\,\text{cm}^{-3}}{17.3\,\mu\text{s/cm}} = 5.799 \times 10^{24}\,\text{s}^{-1}/\text{cm}^2 \cdot \text{mM}$$

A similar procedure yields $4.459 \times 10^{24}\,\text{s}^{-1}/\text{cm} \cdot \text{mM}$ for potassium. The lower speed of potassium has translated into a lower current density of ions per second. Using 145 mM for sodium, the ionic current is 8.408×10^{26} ions/s $\cdot$ cm^2 and using 155 mM for potassium, the ionic current is 6.911×10^{26} ions/s $\cdot$ cm^2. The charge transfer will be proportional to ionic current.

Sodium Electrical Current

Because slower sodium ions will bounce back from the membrane quickly without significant penetration, very few ions are effective in charge buildup. Define a "capture" probability to be T_{Na} for sodium and T_K for potassium. The charge transfer (or electron capture) rate for sodium is thus 8.408×10^{26} $T_{Na}\,\text{s}^{-1}\text{cm}^{-2}$ and for potassium $6.911 \times 10^{26}\,T_K\,\text{s}^{-1}\text{cm}^{-2}$. Effective values for T_{Na} and T_K are going to be determined so that waveforms appear natural. The probabilities for electron capture are going to be very small because only a small number of ions are sufficiently energetic to push into the membrane. Furthermore, stray energetic electrons pushing from the other side are somewhat limited in number. The probability of actual capture is also limited. All of these limiting factors are actually quite fortunate, because it is necessary to have a membrane current that is quite low.

Ion flow is converted into amperes using the fact that the charge on one ion with a single valance electron (q) represents 1.6×10^{-19} C. One ampere is defined to be 1 C/s, where a coulomb is an extremely large number of electrons. Sodium

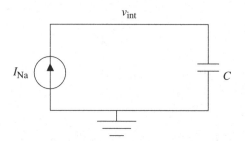

FIGURE 3-3 Model for voltage accumulation.

current density in A/cm^2 may be calculated to be 8.408×10^{26} $T_{Na} \times$ $1.6 \times 10^{-19} = 1.345 \times 10^8$ T_{Na} A/cm^2. To match the known waveform of a measured neural pulse, arbitrarily let $T_{Na} \approx 1 \times 10^{-12}$. The order of magnitude is close to a calculated value assuming quantum mechanical tunneling.* Using this particular value, the current density due to sodium is $J_{Na} \approx 0.1345$ mA/cm^2. A voltage across the membrane, within a soma relative to the outside, accumulates and can be calculated using the model shown in Figure 3-3.

C represents membrane *capacitance*, a measure of a membrane's ability to store charge. A defining equation for capacitance is

$$Q = CV$$

Where Q is charge in coulombs, C is capacitance in farads, and V is the voltage across the capacitor. In free space, a membrane capacitor with an area (A) of 1 cm^2 and a separation (d) of, say, 5 nm, or 5×10^{-7} cm, would have ≈ 0.17 µF/cm^2. This value is calculated from the defining *parallel-plate formula*:

$$\frac{C}{A} = \frac{\varepsilon}{d}$$

Note that permittivity ε in free space is about 8.85×10^{-14} F/cm. The capacitance is higher than free-space capacitance because of polarization within the membrane; 1 µF/cm^2 is used here. Charge Q in coulombs on a surface of 1 cm^2 may be expressed either as $C \Delta V$ or as $I \Delta t$, where I is current in amperes and t is time in seconds:

$$Q = C\Delta V = I\Delta t$$

Because of ferroelectric particles in the membrane, sodium current may be stopped *after a voltage increase from* -70 mV *to* $+130$ mV, *an increase of 0.2 V.*

---

*Probability of quantum penetration of electrons with energy 1 eV into a 5-eV potential barrier 1 nm thick, is about 5.6×10^{-12}, based on standard tunneling calculations. The barrier height is unknown and adjusted to give the desired probabilities.

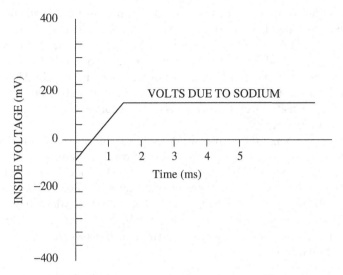

FIGURE 3-4   Internal voltage due to sodium.

The T_{Na} was chosen to provide this much increase in about 1.5 ms, a realistic rise time for a neural pulse. This rise time may be checked by calculating time to increase the voltage from -70 mV to $+130$ mV, or 0.2 V:

$$t = \frac{C\Delta V}{1.345 \times 10^8\, T_{Na}} = \frac{(1 \times 10^{-6})(0.2)}{0.1345 \times 10^{-3}} \approx 1.5\,\text{ms}$$

In summary, ionic current density is $1.345 \times 10^8\, T_{Na} = 1.345 \times 10^8 \times 10^{-12}$. This results in a sodium-induced electrical current of about $0.1345\,\text{mA/cm}^2$ to charge a capacitance of $1\,\mu\text{F/cm}^2$ to a voltage increase of 0.2 V. Included later will be a potassium current going in the opposite direction to discharge the capacitor.

In this, a simple model, the sodium current is zero after 1.5 ms. The resulting voltage due to sodium can be graphed as in Figure 3-4. Sodium transmission was chosen to give an increase from -70 mV to 130 mV, a change of 200 mV and then holding after 1.5 ms.

Potassium Electrical Current

In a simple model, potassium current is triggered at exactly the same time as sodium. Potassium is larger and less penetrating, so potassium current is lower.

Since potassium is concentrated on the inside, potassium current flows from inside out, opposite that of sodium. Potassium current density in A/cm^2 is 6.911×10^{26} T_K $1.6 \times 10^{-19} = 1.105 \times 10^8$ T_K. The transmission factor for potassium can be modeled to be less than that for sodium, because K$^+$ ions, with weight 39, are significantly larger than Na ions with weight 23. To match the known data, we use $T_K \approx 5.5 \times 10^{-13}$, about half that of sodium. Then current density because of potassium becomes $J_K \approx 1.105 \times 10^8 \times 5.5 \times 10^{-13} \approx 0.0608$ mA/cm^2.

Note that at 1.5 ms, the change in the voltage due to sodium is 200 mV; it goes from -70 mV up to $+130$ mV. In 1.5 ms the change in the voltage, defined to be δV, due to potassium must be -90 mV if one desires a pulse peak of about 40 mV, as in the experimental neural pulse. This is because $130 - 90 = 40$ mV at about 1.5 ms. As a check on the calculations, the T_K was chosen to provide a peak of about 40 mV. Note that $T_K = 5.5 \times 10^{-13}$ results in a sodium-induced electrical current of 0.0608 mA/cm^2. Using conservation of charge yields

$$\delta V = \frac{(0.0608 \times 10^{-3})(1.5 \times 10^{-3})}{1 \times 10^{-6}} \approx 90 \text{ mV}$$

In this example, the neural peak is $130 - 90$ or 40 mV; this means that the potential increases by 110 mV in 1.5 ms, going from -70 mV to 40 mV.

This model will choose 20 mV of undershoot below -70 mV, an undershoot to -90 mV. Sodium takes a voltage from -70 up to $+130$ mV and holds. In conjunction with potassium, the voltage moves up to only about 40 mV after 1.5 ms. After this, potassium current causes voltage to decrease. At maximum undershoot, potassium must cause a voltage drop of 220 mV because $130 - 220 = -90$. The time of maximum undershoot can be calculated using conservation of charge as

$$t = \frac{(1 \times 10^{-6})(0.220)}{0.0608 \times 10^{-3}} \approx 3.62 \text{ ms}$$

After about 3.6 ms the ferroelectric membrane snaps back to equilibrium, causing all currents to be reduced to low levels. Low-level charge transport will bring voltage from its undershoot level of about -90 mV back to its equilibrium level of about -70 mV across the membrane. It may be noted that by varying the transmissions through the membrane, the resulting pulse can be fitted to a wide range of neural pulse waveforms. The result in this case is illustrated in Figure 3-5. Note that sodium- and potassium-related voltages combine linearly. Figure 3-6 (a repeat of Figure 2-14), illustrates the measured neural pulse we are trying to get.

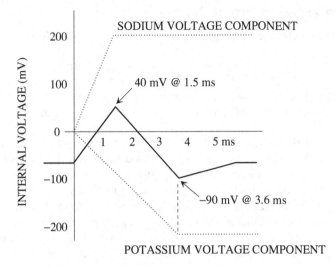

FIGURE 3-5   Calculated voltage pulse internal to a neuron.

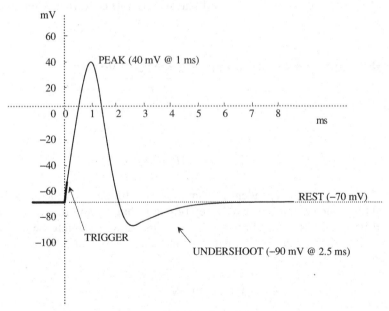

FIGURE 3-6   Reference (lab model) neural pulse (refer to Chapter 2 for more information).

Calculated Versus Reference Pulse

Calculated and reference waveforms may be compared as follows:

	Reference (Lab)	Calculated
Peak	40 mV @ 1.0 ms	40 mV @ 1.5 ms
Valley	− 90 mV @ 2.5 ms	− 90 mV @ 3.6 ms

The rise time of the calculated pulse (1.5 ms) is slower than that of the reference pulse (1.0 ms). This may be because the current due to potassium does not really increase linearly like a ramp. Potassium-induced current may be lower than a ramp because the initial ferroelectric polarization creates a local electric field at the surface of the membrane that repels potassium ions (and sodium electrons). Hence, the capture probability for potassium, T_K, might be lower in the model during the sodium current surge. If there were a reason to do so, a second-order analysis would use a variable T_K to achieve more accurate rise times.

The peaks and valleys of the two pulses at 40 mV and − 90 mV are designed to match. Reference pulse fall time goes from a 40-mV peak to a − 90-mV minimum in about $2.5 - 1.0 \approx 1.5$ ms; for the calculated pulse it is about $3.6 - 1.5 \approx 2.1$ ms, which is relatively slow. This indicates that the capture factor T_K after the peak might be higher in the model above. It appears that an accurate fit to data can result by using variable capture factors for T_{Na} and T_K.

Formal Circuit Model of Membrane Current and Voltage

Technically, the transmission factors T_{Na} and T_K are voltage dependent. They go on and off at given voltages (in this model). The transmission factors can be expressed as

$$T_i = T_{i1} u(M_i - v_{int})$$

where T_i is the voltage-dependent transmission due to ion I, v_{int} the net voltage internal to the neuron, $u(M - v_{int})$ a step function that is unity for $v_{int} < M_i$ and zero otherwise, T_{i1} the fixed probabililty of transmission through the potential barrier, and M_i the voltage at which transmission is disabled. The parameters used above are:

$$M_{Na} = 40 \, mV$$

$$M_K = -90 \, mV$$

$$T_{Na1} \approx 1 \times 10^{-12}$$

$$T_{K1} \approx 5.5 \times 10^{-13}$$

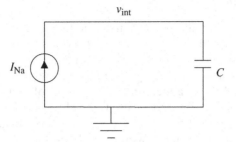

FIGURE 3-7   Charging and discharging with sodium and potassium currents.

In summary:

$$T_{Na} = 1 \times 10^{-12} u(40 - v_{int})$$

$$T_K = 5.5 \times 10^{-13} u(90 + v_{int})$$

The calculation is relatively simple, yet gives reasonable results. Curved peaks and valleys result by going to computer simulation as in Chapter 5, although such refinements are not relevant to a basic model. The overall circuit model appears in Figure 3-7. Here the sodium and potassium current densities are modeled as voltage-dependent current sources in A/cm^2 that charge a membrane capacitance C in F/cm^2.

$$J_{Na} = 1.345 \times 10^8 \, T_{Na}$$

$$J_K = 1.105 \times 10^8 \, T_K$$

The outside of the membrane is assumed to be ground at zero volts.

Resting Voltage

Potassium current decreases radically when the net internal voltage reaches -90 V in this model. At this point, capture probabilities revert back to their equilibrium values; the voltage moves to an equilibrium value of about -70 mV within a few milliseconds. This might involve leakage conductance. The leakage resistance is about $G_L \approx 0.3$ mS/cm^2 or $R \approx 3.33$ kΩ/cm^2, and possibly much higher; the capacitance C is about 1 µF/cm^2; the time for voltage to discharge to about 37% of its initial value is one time constant, equal to C/G_L; the membrane time constant is roughly 3.33 ms. As a rule of thumb, voltage needs about five time constants to return to equilibrium. This much, about 16 ms, might be a little on the long side. Our experimentally obtained neural pulse returns to equilibrium in only a couple of milliseconds.

Continuity Equation

The question is: How would one calculate the time to go from undershoot at about $-90\,$mV to equilibrium at about $-70\,$mV? One possibility is to apply a continuity equation involving not only conduction but also diffusion. It is difficult to believe that relatively large sodium and potassium ions can diffuse in sufficient numbers through a membrane in a couple of milliseconds. Also, one wonders about the diffusion model itself, which depends on collisions in an isotropic volume whose dimensions are well in excess of a mean free path. Membranes are very thin and anisotropic. Nevertheless, a combination of conduction and diffusion could model a neural pulse that recovers in a couple of milliseconds. The continuity equation below assumes that ions diffuse and conduct through the membrane and establish an electric field across the membrane, eventually reaching equilibrium.

Although diffusion does not seem like the best model, at least it is efficient: Energy is not dissipated by diffusion. Let $N = N(x, t)$ be the concentration (ions/cm^3) of a given type of positive ion at a given place and time that diffuse into and through the membrane. The continuity equation is derived in basic texts with sections on diffusion. Within the membrane, a continuity equation can be expressed as

$$\frac{\partial N}{\partial t} = +D\frac{\partial^2 N}{\partial x^2} - \mu\mathbf{E}\frac{\partial N}{\partial x} - RN + G$$

Positive ions are diffusing from left to right, where D is the diffusion constant; μ the mobility for ions drifting through the membrane, $\mathbf{E}$ the electric field (from positive charge to negative charge), $R = R(x, t)$ is a recombination rate or electron capture rate within the membrane, approximated to be zero ($R = 0$); and generation $G = G(x, t)$ of ions within the membrane is assumed to be zero ($G = 0$). Solving the continuity equation is beyond the scope of this book, but its application is clarified to some extent in the exercises at the end of the chapter.

NEURON SIGNAL PROPAGATION

Soma and hillock vary greatly in shape and size but may be modeled as a sphere with a diameter of 25 μm. An axon is modeled as a small fiber (roughly 2 μm in diameter near the hillock) that extends from the soma, reaching perhaps several centimeters, eventually branching into smaller fibers that approach other neurons. Typical axons are covered with myelin, an insulator that develops in about 1-mm lengths with separations of about 2 μm. Capacitance and membrane conductive losses within the axon are insignificant when there is myelination or white matter, so pulses propagate faster. Figure 3-8 is a model of a neuron for the purpose of discussing the propagation of signals along an axon.

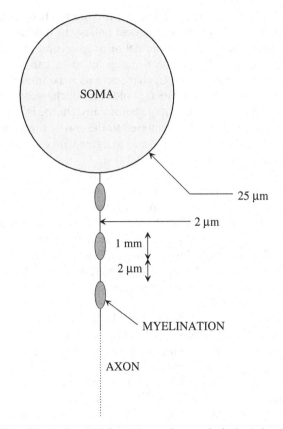

FIGURE 3-8   Physical model for propagation analysis (not drawn to scale).

The physical model may be translated into a circuit model as in Figure 3-9, where C_s represents the soma capacitance; I_s the net current that charges C_s; R_n the axon resistance per millimeter for the first segment; C_n the capacitance at the first node (between myelination), known as a *node of Ranvier* Louis-Antoine

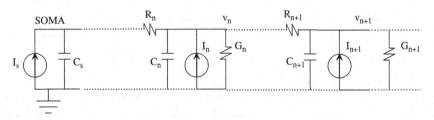

FIGURE 3-9   Model of soma and the first two segments of an axon.

Ranvier, 1835–1922; I_n a restoration current driving the first node; and G_n the conductance at the first node. For subsequent nodes, the index n is incremented.

In a manual analysis, the Elmore model of propagation in an RC transmission line may be applied. Propagation along an axon can be analyzed as a sequence of charge transfers. First, C_s charges to its maximum voltage before a charge to C_n is permitted; then, while C_n holds its full charge, the next C_{n+1} in the line charges to its maximum voltage before any charge is permitted for the next C_{n+2}, and so on in the Elmore model, to the end of the axon. This simple method of manual analysis has been found to agree with computer simulations and is good enough for first-order calculations.

An axon is primarily a passive transmission line. In contrast, a typical dendritic channel has no myelination and is continuously active all along its path. In an axon, small losses because of resistance and conductance are compensated by the I_n sources available through the exposed membrane at the nodes of Ranvier, so that pulses propagate without appreciable attenuation. Since rise and fall times are slow, in the millisecond range, losses in series resistance are very small, as shown in the appendix to this chapter.

A loss in the conductance at a node of Ranvier is very small because the area exposed is very small. Conductive energy losses occur not only in the nodes of Ranvier, but in the soma and dendrites, where myelination is absent. Such losses are common to all neurons and indeed to all cells in the body and are considered a normal part of cellular maintenance. They have little or nothing to do with neural signals, which seem to flutter back and forth in an electrically reversible way without the dissipation of appreciable energy.

The diameters of an axon are continually decreasing, such that $C_{n-1} > C_n > C_{n+1}$. This has certain practical implications. If a stray photon causes a charge to appear in C_n, it is unlikely that it will trigger an action potential. This is because the charge will soon be shared with C_{n-1} and C_{n+1}. By conservation of charge, charge is divided, and in the nodes of Ranvier, voltage is expected to be well below a triggering threshold for C_{n-1} and C_{n+1}. Thus, a stray cosmic ray probably could not begin an action potential in a reliable neuron.

Pulses go down an axon readily but are not reflected or otherwise returned to the hillock and soma. This cannot occur because an axon terminates in a bouton, an organ that develops without a source of energy to trigger a back propagation. Also, it is difficult for a signal to move from a smaller capacitance C_{n-1} to a larger capacitance C_n with enough voltage to trigger a node of Ranvier and gain enough charge for an even larger capacitance, C_{n+1}. The computerized simulation given in Chapter 5 indicates that no reflections are possible from the ends of a neuron, with or without myelination.

In contrast, back propagations (reflections) from dendritic junctions as well as from the soma appear to be quite normal. As a result of a soma pulse, for the purposes of this discussion, C_s may be thought of as holding an excess voltage of about 100 mV (a rounded-off value; the model above used 110 mV). The net magnitude of soma capacitance C_s is surprisingly large. Using a sphere with radius 25 μm, the surface area is πD^2:

$$C_s = \pi D^2 C_m = (1963\,\mu m^2)(1\,\mu F/cm^2)(1\,cm/10^4\,\mu m)^2 \approx 19.6\,pF$$

In contrast to soma capacitance, nodal capacitance C_n at the first node is over 100 times smaller:

$$C_n = \pi DLC_m = (\pi \cdot 2\,\mu m)(2\,\mu m)(1\,\mu F/cm^2)(1\,cm/10^4\,\mu m)^2 \approx 0.125\,pF/mm$$

In an extreme example, assume that all subsequent C_{n+j} are equal to the first C_n. The axon may extend more than 10 cm, yet the resulting nodal capacitance would not quite sum to the soma capacitance. In other words, the voltage pulse from the soma is discharged only slightly, by about 50%. There is enough charge in the soma to deliver a respectable half-voltage pulse to the boutons without the aid of the nodes of Ranvier, although neurotransmitter release could suffer.

G_n is loss conductance; it is usually assumed to be about $0.3\,mS/cm^2$, but it is probably much higher. This seems like a lot of conductance ($3.33\,k\Omega/cm^2$) for what is claimed to be an insulator, but the number is misleading. When scaled properly, loss resistance is extremely large even in the thickest part of the axon. The first node of Ranvier is modeled to have a diameter of 2 μm:

$$G_L = (0.3\,mS/cm^2)(\pi \cdot 2\,\mu m)(2\,\mu m)(1\,cm/10^4\,\mu m)^2 = 3.76 \times 10^{-11}\,S$$

$$R_L = \frac{1}{G_L} = 26.6 \times 10^9 = 26.6\,G\Omega$$

There is also series resistance to consider. The value for R_s depends on the resistivity of the fluid within the axon. Assumptions range from that of seawater ($31.4\,\Omega \cdot cm$) to that of strong salt water ($3.14\,\Omega \cdot cm$). The value assumed is not critical since losses are very small and will be covered by I_n; to begin, strong salt water will be assumed:

$$\frac{R_s}{L} = \frac{\rho}{A} = \frac{3.14\,\Omega \cdot cm}{\pi(1\,\mu m)^2(1\,cm/10^4\,\mu m)^2} = 10^8/cm^{-1} = 10\,M\Omega/mm$$

$R_L \approx 26\,G\Omega$ at a node of Ranvier is very much more than $R_s \approx 10\,M\Omega$ for *strong* salt water or even $R_s \approx 100\,M\Omega$ assuming the equivalent of *weak* salt water inside the axon, so voltage division is insignificant ($v_n \approx v_{in}$ in Figure 3-10). Even with far more segments, voltage loss is insignificant, implying that heat dissipation is also insignificant.

Propagation delay is defined to be the time between a 50% level on the input to a 50% level on the output. In one segment using the parameters above, 1 mm of passive length, a standard Elmore formula (derived in basic texts on circuits)

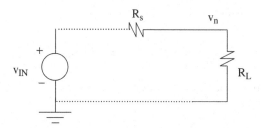

FIGURE 3-10 Voltage-division circuit.

gives propagation delay in one segment as

$$t_p = (\ln 2) R_s C_n = (0.695)(10 \, M\Omega)(125.6 \, fF) = 0.87 \, \mu s$$

One hundred 1-mm segments constitute a length of 10 cm. Assuming that each segment charges in turn from the preceding segment, the propagation delay for 10 cm can be shown to be

$$t_{p(100)} \approx \frac{0.695}{2} R_s C_n N^2 = (0.347)(1.256 \, \mu)(100)^2 = 4358 \, \mu s \approx 4.3 \, ms$$

It may be noted that delay goes up as the *square* of the number of segments, so longer axons have a delay that is more than proportional.

Soma pulses have a width slightly more than 5 ms; thus, if you believe the parameters cited above, propagation delay over 10 cm of axon is comparable to the pulse width in the soma. As the pulse arrives at the tips of the axon, the pulse in the soma is in the process of returning its energy to the ionic solutions. This is interesting but unimportant since neurons work asynchronously, so that propagation delay is noncritical.

Active Aaxon Analysis

An axon is not completely passive. As the signal charges node v_n, current source I_n is triggered. Pulse voltage regulation occurs because if I_n attempts to charge C_n beyond a reference level, which we assumed to be about 100 mV above the equilibrium level, the current through R_n is reversed, which tends to limit the maximum voltage in a pulse. But if v_n is below the reference level, I_n is there to help charge C_n to a higher level.

Eventually, potassium action will reverse the current flow in the soma and lower the soma voltage to a resting value. This lowering of potential propagates similarly along the axon, effectively pulling positive charge back to the soma as the soma voltage drops. A pulse with fixed amplitude and width moves along the axon without noticeable distortion, as observed under laboratory conditions.

Electrical solitons are single, stable pulses that do not change waveform as they travel large distances. Technically, a pulse in an axon is not an electrical soliton, because an axon is passive and linear for about 1000 μm and active for only 2 μm. But an axon pulse looks like a soliton because it appears to retain its waveform. Dendritic pulses, in contrast, are continuously refreshed by membrane unprotected by myelination, and so support true solitons.

At a point of interest, electrical solitons can be created with the help of PN junctions or ferromagnetic beads to send picosecond-width pulses through a circuit without dispersion (a gradual widening of the width of a pulse and a reduction of its amplitude). Optical solitons in optical fibers, for example, routinely transfer large amounts of information over thousands of kilometers with no errors in the signal.

MODELING NEURONS AS ADIABATIC

Neural operations use very few calories as evidenced (indirectly) by the fact that calorie use is difficult to image. Mental activities include such activities as memory searching, recall, memorization, reading, and listening. Mental activity does not include physical movement of any parts of the body or the physical effects of emotion and learning involving synaptic growth. As everyday evidence for the efficiency of neurons as logic devices, mental activity does not make the head warmer nor does it make the heart work harder, certainly not like a muscle that is being exercised. Aside from neural growth and maintenance, there are no chemical reactions in mental activity that are analogous to burning gasoline in an automobile or converting energy in a battery. Ions in a neuron can be modeled as operating in closed cycles.

One rationale for modeling a neuron as adiabatic is the slow rise and fall of a neural pulse. This suggests that the resistance in an axon is unimportant, as it is in an asymptotically adiabatic electrical circuit (refer to the appending to this chapter). Commonly, electrical circuits involving CMOS technology can be made adiabatic in the sense of being asymptotically adiabatic. Being asymptotically adiabatic is good, because power loss can be made arbitrarily low by decreasing the rate at which power supply voltages are permitted to change. Because of loss conductance, unfortunately, real-world circuits can never be asymptotically adiabatic. The best an engineer can design is a circuit that is approximately adiabatic. The word *adiabatic* means either asymptotically zero energy or approximately zero energy. Thus, it is consistent with the use of the word to model neurons as adiabatic, meaning virtually no heat gain or loss.

Calories are a measure of energy dissipation or heat; energy dissipation is the integration of power dissipation. Neural pulses rise and fall slowly, which tends to keep power dissipation negligible in series resistance. But series resistance in an axon is very high compared to resistors used by engineers using submicrometer CMOS standards, so one wonders if energy loss is actually avoided. Consider the loss in one segment of an axon. Using the numbers above, $R = 10\,M\Omega$ and $C = 125\,fF$ for each millimeter. During a neural pulse, the voltage can be assumed to increase at a maximum rate of $100\,mV/ms$. Current in a given segment is therefore

$$i = \frac{C\,dV}{dt} = \frac{(125\,fF)(100\,mV)}{1\,ms} = 12.5\,pA$$

This is the current available to charge the next segment in an axon and thus trigger the next node of Ranvier. At this point, even though R is large, it may be noted that the voltage loss across R in a single segment of axon is very small:

$$\Delta V = iR = (12.5\,pA)(10\,M\Omega) = 125\,\mu V = 0.125\,mV$$

Power dissipated in watts is

$$P = i^2 R = (12.5\,pA)^2(10\,M\Omega) \approx 1.56\,fW$$

This is small. Energy dissipated in joules is

$$J = P\,\Delta t = (1.56\,fW)(1\,ms) = 1.56\,aJ$$

When multiplied by 100 segments (10 cm in length), power and energy dissipations are finite but still miniscule (0.156 fJ). Even if a billion such axons work in parallel, energy is only 0.156 µJ. A single food calorie, on the other hand, is 4.184 kJ, over 1 billion times larger.

Other actions are now considered. When ions impinge upon a membrane, a small amount of kinetic energy is converted into potential energy as the membrane stretches. But as ions bounce back, away, this energy is returned to the external ionic solution. When an ion captures an electron, energy is taken from the electron as it changes states; but when the electron is set free to attach to some other ion, the electron regains its lost energy; the net change in energy is negligible.

Neurotransmitters are modeled similarly. They are pushed away from boutons by a positive voltage pulse, but eventually they are free to return, like a ball tossed into the air that returns to Earth. Average energy use is expected to be inconsequential. If part of a membrane is dielectrically active, it is expected to dissipate some heat. This is equivalent to microwave heating, but at a much lower frequency. Because frequency is so very low, however, heating is insignificant. All appears to be physically reversible in a neuron, a fairly good indication that neurons may be modeled as adiabatic, at least when it comes to electrical signaling exclusive of growth and maintenance.

NEURONS FOR MEMORY

Explicit memory includes both conscious short-term memory and subconscious long-term memory. Refer to Appendix B at the end of the book for a discussion of these types of memory. Another type of memory, termed *implicit memory*, is responsible for reflexive actions that do not necessarily pass through the brain. Learning in the sense of new synapses for new neural connections is a sort of implicit memory that is left for another chapter.

Short-Term Memory

To accomplish fundamental communications with other neurons, short-term memory must provide a signal that can be received by ordinary neurons. For this reason, short-term memory neurons, like any other neuron, are modeled to deliver bursts of pulses on a repetitive basis, but the bursts are a little longer. Short-term memory is probably not charge storage in capacitance, analogous to dynamic RAM (DRAM) in computers. The time for voltage to discharge to about 37% of its initial value is one time constant, equal to C/G, roughly 3.33 ms in a membrane. So the time constant of a membrane is not long enough. Also, discharge through leakage conductance in the membrane would be dissipative, which does not support the outlook that biology tends to be efficient.

A better explanation of short-term memory is readily available. Dendrites in short-term memory neurons have pulses that are wider than average. Dendritic pulses are triggered by excitatory neurotransmitters in the usual way. But within the dendritic receivers and the dendrites themselves is modeled a shortfall of potassium and calcium, so that the dendritic voltage does not recover immediately as it would otherwise. This results in a long dendritic pulse. This longer-lasting voltage becomes an extended trigger to the soma for a second or two, which is an adiabatic process in an ideal case. The resulting long trigger delivers a stream of neural bursts that constitute a short-term memory for a given feature, such as shape or shade. A collection of such features constitutes an entire short-term memory.

The thickness of the membrane in the dendritic receiver area affects the pulse width, since increased width reduces the probability of charge transfer and would spread out the resulting pulse, giving it both a slow rise time and a slow fall time. But a fast-attack, slow-fall time response is needed, so membrane thickness is not expected to be important. An extended trigger to the soma produces *an enhanced rate* of neural pulses. The enhanced rate occurs by applying a steady triggering voltage to the soma. In the ferroelectric hysteric characteristic of Chapter 2, a minor loop is created between the threshold for triggering and the maximum voltage, where sodium-induced charging is stopped. Enhanced rates give lower amplitudes, but not so low as to harm the signaling properties of short-term memory.

A shortfall of dendritic receiver potassium and calcium implies that electrical current is unavailable to reduce the dendritic pulse. But over time, a trickle of charge will penetrate the membrane and reduce the internal positive voltage as electrons return to the interior. Thus, memory fades. Figure 3-11 shows a dendritic pulse expressed as a percentage of maximum voltage and illustrates what the author means by an extended trigger signal. To match psychological data, short-term memory is modeled in the figure with the equation $\eta = 100/\log(10t)$, where η represents the percentage of maximum voltage and t is the time in milliseconds. This is an arbitrary equation to illustrate the logarithmic abscissa, compatible with expectations for short-term memory. As the trigger voltage lowers into a threshold region, the short-term memory neuron will lose its trigger, and thus the memory.

Electrically, a short-term memory neuron is like the *one-shot* used in digital design, presenting its binary output for a few seconds and then shutting down. The figure is an idealization, not real data that are somehow measured. The time at which a short-term memory neuron shuts down is expected to vary slightly from neuron to neuron in this model because of variations in ionic compositions within dendrites, in membrane shapes, and in soma triggering thresholds.

Recent knowledge concerning implicit short-term memory helps somewhat with an understanding of explicit short-term memory. Experiments concerning implicit memory with the sea snail *Aplysia* were conducted over a period of years by Eric R. Kandel (1929–) and others, and suggest that interneurons are involved in implicit short-term memory. An interneuron serves to release serotonin near the synapses of an ordinary neuron, giving the neuron a memory effect. A brief burst of serotonin extends the period of excitatory glutamate release from milliseconds to minutes. Concurrently, the quantity released increases.

Researchers originally proposed that potassium channels are shut down by serotonin. Fewer potassium channels imply a longer neural pulse and an extended duration of neurotransmitter release. Related experiments have indicated that serotonin indeed closes potassium channels if applied directly to the outside of a neuron. But there are other ways to close potassium channels and give a memory effect. In looking for a better explanation of the effects of serotonin in *Aplysia*, it was found that there can be receptors on a neural membrane that receive serotonin and convert it inside a neuron into a substance known as *cyclic AMP* (adenosine 5′-monophosphate). Cyclic AMP results in a measurable memory effect, as described originally. Cyclic AMP inside a neuron shuts down potassium channels and increases the period and quantity of glutamate release.

One is left to wonder whether cyclic AMP changes the membrane itself by shutting down potassium channels, or somehow neutralizes potassium ions,

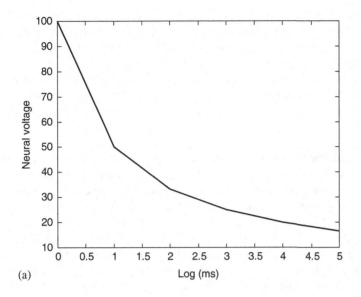

(a)

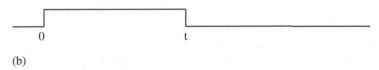

(b)

FIGURE 3-11   (a) Trigger voltage for short-term memory (3 corresponds to 10^3 or 1 s); (b) example output of a short-term memory neuron. Extended trigger produces an extended neural burst.

perhaps by attaching to them, making them less active. The result is a long-duration release of excitatory glutamate. Usually, neurons have action potentials in the form of pulse bursts at the tips of an axon. Normal action potentials are composed of perhaps 10 neural pulses, more or less. The action potential from a neuron for short-term memory is modeled similarly, as a burst of pulses, but a burst that lasts longer. The advantages of neural bursts are neurotransmitter conservation and energy conservation. In contrast, a long-duration release of neurotransmitters over minutes via cyclic AMP suggests the loss of a great many neurotransmitters, raising a question as to how they are replaced so that short-term memory can continue to operate on a regular basis.

The simplest model is to have the dendrites give a long pulse. A long dendritic pulse triggers a long burst in the soma. Significantly, a regular burst is necessary to other neurons in a system, because an excess of neurotransmitter ions beyond normal could disable a dendritic receiver instead of exciting it, perhaps forcing an incorrect long pulse on all downstream neurons. Brain waves do not have periods of minutes, but milliseconds, as commonly observed.

Dendritic operations are discussed in detail in Chapter 5. For the present, a practical model for explicit short-term memory can be described as follows: Dendrites in short-term-memory neurons have a shortfall of internal ions, and this gives a short-term memory effect. Simple and efficient, the short-term memory neuron is just another type of neuron, one with fewer ions in its dendrites.

Energy Dissipation in Short-Term Memory   Short-term-memory neurons are modeled to be adiabatic, as are all other neurons discussed in this book. As in the case of regular neurons, excitatory ions begin a long dendritic pulse, but the pulse itself pushes these ions away and keeps them away, to drift back to their homes. Any action potentially involves the rhythmic release and capture of neurotransmitter ions in response to the presynaptic pulses applied and the postsynaptic pulses generated, but eventually the positive excitatory ions return to their home boutons as they return to a negative rest voltage. The propagating pulses themselves rise and fall sufficiently slowly to avoid loss of charge in the series resistance of the conducting axon. This basic charge recovery concept is presented in the chapter appendix. Overall, very little energy is lost as a result of an action potential, even those with long durations. The senses require external energy in such forms as photons, pressures, molecules, and so on, but this energy is outside the memory system.

There is always a loss in a neural membrane that depends on conductance and the rest voltage ($P_{\text{Loss}} = V^2 G$). This loss is common to all cells and is not counted as being part of an action potential. Surprisingly, during an action potential the $V^2 G$ loss is expected to be less. The average voltage across a membrane decreases when positive peaks counterbalance negative peaks. In the model of this book, losses associated with equilibrium voltages are considered energy for maintenance, growth, and health, but not energy for neural signals. Long-term-memory neurons, discussed next, work on a principle completely different from that of short-term-memory neurons.

Long-Term Memory

It is important to realize that long-term memory and long-term learning are two completely different things. *Long-term learning* involves synaptic growth over a period of time, whereas *long-term memory* happens almost immediately. Many of us have experienced dramatic events that occurred in an instant but that are remembered practically forever. People gifted with photographic memory, for example, remember large quantities of information after only a brief exposure. Explicit long-term memory does not appear to require synaptic growth.

Established practically immediately and lasing indefinitely, long-term memory does not appear to be a variation of short-term memory, which fades within seconds. A completely different model is required. Long-term memory in its simplest form can be modeled as a neural circuit whose output excitatory transmitters are sent to receivers at inputs. The resulting closed circuit may be modeled as shown in Figure 3-12.

A memory cell, by the way, is not necessarily a biological cell; rather, it is a neural circuit involving neural logic gates. Inputs and outputs of long-term memory are pulses of excitatory neurotransmitter ions; gates are coupled by similar bursts. Once excitatory neurotransmitters are applied (S = true), a signal begin cycling through gates 1 and 2 indefinitely. There is no way to stop the cycling in this particular model. Indefinite cycling is physically possible because the neurons are modeled as adiabatic. This means that energy dissipation is inconsequential, since the internal circulating signals within adiabatic neurons never couple their energy to dissipative elements. Circulating signals like this are not unusual in man-made technologies. An analogous condition occurs, for example, when electrical currents cycle indefinitely in a superconducting circuit.

The long-term memory cell is equivalent to a *latch* in digital design. The term *latching memory* is a shorthand way to describe subconscious long-term memory. Inverters are not required, seen later to imply that inhibitory neurotransmitters are unnecessary. The OR gate is connected as a buffer to achieve a circuit delay, because timing is important and since the operation of the circuit is easier to understand with delay. The extra OR gate will be expanded later to create a toggle or T flip-flop, which is sometimes useful in an analysis of the unusual aspects of memory.

In general, biological long-term memory cannot be cleared. Once a collection of information is in memory, it stays indefinitely. The latches cannot be cleared based on what is modeled here. Under unusual conditions, however, such as physical damage or lack of use for a very long time, it is assumed that memory will dissolve. All neural gates have additional controls, not shown here but discussed in a later chapter, that permit them to sleep. Mere inability to recall a memory does not imply that the memory is erased. It usually implies that the memory search process needs more time or is otherwise confused.

The circuit operates as follows: Initially, both S and Q are zero, or false, meaning that the memory cell is blank and ready to be programmed. When

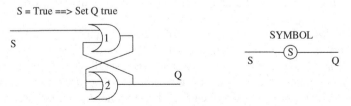

FIGURE 3-12   Long-term memory circuit.

the control signal S goes true, there is a propagation delay through gate 1 and then gate 2 before Q goes true. Q in turn, applies a signal back to gate 1, the OR gate, and latches it. Following this, S is unimportant, and may be returned to zero. Q holds a single feature of an image of memory that is self-refreshing.

In the circuit, timing is important. Neuron 1 is activated by excitatory neurotransmitter ions applied to its input at S; soon after, output neurotransmitter ions emerge from neuron 1 and are applied to the input of neuron 2. Meanwhile, imagine that neuron 1 returns to rest. Shortly after this, neuron 2 emits a package of excitatory neurotransmitter ions that serve to reactivate an input to neuron 1. Now imagine that neuron 2 returns to rest. The circuit is easier to understand by assuming that neurons 1 and 2 alternate between equilibrium and action. The actual number of pulses for each neural action and the delay between actions are parameters that have evolved over millions of years to optimize efficiency.

One arrives at the latching model of memory because other models are untenable. For example, membrane capacitance can store a binary value in direct current form, but only for a short time. Myelination does not change this situation; although it reduces conductance, it also reduces capacitance. Unfortunately, membrane conductance is finite and discharges irreversibly, dissipating all of its energy.

Direct-current (dc) synapses have been proposed, but they would have circulating dc currents, which, over time, would dissipate excessive energy. In this respect they are no better than capacitance, which stores charge only for a short time. As mentioned above, long-term memory is established quickly, far too fast for synaptic growth to be plausible. Ignoring this fact for a moment, it has been proposed that a single large neuron holds a single long-term memory. The problem with this proposal is that it works poorly in a system for memory recall. The axon of a neuron like this might somehow recognize an image but would have difficulty placing it into short-term memory. Also, an excessive number of large neurons are wasted. In Chapter 4 we present a system that uses neurons more efficiently.

There is a theory that a memory cell could consist of free excitatory neurotransmitter ions that surround dendritic receivers. The problem with this theory is that boutons do not generally provide free excitatory neurotransmitters. As soon as boutons go to a negative voltage, neurotransmitter ions are attracted home. Another problem with this theory is that free neurotransmitters would necessitate extra energy for their replacements. The neural latch model is easily created, and costs nothing in terms of energy.

Memorization   To establish a feature of long-term memory, it is necessary to rehearse an image in short-term memory. Rehearsal forces a *memorization enable signal* to go true. The purpose is to create a small obstacle to the creation of long-term memories, forcing memory space to be used judiciously. The memorization enable signal may be generated by a neural digital filter, a simple case of which is shown in Figure 3-13.

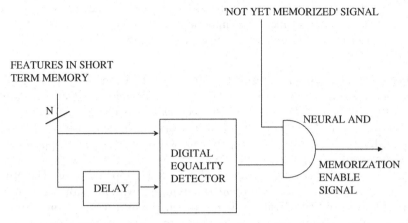

FIGURE 3-13   Generation of a memorization enable signal via rehearsal.

Memorization is enabled only under certain conditions. For example, a *not-yet memorized signal* must be true, as explained in a later chapter: assumed available to prevent exact duplicate memories. Also explained later is the availability of features in short-term memory to be committed to long-term memory. To understand the digital filter concept, think of N features being applied directly to a digital equality detector, and being delayed by a given amount and applied to the second input of the detector. The intended result is a true signal from the digital equality detector if exactly the same image appears in short-term memory more than once with the given delay. As indicated, a memorization enable signal is generated that permits immediate transfer of an image from short-term memory to long-term memory.

What is indicated in Figure 3-13 is a first-order digital filter model, where *first order* means one delay box. A digital filter may be extended to higher orders using additional delays for a more complex system of memorization enable. Delay is available using short-term-memory neurons. The digital equality detector is composed of an array of neural exclusive NORs, obtained formally by placing a NOT gate at the output of an exclusive OR. The basic XNOR with inputs a and b and output c has the following truth table:

a	b	c
0	0	1
0	1	0
1	0	0
1	1	1

Note that the output is true only if the inputs are equal. The neural circuit for detecting the equality of memories may be based on XORs and XNORs. The memory model is elaborated on in subsequent chapters.

Energy Dissipation in Long-Term Memory   If a long-term-memory cell depended on trapping and storing charge, a small amount of energy would necessarily be taken. By definition, *trapped charge* is charge that cannot be recovered in a timely way. Energy held by trapped charge can be analyzed as $\frac{1}{2} CV^2$, where C is the equivalent capacitance where the charge is trapped and V is the equivalent voltage across the capacitor. However, the above neural circuit is modeled as adiabatic and does not depend on trapped charge. Therefore, although an internal action potential circulates without stop, long-term-memory circuits do not dissipate significant energy as a result of this action.

Certain types of neural gates require inhibitory neurotransmitters ions to be placed judiciously on a dendritic branch, usually near the soma. The exclusive NOR might use such ions, for example. These ions tend to stick longer as necessary for the logical operation of a neuron, and so are not returned immediately to their bouton sources. A certain amount of energy was invested in their charge, which is temporarily trapped. But it is assumed that inhibitory ions will eventually be released and returned to their homes for various reasons, such as being pushed away by propagating pulses within the branches they attach to, or being sloughed away by thermal activity in the surrounding ionic solution.

APPLICATIONS

Artificial neurons are generally considered to be the building blocks of an artificial neural network. Unfortunately, artificial neurons differ physically in major ways from biological neurons: They are no more than computer codes or integrated-circuit operational amplifiers, and so do not work the same way as biological neurons. An important goal for the future is the manufacture of *imitation neurons* that are as close as possible to biological neurons, which might be accomplished using a combination of genetic engineering and nanotechnology. An imitation neuron is envisioned as one that supports a triggered action potential as in a biological neuron.

Membranes with suitable properties are being developed slowly but surely. To be an imitation neuron, it is desirable that the membrane possess piezo-electric and ferroelectric properties (the two often go together). Suitable membranes might sense the presence of exciting and inhibiting neurotransmitters and might serve as a new type of logical device—not in the solid state but in a "wet" state. As part and parcel of this new device, imitation boutons might loan neurotransmitter ions during the signaling phase of a logic operation, and then take them back as though the event never happened.

Neurons with input and output neurotransmitters are reminiscent of engineered DNA molecules that can perform logic. When a DNA gate encounters appropriate input molecules, it releases appropriate output molecules. The problem with "DNA logic" is that instead of encoding signals into true and false voltages, signals are encoded in high and low concentrations of short DNA molecules. The gates that perform the information processing are also DNA molecules, each gate being a carefully folded complex of multiple short DNA strands. Because of the nonelectrical nature of the encoding, connections to the outside world of electrical peripherals are a challenge.

If they could be developed, imitation neurons would have important applications to computers and communications. Advantages include nanometer size, efficiency, flexibility, ability to amplify signals from a very large number of other neurons, and the ability to calculate arbitrary Boolean functions with a very large number of inputs. Engineers would find imitation neurons quite interesting, especially their water tolerance and flexibility. Currently, flexible circuits are in great demand; *flex-circuit technology* permits building electronic circuits on flexible substrates such as plastic. In a typical liquid-crystal display fabrication, for example, a thin flexible plastic or metal foil may be used as the substrate instead of rigid glass. The film deposited on top of the substrate is usually very thin, and therefore not rigid. Flex circuits are often used as connectors. They are used in cameras; keyboards made today use flex circuits for the switch matrix.

CONCLUSIONS

In this chapter we show how to calculate a single neural pulse from the bottom up, by hand. This may be done with a simple model that anyone interested in neurons ought to be able to understand. Physically, random energetic ions and stray electrons tunnel into the sensitive parts of a membrane and combine. It is not difficult to create a circuit model, as in this chapter, to predict the transfer of charge back and forth across the sensitive ferroelectric parts of a membrane.

Beginning with a trigger, both sodium and potassium currents flow. Potassium currents are lower, since potassium is less active, thus permitting internal voltages to rise. At the peak of the pulse, the sodium currents are stopped by a new orientation of particles in the membrane. But the potassium-induced current continues on, subsequently reducing the pulse to an undershoot level, below the equilibrium value. During undershoot, molecules in the membrane undergo full restoration of their original orientations, thus stopping the currents driving the pulse. Internal voltage now returns to an equilibrium value.

Of major importance to this book is the model presented for short-term memory, since short-term memory is intimately related to the long-term memory system and cognition. A short-term-memory neuron works much like a regular neuron but is modeled with a shortage of electron-capturing ions in its dendritic receivers and dendrites. This suggests that once triggered, there is a long pulse to the soma. This long trigger to the soma provides an extended pulse burst of a couple of seconds to the axon, with sufficient amplitude to signal other neurons. Like all neurons, short-term-memory neurons are modeled as adiabatic in this books, so an extended burst is physically possible without excessive energy dissipation; neurons borrow energy and then faithfully return it.

Long-term-memory cells are central to a memory model and are modeled to be a neural circuit connected head to tail so that output neurotransmitters are able to shower dendritic receivers in the same circuit. Pulses thus occur that cycle indefinitely, ready to signal other neurons as needed. Such cycling is physically possible because of the adiabatic model.

Future applications include imitation neurons, as opposed to artificial neurons. Imitation neurons are a desirable outcome of genetic engineering and nanotechnology, perhaps to replace damaged biological neurons, but mainly as wet-state devices for everyday communications and computers. They would excel because of small size, mechanical flexibility, and efficiency, and because of an ability to amplify and to calculate any Boolean function for a very large number of inputs.

The adiabatic model of neurons might affect medical practitioners indirectly, helping to explain, for example, fuzzy fMRIs (functional magnetic resonance images; see to Appendix C). An action potential in itself does not consume energy, but energy is still dissipated. Small quantities are continuously dissipated in every membrane in every neuron, if not in every cell of the body. The energy comes from the Nernst or rest voltage as generated across membrane loss conductance. An action potential is expected to result not in an increase but rather a drop in energy dissipation in what otherwise is a steady-state loss in the membrane. This is because an action potential goes positive, thus reducing the average voltage across the membrane.

The adiabatic model of a neuron is not expected to affect neuroscientists as much as computer engineers, those who might be motivated by the idea of a computing machine that requires no energy. Computers today are severely limited by heat dissipation and temperature increases. Because of heat, placing a greater number of computations into a smaller volume has become impossible from an engineering point of view. All this will change by going to adiabatic logic.

EXERCISES

3-1   Assume a temperature of 310 K.

(a) What is the average speed of a calcium ion?

(b) What is the average speed of an electron?

3-2   Explain how to convert ion flow (number of ions/$cm^2 \cdot s$) into electrical current density (A/cm^2). How is current obtained from current density?

3-3 Assume a positive current source of 0.12 mA and a negative current source of 0.03 mA.

(a) How long does it take to charge a 1-µF capacitor to 0.5 V if both current sources are applied to the capacitor? Sketch a circuit with a capacitor and two current sources.

(b) If only the negative current source is applied, how long does it take to discharge a 1-µF capacitor to −0.5 V?

3-4 The basic features of a neural pulse are not difficult to calculate.

(a) Sodium current density is $J_{Na} = 1.345 \times 10^8 T_{Na}$. Repeat the derivation of the neural pulse in the text assuming that the transmission for sodium is 1.5×10^{-12}. The sodium voltage component goes from −70 mV to +130 mV. Calculate time to reach +130 mV.

(b) Potassium current density is $J_K = 1.105 \times 10^8 T_K$. Adjust the transmission for potassium so that the maximum value of a neural pulse is 40 mV. Calculate time for neural voltage to reach −90 mV. Sketch waveforms.

3-5 Instead of potassium ions in a neuron with one valance electron, assume calcium ions with two valance electrons. Apply transmission factors as given in the text (sodium has 1×10^{-12}; calcium has 5.5×10^{-13}).

(a) Derive a neural pulse as in the text, assuming internal calcium, and place it on a graph. Assume neural voltage peaks at 40 mV in 1.5 ms.

(b) Compare two pulses graphically, assuming internal potassium ions and then internal calcium ions.

(c) If the internal calcium ions have concentrations that are 1/10 of the part (a) neurons, calculate and graph the neural pulse. Does this neuron have short term memory?

3-6 The axon model in this chapter may be used to predict the speed of a neural signal. Assuming the chapter model, what is the propagation delay for a nerve that is 40 cm long?

3-7 Show how a single neuron might constitute a cell of long-term memory. Sketch the neuron and refer to the periodic release and reuptake of excitatory neurotransmitters.

3-8 Consider a long-term memory circuit as described in the text.

(a) Design a modification so that Q can go true only if an enable signal E is true while a set signal S is true.

(b) Design a modification so that Q can be reset with a reset signal R. Do not include an enable signal E in this. Show a timing diagram with signals S and R to illustrate setting and resetting Q.

3-9 The neurotransmitter serotonin might be involved in explicit short- and long-term memory.

(a) Create explanations for how serotonin might be involved in short-memory.

(b) Create explanations for how serotonin might be involved in long term memory.

3-10   Consider an asymptotically adiabatic circuit such as the one in Figure A3-1.

(a) Show that the energy dissipated when the ramp for V_{DD} is decreasing is equal to the energy dissipated when the ramp for V_{DD} is increasing.

(b) Show the circuit is asymptotically adiabatic not just for ramp voltages but also for sine-wave voltages with low frequency.

3-11   Classically, a particle cannot penetrate a barrier unless the energy of the particle is high enough to overpower the barrier. Quantum mechanical tunneling implies that indeed there is a certain probability that a particle with low energy will penetrate a barrier; in fact, there is a lower but finite probability that a particle will actually go through a barrier. These probabilities depend heavily on the thickness of the barrier and the energy of the particle.

(a) For a neural membrane, identify the particles involved; identify the barrier.

(b) Refer to a text on modern physics. Show how to calculate the probability that electrons with an energy of 1 eV will pass through a barrier 1 nm thick with a height of 5 eV. The answer is about 10^{-9}.

(c) Why can sodium not pass through the barrier physically like an electron?

3-12   Show that heating in the neural membrane conductance is about 50% more during equilibrium at a fixed $-70\,\text{mV}$ than during the time of a neural burst, which alternates between $-70\,\text{mV}$ and $+40\,\text{mV}$ in a simple model.

3-13   Consider the memorization enable circuit, but assume that only one bit represents a given short-term memory. The digital comparator is a simple XNOR gate. Assume that the not-yet-memorized signal is true. Let the delay be 100 ms. At some point the bit of short term memory pulses true for a pulsewidth of 10 ms. It pulses true again in δ milliseconds. Provide a timing diagram of the AND output assuming that $\delta = 50\,\text{ms}$, $100\,\text{ms}$ and $150\,\text{ms}$. Show only $\delta = 100$ has output.

APPENDIX: ASYMPTOTICALLY ADIABATIC CIRCUITS

A circuit that is common to many systems of logic is shown in Figure A3-1. The resistor R represents resistance in ohms; the capacitor C represents capacitance (in farads), a place where electrical charge (that is, electrons) can be stored. Then power P (in watts) that is lost in the resistance, $P = i^2R$, will be insignificant for small currents i (in amperes). To make i small, the applied voltage $V_{DD}(t)$ must go from zero to V_1 volts with a slow rise time of T, as in

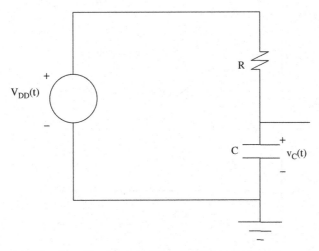

Figure A3-1 Capacitor charging circuit with variable-voltage source.

Figure A3-2. Ideally, charging is so slow that the capacitor voltage is about equal to the power supply voltage; that is, $v_C \approx V_{DD}(t)$. Using calculus, we have

$$i \approx C\frac{dv_C}{dt} = C\frac{V_1}{T}$$

Power lost in the resistor can be estimated as

$$P = i^2 R = \frac{RC}{T^2} CV_1^2$$

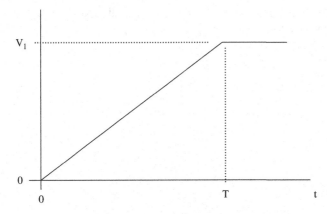

Figure A3-2 Slow rise time.

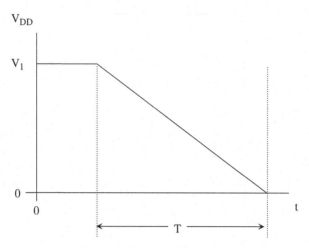

Figure A3-3   Slow fall time.

Energy (in watt-seconds or joules) lost in the resistor can be estimated as

$$E_R = \int_0^T Pdt = \frac{RC}{T}CV_1^2$$

Note that power and energy dissipated in the resistor become arbitrarily less for large values of T. This defines *asymptotically adiabatic*: The dissipation approaches zero as T increases without limit. A similar analysis follows for waveforms other than ramps. Real-world integrated circuits always have leakage conductance and associated dissipation, so practical circuits are correctly termed *approximately* adiabatic.

Once a capacitor is charged without significant energy loss, applying a negative edge (that is, V_1 to zero with a fall time of T as in Figure A3-3) will similarly discharge the capacitor without energy dissipation (hopefully, recharging the power supply V_{DD}).

CHAPTER 4

CIRCUITS AND SYSTEMS FOR MEMORIZATION AND RECALL

INTRODUCTION

By way of explaining how a brain works logically, human associative memory is modeled in this chapter with logical neurons, and these of course correspond to standard digital circuits. The resulting architecture is based on standard digital circuits to incorporate psychological elements including short- and long-term memory. Novel to the architecture are memory searches using cues chosen pseudorandomly from short-term memory. Recalls, alternated with sensory images, many tens per second, are assumed to be analyzed subliminally as an ongoing process, to determine a direction of attention in short-term memory. What is modeled below is not just human memory, but a human memory system that includes the possibility of solving problems and learning: in other words, the beginnings of a cognitive architecture to explain human intelligence.

In this chapter we show how to synthesize circuits for human associative memory, including circuits for memorization and recall, using standard digital building blocks. Inputs to memory circuits are the axons of neurons that encode sensory information, each communicating an encoded feature, shape, shade, tone, and so on, of sensory data true or false. These axons connect in parallel to respective cells in conscious short-term memory assuming a specific but unknown physical location for each feature.

Human Memory Modeled with Standard Analog and Digital Circuits: Inspiration for Man-made Computers, By John Robert Burger
Copyright © 2009 John Wiley & Sons, Inc.

Short-term-memory cells are modeled as connecting to corresponding cells of subconscious long-term memory in a large associative memory. "Cells" in the context of memory are not necessarily biological; rather, they are neural circuits with a special structure to latch the presence of a given feature. Many such cells make up a memory word. The model described below uses long-term-memory words of approximately equal length, comparable to the length of a short-term memory word, in the interests of efficiency.

Associative long-term memory uses a style of search in which a subset of cues held in short-term memory are selected randomly and enabled to retrieve images from long-term memory. A system of *multiple match resolution* is included in case there is more than one response to a given set of cues, thus avoiding a confusing jumble of superimposed images. In the model, many images per second can be recalled and tested for importance and thus for entry into conscious short-term memory.

The same neural paths that conduct cues from short-term memory down into subconscious long-term memory are modeled as serving to convey features for memorization. Neural connections go to all words in parallel, including blank words. Neural circuits are provided to select the next available blank word for features to be memorized. Selecting the next available blank work is accomplished by a system of *multi-write resolution*, since otherwise all available blank words might be identically programmed by one act of memorization, which would eliminate the possibility of additional memorization, at least for the immediate future.

Modeling as above provides a unique perspective on fundamental topics in memory theory: (1) input–output differences, (2) conditions for recall, (3) the role of repetition in memorization, and (4) the meaning of recognition. Beyond such academic issues and beyond neuroscience itself, the models of this chapter point to the possibility of new types of computers to serve humankind. In this book, artificial intelligence goes beyond the concept of computers that act human when queried with a keyboard. In this book the test for artificial intelligence is: Can it learn? Can it learn the equivalent of fetching a ball, for example? Intelligence like this applies nicely to self-contained robots, but it might also apply to immobile systems that follow complex procedures. Prior to attempting to build a system with artificial intelligence, however, it might be reasonable first to analyze biological memory systems and intelligence. Below we review the underlying psychological knowledge that leads to memory system models and, ultimately, to rudimentary models of cognition.

PSYCHOLOGICAL CONSIDERATIONS WHEN MODELING HUMAN MEMORY

Human memory has been described extensively by memory experts, so there is no shortage of information. It is said that we remember things pertaining to the senses, such as melodies, ice cream, perfume, and cold beer. We also remember things we learn. Poems and procedures, once learned, are easy to recall. We can remember a poem, for example, but the same hundreds of words arranged in random order are an impossible challenge.

Long-term recall has been divided into *procedural memory*, such as knowing the procedure to multiply two numbers, and *factual (declarative) memory*, such as knowing how to spell a given word. Factual memory has been defined to include biographical memory of personal episodes, such as remembering your friends from first grade. Factual memory is also defined to include *semantic memory*, memories of symbolic objects, such as words, numbers, names of components in machines, and their relationships. When attempting to memorize disconnected facts, one generally aids memorization by creating a mnemonic (see Appendix B).

We tend to remember procedures better than facts, and this is important to engineers. Test yourself. Multiply 12 × 13! If nothing else, a person may add 12 to itself 12 times to get the answer (156). Most people remember how to multiply, which is a procedure, but might not remember the name of their fourth-grade teacher who taught them to multiply, which is a fact. Factual information is more difficult to retain than learned procedures, partly because procedures such as tying your shoes are used often. From another point of view, a procedure can be learned in the form of a *neural state machine*, which permits a procedure to be executed without excessive recall effort. In a neural state machine, interneurons enable a move from one step to the next within subconscious long-term memory without having to evaluate individual steps in short-term memory. The two types of learning involving synaptic growth are neural state-machine learning and combinational learning, discussed in Chapter 5.

In attempting to identify where memories are stored, Karl S. Lashley (1890–1958) experimented surgically with rats but was unable to find a physical locus of given memory functions in the brain. It was concluded that memory has no "center." As further evidence that memory has no center, various experiments suggest that memory has copies of itself in the half brains, that is, in the right and left hemispheres, as a sort of memory backup.* In an associative memory system, brain functions are naturally distributed. In contrast, a desktop computer sends specific data to specific places.

In a desktop computer, as is quite obvious to a computer engineer, any memory can be located. An expert could trace any word of computer memory and could locate it physically. Thus, we can know exactly where each word is, and we can arbitrarily choose any one for reading or writing: hence the term *random-access memory* (RAM). In contrast, human memory does not have fixed addresses, so we know a lot less about where a given word of memory resides. Human memory is associative; things are recalled not according to

---

* fMRI can picture specific regions of neurons for selected human activities such as moving fingers. However, fMRI cannot indicate the locations of duplicated or backup neurons.

where they are, but according to what they are. Fortunately for computer engineers, associative memory is easy to model with digital circuits.

As evidence that the brain is associative, retrieval from subconscious memory obviously begins with cues. For example, seeing a dog can bring forth a memory of a favorite childhood dog and bring forth details of its face, color, size, and so on. Other such examples are: Seeing your old neighborhood will bring forth memories of stores, houses, rooms, passageways, and so on; reading a page in a book that you studied in college can bring forth what you learned in those days. A component of memory, such as hearing someone's voice, subsequently spurs other components and your knowledge about that person. Cues are essential to memory retrieval.

Human memory is not erasable in the ordinary sense, nor can it be overwritten as we do in RAM. Once something is committed to memory, it is long term. Thus, long-term memory is akin to *read-only memory* (ROM). Under the ROM concept, new memories cannot overwrite old memories; they must be written into blank cells that are grown for that purpose.

When something is remembered, it is passed into conscious short-term memory. Once something is in short-term memory, it is a candidate to become a new long-term memory. When a memory is recalled and subsequently committed as a new, refreshed memory, the older, original memory might never be used again. Such unused words are assumed to be recycled eventually into blank memory words for reuse. Additionally, if a word is damaged, it may revert into a blank word. A few rehabilitated words become available for memory, but the main source for new blank words is expected to be neural growth. In the memory model below, the supply of blank words is assumed to be unlimited.

BASIC ASSUMPTIONS TO CREATE A MODEL

Neurons are modeled as binary devices that are either activated or resting. When activated, they produce a short burst of positive-going pulses. When resting, they hold a steady negative charge; that is, their interior is a negative dc voltage relative to their exterior. Man-made logic is also binary, although it usually relies on voltage levels as opposed to pulse bursts. Man-made computers employ binary codes so that a small number of wires (n wires) can send a large amount of information (2^n codes). In the brain, however, binary codes are unnecessary, since there is an abundance of neurons for parallel connections. Thus, in the model, the rule is: one neuron for one feature.

The process of converting analog sensory inputs into a true or false, denoting the presence or absence of a given feature, is known to engineers as *encoding*. The brain continuously encodes sensory information into features such as shape, shade, coordinate, and color. There are thousands of possible features. Another form of encoding that is completely unrelated to sensory encoding is the creative generation of mnemonics to aid in remembering random facts. Sensory encoding is a complex process represented by a block of logic through which all sensory signals are assumed to go.

Memory search begins with cues. Cues are sent "down" into long-term subconscious memory during a memory search; memories with features that match these cues will come "up" for possible entry into short-term memory. Cues have to be exact, since long-term memories are called forth only for exact matches. Gratefully, old memories are dormant until receiving an exact set of cues. Serious overload would result if we had to see all facts, even irrelevant ones, at all times.

Neurons are active devices that operate one way, in contrast to electrical conductors, which are passive and bidirectional. Often, neurons operate in pairs to establish two-way communications. One sends signals one way; one sends signals the other way. It is assumed that no neuron can transmit more than one feature: that is, that neurons are multiplexed in neither time nor in frequency. This is partly because neurons are quite plentiful and can be dedicated to a given purpose.

In the model below, neural pairs are dedicated to a given feature, where each feature connects to specific locations in short-term memory and corresponding locations in words of long-term memory. These locations must exist physically, although we do not know where exactly. Each location in short-term memory and a corresponding location in long-term memory is reserved for a particular feature. It is unclear that humans are aware of the meanings of individual features in their own memories, but if they are, they may very well realize the meaning of a feature according to its physical location in a word. For example, the color fire engine red might be within a certain location, the 537th cell from the left in the tableau of short-term memory; it is also the 537th cell from the left in each word of long-term memory. This structure is assumed fixed in that axons cannot disconnect and later become reconnected elsewhere.

In case anyone still thinks that they can locate a given memory physically— they cannot, not easily. In reality, there could well be two or possibly three separate neurons distributed spatially to encode a given feature for the purposes of reliability, and certainly there is duplication in the left and right hemispheres. On the other hand, there cannot be excessive redundancy since then a model would be quite inefficient and burdened with many separate neurons for exactly the same feature. As a starting point, the model below assumes one feature for one connecting neuron.

Emotions Are Simply Another Feature

Recalls from long-term memory into short-term memory are dark and subtle; they are not like the bright light and loud noises associated with seeing or hearing. Emotions are an exception. When emotions are recalled, they can be nearly as vivid and primeval as they were originally. In this sense they are special.

Emotions are complex. For example, an emotion described as "satisfaction" follows a well-designed circuit, one of many shades of love. Emotional arousal, if it could be harnessed, is a major aid to memory and learning. Most of us recall where we were when some wonderful or horrible event occurred. For example, what were you doing on September 11, 2001, when you discovered that the World Trade Center and over 3000 civilians were killed by Islamic extremists? Painful emotions are a strong cue to memory. They can bring forth a host of details, even those we would prefer to forget. Strong emotions result in a natural rehearsal of an event, over and over, and thus clear memories.

The small marble-sized amygdala of the brain plays a role in emotions, with the overall result that emotional features have an amplified effect within the body. The amygdala is identified in Appendix A. Emotions are modeled below as a class of features for use by memory. Within a memory circuit, they are no different than any other feature, shape, shade, or color.

SHORT-TERM MEMORY AND CONSCIOUSNESS

Short-term memory lasts only a few seconds and has been termed *working memory*, needed for second-to-second living. Working memory is somewhat analogous to dynamic memory in a desktop computer, which has to be refreshed continuously. In contrast, long-term memory is somewhat analogous to disk memory in a desktop computer; it has no effect until it is recalled. Long-term memory in humans differs radically from long-term memory in machines; human memory is associative, as opposed to machine memory, in which each word has a unique address.

Short-term memories last no more than a few seconds (refer to Appendix B). Consider an experiment. Look at a scene and then close your eyes. You continue to "see" countless details in that scene for a few seconds even if you face the other way. In fact, it seems that any sensory input can be remembered for a few seconds, much like persistence in a cathode ray tube. What you are experiencing is short-term memory. You can become aware of your own short-term memories as storing briefly a very large number of encoded sensations, or alternatively, just a few "packages." A package would be remembering a few new numbers, for example, which is quite different from literal detail in an image. As experiences are rehearsed, they naturally enter into long-term memory, so subjective experiments as above must separate short- and long-term memory.

For the purposes of circuit modeling, and since they have never been proven to differ, short-term memory and consciousness are taken to be exactly the same. Short-term memory can be modeled as a tableau of cells, one for each and every possible feature that the brain can encode. Encoded features from the senses appear in short-term memory. Images from long-term memory use a similar code and also may be recalled into short-term memory. One begins to think that a system might be helpful to edit what enters into short-term memory.

What Will You Think of Next?

Unfortunately, science does not have a satisfactory answer to this basic question. In the memory system model, "important" information is all that will be permitted to enter into short-term memory. Information is important, for example, if it involves strong sensory stimulation or strong emotional content. For example, if you see smoke, images of a fire enter into your short-term memory, based on past experiences with fire. For an instant, fire is more important than anything else, because fire is exciting.

It is the excitement that permits quick entry into short-term memory. Lots of activities are a little exciting. For example, what does 1 + 1 equal? Do you know the answer? That little excitement you just experienced would allow the answer to enter immediately into short-term memory. Even if a person were in the dark without sensory inputs, short-term memory still experiences a sequence of images. Cues selected from an image in current short-term memory naturally result in recalls of related memories from the subconscious.

Memory Search

Memory can be modeled as being searched subconsciously, that is, in the background without a person being aware of the search. Everyone has experienced trying to remember something but being unable to do so. So you go about your business, but unknown to you, a search proceeds within your subconscious long-term memory for what you are trying to remember. Cues keep returning to conscious short-term memory, but are insufficient to recall a full image. When you least expect it, possibly at an inconvenient moment, the correct memory will pop into short-term memory with amazing clarity. This is an indication that the brain has an ability to work continuously in the background without being noticed, adding or subtracting cues from a search until the cues are exactly right, as they must be for recall.

There is a theory that decisions are made not by "free will" in the sense of timely choices, but by a search for a ready-made decision. Often, a ready-made decision may be available based on past similar situations held in long-term memory, as for example when you are asked to contribute to a political cause that you do not believe in. Electroencephalography concerning the timing of finger movements, published by Benjamin Libit and others, indicates that choices are made in the brain without knowledge by the person involved, because the decision was made well before a person realized it. Surprisingly, the brain seems to be in control. In other words, it is not the other way around, in which a "person" makes a decision and then tells the brain what to do.

To synthesize a better cognitive model, it may be noted that the brain appears to search itself continuously in the background not only for forgotten facts and situations, but also for solutions to problems. A "problem" could mean a real problem with no logical solution. For example, it is a problem trying to open a combination lock without the combination. Trying all possibilities requires excessive time. It is more practical to try random combinations and trust to luck. The brain may very well solve problems this way, by a random search for quick solutions.

As further indication that memory searches occur constantly in the background, dreams, as everyone knows, are brief illogical episodes usually soon forgotten. A person is dimly aware of dreams during light sleep partly because there are no overpowering sensory images to block them out as there may be for daydreams. According to one theory, dreams are what we experience as the brain attempts to solve difficult or impossible problems by random search.

Memory searches are modeled as employing a selection of cues centered on features in short-term memory. This suggests an architecture in which a cue editor samples available cues and works tirelessly in the background to recall long-term memories. Recalls may occur at a rate of tens per second, the maximum rate permitted by neural circuitry, so a lot of searching is possible without the full knowledge of the person trying to remember something. A person becomes aware of only the most "important" recalls as they flow into short-term memory.

To retrieve forgotten memories or to solve difficult problems, it is efficient for cues to be selected with the aid of a random variable. Randomly chosen initial values are commonly used in computers to solve difficult optimization problems. Since random starting points are helpful in numerical optimization, they might also be helpful in memory searches. A model is now synthesized, assuming subliminal pseudorandom memory searches.

COGNITIVE ARCHITECTURE

The term *architecture* implies a model not only for input–output behavior but for physical structure. Physical structure refers to size and weight and also to known electrical and logical properties. Neuroscience aside, a useful cognitive architecture can guide engineers to an artificially intelligent robot, that is, an intelligent agent that "reasons" like a human. Toward this end, it is desired to implement cognition in general, not just a computer with voice or picture recognition.

Another implication of the term *architecture* is that cognition must occur in a timely self-contained way as it does in humans. A valid architecture must address information readily available in psychology texts, such as the existence of short-term memory. This is memory capable of holding for a brief time encoded signals from the senses, emotional signals, and signals created by recall from long-term memory.

In a valid cognitive architecture that models physical structure, subconscious long-term memory must be associative; any information may be recalled instantly once proper cues are found in short-term memory. Information is committed to subconscious long-term memory by a process termed *rehearsal* in short-term memory. We note that gifted people have a photographic memory that latches instantly, a sort of proof that long-term memory is unrelated to synaptic growth.

Cognitive Architecture, Including Subliminal Analysis

Figure 4-1 illustrates a system of associative memory based on neural circuits. The objective is to specify the input–output properties of each block, thus permitting it to be synthesized with neurons in the form of digital gates. Examples of neural circuit synthesis are provided below.

Short-term memory is modeled with neurons that produce a long dendritic pulse. This is assumed to be the result of a shortfall of internal potassium in their dendrites and results in an extended electrical trigger to the soma. Short-term-memory neurons are modeled with pulsed outputs to stimulate other

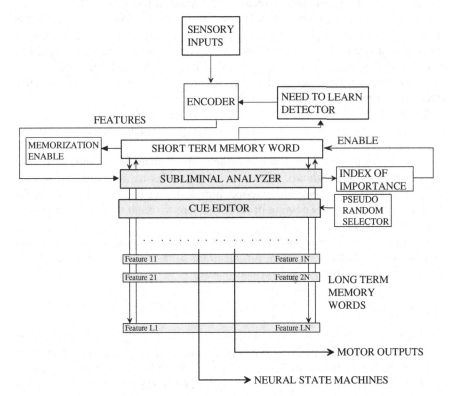

FIGURE 4-1 Human memory system, including subliminal analysis.

neurons, but their action potentials are longer, hundreds of milliseconds, compared to the typical tens of milliseconds.

Long-term memory is modeled with digital neurons that transfer neuro-transmitters from boutons back into dendritic receptors. The result is a digital read-only memory (ROM) neuron that can be set instantly and will latch indefinitely as long as the neuron remains healthy, unless cleared because of lack of use. The indefinite cycling of neural signals in a neuron is physically possible because neurons can be modeled as adiabatic, that is, requiring essentially no calories for electrical signaling beyond what is required for maintenance, heating, and growth in any biological cell. Long-term memory is associative and is organized to be L words each containing N cells. Multiple matches are dealt with via a simple neural circuit, designed later, so that two separate images cannot be recalled at exactly the same instant.

Words in memory are modeled wide enough to accommodate every possible feature that a human can experience: shape, shade, tone, smell, feel, emotional strength, and so on, for thousands of elemental features. Each feature has a given location in a word. Features are encoded from the senses by a functional box labeled the *Sensory Encoder*. If a novel combination of features is used repeatedly, a *need-to-learn detector* signals the sensory encoder to "learn" new features. This detector, used again in Chapter 5, may be based on digital filters, also proposed below for memorization enable. Looking ahead to learning in the sensory encoder, the color chartreuse might be learned as a digital AND of yellow and green. Combinational learning like this (no analog parameters) is assumed driven by a need for efficiency in successful species that cannot afford to waste time first recalling yellow, then green, then a definition of chartreuse.

Another type of learning, *state-machine learning*, involves development of an unconscious procedure that executes automatically. Humans easily execute many such procedures, similar to long poems learned by "heart" to be performed mindlessly. Once initiated, one simply brushes the teeth, drives the car, or operates the keyboard without a lot of pondering, as an aid to survival of the human species. Neural state-machine learning is driven by a need for efficiency, since it avoids passing procedural steps through short-term memory, discussed in detail in Chapter 5.

The cue editor is responsible for selecting useful subsets of cues from the contents of short-term memory for recalling long-term memories. Cues are selected pseudorandomly as described below.

Cue Editor

A cue editor for the random selection of cues appears in Figure 4-2a. Cues are taken from short-term memory and masked using AND gates. The selection of cues used to recall long-term memories is determined by a *shift register counter*, an example of which is given in Figure 4-2b. The space of N features in short-term memory is assumed to be organized into m clusters with n features per

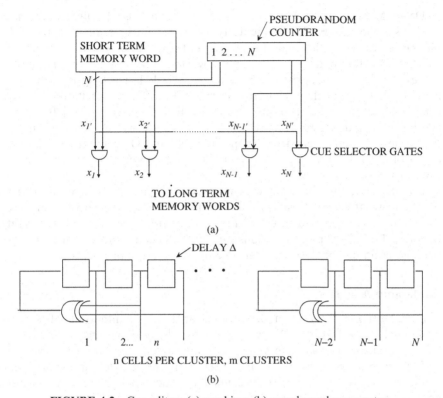

FIGURE 4-2   Cue editor: (a) masking; (b) pseudorandom counter.

cluster, to further randomize the count. An example of $n = 3$ is shown. A typical count sequence for $n = 3$ would be

$$0\ 1\ 0$$

$$1\ 0\ 1$$

$$1\ 1\ 0$$

$$1\ 1\ 1$$

$$0\ 1\ 1$$

$$0\ 0\ 1$$

$$1\ 0\ 0$$

The count then repeats from 0 1 0. The counter is composed of neurons whose details are not worked out here. Each block in the shift register is given a delay identified as Δ. A simple feedback circuit like this may run indefinitely, analogous to a long-term-memory cell, only with additional gates.

Delay Δ, the time between counts, measured in tens of milliseconds, has hidden significance. Evidently, the delay between counts sets the rate at which old memories are recalled, but it may also set the length of a neural burst, that is, when an action potential begins in a downstream neuron, and when it ends. If the cue editor did not exist, action potentials would last as long as short-term memory in this model. A neuron will respond as long as excitatory neuro-transmitter ions are being pushed back and forth in a synaptic cleft, which continues until driver neurons return to rest. This can occur only when the triggering of action potentials is stopped at its source. Overall, the cue editor is a sort of clock for brain memory to initiate and terminate what otherwise is asynchronous processing.

Counters like this can produce a unique subset of cues that recall images related to what a person currently has in mind. These associative recalls are assured to have some features of interest, but not necessarily all the right features. Therefore, prior to admission into conscious short-term memory, there is subliminal analysis to determine the importance of each recall.

Subliminal Analyzer

The analyzer has the task of determining an index of importance for each subliminal set of features. Digital signals from long-term memory as well as from the sensory encoder are assumed to appear on interneurons associated with short-term memory. These signals are ready to be gated into short-term memory, but first their importance must be calculated. Importance is just another encoding operation, as suggested in Figure 4-3. The importance encoder is akin to a priority encoder in a desktop computer: to decide which peripherals can interrupt a running program.

Importance is digital evaluation for (1) brightness of sensory images, (2) magnitude of emotional content, (3) quantity of matched cues, and (4) recency of experiences. Importance encoders assign a numerical value to candidate recalls. It is misleading to think of importance as conflict resolution. There are no conflicts here, just data. The output of the encoder is an index for each interneuron image, to be compared with a index computed similarly for the current contents of short-term memory.

The current contents of short-term memory have previously been encoded for importance, but as short-term memory fades, importance is going to drop. Since the importance of the contents of short-term memory is variable, a second encoder is necessary to compute a running value. When the index for short-term memory is comparable to the index for interneuron images, this new image enters short-term memory. Thus established is a moving picture within short-term memory, and since a person is aware of this picture, it constitutes a direction of attention.

Recalls are selected pseudorandomly, perhaps tens per second. Recalls are assumed to alternate with sensory data for subliminal analysis (the switch for this purpose is not shown). An index of importance for each image is computed

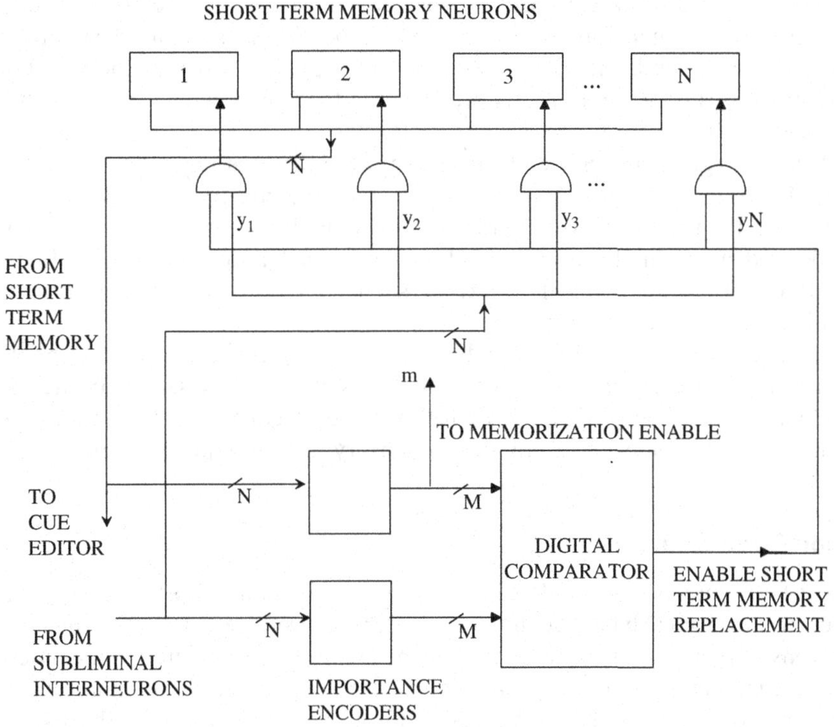

SHORT TERM MEMORY NEURONS

FIGURE 4-3   Short-term memory updating circuit.

by encoders especially for this purpose. To recapitulate, when the index of importance for a subliminal image approaches that of current short-term memory, a transfer occurs. A new set of attributes is thus enabled to enter short-term memory, with a new set of cues, thus defining a direction of attention. Neurons have memory and they accomplish logic, and since there are billions of them, the amazing calculations suggested above are available biologically.

DISCUSSION OF THE MODEL

It is practically impossible to trace brain circuits with a probe; they are very small, soft, and intertwined. However, well-known circuit models for man-made associative memory suggest the probable structure of the brain.

Sensory Inputs

Sight, sound, touch, taste, and odor send over 1 million parallel signals via appropriate neurons to respective parts of the brain. Basic brain areas for senses are identified in Appendix A. Sensory signals are processed by respective organs of the brain as follows. The occipital lobe processes vision; the temporal lobes process sound; the somotosensory cortex processes touch; the olfactory bulb processes odor; and taste is processed in the insula, which is deep within the folds of the cerebral cortex.

Sensory signals are encoded using distributed processing. The 1.2 million axon fibers in each eye's optic nerve, for example, are first processed in the thalamus, then in the amygdala for emotional analysis, and then within credit card–sized areas in the occipital lobes. Additional processing occurs in the cerebral cortex. As a result, features such as shapes and shades become available to short-term memory.

If subconscious memory is enabled, the sensory encoder system is briefly disabled. Most everyone can remember things even if their senses are heavily loaded: during a Steven King movie for example. Recollections from long-term memory are not blocked in practice by sensory images, and vice versa.

Short-Term Memory

Short-term memory is modeled as a word with many short-term memory neurons, one for each feature that an encoder can produce. Short-term-memory neurons have a fast attack time, that is, the ability to be activated immediately. Because information fades within seconds, new images tend to dominate short-term memory even though remnants of an old image are present. Short-term-memory action potentials in this model are slightly higher in frequency and slightly lower in amplitude; even so, connecting neurons are assumed to respond without a need for special amplification.

Long-Term Memory

N and L for associative memory are not necessarily small numbers; they are variable to leave room for expansion as a result of memorization activities to expand the length L; learning to detect new features expands the width N. Width N expands because a recently learned feature is assumed to require a memory word that is wider by one memory cell. There is fMRI evidence that portions of the brain are reserved for particular purposes: for example, face recognition. Models could easily be organized according to function, such as face recognition. But for the purposes of this book, the model is left unstructured, meaning that anything can go anywhere physically and still remain tightly linked to related memories associatively.

Recognition

In everyday experiences, there seems to be a subtle satisfaction, a "eureka" moment, when a memory is found in all its completeness. This satisfaction has also been described as a minor excitement, such as occurs when you actually know the answer to a question. An interesting theory is that the excitement of recognition is connected to importance and entry into short-term memory, and perhaps excitement is released when many cues are matched completely. Alternatively, when recognizing a person you know and see often, a neuron could theoretically learn to detect that person as though he or she were just another feature. In addition to possible responses relating to the index of importance, it is theoretically possible for endorphin to be released whenever recognizable images move into short-term memory. It is unknown which, if any, of these theories are correct.

ENABLED NEURAL LOGIC

In Chapter 5 we show that neurons are capable of arbitrary Boolean logic. Neurons become active, execute their logic functions for a short period of time, then return to a state of inactivity. Logic like this may be termed *enabled logic*. Figure 4-4 shows logic symbols used in this book in case someone is unfamiliar with standard logic symbols. Not shown in these symbols, but implied, is a method for enabling. Loss of an enable signal effectively puts a neuron to sleep with an output at the rest voltage, logic zero.

Inputs for AND and OR gate symbols may be generalized to any *fan-in*, that is, any number of inputs. NOT can have only one input; XOR, the exclusive OR, can have only two inputs, although trees of XOR accepting any number of inputs are possible. Gate outputs go *only* to the inputs of other gates. As in standard hardware, logic outputs are *not* permitted to connect together. This is permitted only in a special class of hardware logic known as *open drain logic*, *open collector logic*, or generally, *hardwired logic*, generally used for driving a data bus. Neural circuits internal to the logic symbols are explained in Chapter 5.

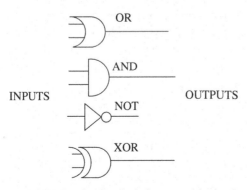

FIGURE 4-4   Symbols for neural logic.

Recall Circuits

First we model *recall*, that is, remembering something that has been committed to long-term memory. After this, memorization to long-term memory is modeled.

Memory Cell

Long-term memory is an organization of brain *memory cells*, not to be confused with biological cells. A memory cell may or may not be a single neuron. Long-term memory cells can be modeled as a neural circuit that sends excitatory neurotransmitters back to its own input, similar to a cell of read-only memory (ROM) (Figure 4-5), described in Chapter 3. By moving S, the set signal, true briefly and than back to rest, the output Q goes true and holds indefinitely. It is relatively difficult to reset Q back to false since there is no reset or toggle input, consistent with the fact that long-term memory cannot easily be erased. To reset this cell so that its output Q is false, the chief approach is to reduce the precharge on one or more of the gates, a topic of Chapter 5. Once set, a pulse burst circulates indefinitely using very little energy in an adiabatic model.

Memory Standard Cells

Long-term memory can be modeled as a connection of standard cells, as shown in Figure 4-6. In circuit parlance a *standard cell* is one that is designed to connect directly to other, identical standard cells. The Q in this figure represents a memory cell. The standard cell may be synthesized based on input and output behavior as defined below. The method discussed below yields a slightly different circuit if behavior is defined differently, so it is important to choose the correct behavior to begin. The signals are defined in Table 4-1.

Note that neural buses often work in pairs: Cue signals from the short-term memory system, the x signals, travel down from x to x_0. Recalled features, the y signals, travel up from y to y_0 and on to the short-term memory system. Word bus signals also work in pairs: A right-going bus signal travels to the right, from R_{in} to R_{out} along a local bus. A left-going bus signal travels to the left, from L_{in} to L_{out}. The desired logic can be expressed technically as shown in Table 4-2.

In Boolean terms, false is 0, true is 1. The first entry means that if there is no bus signal coming from the left ($R_{in} = 0$), none is transmitted to the right

S = SET

Q

FIGURE 4-5 Long-term (read-only) memory circuit (cell).

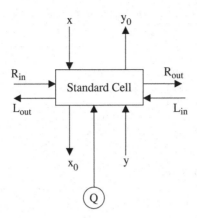

FIGURE 4-6 Standard cell for human memory modeling.

($R_{out} = 0$). This keeps a memory word dormant until needed. The second entry in Table 4-2 means that if there is no cue ($x = 0$), there is no change in R_{out}, and $R_{out} = R_{in} = 1$. The third entry means that if there is a cue for a feature ($x = 1$) but there is no memory of this feature ($Q = 0$), bus operations terminate ($R_{out} = 0$). The fourth entry means that if there is a cue for a feature ($x = 1$) and if there is also a memory of this feature ($Q = 1$) there is no change in Rout, and $R_{out} = R_{in} = 1$. A binary truth table for all this is constructed in Table 4-3.

The appropriate Boolean equation for R_{out}, derived from the truth table using standard symbols ($\bullet$, $+$, $'$ for AND, OR, NOT), is

$$R_{out} = R_{in}[x' + Q]$$

x' represents a NOT function of x. A logic circuit corresponding to this equation is shown in Figure 4-7. This, like any logic, may be implemented using neurons. A similar neural logic circuit applies to L_{in} and L_{out} (not shown).

TABLE 4-1   Definitions of Memory Cell Signals

Q	Memory signal from memory neuron
x	Cue for given feature (input)
$x_0 = x$	Cue to cells below (output)
Y	Memory from cells below (input)
$y_0 = y$	Memory of a given feature (output)
R_{in}	Right-going local bus signal (input)
R_{out}	Right-going local bus signal (output)
L_{in}	Left-going local bus signal (input)
L_{out}	Left-going local bus signal (output)

TABLE 4-2   Desired Logic for a Standard Cell

	Conditions	R_{out}
1.	R_{in} = false x = either true or false Q = either true or false	$R_{out} = R_{in}$ = false
2.	R_{in} = True x = false, no feature Q = either true or false	R_{out} = true
3.	R_{in} = true x = true Q = false	R_{out} = false
4.	R_{in} = true x = true Q = true	R_{out} = true

Readout Details

The output of a standard cell is y_0. This output will be true only if both R_{out} and L_{out} are true for a given cell, and also if Q is true. Testing the truth value of R_{out} and L_{out} as well as Q prevents spurious readouts. The standard cell is applied in such a way that R_{out} and L_{out} cannot both be true unless there is a match in every cell. Figure 4-8 illustrates an appropriate readout circuit.

The logic in a standard cell can now be summarized as shown in Figure 4-9. The R_{out} and L_{out} signals are assumed connected to give a word with any number of standard cells. An example of four cells is provided in Figure 4-10. Note that the x_i inputs from above are also the x_i outputs to below (i = 1, 2, 3, 4). E represents an enable that energizes R_{in} entering on the left and L_{in} entering on the right. When E goes true, it begins a memory search in all words of memory. Cues should be selected before an enable is issued. If there are no cues during a memory search, both R_{out} and L_{out} will indicate true unconditionally. This involves attempted recall of all possible memory words. Attempted recall

TABLE 4-3   Boolean Truth Table for a Standard Cell

R_{in}	x	Q	R_{out}
0	0	0	0
0	0	1	0
0	1	0	0
0	1	1	0
1	0	0	1
1	0	1	1
1	1	0	0
1	1	1	1

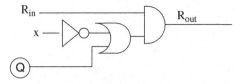

FIGURE 4-7 R_{out}–R_{in} logic.

of more than one word of memory sounds bad, but it is handled by a multiple match system as below, and the short-term memory system above.

Multiread Circuit

When an inadequate number of cues are presented to an associative memory, one normally expects multiple matches to the cues and thus multiple images. Multiple matches in hardware associative memory are handled quite easily by a circuit for multiple match resolution. Often, unfortunately, the images retrieved have to be examined one a time by the person who wants the information.

In a computerized database of the nonassociative, conventional addressing type, ordinary addressing can be more involved. A hashing function serves to convert keywords or questions into addresses where information might be stored. Unfortunately, since addresses are short compared to the formal code associated with a fully encoded keyword, unique keywords often produce the same identical address into which data are written and read. So in a given address, several categories of information have been jammed in. This is known as a *collision*. With collisions, one obtains a *bucket* of information, some important, some not. Web searches, for example, commonly frustrate a user with many choices as he or she sorts through a "bucket" of information.

In the model of human memory described below, inadequate addressing space and hashing functions are avoided entirely because memory is content-addressable. However, we still require a multiple-match resolution circuit because a person cannot actually think of two things at once. Try to create a mental picture of your favorite automobile and also think of a friend's face, for

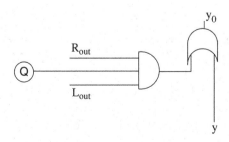

FIGURE 4-8   Readout logic.

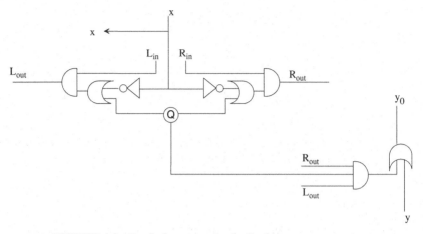

FIGURE 4-9 Logic for a standard cell of long-term memory.

example. As an experiment in differentiating multiple recalls, try to think of two such things at once. You will notice that perfectly clear images seem to alternate rapidly. Images seem to arrive from memory one at a time, although in rapid succession. Thus, in the book's memory model, we postulate that two separate things cannot be recalled at exactly the same instant.

The short-term memory system helps sort out images recalled in rapid succession. However, the model does not permit two images that overlap to be recalled simultaneously. In Figure 4-10, with its four standard cells, the y inputs arising from other words were assumed to be false, and will be false as long as there are no other matches to the cues given. If there are other matches to the cues in the circuits that follow, an additional support circuit will be required.

Multiple match circuits such as that shown in Figure 4-11 utilize a neuron that connects across the length of each word. A match between cues and stored memory words means that R_{out} is true. A complement of R_{out} is calculated and sent to the inputs of AND gates on each y signal. The complement is assumed accomplished with a NOT gate as implemented by neurons, although an XOR

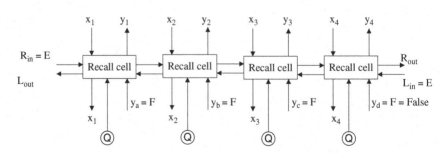

FIGURE 4-10 Circuit model for reading brain memory.

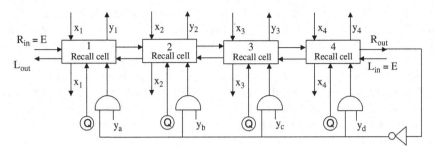

FIGURE 4-11   Multiple match resolution.

would also accomplish a NOT. This will lock out all other matches to memories below the first recall.

This system of multiple match resolution differs from man-made associative memory in that only the top matching word is permitted to be recalled. If it is not used, it may or may not be called again, because cues taken from short-term memory are modified continuously. Effectively, new cue combinations will tend to exclude previous recalls in a memory search since cues have an exacting nature.

Basic Memory Search

In attempting to recall the details of a particular little creature, as an example, short-term memory contains some but not all of the creature's features. Say that it holds the color red and a texture of little black spots.

x_1 = red (true)
x_2 = green (false)
x_3 = little black spots (true)
x_4 = legs (false)

Example signals in Figures 4-10 and 4-11 can be traced as follows:

- There is a cue x_1 for red and a memory of red, so cell 1 sets its R_{out} to true.
- There is no cue x_2 for green and also no memory of green, so cell 2 sets its R_{out} to true.
- There is a cue x_3 for spots and a memory of spots, so cell 3 sets its R_{out} to true.
- There is a no cue x_4 for legs but there is a memory of legs, so cell 4 sets its R_{out} to true.

R_{out} on the right of each cell indicates that a match has been found. Meanwhile, a similar signal has worked its way across the word from the right to the left, so

L_{out} on the left of each cell indicates that a match has been found. Both L_{out} and R_{out} are true in each cell, a condition for the recall of a word of memory to the short-term memory system. The features y_1, y_3, and y_4 are sent to short-term memory via the y outputs. Because of the way the circuit works, y_3 is sent up first, because L_{out} and R_{out} for y_3 are the first to go true together.

Note that there is no recall of green (y_2) and it is not sent up to short-term memory. Short-term memory now contains the sought-after memory. What is recognized is a red, spotted little creature with legs, a ladybug.

Pseudorandom Memory Search Example

Pseudorandom shift register counters are standard logical devices. Figure 4-12 shows how a small search for the image of a ladybug could be implemented using a pseudorandom counter. Shown is a shift register counter that, to begin, is initialized to all 1's. Initially, none of the cues are masked (blocked) and the count begins in this model with a count of 1111, and this basically refreshes the current image in short-term memory. Soon after, the count jumps to 0111. This takes the feature red away. Now the cues are x_3, little black spots. Brain memory might pop forth a dalmatian, a type of dog, or a leopard, a cat with spots. These images are subliminal at this point. What has happened is that spots are now associated with a dalmatian, a creature with spots, or a leopard.

However, cats and dogs do not match many of the available cues, so their importance is low. They are not the sought-after image and thus do not enter short-term memory. When there are hundreds of features, a pseudorandom search will tend to change only a few features at each step; so usually, one does not expect a radical change of subject, although it could happen.

As the pseudorandom count proceeds, a variety of different recalls flash into short-term memory at a rate of several per second, as fast as memory can work.

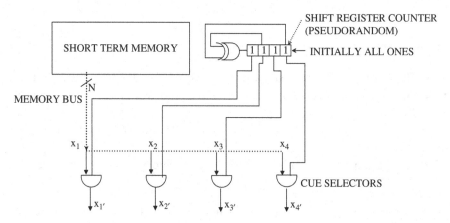

FIGURE 4-12 Pseudorandom memory search example.

One of these test images, the ladybug, will have a high index of importance and will become the new image in short-term memory, thus changing subjects.

Richard Semon's Memory Theory

Theoretical possibilities concerning recalls were noted by Richard Semon (1859–1918), a source of ideas about memory. When unrelated images alternate or form a sequence in short-term memory, the result may be described as *differentiating multiple recalls*. In contrast, *nondifferentiating multiple recalls* constitute a sequence of related images in which slight differences in detail exist but are ignored. Nondifferentiating multiple recalls with differing details, if recalled frequently, can form a new, refreshed memory. This is possible in the book's model only if the resulting image in short-term memory does not already have an exact copy in long-term memory. Thus, small changes in a refreshed memory are expected, reminiscent of a phenomenon called *serial reproduction*, analogous to gossip that changes each time it is told repeated.

Occasionally, multiple recalls are very close to identical, a phenomenon termed *resonance*. Conflicting details are not noticed. Resonance is one way to define a clear memory, possibly the result of study to memorize a given image from many different, nearly identical points of view. A long-term-memory word seems to the author to be similar to Semon's *engram*, an *impression* that is stored subconsciously. The term *engram* apparently captures the imagination, since it has been applied in differing ways over the past century in the literature of religion and science fiction. Currently, the term is ignored in scientific circles.

MODELS FOR MEMORIZATION

How long is a word of memory? If a student is memorizing world history, for example, does it all go into one ultralong memory word? If so, a word of memory might be quite long indeed. An exceedingly long word is inefficient because identical neural networks would have to be repeated over and over throughout the word. Also, words might end up with differing random lengths, making recall difficult and inefficient. For efficiency, the model described below assumes words of approximately equal lengths, all related associatively.

Memories from before or after the moment at which an image is memorized are modeled as going into different words. Possibly, words are linked with such items as when, why, and where memorization occurred, although it is not certain that they will be so linked. Most probably there is no time stamp for each word as there might be with machine hardware.

A circuit model must reflect the observation that memories cannot be erased easily, nor can they be overwritten. Also, new memories must go into new blank words. Blank neurons for words of memory are assumed to grow profusely. It is reasonable to assume that nature works this way for new memories, since otherwise humans could neither remember nor learn much. The model assumes an unlimited count of blank words to avoid the issue of what might happen when there is no longer space for new memories.

New blank words of memory must have access to all possible encoded features, given that anything can be committed to memory, as is common experience. Combinational learning is modeled in Chapter 5 as growing additional interneurons and synapses to detect new features. New neurons for new features are modeled as extending to new memory words but not to old memory words. Thus, new blank words must be slightly longer than old words as a result of learning new features. This is consistent with the tenet that the contents of old memories are unchangeable and cannot be adorned with new features.

Memorization Enable

In the architecture described above, memorization is triggered by a *memorization enable,* which is sensitive to recurring images in short-term memory, that is, rehearsal. A memorization enable may be accomplished with a simple digital filter. In the example circuit in Figure 4-13, conditions for committing a given image to memory are true if cues are presented but there are no matches or recalls. This implies that the image has not yet been memorized. Additionally, if an image identified by the importance encoder above appears in short-term memory twice, separated by a delay, it will automatically be committed to long-term memory. The delay can be implemented by short-term memory neurons applied to a standard digital filter circuit.

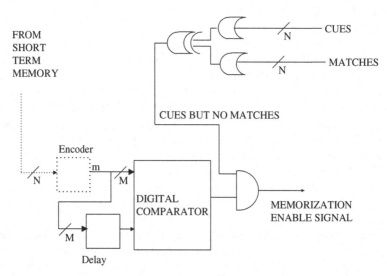

FIGURE 4-13 Proposed memorization enable circuit based on a digital filter.

Circuit Model for Memorizing New Memories

The neurons that convey cues for recall may also serve as conveyers for features in new long-term memories. Figure 4-14 shows how the cellular recall model works for memorization. The little circle with the large Q represents a blank memory cell. In order to memorize a feature, a memorization enable must be made true whenever it is appropriate to memorize. Memorization cannot overlap a memory search.

Programming a blank word with a new memory is not quite as easy as recalling. Rehearsal is necessary to force the memorization enable to go true. A circuit that calculates a true signal based on repeated memorization attempts was modeled in an earlier chapter. Memorization, in the sense of programming a blank word filled with blank memory cells, begins when the memorization enable goes true.

Multiwrite Circuit

Additionally, there have to be controls so that not all available blank words are programmed with the same information. Such a situation would leave no room for additional memory. It is avoided using a simple neural multiwrite circuit, which ensures that only one word is programmed for a given memorization enable. Memorization is regulated by a set of neurons constituting the *memorization control line*, whose purpose is to give multiwrite capability. A multiwrite system is modeled as in Figure 4-15. Each blank word is modeled with a memorization control cell that is set to false. But one blank word has its

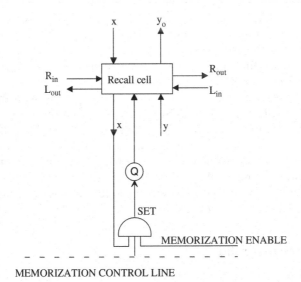

FIGURE 4-14   Memorization circuit.

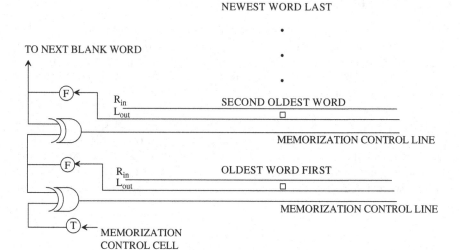

FIGURE 4-15   Programming blank words one at a time.

memorization control cell set to true. If the memorization control cell is true, the memorization control line is also true for one blank word. This blank word is ready to receive a new memory.

Immediately after a word has been programmed, the applied features, interpreted as cues from short-term memory, will permit L_{out} and R_{out} to go true. L_{out} in this circuit permanently sets the next memorization control cell to true. This makes the next blank word ready to be programmed. Once set, the memorization control cell cannot be reset, at least not easily. This prevents previously programmed words from being modified. The XOR associated with a programmed word serves to prevent it from being modified, while the XOR associated with the current blank word makes it ready to be programmed. Newly programmed (memorized) words are available immediately for purposes of memory search and recall.

The implication is that words come (that is, are grown) with their memorization control cells reset to false. Similarly, long-term memory words come blank with their outputs false. Once programmed, this control cell is set true for the long term. As a result, the older blank words of memory are the first to be enabled for new memories; newer blank words of memory are the last to be enabled for programming. Memorization is another manifestation of associative processing. Note that the memorization control cell described here is a sort of toggle, known as a *one-shot* because it toggles forward and back exactly once.

Calories for Memorization

At the moment of memorization, only neurons modeled as adiabatic are involved. Within the brain, the energy for neural signals approximates zero.

This energy excludes leakage of current through membrane conductance, which is common to all neurons, and indeed, all mammalian cells. Leakage energy in the membrane is assumed to be for maintenance, growth, and cellular health. Calories for neural logic, and hence for memory circuits, approach zero.

APPLICATIONS

Future applications of the memory models described above are envisioned as follows.

Robotics

Building a credible brain is a difficult task that is considered a distant goal. However, the author is advocating a robot based on a human memory system, models of which may be applied now to enhance robotic autonomy. The model above suggests that all sensory inputs should be processed simultaneously for presentation to short-term (or *core*) memory. If it meets a memorization criterion, basic information from core memory should be sent immediately to long-term (or *mass*) memory for later use, making room for new sensory inputs. Associative processors are essential for a fast response. Microprocessors, typically used in robots, are basically serial and inefficient.

Ideally, both sensory inputs and motor outputs are massively parallel. A robot needs to register data from many local sensors for feeling, seeing, and hearing, if not smelling and tasting, as humans do. At some point, robots make decisions. An example of a decision would be, "reverse direction to avoid wall." A decision requires consultation with long-term memory for similar situations with a favorable outcome, much as a human would do. In this way a robot, such as a wheeled vacuum cleaner, might someday be designed to avoid cleaning an area already clean or to avoid getting stuck under a bed.

Artificial Intelligence in a Robot

If a robot encounters a problem and recalls a procedure to solve the problem, it seems intelligent. Unfortunately, this is minimal intelligence. Important to true intelligence is the ability to learn. An important step in the evolution of man-made brains is the ability to learn procedures without having to bring into core memory a large number of steps. In this way, core memory remains dedicated to monitoring the environment rather than to procedures. Robots of the future will need the ability to develop automated procedures that do not tie up core memory.

Robots might also learn to recognize new combinations of sensory inputs without having to tie up core memory for their meanings. A human, for example, can learn to play middle G on a violin without hesitation as well as all other notes instantly for all future occasions. There is no need to saturate short-term memory.

Learning is the last major frontier in robotics. The architecture described above introduces a need-to-learn circuit, but this is only a first step. Future work includes the design of reconfigurable circuits that can respond to a need to learn. This is quite possible for new attributes that can be identified as combinations of existing attributes. A similar approach would apply to new procedures implemented as neural state machines that execute automatically when called upon.

CONCLUSIONS

The goal is to model human memory for the amusement of those who might be interested. To begin, brain memory is topped off with a word of short-term memory, below which is modeled a stack of words of approximately equal lengths. Each cell in each word has connections from feature-detecting neurons whose only task is to detect features and to communicate to long-term memory features such as shape and shade. Each feature connects to a definite but unknown location in a word of short-term memory and to corresponding locations in words of long-term memory.

The model of the human memory system presented here includes a variety of memory operations, including memory searches. Here a cue editor is assumed to select cues randomly and in rapid succession. A circuit model was synthesized for a cue editor in which edited cues are used to recall images from subconscious long-term memory. If there are multiple matches, the match nearest the top of the memory stack is analyzed first. Multiple match circuits are used to prevent memories from being returned at exactly the same instant, and being confused.

Recalls are returned within fractions of a second for a calculation of their index of importance. A circuit model was synthesized to calculate an index of importance, which is somewhat similar to a priority encoder. A recalled image is permitted into short-term memory only if its importance is higher than that of current short-term memory. This index is a measure of all features, including bright and strong sensory information, emotional responses, and recalls with compelling features.

Words filled with old memories cannot be erased and rewritten, although over a great span of time they may be dissolved for routine maintenance. Fortunately, the brain is constantly growing new neurons and creating blank words. In this chapter we have examined logic circuits to accomplish the programming of blank words, one at a time. A multiwrite circuit ensures that one word holds one memory. Without this circuit, all available blank memory would be used up in a single act of memorization, preventing additional memorization until new blank words grow.

As new features are learned, new blank words become slightly longer, to include the possibility of memories that include newly learned features. Newly learned features are available only to new words of memory, since old memory is assumed unchangeable. A memorization enable circuit is used to install the contents of short-term memory into a word of long-term memory. This circuit contains a digital filter to effectively impose a requirement for rehearsal before automatic memorization occurs.

The model discussed in this chapter is self-contained and manages to avoid mysterious signals from the cerebral lobes and the soul. Since the model includes memory searches for problem solutions and decisions and a way to select the next image in short-term memory, it is a rudimentary cognitive architecture. Thus, since it is founded on standard logic, it introduces the possibility of building something new, a robot whose brain imitates a human memory system.

EXERCISES

4-1 A man-made encoder uses a microphone with amplifiers and filters to encode sound into tones on a musical scale covering one octave. The detection of each note (A, B, C, D, E, F, G) is either true or false. Each note is represented by one of 7 bits in a 7-bit register, with one bit per note.

(a) Suggest practical applications of this particular analog encoder.

(b) Sketch a circuit for a digital encoder circuit that encodes 7 bits, but with only one bit true at a time, into a 3-bit binary count from 1 to 7. AND, OR, and NOT gates may be used.

(c) List two major differences between an analog and a digital encoder.

(d) What is the difference between a digital encoder and a digital decoder? Illustrate by showing an example of a decoder for a 2-bit address.

4-2 An analog image encoder is based on squares of variable size and shade. A square is fitted to objects in a picture using an optimization procedure that is unimportant to this exercise. Assume 16 squares. Each square is located by an x-coordinate of 5 bits for a binary count from 0 to 31 and a y-coordinate of 5 bits for a binary count from 0 to 31. For each square there are 10 size bits, corresponding to 10 possible sizes, and 6 shade bits, corresponding to 6 shades available. Only one of the size bits is true at a time; only one of the shade bits is true at a time.

(a) What is the maximum number of binary outputs for this analog encoder?

(b) The size bits and shade bits are run through a digital encoder so that they are binary counts. How many bits are necessary in a word of RAM to store a single picture?

4-3 A neuron is capable of Boolean logic.

(a) List major differences between neurons and CMOS.

(b) The XOR is generated by a standard Boolean equation:

$$z = xy' + x'y$$

Synthesize a logic circuit for z.

(c) Modify the XOR circuit to give a nonzero output only if an enable signal E is true. This is an example of enabled logic, where E goes true briefly and then returns to false.

(d) Demonstrate with reference to the XOR equation that it can be used to generate a NOT function of x. Illustrate the NOT using an XOR circuit.

4-4   Human memory and man-made memory have much in common.

(a) Compare human short-term memory to dynamic random-access memory (DRAM). How is DRAM refreshed? Can human short-term memory be refreshed?

(b) How many words are there in the short-term-memory model? How many in DRAM? Explain how a word is read from DRAM using conventional addressing.

(c) Compare human subconscious long-term memory to read-only memory (ROM). How is addressing accomplished in human memory; in ROM?

4-5   Refer to the memory system presented in the text. Assume that there is an address field in the 32 leftmost cells, that is, 32 binary features.

(a) If each unique set of features results in exactly one memory recall, how many memories are held?

(b) If each unique set of features corresponds to two possible memories, how many memories are there?

(c) When two memories are activated, one of them is blocked out. How would you identify the one that is blocked out?

(d) Explain, with reference to a circuit, how neural logic handles conflicting memory recalls.

4-6   Refer to a standard textbook to locate a digital circuit (or design a digital circuit) for associative memory.

(a) Sketch the overall architecture of traditional associative memory, labeling all components.

(b) Illustrate the logic for a traditional associative memory and explain its function.

(c) Identify differences from the system given in this chapter?

4-7   Redesign the memory system given in the chapter so that

$$R_{out} = R_{in}x' + R_{in}Q$$

This subtle difference results in a different circuit. Redesign the circuit to include multiple read and write.

4-8 It was suggested that cerebral editing results in cues for recall. Assume that you meet an old friend but cannot remember his name.

  (a) List a sequence of cues to aid memory. Begin with six names in *alphabetical* order and end with his actual name: Zinzendorf.

  (b) If items from the list above are organized *randomly* and then processed from the top, is recall faster or slower? Give an example involving a 3-bit pseudorandom counter.

4-9 Provide an example of recall that is modeled after a classic car, in which you remember the chrome hood ornament and the red- and-white two-tone body, but not the other features of the car. Then trace the recall signals in four cells as done in the chapter's example.

4-10 The memory cell described in the text depends on adiabatic neurons. Why are adiabatic neurons important here?

4-11 A pseudorandom shift register counter was suggested in this chapter.

  (a) Employ four toggle circuits and an XNOR to design the logic circuit for a shift register counter.

  (b) Give the count sequence.

4-12 An encoder was used to determine an index of importance. Assume four attributes that are labeled red, white, blue, and black. Red is most important; white is second; blue is third; black is fourth in importance. Design or find a digital circuit that encodes these priorities. It is all right to use a basic priority encoder circuit. Make a truth table of encoder input and output.

4-13 A digital filter can be made to enable memorization if an image occurs twice in short-term memory at given times. Provide a block diagram of the digital filter. Explain with reference to the circuit:

  (a) What happens if an image occurs only once?

  (b) What happens if an image occurs twice but at the wrong times?

  (c) What happens if an image occurs twice at exactly the right times?

CHAPTER 5

DENDRITIC PROCESSING AND HUMAN LEARNING

INTRODUCTION

In this chapter we examine a dendritic model that generates arbitrary Boolean logic and then applies it to learning. In the model, pulses are recognized to be electrical solitons, pulses that propagate with neither dispersion nor amplitude reduction, owing to an assumed continuity of the dendritic membrane. Electrical solitons can be activated by excitatory neurotransmitters, but inhibitory neurotransmitters are able to stop their propagation toward a soma.

Simulations indicate that solitons can be reflected by dendritic junctions and by the soma itself. Reflected pulses "back propagate" toward the dendritic receivers but do not pass through oncoming solitons as solitons in electrical wires generally do. Colliding dendritic solitons annihilate each other, clearing the way for additional oncoming pulses. Back-propagating solitons arriving at a receiver help to regulate neurotransmitters. Like recently generated pulses, they are positively charged and effectively repel positive neurotransmitter ions. This, in combination with a negative voltage in the presynaptic bouton as its action potential finishes, pushes and pulls excitatory neurotransmitter ions away from a postsynaptic receiver and terminates an action potential.

Artificial intelligence (AI) today is beginning to accomplish scene and sound recognition, but this is only one aspect of AI as defined in this book, the ability

Human Memory Modeled with Standard Analog and Digital Circuits:
Inspiration for Man-made Computers, By John Robert Burger
Copyright © 2009 John Wiley & Sons, Inc.

to learn being paramount. The ready availability of neurons as logic devices creates the possibility of *all-digital learning*, discussed later in the chapter. We begin with an overview of the neural circuits associated with learning. Once these are delineated, reconfigurable circuits suitable for learning are proposed. Learning has several meanings, including reflexive actions independent of the brain: for example, automatic recoil from a hot pan. Since reflexive learning apparently does not pass signals through short- or long-term memory and appears to be independent of the brain, it is not considered a part of brain theory.

What drives biological learning is a need to accomplish a *task* efficiently, since efficiency is essential to species survival. Related to learning, but not learning itself, is *memorization*, the committing of events to long-term memory for recall when needed. Memorization relating to learning is modeled as occurring instantly with no need for synaptic growth. True learning is modeled as requiring new neurons and synapses. Two types of learning are fairly obvious:

1. *Combinational learning.* Here a special new feature is detected automatically as a combination of signals from existing neurons, the result being that a person done not have to ponder a new special feature in short-term memory.
2. *Neural state-machine learning.* Here the steps of a procedure can execute directly in long-term memory without having to pass all details through short-term memory.

The resulting new abilities can be modeled to be the result of new neurons with new synapses to existing neurons. Learning is assumed to take place in an environment with an abundance of interneurons. An analogy is the field-programmable gate array (FPGA), or the application-specific integrated circuit (ASIC), in which an abundance of overhead circuitry is helpful. The purpose of overhead circuitry is none other than to direct synaptic development where it is needed. Most of the time, most of the circuits are dormant. But when directed to do so, they make critical connections at critical localities. Before connections are permitted, however, there must be a need-to-learn signal.

A need-to-learn signal is assumed to exist as a result of having to recognize or execute something repeatedly using short-term memory. A digital filter picks up the fact that something is being used regularly and triggers a need-to-learn signal. This signal begins the learning process. A decoder spurs appropriate interneurons to release neurotransmitters at locations where they are needed, effectively connecting stray unused neurons into those circuits where they are needed. Learning seems to occur like this, and it can be modeled like this, but the actual physics of learning continues to be a subject for additional investigation.

Learning as modeled below begins in the brain, in short-term memory, with a need-to-learn signal. Before we expand on learning models, it is important to clarify certain confusing issues relating to artificial neurons, and to clarify what is meant by combinational learning and neural state-machine learning.

BIOLOGICAL VERSUS ARTIFICIAL NEURAL NETWORKS

Biological neural networks for feature-detecting tasks and speculation about their operations have spurred the field of artificial neural networks. Artificial neural networks, the subject of Chapter 6, are potentially valuable for speech recognition, picture recognition, and a host of other useful applications. Single-layer artificial neural networks can achieve AND, OR, NOT logic; multilayer artificial neural networks can achieve XOR (exclusive-OR) logic. Artificial neural networks do all this, but they are not used for processing or learning as modeled in this book; they are not correct biologically.

Artificial neural networks have the ability to learn, but this learning is very different from what occurs in a brain. It is mainly a type of mathematical optimization in which many analog variables are adjusted in an attempt to minimize an *error function*. A typical error function is usually a sum of the squared differences between actual outputs and desired outputs of an artificial neural network. Optimization like this requires considerable computational effort in large computers, and quite often, optimization is impossible given an intractable error function that will not be minimized.

Artificial neurons are computer subroutines, or operational amplifiers, one op amp per artificial neuron. The inputs to each op amp are analog signals whose amplitudes or weighting factors are continuously variable. Linear summation is assumed. In contrast, biological neurons as modeled in this chapter are restricted to positive weighting factors that are either zero or one. This is because the voltage pulses in dendrites are regulated by the active membrane to have identical positive amplitudes. A similar principle applies to pulses in soma and axon.

Linear summation is difficult to visualize in a synaptic receiver, although one may visualize an integration of excitatory ions as released from a given particular bouton, not at all what is suggested by an artificial neural network. Summation in the form of charge accumulation may occur in the capacitance of the soma, but only in a limited sense of positive quantities of fixed steps. Overall, artificial neurons, although successful in engineering terms, relate poorly to biological neurons.

Neural codes were discovered by Edgar Adrian, who found that increased pressure on neurons involved in the sense of touch resulted in an increased firing rate, that is, an increased number of action potentials or pulse bursts per unit time. Neuroscientists have speculated that neural waveforms carry subtle bits of information, for example, not just in the rate of firing but also in the timing between spikes. Codes like this work well enough in information theory but are difficult to imagine physically in a neuron. Waveforms are generally fixed by ionic composition, by membrane thickness, and to some extent by the size and shape of a neuron. The net result is a very restricted range of frequencies within a pulse burst with no way to create pulse code modulation.

The length of a "standard" neural burst of the type most often published depends on a natural rhythm associated with short-term memory. Usually, there are about 10 pulses with a characteristic spacing as shown later in the chapter. Random isolated spikes are possible, and their purposes, if any, are poorly understood, but they seem to be very much in the minority of neural actions. When many neurons fire at the same time, this can be interpreted to be not a code, but rather, an indication that the brain is working normally. Thus, we arrive at the simplest of codes: One action potential equals one bit of information, as assumed in Chapter 3.

The model of a biological neuron developed in this book uses no analog weighting factors, no negative weighting factors, only Boolean values, and no summations, linear or otherwise. It is a simpler sort of digital model that serves adequately for biological learning.

Neurons with Combinational Abilities

Combinational learning is defined below to involve the growth of new neurons and synapses that are dedicated to detecting new features, and doing so without pondering in the short-term memory system. Dedicated feature-detecting neurons, the neurons represented by the encoder box of Chapter 4, are activated only when they detect a given feature, such as a shape, shade, or color. Assumed to be the result of learning over many decades, feature-detecting neurons do only one thing in this model: Each is dedicated to detecting a given feature. When they do so, they send a signal into a particular location in conscious short-term memory. As appropriate, signals in short-term memory are transmitted to corresponding locations in subconscious long-term memory for memory searches and possible memorization.

Sensory encoders are analogous to analog-to-digital conversion in man-made computers, although both the analog and the digital codes in a biological system are quite different from those used in man-made computers. The signal produced by a feature-detecting neuron is a standard pulse burst that is easily recognized by neurons in the memory system. Once created by a process of learning, new dedicated neurons will detect new features automatically without analysis in the short-term memory system.

Neurons with State-Machine Abilities

Neural state-machine learning is defined here to involve the growth of new neurons and synapses within long-term memory used to jump between words of memory automatically, without going through the short-term memory system. Neural state machines, mentioned previously but not discussed until now, are another result of learning over a period of many decades. Neural state machines are relevant to a human's strong ability to learn, that is, to remember procedures and sequences—a long poem, for instance. In a biological context, a *state* refers to a particular word of subconscious long-term memory; when a person performs a step in a procedure under state-machine control, a particular word of memory is activated. In a state machine, a state is activated only if related states have been activated previously. As modeled below, interneurons will signal when previous states have been activated and thus enable the next word of long-term memory, that is, the step of a procedure.

Clearly, humans depend heavily on automatic procedures, including a basic procedure for walking, talking, and thousands of others. Learned procedures relate to advanced abilities, such as playing a musical instrument, hitting a golf ball, or learning complicated dance steps. Neural state machines increase efficiency because they avoid bringing procedures into short-term memory for evaluation; they may execute without thinking when a person is well practiced.

DENDRITES

Before attempting to explain neural logic and learning, an introduction to dendrites is necessary to clarify the nature of dendritic processing. The word *dendrite* derives from the Greek *dendron*, meaning a tree with branches. Dendrite segments are named relative to their position from the soma. The initial segment is called a *first-order segment* or sometimes a *trunk*, its daughter segments are termed *second-order segments* or *branches*, daughter segments of second-order segments are *third-order segments* or *branches*; and so on. The terminal nonbranching dendritic segments are *tips*, sometimes termed *leaves*. Figure 5-1 shows an artist's rendition of a dendritic tree, upside down from trunk to tips, although note that dendritic trees, like botanical trees, do not look the same.

Dendrites usually do not extend as far from the soma as axons; however, they can be quite extensive. The dendritic arbor can account for up to 98% of the phospholipid surface area of a neuron. Excitatory and inhibitory synapses are distributed across the arbor such that excitatory synapses are usually uniformly distributed out to the distal locations, whereas inhibitory synapses are typically proximal, located closer to the soma. Neurons display two classes of dendrites. *Apical dendrites* extend outward from the apex or top of a pyramidal soma. *Basal dendrites* project laterally from the base of a pyramidal soma. In the model below, basal and apical dendrites are capable of limited logic in conjunction with soma capacitance: for example, AND logic. Located on the dendrites are many *spines*, the targets of excitatory neurotransmitters sent by the boutons of other neurons. Excitatory neurotransmitter ions that approach a receiver will trigger an action in the active membrane of the receiver, resulting in solitons propagating toward the soma.

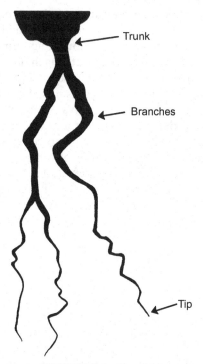

FIGURE 5-1 Dendritic tree.

Dendritic Pulses

A simplified model for neurons as logic devices depends on a clear role for neurotransmitters. The model below assumes nothing new: Neurotransmitters, in the form of excitatory ions attach briefly to spines and receivers on dendrites, triggering pulses as modeled in Chapter 3. Neurotransmitters in the form of inhibitor ions attach closer to the soma, where they serve to hinder the propagation of a dendritic pulse. They do this by inhibiting the active properties of the membrane, effectively converting the path where they attach to a passive channel.

Dendrites lack *myelination*, so are active all along their lengths, except where inhibitory neurotransmitter ions become attached. Ionic compositions and membrane properties are the chief factors in dendritic pulse widths. In the model below, the diameter of a neural path will have little effect on dendritic pulse waveform because both charging currents and membrane capacitance are proportional to surface area, not volume.

Solitons

Dendritic pulses are technically electrical solitons. They are characterized by the fact that they do not disperse as they propagate as do electrical pulses in linear circuits. Dispersion results in a spreading out of the width of the pulse and a reduction in amplitude. Electrical solitons can exist in dendrites because they are refreshed by membrane activation. When two electrical solitons approach each other from opposite ends of a neural path, a soliton collision occurs that results in the disappearance of both pulses, according to the author's simulations (see the soliton simulations in the appendix to this chapter). In contrast, electromagnetic solitons in nonlinear media usually pass through each other with little apparent change.

Soliton logic is readily produced within dendrites, so the propagation of any soliton depends on Boolean logic. Soliton logic in a limited sense is also possible in the soma, as explained next. In the model used below, there may be a partial charge buildup in the soma as a result of an incoming soliton, but not quite enough charge to trigger the soma. This charge is positive and quantized by the charge available in a soliton but otherwise analogous to the bias in an artificial neuron. The charge transferred by the first incoming soliton may serve effectively as an enable signal but not as a triggering signal. Triggering in such cases depends on a second dendritic pulse arriving at the soma, implementing what is essentially a soma AND gate. Assuming that Boolean logic is satisfied, a trigger occurs in the soma and thus action in the axon.

Starting and Stopping an Action Potential

To begin, a pulse burst in a driving axon results in an initial release of excitatory neurotransmitter positive ions. These are attracted to a negatively charged dendritic receiver, where they instigate a pulse. As the dendritic pulse goes positive, its positive charge repels the positive neurotransmitter ions back into the synaptic cleft. With oscillatory timing they are attracted back and then repelled again by their home boutons and the driver axon undergoing its own action potential.

The pulse triggered in the receiver becomes a soliton that propagates away from the vicinity where it was triggered. Once it moves away, positive excitatory ions are able to drift back to the negative receiver and trigger another pulse, and the cycle repeats. The action potential in this model is ended when the driver neuron returns to its rest potential, which is negative, thus attracting positive excitatory ions away from the postsynaptic receiver and docking them where they came from.

One may visualize a ball connected by a rubber band to a paddle. The rubber band is analogous to electric force; the paddle is analogous to a receiver. The ball is kept in motion by an action of the wrist, analogous to neurotransmitter ions bouncing repeatedly to and from a membrane. Eventually, the rubber band breaks and gravity brings the ball to Earth, analogous to ions returning to their homes.

Negative charge attracts positive neurotransmitter ions back to the boutons where they came from, a process termed *reuptake*. This simple model based on positive and negative charge suggests that excitatory ions ideally work in a closed cycle. Neurotransmitter exciters are encouraged to return to their homes by the very pulses they generate, and also by reflected solitons. The last of the solitons will probably have a reflected soliton that soon reaches the site of generation to assure the removal of stray positive neurotransmitter ions.

An action potential ends when the presynaptic bouton returns to equilibrium. This occurs indirectly through a circuit of neurons when signals from the short-term memory system change course. As soon as the information released from short-term memory is gated off, all downstream neurons begin to clear, returning to rest.

According to simulations, reflected solitons are quite common. A discontinuity where dendritic branches meet, where there is increased capacitance and reduced resistance, is sometimes enough to cause a reflection and usually, also a forward propagation. In this case, one soliton becomes two solitons, which is not unusual given the activity of the membrane. A soliton that reaches the dendrite–soma interface generally produces a reflection propagating back toward the tips. This is caused by the discontinuity of higher soma capacitance and lower equivalent resistance, which is present whether or not the soma is triggered.

Simulations show that no reflections are expected back from dendritic tips, however, since a neural path ends with little or no capacitive load to cause retriggering. Like their forward-propagating relatives, reflected solitons push neurotransmitter ions away from the surface of the dendrites, and help to ensure that neural activity ends cleanly. Propagation in a dendrite is considerably slower than in an axon, mainly because dendritic capacitance is not reduced by myelination and is significantly larger. To begin analyzing a dendritic branch, it may be modeled as a series connection of many short segments (see Figure 5-2).

Each segment waits to be triggered by an adjacent segment. To be triggered, sufficient voltage must accumulate in the capacitance (C_1) of the segment, about $1 \, \mu F/cm^2$ of the surface area. In a cylindrical segment, C_1 is proportional to $\pi D L$, where D is the segment diameter and L is the segment length. The cross-sectional area A is $\pi(D/2)^2$. The series resistance (R_1) in the segment is $\rho L / A$ or $\rho 4 L / \pi D^2$, where ρ is resistivity, assumed to fall between 3.14 and $31.4 \, \Omega \cdot cm$. Thus, $R_1 C_1$ is the time constant, and as derived for the axon in Chapter 2 using the Elmore approximation, one expects a propagation delay

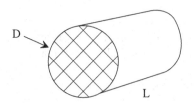

FIGURE 5-2 Model of a segment of a dendritic branch.

equation of the form

$$t_p \approx \theta_1 R_1 C_1 N^2 = \theta_2 \cdot 4L^2 \frac{N^2}{D}$$

Here N represents the number of segments, or the length of a dendritic branch, and θ_1 and θ_2 are constants whose evaluation is unimportant here. The equation shows that if diameter D is small, the delay is greater; if L (or N) is large, meaning a longer path, delay increases as the square of L or N, that is, geometrically. Pulses that are generated far from the soma are expected to take disproportionately longer to arrive at the soma based on this analysis.

After the first soliton that is generated leaves the region of excitation, another may occur, and perhaps several more as neurotransmitters oscillate back and forth to the receiver. But each soliton arriving at the soma produces a reflection; and each reflection will annihilate one approaching soliton. Therefore, every other soliton will periodically reach the soma in an ideal situation, and this affects the frequency of pulses within a burst.

Pulse Frequencies Within a Burst

Electrical pulses in soma and axon are instigated by dendritic activity and usually occur in groups of pulses known as *pulse bursts*, also known as *action potentials*. A soma pulse may correspond to a soliton impinging on the soma, so the rate of solitons sets the rate of pulses within a burst, a situation assumed to be fairly common. Ideally, soma pulse frequency within a burst will be below the *maximum amplitude rate* (MAR), the number of regular-sized spikes per second that can occur within a given burst (not to the rate of the bursts). MAR depends on membrane and ionic conditions, so it can vary for different types of neurons, although it is not expected to very by orders of magnitude. As an example of calculating MAR, consider the model action potential waveform of Chapter 2. The pulse width is perhaps 3.3 ms according to the model. Thus, MAR is in the range $1/3.3$ ms ≈ 300 Hz. Above this rate, amplitudes will be less than full value.

MAR implies that another pulse is triggered shortly after the preceding pulse reaches undershoot. Early triggering before that pulse reaches undershoot is also possible given a sustained triggering voltage, but the resulting pulse will have less than maximum amplitude and a higher frequency than the MAR. Rates greater than the MAR might be obtained as follows: As a soma pulse reaches its peak at about $+40$ mV and begins to decrease, it might not reach the undershoot value (-90 mV) before another trigger occurs. Instead, it may trigger as soon as possible at the threshold of triggering at -55 mV. It thus will oscillate between -55 and $+40$ mV, an amplitude of 95 mV, not between -90 and $+40$ mV, an amplitude of 130 mV. Since the range of voltage is less, the width of the pulse is less, and the frequency exceeds the MAR. Thus the frequency is higher, but the amplitude is lower.

The short-term-memory neuron provides an example of rates above the MAR. Here the soliton is modeled as a long pulse that goes up fast but drops very slowly. This implies sustained triggering in the soma. A long dendritic pulse is expected to trigger shorter, reduced-amplitude soma pulses, higher than the MAR but with lower than maximum amplitude. Basically, the pulse width of a dendritic soliton is set by the membrane and ionic properties in the dendrites. When a soliton arrives at a soma, a soma pulse occurs, although multiple or distorted soma pulses may occur in some cases. More often than not, solitons arrive at a rate lower than the maximum amplitude rate, judging by published action potential waveforms. In this case, the soma voltage decreases to an undershoot value, returns to equilibrium, and waits to be triggered by the next available soliton. In this situation, the frequency of pulses within a burst will be lower than the maximum amplitude rate. A typical burst of axon spikes, distorted by oscilloscope limitations, is pictured in Figure 5-3.

Triggering considerations as above help to explain spikes per second within a given burst as observed in Purkinje and pyramidal neurons. For example, Purkinje neurons (Figure 5-4) have been observed to produce a higher frequency than a pyramidal neuron (Figure 5-5). The higher frequency demonstrated by a Purkinje neuron apparently approaches a maximum amplitude rate for this neuron.

Purkinje Neurons

Johannes Evangelista Purkinje (1787–1869) was a pioneer in experimental physiology and the study of cells, particularly after he acquired a compound microscope in 1832. Purkinje neurons are found in the cerebellar cortex, this being the dominant type of cell in the cerebellum (see Appendix A). Purkinje neurons are relatively large, with dendrites that extend from the soma in two dimensions (that is, a Purkinje neuron is nearly flat). A particularly impressive dendritic arbor accompanies an artist's rendition of a Purkinje cell in Figure 5-4.

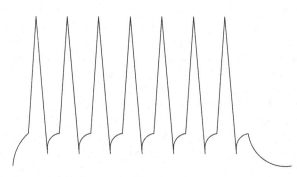

FIGURE 5-3 Example of a burst of spikes (amplitude, 50 mV; burst duration, 70 ms).

FIGURE 5-4   Cerebellar Purkinje cell.

Purkinje neurons are stacked in the cerebellum with their dendritic arbors parallel to each other. Granule cells (*parallel fibers*) form excitatory synapses to dendritic spines. In addition, *climbing fibers* make about 200,000 excitatory synapses to receivers in the proximal dendrites and the soma itself, one synapse per fiber. Stellate (starlike) and basket neurons provide inhibitory input to the Purkinje neurons; stellate neurons synapse with the proximal dendrites, while basket-shaped neurons actually synapse with initial parts of the axon.

Web data indicate that Purkinje neurons demonstrate simple spikes with equivalent rates of roughly 17 to 150 per second, perhaps an average of 50 Hz either spontaneously or when activated via the parallel fibers of granule neurons that form synapses with the spines. These simple spikes, apparently, are triggered by propagating solitons coming in from dendritic spines. But when activated directly in the proximal dendrites or soma by the climbing

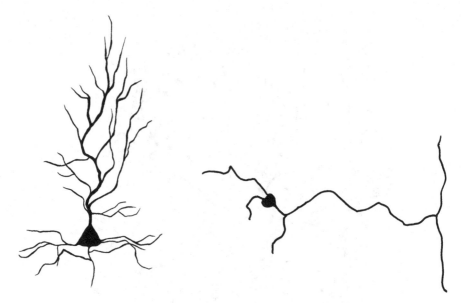

FIGURE 5-5 Pyramidal and granule neurons.

fibers, the spike rate is in excess of 300 per second, approaching the maximum amplitude rate. This rate is apparently approached because of synapses directly to the soma (that is, the rate is not regulated by solitons from dendrites). Synapses directly to the soma may very well experience a higher frequency of neurotransmitter oscillation, since the soma area is far greater than the dendritic receiver areas, resulting in stronger electric forces to speed the movement of excitatory ions.

In contrast, a train of solitons from the tip of a dendrite results in a lower rate of pulsating within a burst. Analysis is possible in a limited sense by assuming one ideal soma triggering per soliton. Very likely the rate at which solitons arrive at the soma is lower than the maximum amplitude rate in a soma. Each incident soliton creates at least one reflected soliton from the soma. The reflected soliton annihilates an oncoming soliton, according to simulations, effectively cutting the rate of the incoming soliton in half. In this case, after a single pulse, the soma will have to wait for the next soliton. As a result, frequency within a soma burst is less than the MAR meaning that there is more time between pulse peaks.

To increase the confusion, an incoming soliton may have a different waveform than a soma pulse and could easily have a width beyond 10 ms, depending on the characteristics of membranes and ions. Considering the discussion above, incoming solitons may be spaced roughly every 10 ms or more. If every other one is annihilated by a back-propagating soliton, the soma will be trigged every 20 ms, or a frequency of 50 Hz, reasonably close to what is reported experimentally. A pyramidal neuron, according to Web data, experiences a lower frequency of triggering (50 to 100 Hz) within a burst and is assumed to be regulated by a train of solitons from conventional synapses on its dendrites.

Pyramidal Neurons

Pyramidal neurons constitute 80% of all neurons in the cortex; they release glutamate as their neurotransmitter, making them a major excitatory component of the cortex. A pyramidal neuron with many tips is illustrated in Figure 5-5. Look at the soma; it is shaped like a pyramid. Somas can range from 10 to 100 μm at the base. There are several hundred tips (not all shown). There are many tips in the axonal arbor (bottom) as well as the dendritic arbor (top). The pyramidal neuron develops in three dimensions. This cell is potentially a complex logic gate with many inputs. In comparison, the granule neuron, shown to the right in the figure, suggests only two inputs. This cell is potentially a simple logic gate.

Pyramidal neurons, the prevalent neurons in the cerebral cortex, have two classes of dendrites as described earlier. Apical dendrites, which extend outward from the apex (top) of the pyramide-shaped soma, typically receive input from distant sources such as the thalamus. Basal dendrites, which project laterally from the base of the soma, may receive enabling inputs from nearby cortical areas. Basal dendrites in the primary sensory areas are shorter in total length and have fewer segments and fewer dendritic spines. Basal dendrites in the prefrontal cortex are longer with more segments and more spines. The complexity of the dendritic arbor is said to be related to the functional complexity of the area in which it is embedded.

Dendritic diameters are a few micrometers near the soma and range down below 0.3 μm, often reaching 1 mm in length. Many but not all dendrites are studded with small appendages called spines (ranging widely from 300 to 200,000 in number per neuron).

Spines

Spines, micrometer-sized bulbs connected to the parent dendrite through a thin neck, are believed to be the main postsynaptic targets for neurotransmitter input. Figure 5-6 represents the general shape of a spine. Spines occur in densities of about one every square micrometer; the spine membrane area is up to 60% of the total neuron area. Spines have an average length of 1.5 μm. Average bulb dimensions relate to an equivalent sphere with a diameter of 1 μm or a surface area of about 3.14 μm². Spines have a higher percentage of calcium ions than other parts of the neuron. It is thought that the trunk prevents excessive calcium from diffusing into other parts of the neuron. Calcium has two electrons rather than one; both are available for ionization, and in this sense calcium is more active than potassium.

FIGURE 5-6   Mushroom-shaped spine example.

Excitatory receptors, in conjunction with appropriate excitatory neurotransmitter ions, function as excitatory inputs, tending to trigger an internal action potential within the dendrites. Inhibitory receptors, in conjunction with appropriate inhibitory neurotransmitter ions, tend to prevent an internal action potential from propagating through a given segment of a branch. The excitatory inputs are chiefly distributed on spines and amount to roughly 75% of the inputs. The inhibitory receptors are mostly near the soma and constitute about 25% of the total. The density of spines, especially the density of smaller spines, is known to change over time. Changes in spine receptor density plus formations of new synapses are related to learning.

NEURONS FOR COMBINATIONAL LEARNING

Neurons for basic survival have evolved over millions of years, and fundamental neural structures apparently are present at birth. Beyond this, all else is learned over a lifetime. What follows is a model of the result of learning.

Learning to detect a new feature such as the color chartreuse, a mixture of yellow and green, can be modeled as follows. Assume the existence of a neuron in the encoder block that is dedicated to green and another that is dedicated to yellow. At first a person may recall words involving green and then words involving yellow into short-term memory and then alternate these words with a definition of chartreuse to identify chartreuse. But going through short-term memory this way is inefficient. A person who needs to identify chartreuse eventually learns to recognize it automatically, without having to ponder the components of green and yellow and tie up short-term memory.

In order to "learn" chartreuse, a new unused neuron must develop near those two neurons in the encoder block dedicated to yellow and green. As chartreuse is brought repeatedly into short-term memory, a need-to-learn signal is made to occur. This signal and the cues for yellow and green are able to pinpoint those locations on the yellow and green neurons where synapses are needed. With the aid of interneurons for learning, described below, the yellow and green neurons develop synapses to the new neuron, as

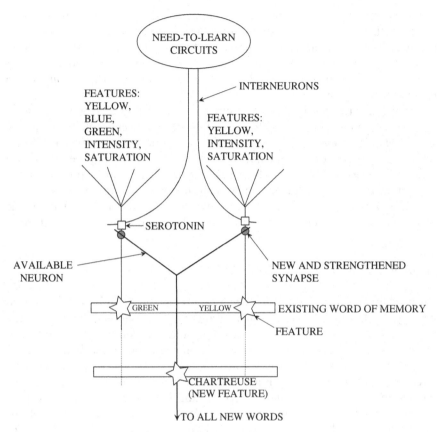

FIGURE 5-7   Learning as building combinational gates.

shown in Figure 5-7. The new neuron, now dedicated to chartreuse, is activated only when both yellow and green are present. There are no assumed analog weighting factors. The new neuron is an AND gate with yellow and green signals as input. The axonal output of the new neuron goes to all new words in long-term memory so that chartreuse may have features of a new memory. Any new memory referring to chartreuse can still refer to green and yellow but will not if they are not part of the memory word.

Chartreuse will, however, be unavailable to old memories, because old memories are assumed long term and unchangeable. Common sense says than an old memory will not contain something recently learned after the old memory was created. However, it may be possible to recall an old memory and to include a new attribute recently learned, and then to create a new refreshed memory. To develop synapses as above, an interneuron is modeled as depositing the neurotransmitter serotonin near the dedicated green and the dedicated yellow neuron, and also near a new neuron that is about to be dedicated to chartreuse. Serotonin has been found to encourage the growth of new synapses. The breakthrough realization that serotonin is involved in synaptic growth was advanced by Kandel and others after years studying the sea slug *Aplysia*. Pulses of serotonin are proposed to cause molecular messengers to move into the nucleus of a neuron. This was observed to result in *gene expression* for the growth of new synapses.

The driving force for learning is efficiency. Learning frees up short-term memory, enabling it to be used for more important current issues, such as the sensing of new dangers. In a basic neural model, a synapse either triggers a pulse in a receiver, or it does not; it's digital. But there may be many new synapses, corresponding to brightness, luster, intensity, and so on, associated with yellow and also with green. A new dedicated neuron thus becomes a multi-input AND gate that provides output only for the correct inputs. This simple model explains what happens when a person learns to detect a new feature.

NEURONS FOR STATE-MACHINE LEARNING

Much of life revolves around learned procedures. To be efficient, procedural memory must act like a state machine and not necessarily pass through the apparatus of short-term memory. Neural state machines are unrelated to feature-detecting neurons. A neural state machine is a logical machine that steps through a procedure or a poem learned by "heart," by choosing the next step based on past steps. Each step is assumed to be in a word of long-term memory. Short-term memory is essentially bypassed and is thus free to deal with more important issues. A neural state machine uses interneurons to control the sequencing of words. These interneurons have propagation delay and perhaps a short-term memory effect to regulate the speed at which a procedure is performed. In contrast to a desktop computer, which is clocked, a neural state machine is self-timed. If the procedure does not execute in the standard way, short-term memory comes into play to correct a person's activity.

Consider a procedure to open a door. This can be modeled simplistically as two steps: (1) turn the doorknob; (2) pull the door. Somewhere in the brain there is a memory word for what a doorknob is and how to turn it. Once this is done, there is another memory word that indicates what a door is and how to pull it open. Two steps are involved. Before the learning takes place, a doorknob and its workings are recalled to short-term memory. Within this doorknob memory is a link to the next step, a memory about how to open a door. This is a classical two-step procedure; at first it is brought sequentially into short-term memory in order to implement it. However, as this is done repeatedly, a need-to-learn signal occurs. New neurons are linked into long-term memory in an appropriate way to automate the learned procedure. A person thus learns to accomplish such procedures without thinking, that is, without tying up short-term memory with such minutia as finger placement on a doorknob, for example.

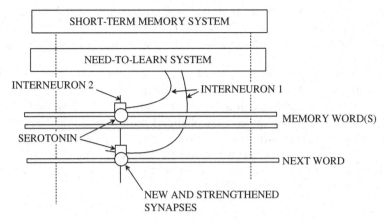

FIGURE 5-8 Learning as building neural state machines.

Figure 5-8 shows how a two-step procedure may be executed in a neural state machine. During the activation of the "doorknob" word, a word-jumping neuron becomes activated. This interneuron, interneuron 2, after suitable delay, serves to enable the "open-the-door" word. Essentially, interneuron 2 becomes a multi-input AND gate that activates only if the past steps of a procedure are first activated. To accomplish neural state-machine learning, a need-to-learn signal first occurs because of repetition of a procedure in short-term memory. This signal and the cues taken from short-term memory are enough to locate in long-term memory those words that need linking. Interneurons, similar to interneuron 1 in the figure, release serotonin, causing new neurons to develop synapses so as to implement an embedded state machine.

There is a force in nature that is very different from gravity, electromagnetic, or nuclear forces. It is a force that encourages efficiency, thus aiding survival. This force is what drives the creation of new dedicated neural networks in the encoder block as well as new neural state machines within subconscious long-term memory.

LEARNING CIRCUITS

A healthy adult brain contains about 100 billion neurons, each neuron linking via synapses to as many as 100,000 other neurons. Calculating numbers gives quadrillions (multiples of 10^{15}) of connections. One quadrillion pennies side by side would go from the Sun to Jupiter. Evidence suggests that new neurons are constantly being born and new synaptic connections are forming continuously, while old connections dissolve and old neurons die. A good many neurons apparently are crammed into the cerebral lobes, a likely location for learning circuits. In the context of such unimaginably large numbers of neurons and connections, it must be realized that overhead circuits involving AND gates are extremely easy to have. A few trillion AND gates is not a big problem. What is a big deal, however, is attempting to draw a logic circuit for a few trillion gates. Simple models must suffice to convey how learning occurs.

To study a learning circuit, consider four features, the colors blue, red, green, and yellow. Assume that these are features in a group of n features, where n is the unspecified size of a block with learning capability, one of many such blocks. If it should happen that blue and red are used, this fact may be identified by a circuit known as a 2-out-of-n detector, illustrated in Figure 5-9, where the top AND gate detects when blue (B) and red (R) go true. Any two of the n features is decoded this way. The number N_{AND} of AND gates will be a combination of two things in n objects:

$$N_{AND} = \frac{n(n-1)}{2}$$

The outputs of the ANDs go to digital filters identified as need-to-learn filters. In the figure, only the first and last outputs are illustrated for the need-to-learn

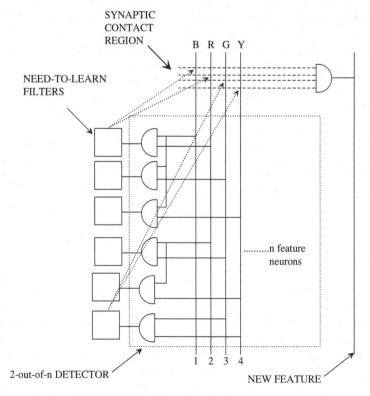

FIGURE 5-9 Learning circuit concept.

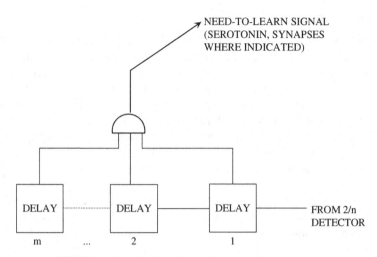

FIGURE 5-10   Need-to-learn detector circuit concept.

blocks. If a need to learn is sensed by these filters, interneurons will deposit neurotransmitters to facilitate synaptic growth in exactly the right spot to cause learning. Learning a new feature is simply a matter of linking the components in another AND gate whose output is the new feature neuron. The new feature line is shown on the right of the figure. The new feature becomes an element in short-term memory and is also a candidate for placement in new long-term memory words. New words thus are slightly longer because of such new feature neurons.

A need-to-learn filter might be implemented as illustrated in Figure 5-10. The figure suggests that pairs of features become important when used quite often on a regular basis. Once this criterion is satisfied, learning occurs automatically. Shown in the figure is a filter that requires pairs such as blue and red to be used in short-term memory a number of times equal to m, where m is not specified exactly but must be large enough to establish a limit to learning compatible with the number of new neurons available for learning.

The delay blocks are versions of the memorization enable circuit based on short-term memory neurons with random durations, as discussed earlier.

Presented above is an all-digital circuit concept for learning. This circuit was arrived at only because there is a shortage of better circuits for this purpose. From a neural view, it is easy enough to detect three or more uses of n features because digital filters of greater complexity are readily available. Potential applications include learning circuits for robots.

DENDRITIC PROCESSING MODELS

Next, we develop a model for dendritic logic, illustrating the roles of excitatory and inhibitory neurotransmitters.

Neurotransmitter Ions

Neurotransmitters have various purposes. For those that serve chiefly for logic purposes in a simple model, it has been estimated that the majority of neurotransmitters are molecules similar to those of *glutamate* (GLU), associated with excitatory receptors, and *gamma-aminobutyric acid* (GABA), associated with inhibitory receptors. Thus, for modeling purposes, our attention will be limited to generic excitatory and inhibitory neurotransmitters.

As a result of neural activity, a pulse burst reaches a presynaptic bouton. When the pulse burst arrives, it carries a positive charge, so there is a positive electric field within the presynaptic region. Ordinary electrostatic repulsion drives positive ions away from their boutons. They drift and perhaps diffuse a very short distance, only about 20 nm, to a receiver located on a dendrite or spine of another neuron, resulting in an assembly of large, slow-moving neurotransmitter ions drifting across the synaptic cleft and toward a postsynaptic receiver. The receiver is in equilibrium and thus negatively charged, so it is in a position to attract positive ions the smaller of which usually bounce away in thermal chaos. But larger neurotransmitter ions drift in slowly and interact with the receiver long enough to modify the alignment of sensitive particles within the dendritic membrane.

Receivers are said to be *ionotropic*, meaning that they are sensitive to neurotransmitter ions. Excitatory receivers work with excitatory ions such as GLU, which triggers a dendritic action potential. Figure 5-11 shows a model of how this might happen. Initially, sensitive particles within the membrane are held together tightly by the strong intrinsic electric field within the membrane,

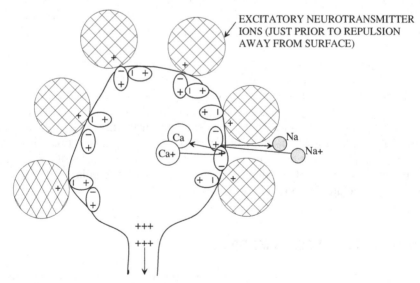

FIGURE 5-11 Randomly attached neurotransmitter ions result in triggering.

as they were for the soma in Chapter 2. But neurotransmitter ions that approach a receiver are large and slow enough to disrupt the alignment of molecules within sensitive parts of the membrane. This disruption is enough to trigger a dendritic action potential. The action potential, of course, is not energized by neurotransmitters, but rather by local sodium, potassium, and calcium ions and probably by a few other ionic elements.

Another type of receiver is known as *inhibitory,* meaning that it works with inhibitory neurotransmitter ions. Inhibitory ions (for example, GABA) have the power to suppress an action potential. Figure 5-12 models how this might happen. Large neurotransmitter ions cover the surface of a short dendritic segment in a structured formation. The protective ring of neurotransmitter ions is sufficient to prevent a trigger even when the internal voltage goes positive. Inhibitory ions effectively thicken the membrane; their action is vaguely similar to that of myelination. They protect it from sodium ions and stop the propagation of a local action potential as envisioned in the figure.

When a segment goes passive, attenuation is significant. Consider an electrical pulse moving from the left through the resistance R in Figure 5-12. The pulse will have a slow millisecond-range rise and fall time and a low current that minimizes loss in the series resistance. Pulse voltage is attenuated as it attempts to charge capacitor C because the low current through R is the only source of charging current. Normally, without the inhibitory ions, the membrane provides significant charging current. The amplitude is not rejuvenated in this segment because the membrane is disabled; it has been pacified by the inhibitory neurotransmitter ions. A single pulse that enters the segment will emerge too weak to trigger its own self-sustaining action potential.

Logic generation in dendrites depends on the relative locations of excitory and inhibitory ions. It is found below that the locations of inhibitory receivers must not be far from the soma. This reflects the observation that excitatory

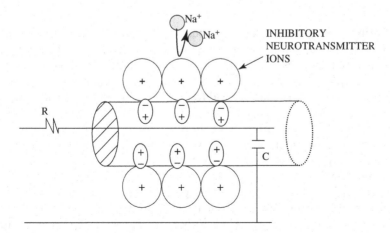

FIGURE 5-12   Structured sheath of neurotransmitter ions prevents a trigger.

receivers tend to be toward the tips of the dendrites, whereas inhibitory receivers tend to be near the soma. Inhibitory ions are needed for certain types of logic: for example, AND and NOT gates.

Consistent with the adiabatic model of a neuron, neurotransmitters in our model are eventually set free and drift back to their homes in the presynaptic boutons, thus completing a cycle. Excitatory neurotransmitter ions will drift home because the presynaptic region has returned to a negative voltage due to equilibrium in the presynaptic boutons. A negative potential within the boutons thus attracts and accelerates the free positive neurotransmitter ions and encourages them to "dock" where they came from. The return of excitatory neurotransmitters has given us the word *reuptake*.

A portion of inhibitory neurotransmitter ions might be knocked loose by the solitons they regulate. But generally, inhibitory ions are not released immediately. They create a certain Boolean gate, and this gate stays in place for awhile. Having a gate in place for awhile is consistent with the memory model of Chapter 4, which does not depend on reconfigurable logic. Unfortunately, leaving ions in place for awhile is equivalent to trapped charge and a small energy loss. Trapped inhibitory ions are expected to erode away over time because of thermal activity, so they also return home within a reasonably short time frame. Subsequently, a new batch of inhibitory neurotransmitter ions appears upon the next use of the neural gate.

The life cycles of neurotransmitters are a subject of modern research, so neurotransmitter theory is still evolving. The foregoing model has advantages. It is simple and understandable, with all the advantages of a closed cycle. This supports the contention that virtually all neural actions are reversible and that essentially no calories are consumed in a neural event. Another advantage of a cyclic model is that neurons may be reused immediately over and over, with no dead or recovery time.

Dendritic Waveform

A dendritic soliton is modeled as being triggered by positively charged neurotransmitters appearing on the surface of a receiver. Once triggered, this action potential operates with ions from the ionic solution much as it did for the soma in Chapter 3. However, a difference in waveforms between soma and dendrites could occur because of a different, possibly thicker membrane and because of a different, possibly more active type of ionic makeup involving internal calcium. The waveform of a dendritic pulse is not calculated here, since this was done in Chapter 3, but a waveform may be modeled or guessed at according to expectations, as in Figure 5-13.

This modeled pulse has a lower amplitude and a greater pulse width, consistent with the observation that spikes in a soma burst often have separations of perhaps 12 ms, driven by solitons whose pulse rate within a burst is in the range of 167 Hz. Undershoot is shown as going more negative, which does not hurt but only aids in properly realigning the sensitive

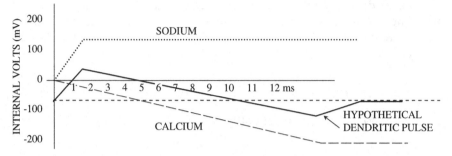

FIGURE 5-13 Artist's concept of a dendritic pulse.

ferroelectric particles in the membrane. This is a waveform model based on expectations, not calculations; fortunately, the dendritic waveform is not critical to neural operations.

Next we go into detail about how dendrites produce a Boolean function. To understand the context of this analysis, consider the model of a simplified dendritic system with two branches.

Physical Model of a Logic Gate

The objective of this section is to derive typical physical parameters for a trunk and two branches, as in Figure 5-14. The diameter of a dendrite is assumed to be $1\,\mu m$; the length of a branch is assumed to be $1\,mm$. The membrane capacitance is $C_m = 1\,\mu F/cm^2$ (or $10\,fF/\mu m^2$); the resistivity is about $3.14\,\Omega \cdot cm$ as a lower bound. The conductance of the dielectric membrane is about $G_m = 0.3\,mS/cm^2$ as an upper bound. The conductance might be expected to be lower in an insulating membrane that does not pass much electricity.

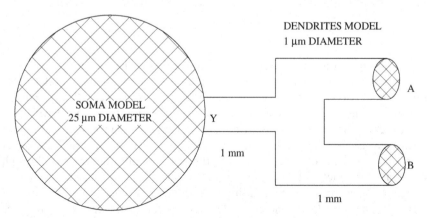

FIGURE 5-14 Model of a dendritic tree (not drawn to scale).

Dendrites differ from the axons in Chapter 3 in that they are unprotected by myelination. This means that capacitance and conductance to the outside regions are larger, although the total lengths involved may be shorter. Calculations for a segment 1 mm long and 1 μm in diameter are

$$C_1 = \pi DLC_m = (\pi \cdot 1.0\,\mu m)(1000\,\mu m)(10\,fF/\mu m^2) \approx 31.4\,pF$$

$$G_L = \pi DLG_m \approx (\pi \cdot 1.0\,\mu m)(1000\,\mu m)(0.3\,mS/cm^2)(1\,cm/10^4\,\mu m)^2$$

$$\approx 9 \times 10^{-9}\,S$$

$$R_{\text{Loss1}} = \frac{1}{G_L} \approx 106\,M\Omega$$

$$\frac{R_s}{L} = \frac{\rho}{A} = \frac{15.7\,\Omega \cdot cm}{\pi(0.5)^2\mu m^2}\frac{10^8\mu m^2}{1\,cm^2}\frac{1\,cm}{10\,mm} \approx 196\,M\Omega/mm$$

R_s for a segment that is 1 mm long will be 196 MΩ.

These parameters are used in Figure 5-15 to illustrate the sort of circuit that results. I_{A+} and I_{A-} are voltage-dependent current sources that can be triggered to generate a dendritic pulse. Analogous currents may occur for the B and Y segments. The pulse, once triggered, will go from a negative equilibrium value up to some positive value for the dendrites. I_{s+} and I_{s-} in the soma region are such that if triggered, a pulse is generated that moves from a negative equilibrium value up to a positive voltage for the soma; within the soma, $C_s = 19.6\,pF$, using a value from Chapter 3.

A pulse in segment A will trigger a pulse in segment B that may trigger a pulse in the soma. R_{sL} is leakage resistance in the soma area, calculated assuming 0.3 mS/cm^2 as follows:

$$G_{sL} = \pi \cdot 25^2\,\mu m^2(1\,cm/10^4\,\mu m)^2(0.3 \times 10^{-3}/cm^{-2}) = 5.88\,nS$$

$$R_{sL} \approx 170\,M\Omega$$

A model with only three segments is not going to be accurate. Although lacking accuracy, it shows the basic structure of a segmented model. This simple model shows that in a worst case, the shunt resistances R_{Loss1} and R_{sL} are comparable to R_1, the series resistance, so the shunt resistance will have some effect on the resulting pulse. But using 0.3 mS/cm^2 is a worst case. If shunt resistances are actually higher, the effect is reduced. In general, the effect expected is that some of the current from the active membrane will leak through the shunt resistance. The remainder of the current will charge membrane capacitance at a slower rate, resulting in a slower rise time.

This simple model also indicates that a potential in the trunk where $C_1 \approx 31.4\,pF/mm$ will easily build up a triggering voltage in the lumped soma capacitance, $C_s \approx 19.6\,\text{pF}$. There is plenty of charge in C_1 to be shared with C_s. If C_1 were orders of magnitude smaller than C_s, one might expect an inadequate triggering voltage for the soma. Fortunately, these capacitances are well matched.

Physical Model of a Dendritic AND Gate

Assume that part of branch Y in Figure 5-14 is pacified by inhibitory neurotransmitters near the intersection of branches A and B, illustrated in Figure 5-16. Branch A has a voltage pulse $v(t) > 0$, while branch B has none, $v(t) = 0$. Propagation of a voltage pulse from branch A to the soma is stopped because of the extra capacitance in the passive region. This occurs because the current available from the membrane is limited, so voltage in a pulse depends directly on passive capacitance. Higher net capacitance will reduce the peak voltage according to conservation of charge.

Reduced voltage will stop the self-triggering in branch Y and thus stop the propagation of an action potential through branch segment Y. Only a small charge trickles through passively, not enough to trigger the soma. We note that although branch Y is blocked, pulses can be triggered in branch B in this situation.

If branches A and B both have voltage pulse inputs, the situation can be quite different. When A and B work together, there is additional current to charge the passive region. A dendritic action potential will continue its propagation toward the soma and trigger it. This explains why inhibitory receptors are closer to the soma, as observed in the laboratory, since inhibitory receptors, working as above, have be closer to the soma to be effective.

Define A, B, and Y to be Boolean variables. If A is true and B is false, Y is false, as described above because of charge sharing. Reversing this, if B is true but A is false, Y is false, because B cannot by itself send enough charge through a passive segment to trigger segment Y. But if both A and B are true, Y can be true, because by working together, sufficient charge accumulates in the inhibited segment to continue the propagation of the dendritic pulse.

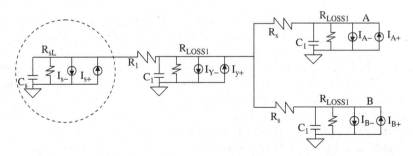

FIGURE 5-15 Circuit model for two branches of a dendritic tree.

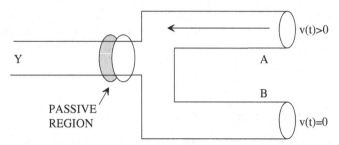

FIGURE 5-16   Effect of inhibitory neurotransmitters.

The result is

$$Y = AB$$

Note that voltage pulses are timed to arrive at a pacified region at about the same time. The length of the passive region has evolved to fall within a certain range. If it is too short, its capacitance will not stop an action potential; if too long, it will always stop an action potential even when branches A and B work together.

Physical Model of a Dendritic OR Gate

An OR gate model is almost trivial because it needs no inhibitors in either branch. In this case the soma will be activated if either input to A or input to B is active, or if inputs to both are active. In this case, the Boolean logic is

$$Y = A + B$$

The appendix to this chapter illustrates simulations of dendritic logic.

ENABLED LOGIC DIRECTLY AT THE SOMA

Neurons have evolved to be most efficient. They turn on when needed and go to sleep otherwise. They are analogous to *enabled logic*, with an *enable* signal to wake them before they can generate any logic. Enabled logic is possible in CMOS technology. To understand enabled logic, it is helpful to have symbols denoting the presence of excitory or inhibitory neurotransmitters, and another symbol for the absence of neurotransmitters:

Presence of excitatory neurotransmitters $(+)$
Presence of inhibitory neurotransmitters $(-)$
Absence of neurotransmitters (0)

AND Gate with Enable

All neural logic will be modeled as enabled, that is, as being of finite duration. Enabling can be emphasized with a bias voltage to the soma, although there may be other ways to enable a neuron. Figure 5-17 gives voltage possibilities (relative to zero volts) for enabling. In the figure, branch e charges the soma to 50 mV. This is taken to be the result of solitons or dendritic pulses. One precharge, however, is not enough to trigger the soma, which in this example is assumed to require at least 75 mV. If solitons from branches a and b give the accumulation of another 50 mV, soma triggering occurs. The soma is assumed to trigger at 70 mV, so an accumulation to 100 mV by solitons from branches a and b will trigger it.

In this model, other neurons are involved. Some must provide excitory inputs via branches e and a and another to branch b and perhaps another must provide inhibitory input to branch y. If there are signals working together from both branches a and b, the soma will receive an action potential and will be triggered, as in the AND gate explained above. The Boolean logic thus generated is

$$z = e(ab)$$

where z, e, a, and b are Boolean signals. Signal e is considered to be an enable signal. Other arrangements also provide an enabled AND gate, although it is enough for our purposes to show only one.

In the example above the soma is used for enabled logic. For a large number of inputs, it might be unusual to have a large number of dendritic trunks going to the soma. Physically, there is not enough space for a large number of trunks directly on the soma. Electrically, the thresholds become critical for a large number of inputs directly to the soma. For these reasons, most logic is generated in dendritic branches.

Keeping Neurons Asleep

Normally, neurons naturally sleep until they receive a pulse of neurotransmitters. Beyond this, there is a way to prevent waking. Lack of a precharge in the

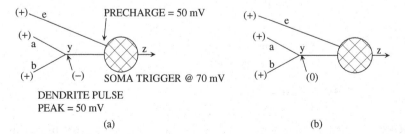

FIGURE 5-17   Application of neurotransmitter symbols: Voltages are relative.

neural model above means, effectively, that the neuron cannot be triggered by dendritic pulses. Neurons that depend on precharge can be kept asleep by withholding precharge.

OR Gate with Enable

The OR gate needs no inhibitory neurotransmitters according to our analysis here. Input e in Figure 5-17 is essentially an enable signal. The Boolean result is

$$z = e(a + b)$$

where z, e, a, and b are Boolean signals. Note that there are other ways to generate an OR logic, so this is simply one example among several.

NOT Gate with Enable

A precharge in the soma is restricted to be positive; it cannot, of course, exceed the triggering voltage for the soma; otherwise, the logic operations of other dendrites will be bypassed. Without the availability of negative voltage as commonly used in artificial neurons, one wonders if a NOT gate is possible in a biological neural network. To investigate NOT gates, consider Figure 5-18. Assume that branch b always receives dendritic solitons, and that precharging is completed via branch e. Let branch a in part (a) have solitons from an external neuron. When branch a is excited, the propagation of solitons to the soma is stopped at branch y, because, linked to neural input a is an inhibition for branch y. This linking is denoted by the primes in Figures 5-18. The action potential applied as in input to branch b is also stopped for similar reasons, so there is no chance of signals a and b giving an AND gate. Thus, the output of axon z is false (no action potential from this neuron) when the inputs going to branch a are true.

If branch a is not excited, as in part (b), the inhibitory neurotransmitters from the primed input are not applied; branch b is now free to propagate an action potential. This signal is not stopped by branch a where an action

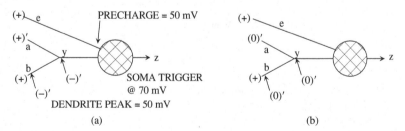

(a)   (b)

FIGURE 5-18 NOT gate concept for a neuron: (a) a = true ⇒ z = false; (b) a = false ⇒ z = true.

potential merely propagates harmlessly down the branch and, most important, also toward the soma. Thus, when the inputs to branch a are false, the soma is activated. What is accomplished is a neural NOT gate.

During a NOT operation, the input to branch b must be solitons. The external neuron driving branch a must also control or provide inhibitory inputs to branches b and z. The inputs to branches e as well as b may be obtained from a single neuron. The input to branch e is basically an enable, as is the input to branch b. To summarize using Boolean notation, we have

$$z = e(a')b$$

where z, e, a, and b are Boolean signals and a' means NOT(a). It may be noted that the timing of the precharge due to branch e is not critical; it may arrive before or after the other signals arrive, for example. As in all neural logic, signals are present only during a certain time frame, giving the expected enabled logic.

To summarize, there exists a complete set of basic logic gates (AND, OR, and NOT) that can provide any Boolean function.

COMMENTS ON THE ADIABATIC NATURE OF DENDRITES

Adiabatic neural models are suggested not only because of the obvious fact that human calorie use is not increased substantially during mental exercise but because pulse rise and fall times are relatively slow, in milliseconds, and will minimize the dissipation of energy in series resistance. Only positive pulses are involved, so that positive and negative charges never short circuit and dissipate energy. Heating is expected because of equilibrium voltages across the neural membrane, but this is reduced by action potentials. Membrane heating is not counted for neural operations. It is common to all cells for health, growth, and maintenance.

Excitatory ions are released by the pulses they generate and are not trapped in this model. Inhibitory neurotransmitters, in contrast, are modeled as not being released appreciably by forward- and back-propagating solitons. It seems possible that inhibitory ions will be temporarily trapped after a neural action, but before long, thermal agitation will cause them to be released and to drift back to their bouton homes. The energy due to trapped charge is assumed to be low. Irreversible chemical reactions are avoided in this model, so neurotransmitters should be reversible and reusable. They are modeled as operating in a closed cycle.

All aspects of neural signals in this model are approximately electrically reversible. When a system is approximately electrically reversible, engineers idealize this to a system that is adiabatic for all practical purposes.

APPLICATIONS

Modeling neurons as logic devices is an interesting endeavor if for no other reason than to spur the creation of new methods of computing. Engineers have long sought better logic devices, and this continues to be a hot topic of research. For constructing molecular-sized gates for computer logic, genetic engineering and nanotechnology are promising. An active area of research today involves the development of DNA circuits. As mentioned in Chapter 3, DNA molecules can perform logic. Rather than encoding signals with high and low voltages, they may be encoded with high and low concentrations of short DNA molecules. The chemical logic gates that perform the information processing are also DNA molecules: each gate a carefully folded complex of multiple short DNA strands. When a gate encounters the certain molecules as input, it releases a characteristic output molecule. It appears that DNA gates will work in salt water, in contrast to solid-state logic and so may have applications in human tissue such as detecting molecules associated with cancer. A drawback of DNA circuits is the difficulty of interfacing them to ordinary peripherals.

The biological neuron is a miraculous logic device that is nanometer-sized, flexible, immersible, and efficient. A neuron borrows neurotransmitter ions, and if conditions are logically correct, a neuron provides output neurotransmitters available for loan. Biological neurons differ from artificial neurons, with their positive and negative voltages, positive and negative weighting factors, and their integrated circuit and software implementations. Imitation neurons as logic devices based on excitatory and inhibitory forces are a goal for the future.

A new class of logic, vaguely reminiscent of a neuron, involves carbon nanotubes as pursued by IBM and others. An interesting development is being pursued by Nantero, Inc. using billions of nanometer tubes in a memory device. The wall of each nanotube is only one carbon atom thick; prototypes have been made in the laboratory with diameters of about 20 nm. Nanotube random-access memory (NRAM) is accomplished via suspended carbon nanotubes that can be oriented to represent true or false using local electric fields. If production can be perfected, NRAM may replace all memory used in computers, including DRAM, SRAM, flash memory, and ultimately, hard disk storage. Unlike DRAM and SRAM, NRAM is nonvolatile.

CONCLUSIONS

This chapter provides a model of all-digital learning for human brains. A similar model could be applied to artificially intelligent machines. Driven by a need for efficiency and survival, learning is important. It happens in at least two categories: combinational learning and state-machine learning. Both increase mental efficiency by avoiding monopolizing short-term memory.

- *Combinational learning.* This involves new neurons and synapses for detecting new features as part of the sensory encoding block. These are implemented when synapses link existing feature-detecting neurons into a new neuron. Such new neurons are essentially multi-input logic gates. Each new neuron is dedicated to a new feature and never serves any other purpose.

- *State-machine learning.* This involves new interneurons and synapses for neural state machines within subconscious long-term memory. It is noted that humans excel at remembering procedures and logical sequences such as long poems, and can perform them without having to think about them in short-term memory. Links between words of long-term memory, representing steps in a procedure, are the result of interneurons that detect the completion of previous steps. In general, all previous steps of a procedure may be involved in determining the next step. The interneurons involved are essentially multi-input AND gates.

Learning, like memory itself, depends on logic operations as generated by dendritic branches and the dendrite–soma interface. Dendritic pulses or, more precisely, electrical solitons are triggered by excitatory neurotransmitter ions and generate arbitrary Boolean algebra under the influence of inhibitory neurotransmitter ions. Physical models and simulations were provided to demonstrate basic AND, OR, and NOT logic using both excitatory and inhibitory ions.

Simulations indicate that propagating solitons derive current from a continuous active membrane to maintain a fixed amplitude and width. Solitons are easily reflected from the soma and from dendritic branches, producing back-propagating solitons. Simulations indicate that when solitons collide, both are annihilated.

Neurons are naturally at rest when not in use. Excitatory neurotransmitter ions bring them alive for a given purpose, and afterward, they return to their sleep. Dendritic connections directly to the soma may produce AND–OR logic but not NOT logic. It is conjectured that neural logic is enabled by a positive precharge to the soma, analogous to a bias in an artificial neural network. This type of logic uses a separate trunk to the soma, that is, a basal dendrite, for a precharge delivered by solitons. Neurons that depend on precharge to the soma will stay asleep as long as there is no precharge, even though pulses are present in other dendritic trunks.

Dendrites, soma, and axon are modeled to work in a cycle; their signals are modeled to be electrically reversible and hence adiabatic. This seems to be an accurate model as long as one does not count calories dissipated in the membrane and for routine cellular maintenance, synaptic growth, and health, common to all cells. Calories are conserved for information processing, but more important, adiabatic neurons suggest a new type of computer, one that engineers can pack into a very small space without concern for heat dissipation. In subsequent chapters, design is initiated on this novel computer concept.

EXERCISES

5-1 The color magenta is a purplish red that is technically a mixture of red and blue wavelengths.
(a) Discuss ways in which a neuron might learn to recognize magenta.
(b) Make a diagram to indicate how a neuron might learn to recognize magenta automatically.

5-2 An A-minor chord is composed of the musical notes A, C, and E.
(a) Discuss ways in which a neuron might learn to recognize an A-minor chord.
(b) Make a diagram to indicate how a neuron might learn to recognize an A-minor chord automatically.

5-3 Certain procedures in life are automatic. Make diagrams of neural state machines for:
(a) Brushing your teeth.
(b) Adding 7 and 11.

5-4 Consider the problem of multiplying 16 by 32.
(a) Explain how this is usually done and give the result.
(b) Illustrate with a diagram how parts of the multiplication might be done concurrently assuming that computers are available to work on the independent parts of the multiplication in parallel, with addition as the final step.

5-5 A neuron uses both excitory and inhibitory receptors and neurotransmitters for logic.
(a) Explain in a paragraph what excitory receptors do.
(b) Explain in a paragraph what inhibitory receptors do.
(c) Show in a diagram how the two work together to achieve a neural AND gate.

5-6 Explain the actions of a neural AND gate with an enable (precharge) signal.

5-7 Show in a diagram how biology achieves a neural OR gate with three inputs.

5-8 Biological neural networks have differing forms.
(a) Design an AND gate using the chapter's excitory and inhibitory notation.
(b) Design an OR gate using the chapter's excitory and inhibitory notation.
There is extra credit for original designs that differ from those given in the text.

5-9 The NOT gate was explained using both excitory and inhibitory receptors and neurotransmitters.

(a) Explain in your own words how a neural NOT works.

(b) Design another NOT using the book's excitory and inhibitory notation.

5-10 The XOR output is true if one and only one of the inputs is true. Design an XOR using the book's excitory and inhibitory notation.

5-11 Energy dissipation in a membrane is finite but is less during an action potential. Assume that dendritic voltage moves from –70 mV to –5 mV during a pulse burst with an ideal 50% duty cycle. That is, the voltage is low for half the time and high for half the time. The pulse burst goes for 10 pulses. Compare energy dissipations before, during, and after a pulse burst in units of J/cm^2 in a membrane with $0.01\,mS/cm^2$.

5-12 Can energy be dissipated in a neural AND gate?

(a) Explain the losses due to series resistance.

(b) Explain the heating in the membrane because of ferroelectric actions.

5-13 A certain neuron has 98% of its membrane surface area occupied by dendrites. Note that energy in joules is $\frac{1}{2}CV^2$, C in farads and V in volts. A food calorie is a kilocalorie, equal to 4.184 kJ.

(a) Calculate the maximum energy in food calories in the membrane capacitance of a single neuron in equilibrium using the following assumptions:

- A 25-μm-diameter soma.
- A $1\,\mu F/cm^2$ membrane capacitance.
- The equilibrium voltage is $-70\,mV$.
- The axon energy can be ignored.

(b) Does this energy increase or decrease during a neural action?

(c) After a neural action, what is the maximum energy in food calories?

APPENDIX: CIRCUIT SIMULATIONS OF NEURAL SOLITON PROPAGATION

Simulations provide a useful insight into electrical activity in neurons that otherwise is unavailable. Here we use a basic WinSpice simulator. The simulations below assume that sodium and potassium currents switch on and off as a function of the voltage across a membrane.

The main parameters may be chosen based on published data and basic physical calculations. The rest potential is assumed to be $-70\,mV$. Both sodium (Na) and potassium (K) currents are assumed triggered at $-55\,\text{mV}$ for simulation purposes. Listed below are the major parameters:

Rest potential	$-70\,\text{mV}$
Trigger voltage (both Na and K currents)	$-55\,\text{mV}$
Na current cutoff voltage	$+50\,\text{mV}$
K current cutoff voltage	$-95\,\text{mV}$
Sodium current	$0.1345\,\text{mA/cm}^2$
Potassium current	$0.0608\,\text{mA/cm}^2$
Membrane capacitance	$1\,\mu\text{F/cm}^2$
Membrane conductance	$0.3\,\text{mS/cm}^2$
Internal resistivity ρ	$15.7\,\Omega \cdot \text{cm}$

Manual analysis of a single neural pulse is given in Figure A5-1. The figure assumes that Na and K currents are triggered simultaneously at $t = 0$. First, Na cuts off at roughly 1.6 ms; then K cuts off at roughly 3.9 ms, allowing the voltage to relax to its rest potential (equilibrium) value of about –70 mV. This analysis does not include the effects of membrane loss conductance.

The switching properties of a neural membrane may be simulated using elementary nonlinear amplifiers to generate hysteresis loops. Figure A5-2 shows the necessary control signals. Triggering (of both Na and K currents) results when internal voltage exceeds $-55\,\text{mV}$, sending V_1 high. The simulation model cuts off the Na current at roughly $+50\,\text{mV}$, as regulated by V_2, which is the STOP sodium current signal; retriggering is impossible until the internal voltage drops below about $-55\,\text{mV}$ because of V_2. Below a voltage of about

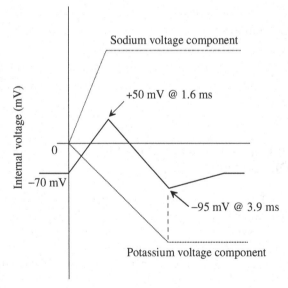

Figure A5-1 Simplified analysis of a neural pulse in terms of Na and K currents.

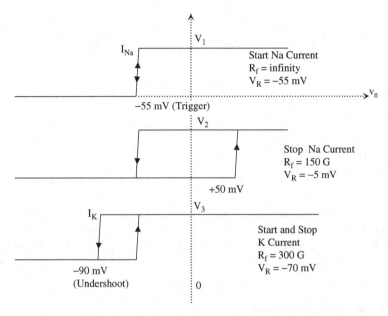

Figure A5-2   Control signals for membrane current switching.

-55 mV the pulse can always be retriggered. The K current is stopped at about -90 mV as regulated by V_3.

Each control signal (V_1, V_2, V_3) is generated by a subcircuit as in Figure A5-3. The resistances involved in the voltage-controlled voltage sources are chosen in the gigaohm range to avoid loading the high-resistance model of the neural path. The circuit is initialized via 100 pF to force $V_i = 0$ for $i = 1, 2, 3$ at $t = 0$.

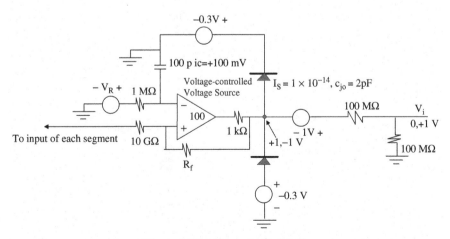

Figure A5-3   Control subcircuit.

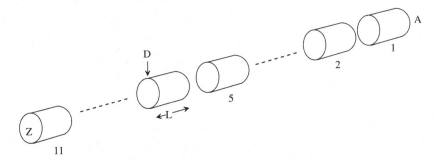

Figure A5-4   Segments model of a neural path.

The simulation approach is to model the neural path, assumed to be dendrite, as short segments that are connected in series. Series segments are illustrated in Figure A5-4. This simulation used 11 segments to study propagation going from segment A to segment Z. Each segment has circuit elements as in Figure A-5.

Scaled Values for a Segment

$$R_1 = 200\,\text{M}\Omega$$

$$C_1 = 31.4\,\text{pF}$$

$$R_{\text{Loss1}} = 106\,\text{M}\Omega$$

$$I_{\text{Na1}} = 4.225\,\text{nA}$$

$$I_{\text{K1}} = 1.910\,\text{nA}$$

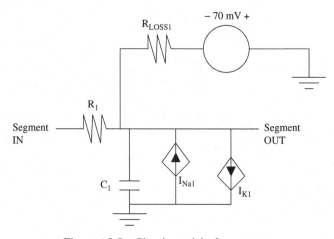

Figure A5-5   Circuit model of a segment.

The leakage conductance of a segment is used to model the charging attributed to the Nernst potential across the membrane. A segment can be scaled to any convenient size since it is a linear circuit model. Parameters are calculated as follows:

$$L = 1\,\text{mm} = 0.1\,\text{cm}$$

$$D = 1\,\mu\text{m} = 1.0 \times 10^{-4}\,\text{cm}$$

$$A_{CS} = \pi(D/2)^2$$

$$R_1 = \rho L/A_{CS} = 15.7L/A_{CS}\,\Omega$$

$$A_{side} = \pi DL$$

$$C_1 = 1\,\mu\text{F/cm}^2\,A_{side}$$

$$R_{Loss1} = 1/(0.3 \times 10^{-3}\,A_{side})\,\Omega$$

$$I_{Na1} = 0.1345\,\text{mA/cm}^2\,A_{side}$$

$$I_K = 0.0608\,\text{mA/cm}^2\,A_{side}$$

The current sources are modeled with voltage-controlled current sources; I_K is under the control of V_3 in Figure A5-5. I_{Na} is started by V_1; but as v_n approaches its maximum ($\approx 50\,\text{mV}$), V_1 is zeroed by V_2 using a voltage-controlled switch. This stops the sodium current; the circuit for this is given in Figure A5-6.

Segment A was triggered by assuming a 10-nA current pulse for about 0.2 ms. The result was a propagating pulse as in Figure A5-7. The waveform of the pulse is quite interesting. As those who perform this simulation will discover, this is by definition a soliton, a solitary pulse whose general waveform resists dissipation as the pulse propagates. There are no reflections in Figure A5-7, presumably because the terminating segment does not present a capacitive load. Each segment has a capacitance of about 31 pF and a resistance of about 200 MΩ. Loss resistance is about 106 MΩ. If an additional 60 pF is

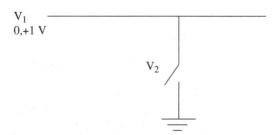

V_1
0,+1 V

V_2

Figure A5-6 Sodium current stop switch.

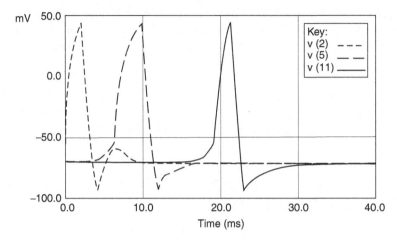

Figure A5-7   Propagating pulse from A to Z.

presented to the last segment only, with no change in resistance, there is a reflection as in Figure A5-8. This suggests that pulses arriving at the larger capacitance of a soma are reflected (back-propagated) back down dendrites. This occurs whether or not the soma is triggered. Simulations with the model above indicate that reflections are quite common for a variety of discontinuities in the series resistance and shunt capacitance.

Colliding solitons cannot pass through each other as electromagnetic solitons do. Typically, membrane-supported solitons will be annihilated as

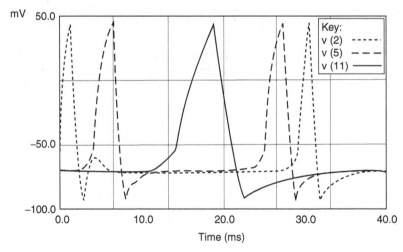

Figure A5-8   Soliton reflected by a load capacitance of 60 pF.

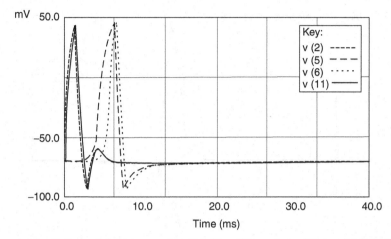

Figure A5-9 Solitons injected at each end will collide and annihilate; V(11) indicates input but no output.

shown in Figure A5-9. Note that just before the annihilation, the pulses become steeper. Compare V(5) to V(6). This is because the charges in the pulses are attracted to each other through the series resistance and pull each other down, preventing a trigger to continue the propagation.

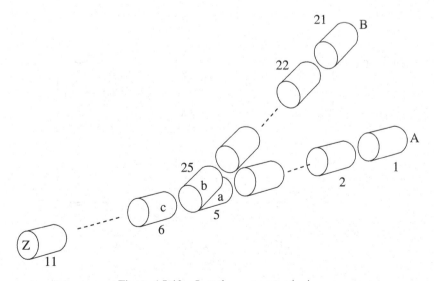

Figure A5-10 Junction generates logic.

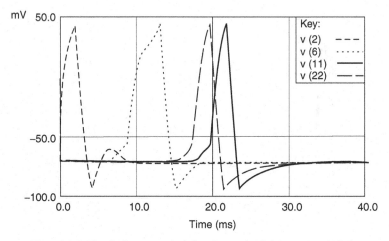

Figure A5-11   Only segment A is triggered, giving output V(11).

Logic Generation in Dendrites

Neural paths in dendrites are natural logic gates without having to rely on soma behavior. Two input paths beginning with segments A and B can be constructed as shown in Figure A5-10. In the first example, all segments are assumed identical. Segments 5 and 25 are joined to the input of segment 6. First, only segment A is triggered. The result is a propagation that travels to the junction, splits, and travels to both B and Z as shown in Figure A5-11. Z receives a pulse if segments A and B are both triggered (Figure A5-12), giving a form of the OR gate.

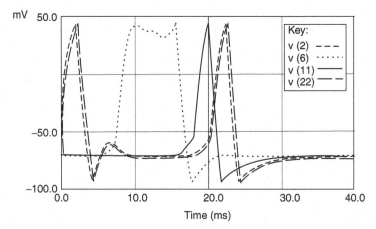

Figure A5-12   Segments A and C are both triggered, giving an output V(11).

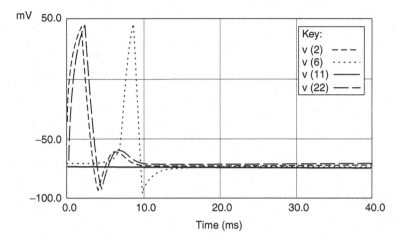

Figure A5-13 A and C are triggered but there is no output V(11); XOR because of capacitance reduction in segment 6.

It may be noted in this model that if the capacitance at the input to segment 6 is reduced by about 33%, the exclusive OR gate results. A single pulse will go through, but two pulses will "collide" and be annihilated (Figure A5-13). This sort of reduction in local capacitance could involve local myelination, although it could also result in a change in the geometry of the junction. Given an XOR gate, the NOT function may be constructed without difficulty.

AND Function Segment 6 may be modified to achieve an AND function: Let $L = 0.5 \times 10^{-1}$ cm. Then $C_1 \approx 15\,\mathrm{pF}$, $R_1 \approx 100\,\mathrm{M\Omega}$, and $R_{\mathrm{Loss1}} \approx 212\,\mathrm{M\Omega}$.

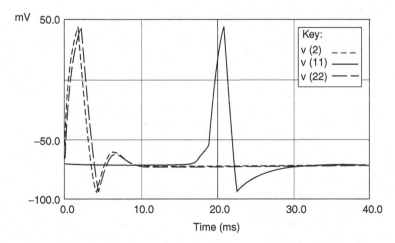

Figure A5-14 The AND results by shortening and deactivating segment 6.

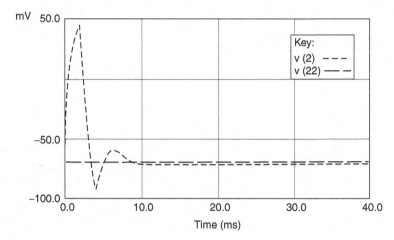

Figure A5-15 Only V(2) is present; V(22) is zero; V(11) = 0 (not shown).

The current sources in segment 6 are set to zero to model the effects of inhibitory neurotransmitters. Thus, to propagate a pulse to Z, there must be enough charge to move passively through the shortened segment 6 and to trigger segment 7. The result is that two inputs, one from A and one from B, are required to propagate a pulse to Z, as in Figure A5-14. Triggering only input A, for example, is insufficient to propagate a pulse to Z as shown in Figure A5-15.

Tapered Circuits

A tapered circuit is a tube that begins with a given diameter and ends with a smaller diameter, as in Figure A5-16. Simulations of tapered circuits suggest that it is slightly easier for a soliton to propagate from the larger end to the smaller end. This is reasonable because it is easier to charge a slightly smaller capacitor through a slightly smaller resistor, and hence to trigger the segment.

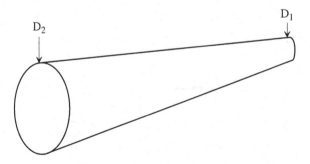

Figure A5-16 Tapered circuit.

If propagation is possible from the smaller end to the larger end, back propagation is certainly possible from the larger end to the smaller end. Dendritic logic as above produces pulses only when needed. Otherwise, the excitatory neurotransmitter ions are attracted home to their resting places and the neuron goes into standby mode.

CONCLUSIONS

Millions of years of evolution have produced the modern neuron, the basic element of the human brain. Covering the neuron is a ferroelectric membrane that was modeled with current sources to produce electrical solitons. The propagation properties of electrical solitons were investigated using a circuit simulator. In general, solitons in dendrites and axons were found to depend on a judicious balance of resistance and capacitance. An example of a useful balance was simulated above, although other voltage levels and pulse widths are possible. It was shown that solitons obey arbitrary Boolean logic using fairly obvious assumptions about the roles of excitatory and inhibitory neurotransmitter ions. This style of neural logic points to artificial membranes and indeed, artificial neural logic for the future.

CHAPTER 6

ARTIFICIAL LEARNING IN ARTIFICIAL NEURAL NETWORKS

INTRODUCTION

Computer engineers and scientists have long recognized that the brain computes in an entirely different way than that used by classical digital computers. The brain is a parallel computer many times faster than any modern computer. It performs routinely, within milliseconds, pattern recognition tasks such as recognizing a face in a crowd, whereas sequential computers may spend days on a recognition task of much lesser difficulty, and then fail to converge.

In 1943 McCulloch and Pitts introduced the idea of an artificial neural network, modeled after the perceived behavior of the brain. An artificial neural network is usually trained for a given task, such as recognizing a specific pattern in their input signals, but with effort, they can be trained to recognize several different patterns. They are quite adaptable, and if designed to do so, they can recognize a completely different set of patterns.

Artificial neural networks employ standard cells of artificial neurons usually connected as a tree with a great many inputs. Cells work in parallel and must be trained to meet given requirements. Training occurs by systematically varying the *synaptic weights* associated with each artificial neuron. Synaptic weights are analog, real numbers, positive or negative. Overall, the synaptic model is best described as an analog-to-digital converter. This is in contrast to the all-digital model for learning presented in this book.

Artificial neural networks differ radically from biological neural networks, yet this is no problem to engineers. The very thought of how neurons might work was enough to inspire engineering advances. Artificial neural networks have been applied to system identification and control (vehicle control, process control), game playing and decision making (backgammon, chess, racing), pattern recognition (radar systems, face identification, object recognition), sequence recognition (gesture, speech, handwritten text recognition), medical diagnosis (tumor recognition), financial applications (recognition of trends in the prices of stocks), data mining (or knowledge discovery in databases), visualization, and e-mail spam filtering.

These successes accrue because artificial neural networks can be used in many different ways. For example, they may be implemented in very large scale integration (VLSI) or computer software. Artificial neural networks may be linear, although usually they are nonlinear. During design, the synaptic weights for given applications can be established through a process of supervised learning (or training). Under this process, known inputs and desired outputs are made available to a design process; weights are then modified to minimize differences between desired and actual outputs. Artificial neural networks are easily retrained should requirements change; they are adaptable to change. Artificial neural networks are fault tolerant and continue to function with graceful degradation even if one or more cells fail. They have been described as robust.

A better understanding of biological neurons may be achieved by studying artificial neural networks. Chief concerns in this chapter are the methods by which an artificial neural network "learns." Do any of these methods apply to a model of human learning? To investigate this interesting question, we begin a presentation of artificial neurons and neural networks.

ARTIFICIAL NEURONS

Figure 6-1 shows a model that describes an artificial neuron. Signals from other artificial neurons enter on the left and are applied to synapse k. Usually, the signals are envisioned as analog voltages or as digital simulations of analog signals. The synaptic weights usually are multipliers that can take any numerical value on the real line. Note how they are written: w_{ki}; the first subscript refers to the synapse (summing junction) being approached and the second subscript refers to the sources of the input signal, the outputs of other artificial neurons.

The strength of a synapse in an artificial neuron equals the numerical value of the multiplicative weighting factor w_{ki}. What does *strength* mean for a synaptic connection? What does *summation* mean for a synaptic connection? One can learn much by trying to answer such questions.

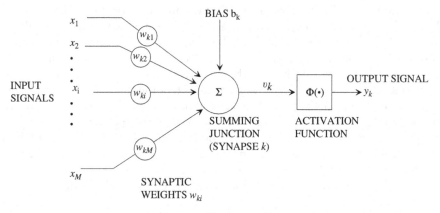

FIGURE 6-1   Model of an artificial neuron.

From a biological view point, synaptic strength has several possible inter-pretations. Strength could mean number of the attached excitatory neuro-transmitter ions on a receiver. However, it seems clear that what is released by a given bouton depends only on the neuron to which the bouton belongs, not on a large number of other neurons, as in the artificial neural model. In the model of this book, neurotransmitter ions from a given bouton are either released in sufficient quantities to cause a postsynaptic action potential, or they are not.

Strength, some say, is a number of spikes within a burst, proportional to spikes per unit time within a burst. However, the number of spikes can be observed to be about 10 on the average, although single random spikes are possible. Spikes per unit time within a burst are fixed for the most part by a combination of membrane and ionic properties and by the length of an action potential in the exciting bouton. Another interpretation that carries consider-able currency is that strength is the number of action potentials per unit time (the number of bursts per second). However, bursts per second depend on how often a neuron needs to be used, determined by the process being executed and the timing of the information released by the short-term memory system.

In considering a biological neuron, summation may be imagined to be the result of accumulation of neurotransmitter ions in a dendritic receiver. Summation is also possible in a limited way by charge integration when signals arrive at the capacitance of the soma via separate paths: for example, the basal and apical dendrite paths. These possibilities are discussed again later, but for now it is enough to interpret strengths and summations as belonging to an artificial neural network and not necessarily as belonging to a biological neural network. There is a bias b_k that serves to raise or lower the average level of the summation and thus control the switching threshold of the output. Assuming analog signals, the summing junction is a linear combiner, meaning that positive inputs are added whereas negative inputs are subtracted.

The *activation* function $\Phi(\cdot)$ models the threshold for triggering a membrane. The activation function is represented in the diagram by a box with the symbol $\Phi(\cdot)$. It is easiest to understand in the context of a comparator with a threshold for true or false output. In this sense, it is a simple one-bit analog-to-digital converter. The threshold of the converter is adjusted by varying the bias parameter b_k. Figure 6-2 illustrates a typical activation function. It operates on v_k to provide the output y_k. The activation function in this case may be recognized to be a nonideal comparator whose output approaches -1 if v_k is negative and is $+1$ if v_k is positive. Logic levels may be defined: -1 is false; $+1$ is true. As β increases in magnitude in the figure, an ideal step is approached between -1 and $+1$ with a threshold at $v_k = 0$.

In mathematical terms, neuron k is characterized by the following equation:

$$y_k = \Phi\left(\sum_{i=1}^{M} w_{ki}x_i + b_k\right)$$

where i is an index and M is the number of inputs. As a convenience, the bias is usually relabeled to be w_{k0} and combined with the weighting factors by defining $x_0 = 1$:

$$y_k = \Phi\left(\sum_{i=0}^{M} w_{ki}x_i\right)$$

It often is convenient to represent an artificial neuron as a directed graph (Figure 6-3). This has the same meaning as Figure 6-1; multiplicative factors and the activation function are indicated next to the arrows on signal lines; linear summation is implied by a junction of signal lines.

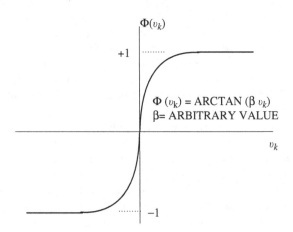

FIGURE 6-2 Activation function example.

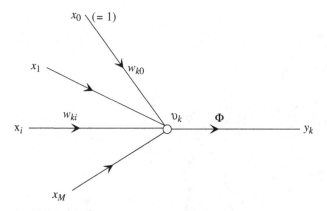

FIGURE 6-3   Artificial neuron as a directed graph.

Artificial neural networks have a treelike architecture. Figure 6-4 illustrates what is meant by a one-layer artificial neural network. Note that the bias, weights, summation, and comparison are now assumed to be in the circle.

A one-layer network can be characterized by a given time delay Δ expressed in seconds. In contrast, a two-layer network is characterized by a delay of 2Δ. An example of a two layer neural network is illustrated in Figure 6-5. This network is said to be *fully* connected because every node in a given layer is connected to every node in an adjacent layer.

Hopfield Networks

The networks above are classified as *feedforward networks*. A recurrent neural network will have at least one path from the output back to the input.

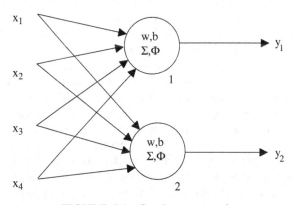

FIGURE 6-4   One-layer network.

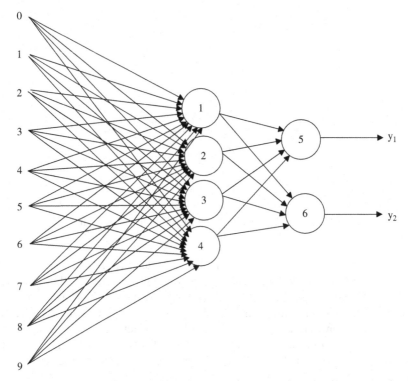

FIGURE 6-5   Two-layer artificial neural network.

Recurrent networks in which the number of feedback loops equals the number of artificial neurons are termed *Hopfield networks*. A Hopfield with two artificial neurons is illustrated in Figure 6-6. Recurrent networks such as Hopfield networks have stable states and *these* have been proposed to model brain memory. The long-term memory cell model of Chapter 3 could be said to be a Hopfield network but with only one neuron. A related feature of the Hopfield network is its potential to become a content-addressable memory: better yet, a content-addressable memory that might retrieve correct information even if cues are inconsistent. Analysis indicates that the storage capacity of a Hopfield network scales with the number of artificial neurons in the network.

One drawback of any feedback network with recursion like this is going to be its delay. In other words, a serial procedure must ripple through a feedback network to find the desired stable state. N artificial neurons delay by $N\Delta$ seconds. If N is large, say a few billion, as expected in a human memory system, the delay is unacceptable in a practical model. Another drawback for brain modeling is that in order to write information, an $N \times N$ a synaptic weight matrix must be processed. The main limitation of a Hopfield network is its delay.

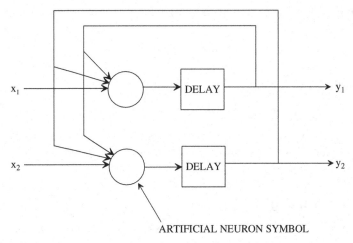

ARTIFICIAL NEURON SYMBOL

FIGURE 6-6   Hopfield network.

ARTIFICIAL LEARNING METHODS

There are two type of artificial learning of interest in this chapter: Hebbian self-organized learning and Rosenblatt supervised learning.

Hebbian Learning

Hebbian learning depends on activity in a network as proposed by psychologist Donald Olding Hebb (1904–1985). According to Hebb, if two neurons on either side of a synapse are activated simultaneously, the strength of that synapse is increased selectively. As a useful generalization, if two neurons on either side of a synapse are activated at differing times, the strength of that synapse is selectively weakened. Hebb assumed that his neurons were constantly being triggered. Strength in the Hebb concept refers not to the amplitude of an input signal, but rather, to the frequency of the signal.

Hebb proposed the concept of a *learning rule*. Hebb's rule is to increase the weights for those branches that are used most frequently. In an attempt to make this more exact, assume that w_{ki} represents the weight of a connection from input i to output k; let y_k be bursts per second of output k; let x_i be bursts per second of input i. The relationship can be formulated as a linear system:

$$y_k = w_{ki}x_i$$

Note that x_i and y_k represent frequencies of neuron activations, the number of bursts per second; they do not mean spike frequencies within a burst, nor do they mean voltage levels. The variables k and i are convenient indices.

As learning proceeds, the weights develop with a variable of proportionality α_{ki} as follows:

$$\Delta w_{ki} = \alpha_{ki} y_k x_i$$

Learning is equivalent to an adjustment of weights:

$$w_{ki(\text{new})} = w_{ki(\text{old})} + \Delta w_{ki}$$

The variable of proportionality α_{ki} can be either positive or negative, a vague analogy to the idea of excitatory and inhibitory receptors. Hebb's idea was inspirational to many.

Rosenblatt Learning

Computer scientist Frank Rosenblatt (1928–1969) introduced the concept of a *perceptron* in 1956 as a model of a neuron. This model is basically electronic and can be simulated in general-purpose computers. It is capable of supervised learning. A perceptron takes account of the fact that a neuron is inherently nonlinear and must be excited to a threshold for triggering. The perceptron is essentially another name for the artificial neuron shown in Figure 6-1.

Its mathematical formulation is a linear combination of the inputs x_i, $1 \leq i \leq M$, with a bias $x_0 b_k$ included. Bias b_k is considered an internal parameter of the perceptron and is not considered an input. The x_i are voltage levels from sensors; v_k is voltage after linear summation. There may be K such artificial neurons: $1 \leq k \leq K$, although only one is shown. The variables i and k are convenient indices. A mathematical expression for v_k is

$$v_k = \sum_{i=0}^{M} w_{ki} x_i$$

Then

$$y_k = \Phi(v_k)$$

Single-Layer Networks Each perceptron input line will have weighting factors w_{ki}, the design of which is equivalent to learning. Rosenblatt proved that a single perceptron can classify input patterns if they come from one of two classes. The two classes are

$$v_k > 0$$

$$v_k \leq 0$$

as separated by an activation function or comparator. This defines what is meant by the term *linearly separable*.

Perceptron Convergence Algorithm Those who are mathematically inclined will find the algorithms below quite interesting. The synaptic weights w_{ki} can be determined by iteration using an error correction rule known as the *perceptron convergence algorithm*. The algorithm assumes the availability of training vectors. These are desired outputs, true or false, for given inputs. The perceptron convergence algorithm is summarized below.

Definitions:

$\mathbf{x}(n) = M + 1$ by 1 input vector $= [+1, x_1(n), x_2(n), \ldots, x_M(n)]'$

$\mathbf{w}(n) = M + 1$ by 1 weight vector $= [b(n), w_1(n), w_2(n), \ldots, w_M(n)]'$

$b(n) = \text{bias}$

$y(n) = \text{actual response}$

$d(n) = \text{desired response } (+1 \text{ or } -1)$

$\eta = \text{perceptron learning-rate parameter, positive and less than unity}$

Step 1: Set $\mathbf{w}(1) = \mathbf{0}'$; $n = 1$; perform the following computations for time step $n = 1, 2, \ldots$: MAXN.

Step 2: Compute the actual response of the perceptron:

$$y(n) = \text{sgn}[\mathbf{w}'(n) \cdot \mathbf{x}(n)]$$

$\mathbf{w}(n)' \cdot \mathbf{x}(n)$ is a vector inner product in which corresponding elements are multiplied and then all products are added. This accomplishes linear summation. $\text{sgn}(v) = +1$ if $v > 0$ and -1 if $v \leq 0$; this accomplishes the activation function or comparison.

Step 3: Update the weight vector:

$$\mathbf{w}(n + 1) = \mathbf{w}(n) + \eta[d(n) - y(n)]\mathbf{x}(n)$$

where $d(n) = +1$ if $x(n)$ belongs to the first group; $d(n) = -1$ if $x(n)$ belongs to the second group.

Step 4: Increment the time step n by one and go to step 2.

In this procedure $d(n) - y(n)$ is the error signal. The learning-rate parameter η is a positive constant between 0 and 1, chosen so that the weights do not change too fast in an unstable way, yet fast enough for quick convergence of $y(n) \to d(n)$. The perceptron convergence theorem proves the iteration can be made to converge by proper choice of η.

An interesting application of the algorithm is to enable an artificial neuron to learn to be a logic gate. To do this, one must enter a truth table. The AND truth table, for example, is

x_1	x_2	d
-1	-1	-1
-1	$+1$	-1
$+1$	-1	-1
$+1$	$+1$	$+1$

The algorithm may be executed on these entries one at a time going through all four and then repeating until the weights no longer change. We have assumed a bias of zero and $\eta = 0.5$ for an example of the setup. We begin by using the fourth entry in the table:

Step 1:

$$\mathbf{x}(1) = [+1, +1, +1]'$$
$$\mathbf{w}(1) = [0, 0, 0]'$$
$$d(1) = +1$$
$$\eta = 0.5$$

The prime denotes a transpose that converts to a column vector.

Step 2:

$$y(1) = \text{sgn}[\mathbf{w}'(0)\mathbf{x}(0)] = \text{sgn}[(0)(1) + (0)(+1) + (0)(+1)] = \text{sgn}[0] = -1$$

Step 3:

$$\mathbf{w}(2) = [0\,0\,0]' + \{0.5[1 - (-1)]\}[+1 + 1 + 1]' = [+1 + 1 + 1]'$$

The iteration proceeds through each entry in the truth table and repeats until it converges, as indicated by the fact that $\mathbf{w}$ no longer changes. As an example of the results from the algorithm, simple implementations of AND and OR gates appear in Figure 6-7, assuming an ideal comparator. In this simple example, the logic levels are -1 false and $+1$ true, and the weighting factors all turn out to be unity.

It is easily verified by tracing the voltages that the logic specified is generated for any combinations of -1 and $+1$ as inputs. Examples are AND($+1$, $+1$) = true; AND($+1$, -1) = false; OR($+1$, -1) = true. Other levels are also available, although differing weighting factors and biases are required. Simple two-input ANDs and ORs like this are fundamental to any logical system.

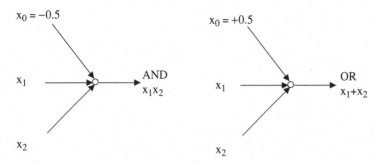

FIGURE 6-7 Basic logic generation using the perceptron model of a neuron.

Multilayer Networks A single perceptron will not implement the XOR. The XOR is a Boolean function that is true if one or the other input are true, but not if both are true. What is required for the exclusive OR is a two-layer neural network such as that shown in Figure 6-8. Figure 6-9 is an example of an XOR (obtained by an unspecified process of design).

In the flow graph, the comparator $\Phi(\cdot)$ is ideal (either true or false) and switches at a threshold of zero; the logic levels are $+1$, -1. An interested reader may demonstrate that these two layers can generate an XOR by tracing inputs through Figure 6-9. The NOT function results from the XOR if one of the inputs is held true ($+1$). An arbitrary Boolean function may result for any number of inputs by combining basic AND, OR, and NOT.

Learning in a multilayer artificial neural network is equivalent to designing weighting factors. Unfortunately, the number of weighting factors grows exponentially with the number of layers used. Computers apply an algorithm to force the actual output to approach the desired output. The output desired for given inputs must be available for training the network.

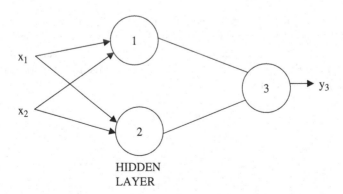

FIGURE 6-8 Two-layer perceptron network to implement an exclusive OR.

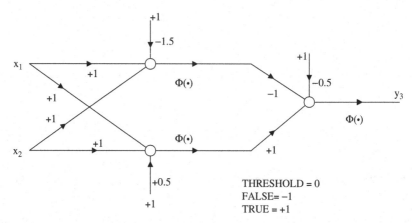

FIGURE 6-9   XOR flow diagram.

Back-Propagation Algorithm   An algorithm known as *back propagation* may be applied to find weighting factors in a multilayer artificial neural network. This is mathematical back propagation which has nothing to do with the back propagation of electrical solitons. Our focus will be on two layers. If one can design weighting factors for two layers, one should be able to design for any number of layers. Back propagation is an example of mathematical optimization that applies to a variety of design problems. It is going to be derived from basic considerations in the hope that the algorithm will become understood. It is an iterative algorithm. To simplify the notation, the index of iteration is not going to be shown, although it will be necessary when writing a computer program to run the algorithm. We begin with step $n = 1$.

Error is defined to be the difference between the d_k desired and the output y_k of neuron k; the error equation is

$$e_k = d_k - y_k$$

The equation for y_k is similar to those above for the perceptron except that the inputs are defined here to be y_i and not x_i, because having the same symbol with a different subscript is a convenient notation for multilayers. Note that the subscript i does double duty. It identifies input signals and it also serves as an index to count the inputs.

$$y_k = \Phi(v_k)$$

with

$$v_k = \sum_{i=0}^{M} w_{ki} y_i$$

The error e_k can be positive or negative. To remove the sign we square e_k. In general, there may be several output neurons over a range of k. Thus, we are led to the following error function E, the famous *sum-of-squares* function summed over all output neurons:

$$E = \frac{1}{2} \sum_{\forall k} e_k^2$$

The goal is a least-squares estimation of the weighting factors w_{ki}. A *gradient* is a concept from calculus similar to a differential. Adjusting the weighting factors in a direction opposite the gradient will tend to reduce the error function E. A gradient involves several variables and may be calculated using partial derivatives in a chain rule of calculus as follows:

$$\frac{\partial E}{\partial w_{ki}} = \frac{\partial E}{\partial e_k} \frac{\partial e_k}{\partial y_k} \frac{\partial y_k}{\partial v_k} \frac{\partial v_k}{\partial w_{ki}}$$

The components of the gradient $\partial E / \partial w_{ji}$ can be calculated one at a time from the foregoing equation:

$$\frac{\partial E}{\partial e_k} = e_k$$

$$\frac{\partial e_k}{\partial y_k} = -1$$

$$\frac{\partial y_k}{\partial v_k} = \frac{\partial \Phi(v_k)}{\partial v_k}$$

$$\frac{\partial v_k}{\partial w_{ki}} = y_i$$

Thus, the gradient becomes

$$\frac{\partial E}{\partial w_{ki}} = e_k(-1)\frac{\partial y_k}{\partial v_k}y_i$$

$$= -\delta_k y_i$$

where

$$\delta_k = e_k \frac{\partial y_k}{\partial v_k}$$

$$= e_k \frac{\partial \Phi(v_k)}{\partial v_k}$$

Weighting factors are corrected by what is known as the *delta rule:*

$$w_{ki}(n+1) = w_{ki}(n) + \Delta w_{ki}$$

$$\Delta w_{ki} = -\eta \frac{\partial E}{\partial w_{ki}}$$

$$= \eta \delta_k y_i.$$

η is a learning-rate parameter, usually positive and less than unity. δ_k may be calculated as a product of e_k and $\partial \Phi / \partial v_k$ and is easily computed numerically.

A useful relationship is available when multilayer networks are designed:

$$\delta_k = e_k \frac{\partial y_k}{\partial v_k}$$

$$= \frac{\partial E}{\partial e_k}(-1)(-1)\frac{\partial y_k}{\partial v_k}$$

$$= \frac{\partial E}{\partial e_k}(-1)\frac{\partial e_k}{\partial y_k}\frac{\partial y_k}{\partial v_k}$$

$$= -\frac{\partial E}{\partial v_k}$$

Therefore, δ_k is the negative of a gradient that is termed the *local gradient*. It is needed for multilayer analysis.

For a single-layer network the calculation is a lot simpler. Usually, there is an initial guess for the weighting factor matrix. This guess could very well be a pseudorandom selection of weights. The algorithm uses a "forward" pass to calculate e_k using current w_{ki} and then a "backward" pass to update w_{ki}. After this we replace n with $n + 1$ and continue the iteration a few hundred times. With luck, the w_{ki} will all converge to a stable value.

When there are two layers, a j-layer of neurons is taken as hidden and the k-layer is the output. This setup is suggested in Figure 6-10. The following relationship was suggested above and can be shown to hold true:

$$\Delta w_{ji} = \eta \delta_j y_i$$

We need to calculate δ_j:

$$\delta_j = -\frac{\partial E}{\partial v_j}$$

$$= -\frac{\partial E}{\partial y_j}\frac{\partial y_j}{\partial v_j}$$

$$= -\frac{\partial E}{\partial y_j}\frac{\partial \Phi(v_j)}{\partial v_j}$$

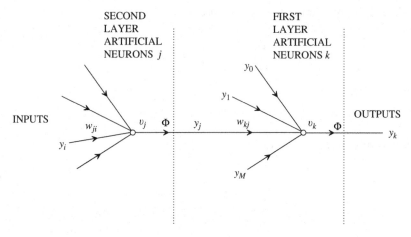

FIGURE 6-10   Flow graph showing two layers of artificial neurons.

The second factor is known, but we need $\partial E/\partial y_j$.

$$E = \frac{1}{2} \sum_{\forall k} e_k^2$$

$$\Rightarrow$$

$$\frac{\partial E}{\partial y_j} = \sum_{\forall k} e_k \frac{\partial e_k}{\partial y_j}$$

$$= \sum_{\forall k} e_k \frac{\partial e_k}{\partial v_k} \frac{\partial v_k}{\partial y_j}$$

But since $e_k = d_k - y_k$ and $y_k = \Phi(v_k)$;

$$\Rightarrow$$

$$\frac{\partial e_k}{\partial v_k} = -\frac{\partial \Phi(v_k)}{\partial v_k}$$

and

$$v_k = \sum_{j=0}^{M} w_{kj} y_j$$

$$\Rightarrow$$

$$\frac{\partial v_k}{\partial y_j} = w_{kj}$$

The result completing the definition of δ_j is

$$
\frac{\partial E}{\partial y_j} = -\sum_{\forall k} e_k \frac{\partial \Phi(v_k)}{\partial v_k} w_{kj}
$$

$$
= -\sum_{\forall k} \delta_k w_{kj}
$$

Using δ_k as defined above yields

$$
\delta_k = e_k \frac{\partial y_k}{\partial v_k}
$$

$$
= e_k \frac{\partial \Phi(v_k)}{\partial v_k}
$$

This permits the hidden layer δ_j to be expressed in terms of the output layer δ_k:

$$
\delta_j = \frac{\partial \Phi(v_j)}{\partial v_j} \sum_{\forall k} \delta_k w_{kj}
$$

Hence, one may easily calculate the changes in the weighting factors for the second layer:

$$
\Delta w_{ji} = \eta \delta_j y_i
$$

Again, there is an initial guess for the weighting factor matrix. This guess could very well be a pseudorandom selection of weights. There is a forward pass to calculate e_k using current w_{ji} and w_{kj} and then a backward pass to update w_{ji} and w_{kj}. Then n is replaced with $n + 1$. With luck, the w-factors will converge to make the error function zero. However, there is no law that forces convergence; sometimes there is a loop in which the error function will not decrease below a given value. Such results have been termed *false* minimums. In such cases, the initial values used for w_{ji} and w_{kj} must be chosen again, usually with the aid of another call to the random number subroutine. For difficult input patterns a false minimum might be good enough to accomplish the needed recognition with good probability. A gradient method like this will never actually increase the value of the error function as long as η is chosen small enough.

Activation Functions The derivative of the activation function Φ is used in the back-projection algorithm. For this derivative to exist, the function has to be continuous. One useful function is the hyperbolic tangent function, defined by

$$\Phi(v_j) = a \tanh(bv_j)$$

where a and b are constants. Its derivative with respect to v_j is

$$\frac{\partial \Phi(v_j)}{\partial v_j} = ab \ \text{sech}^2(bv_j)$$

$$= ab(1 - \tanh^2(bv_j))$$

$$= ab\big[(1 - \tanh(bv_j))(1 + \tanh(bv_j))\big]$$

In the context of a calculation in an artificial neural network,

$$y_j = \Phi(v_k)$$

$$= a \tanh(bv_j)$$

so

$$\frac{\partial \Phi(v_j)}{\partial v_j} = \frac{b}{a}\big[(a - y_j)(a + y_j)\big]$$

As an approximation, sometimes a programmer uses

$$\left(\frac{\partial \Phi(v_j)}{\partial v_j}\right)^n = \left(\frac{b}{a}\big[(a - y_j)(a + y_j)\big]\right)^{n-1}$$

This means that the algorithm at the nth step is modified a little to calculate the derivative of the activation function based on the y_j at the $(n-1)$th step. The error in doing this is unknown.

DISCUSSION OF LEARNING METHODS

Adjustments of weighting factors in artificial neural networks are described as supervised learning, or learning with a teacher. This learning causes the network to recognize certain input patterns, those for which it can be trained to recognize. This type of learning differs from biological learning.

Biological Versus Artificial Learning

In a simple biological model a group of neurotransmitters are either sent across the synaptic cleft by a presynaptic action potential or they are not. Analog weighting factors are difficult to envision. There might be a way to release only a few excitatory neurotransmitter ions, depending on mechanisms not yet understood. Then neurotransmitter ions would be attracted to a postsynaptic receiver and accumulate there until enough are released to initiate an action potential in the receiver. However, there is no reason for such a complicated model.

The release of neurotransmitter ions into a synaptic cleft depends on a single bouton on a single neuron, not on a large number of connecting neurons. The cleft is only a few nanometers wide and is quite far from other neurons, which are not likely to have an input. In the artificial model, signals are supposed to enter from many other neurons to be weighted and summed. Many separate neurons contributing to a given synapse seem physically impossible.

Thresholds are not just in postsynaptic receivers as in artificial neurons, but everywhere. There is a built-in threshold within each ferroelectric membrane not shielded by insulating material. Membranes respond only to strong signals, like a Schmitt trigger in electronics, not to noisy random analog events. In this way, digital reliability is vastly increased. A threshold exists wherever a membrane exists with no myelination, not only in receivers on spines, but on the surfaces of dendrites and soma and on exposed axons.

Dendrites have many branches, and at first sight, summation is suggested where two branches meet. However, a branch has been modeled as either activated with propagating solitons or at rest. Furthermore, the waveform of a soliton is fixed by membrane properties. Two or more solitons that happen to meet at a junction merge into a propagated soliton in the forward direction (and possibly a reflection) with exactly the same amplitude and width. Simulations discussed in Chapter 5 also indicate that colliding solitons, one moving forward, one moving backward, will be annihilated. Summation does not exist in dendrites except in a Boolean sense, although it is part and parcel of the artificial neural network model.

An iterative algorithm for learning could be wired, since there is always a way to implement a sequential procedure using basic logic. The problem is that algorithms of this type converge slowly or not at all, so there is an element of inefficiency. This violates the rule that evolved intelligence is efficient.

Learning with a teacher is essential to an artificial neural network. In contrast, the model in this book leaves it up to the brain to collect information and eventually to internalize it. Useful information certainly comes from an experienced teacher and elsewhere, but merely having the information in long-term memory does not mean that it is learned in the sense of growing new neurons and synapses.

It is difficult to imagine supervised learning at the neural level, because there is no teacher at this level. For example, one observes a violin master to learn fingering. Presumably this knowledge is committed to long-term memory and recalled to short-term memory as appropriate. But memorization is not learning. Interneurons and synaptic growth are necessary for learning, which is a physical thing. Physical learning means that a new feature in a scene will be recognized automatically, or a new procedure will be executed automatically without necessarily passing information through short-term memory.

Learning using the memory model of this book is all-digital and completely different from learning in an artificial neural network. All-digital models of learning are feasible because there are billions of neurons and trillions of synapses eager to make connections.

To recap, *combinational learning* is modeled as configuring logic gates for encoding new sensory features; *sequential learning* is modeled as configuring logic gates for a new neural state machine within long-term memory. First there has to be a need-to-learn signal as calculated by recurrent recall of given information in long-term memory. This signal begins an automatic reconfiguration process in which synapses develop in targeted locations. Digital learning operates roughly like a field-programmable gate array in digital electronics, only the programming is self-contained. The locations of the new synapses are guided by an overlaid network of cerebral interneurons for the purposes of decoding relevant features into specific learning signals.

Hebbian Self-Organized Learning

Hebbian self-organized learning depends on burst rates. Spike rates within a burst must not be confused with burst rates; spike rates within a burst are essentially fixed by soliton properties, membrane properties, and ionic compositions. Burst rates, action potentials per second, are quite different. Ultimately, the action potentials per unit time are going to depend on how often a particular neuron is needed in a given process. This is determined by such issues as the process being executed and the timing of the short-term memory system.

We note that neurons of importance to learning seldom experience constant bursting, although simple random spikes have been observed. Purkinje neurons stacked in the cerebellum have been observed to exhibit simple spontaneous spikes at a rate between 15 and 150 Hz, although these simple spikes are not always there. Pyramidal and other neurons associated with memory processing appear to be more or less calm until triggered. The concept of higher and lower burst rates, proposed to be a mechanism of learning, apparently must wait until a neuron is being used. But, as mentioned above, in this book usage is fixed by the process being executed and the timing of the short-term memory system.

As a further comment on Hebbian self-organized learning, when something is learned, the average burst rate is supposed to increase. But does the average frequency of action potentials in a brain depend on learning? An experiment needs to be carried out using basic electroencephalography to see if a college education, for example, results in brain wave frequencies that are higher than average. Dealing with burst rates and frequencies is poorly suited to the artificial neural network or perceptron concept. Frequency weighting and summation would have to be related to Fourier integrals and nonlinear mixing, which is far from amplitude processing. Nonlinear activation functions with Fourier inputs would be a puzzle.

Hebbian self-organized learning applies when neurons are used repeatedly and need to build up their frequency of firing. This concept is remotely related to a need-to-learn signal enabled by frequent neural usage. Unfortunately, Hebbian learning relies on modulating the frequency of bursts, something that is difficult to explain physically. What *can* be explained physically is that a standardized burst is instigated by a connecting neuron whose frequency of action potentials depends entirely on how often it is excited by a connecting neuron.

Artificial neural networks tacitly assume that neurons for learning are already in place and only need to be adjusted. The real question is: What causes the growth of the first synapse that creates the first burst in the history of a new neuron?

Finally, when designing self-contained self-directed robots, an all-digital system, which admittedly has a large overhead of gates, and so seems impractical, might eventually prove easier to design than a large artificial neural network. A digital VLSI chip, for instance, has millions of gates and continues to grow in capacity, doubling approximately every two years, as predicted under Moore's law.

CONCLUSION

Working through this chapter provides a nontrivial appreciation of artificial neurons and artificial neural networks. The successful concept of artificial neural networks was inspired by early brain models. What is special about artificial neural networks is their ability to be trained to recognize a given pattern. Training methods must have available a set of desired outputs for given inputs. An algorithm will then choose the correct weighting factors in the network.

For example, perceptrons can be trained to be logic gates for a class of Boolean functions such as the AND. The perceptron convergence algorithm, given above, shows how a computing machine can train a single artificial neuron to distinguish between differing inputs that are linearly separable. The XOR is an example of a gate that cannot be implemented with a single perceptron; it must be implemented using two layers of an artificial neural network. An example of a two-layer XOR is provided above for interested readers.

A style of optimization known as back propagation applies to a neural network with more than one layer. The back-propagation algorithm is delineated above for interested readers. Desired outputs for given inputs must be supplied. In this style of optimization the weighting factors are adjusted in proportion to their gradient on an error function, a sum of the differences between desired and actual outputs. Weights are adjusted in a direction that reduces the error function. A drawback of back propagation is that iterations sometimes do not converge to zero error when attempting to recognize complex patterns.

The mathematical ways in which artificial neural networks "learn" is very different from the ways in which humans learn. An artificial neural network is said to learn when it finds a useful combination of analog weighting factors. Finding a useful combination of weighting factors involves numerical iteration to adjust them to achieve desired outputs from known inputs. Human learning, in contrast, is modeled in this text as all digital. Learning circuits are possible because neurons are plentiful, pervasive, and eager to make new contacts. From the point of view of building a smart robot the all-digital approach has advantages in this age of VLSI chips. These chips are dense with logic and relatively inexpensive to apply.

EXERCISES

6-1 How does an artificial neural network differ from a general-purpose computer?

6-2 Artificial neural networks for AND and OR gates were implemented in this chapter with particular weighting factors and biases.

    (a) Provide flow diagrams that will accomplish the AND in another way using a perceptron.

    (b) Provide flow diagrams that will accomplish the OR in another way using a perceptron.

    (c) In each case above, what must the bias x_0 be changed to in order to disable the perceptron so that its output is always false (metaphorically to put it to sleep)?

6-3 Consider the perceptron convergence algorithm.

    (a) Apply the algorithm to machine-design an AND gate.

    (b) Apply the algorithm machine-design an OR gate.

    (c) Is it possible to machine-design a NOR gate? How?

6-4 The XOR requires two levels of perceptrons.

    (a) Trace the flow diagram in the chapter to prove that the XOR, as given, indeed works with logic levels of -1 and $+1$.

    (b) Redesign the XOR with logic levels of 0 and 1.

6-5 Draw a block diagram of a Hopfield feedback network with four elements.

6-6 Artificial neural networks can be used for analog-to-digital conversion (ADC) using a network reminiscent of a Hopfield network. Figure E6-6 shows a 4-bit converter; it assumes ideal comparators and a logic system such that F $= -8$ and T $= +8$. An offset of -0.5 V is applied to each positive input of the comparators. Multiplicative weighting factors are the fractions placed by the arrows at the bottom of the figure.

(a) Trace the output signals for each amplifier as v_{in} moves from -8 V to $+7$ V in 1-V steps. Place the results in a table.

(b) Determine which input voltages provide the output T, F, T, F, which is the same as $+8$, -8, $+8$, -8.

6-7 Design a neural network ADC with two output bits. Begin with the circuit shown in figure E6-6; trim it down to size and adjust the voltage levels in a convenient way. Logic levels of ±2 V are suggested.

6-8 Consider the back-propagation method for calculating weighting factors when there are two layers of perceptrons. Assume an arctan type of

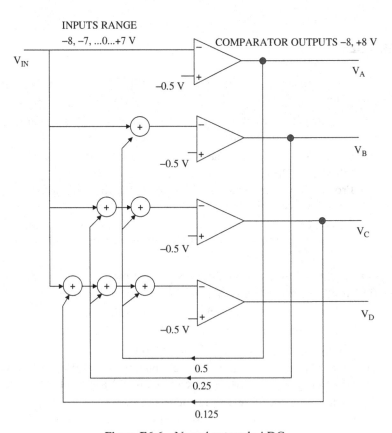

Figure E6-6 Neural network ADC.

activation function to model a comparator that switches with a threshold of zero volts.

(a) Apply the back-propagation method to machine-design the weighting factors for a one-layer neural network for the OR. Assume logic levels of -1 and 1.

(b) Apply the back-propagation method to machine-design the weighting factors for a two-layer neural network for the XOR. Assume logic levels of -1 and 1.

A program for back projection may be written in a computer language of your choice or purchased: for example, the MATLAB package for neural network design.

CHAPTER 7

THE ASSET OF REVERSIBILITY IN HUMANS AND MACHINES

INTRODUCTION

In past chapters we have presented a model of the human memory system based on physical and logical concepts in an attempt to shed light on such everyday events as memory searching, direction of attention, memorization, and learning. The model is built on neurons as logic devices activated by ions and ferroelectric membranes. The modeling effort points to a brain circuit that could conceivably be built in solid-state technology. However, it is doubtful that any such machine would ever be considered gifted, although a robot might be considered quite intelligent, especially if it has the ability to learn. But how can a machine be designed to be gifted, equivalent to a special talent in some narrow area? In seeking an answer this question, it is helpful first to consider gifted humans.

To gauge giftedness, the abilities of savants are now investigated. The causes of savant syndrome are not the focus in this chapter except to say it is often associated with autism and occasionally with head injuries. What is important here is that savants sometimes have unusual mental abilities far beyond those of the average person. Often, their abilities are in a very narrow area, so are termed *splinter skills*. Some savants have photographic memories and are able to recall vast amounts of information after seeing it only briefly. Indeed, this

Human Memory Modeled with Standard Analog and Digital Circuits: Inspiration for Man-made Computers, By John Robert Burger
Copyright © 2009 John Wiley & Sons, Inc.

fact takes us away from the synaptic-growth theories of explicit memory and to models using neural latches. As examples of photographic memory, a musical prodigy might play a complex piano piece in a respectable way after hearing it only once, thus displaying superior memory coupled with musical talent. Others might recite an entire book after reading it only once. Gifted savants may excel at foreign languages, often with no trace of an accent. Savants occasionally excel at rapid multiplications, divisions, roots, powers, and prime number recognition, which are computer-related operations of special interest here.

Many savants demonstrate calendar skills. They enjoy asking people for the date of their birth and then telling them on which day of the week they were born. There are 14 different calendars, seven for regular years and seven for leap years—one for a year that starts on a Sunday, another for when it starts on Monday, and so on. Memorizing all these calendars seems possible, but not easy. One wonders if there is a shortcut way to do it.

Those with splinter skills are often handicapped in other ways. Fortunately, many savants are supported by friends and relatives who care about them and who appreciate their special abilities. Especially to be applauded are savants with communication skills who allow themselves to be studied scientifically.

In this chapter we introduce three well-known savants with an eye to imagining how they do it. The resulting models are highly speculative but still inspiring. There are plenty of examples in which brain-related models have inspired inventions for everyday life. For example, models of the neuron have resulted in artificial neural networks that are quite useful for recognizing patterns. For example, they may identify e-mail spam, among other things. Similarly, brain models led to cybernetics* and to the electronic brain, otherwise known as a computer. Computers grew with technology after World War II along with frequent attempts to relate computers to brains, and vice versa. Brain models of the past were far from perfect, but nevertheless they were inspiring, and they served a purpose in the world of design engineering. Models do not need to be perfect to inspire practical machines.

In an attempt to explain computationally gifted savants, we introduce a particular system of parallel processing. The particular system envisioned turns out to be logically reversible and so takes us to explanations of electrical and logical reversibility and to an explanation of *Landauer's limit*. This is the energy associated with a lost bit of information in an irreversible computer. In preparation for practical implementations of logical reversibility, the chapter concludes with an introduction to the programming of a logically reversible computer.

---

* Cybernetics was defined by Norbert Wiener (1894–1964), in his book of that title, as the study of control and communication in the animal and the machine.

SAVANTS

Benjamin Rush (1746–1813) was a founding father of the United States and signer of the Declaration of Independence. In addition to many other activities, he was far ahead of his time in the treatment of mental illness. He is considered the father of American psychiatry, publishing the text *Medical Inquiries and Observation upon the Diseases of the Mind* in 1812. Rush was an advocate of hospitals for the cure of mental diseases; he promoted the idea that alcoholism is a form of medical disease; and he was an early opponent of slavery and capital punishment.

Thomas Fuller

Among other things, Rush described the lightning calculating skills of Thomas Fuller, "who could comprehend scarcely anything, theoretical or practical, more complex than counting." When Fuller was asked how many seconds a man had lived who was 70 years, 17 days, and 12 hours old, he gave the correct answer (2,210,500,800), even correcting for the 17 leap years involved, taking less than 2 minutes to perform this mental calculation.

Abilities such as this are of interest in this chapter, where we now review a few common observations about savants. Recall that the brain is divided into two hemispheres, left and right, connected by nerve fibers called the *corpus callosum*. This is a band or *commissure* of myelinated axons, estimated to be a 4- by 1-inch band of roughly 200 million axons. Thoughts and actions are processed in the two cerebral hemispheres; they typically function as an integrated unit that may be described as highly connected. Left and right brains are like a married couple who each have certain household chores but who constantly discuss possible solutions to problems that involve the family.

The right hemisphere is thought to deal with literal information and new problems. The left processes neural state-machine routines involving symbols: for instance, those of mathematics and language. Unfortunately, symbols can be inefficient. A symbol typically is connected to several words of memory to delineate multiple meanings, all of which must be processed through short-term memory. As an example, ♥ is a symbol with a complex of meanings, including past relationships with things, relationships with people, or simply a medical reference. What is supposed to be a precise symbol, β, has countless meanings: It could be a letter in the Greek alphabet, the gain of a transistor, refer to a type of brain wave, on refer to a type of atomic ray. The point is that symbols in the usual sense of the word are, in fact, quite inexact. One must analyze the context in which the symbol is used.

There is brain-scanning evidence that a savant's right hemisphere, which specializes in literal information, is compensating for underdevelopment or damage in the left hemisphere, which specializes in symbols. Researchers theorize that limited activity in the left anterior temporal cortex allows the brain to be stronger with literal data and weaker with symbols. An example might be grouping stars into constellations. This could interfere with an accurate count of the stars.

Symbols in the savant brain may very well be limited to exact meanings, such as given geometric shapes for each number, for example. A given shape is never used in any other way. Thus a savant symbol is unambiguous, unlike ordinary human symbols. Having a given shape for a given prime number, for example, is useful in arithmetic but not for everyday functioning. Magnetic resonance imaging shows other neurological differences in the savant brain. The hippocampus (associated with memory) and amygdala (associated with emotion) constitute the *limbic system*, which is thought to be responsible for relaying information throughout the brain while correlating emotion to the information. In the autistic brain these neural structures are immature and often incapable of functioning normally. This causes unresponsive, emotionless expressions often associated with autism.

On the other hand, greater mental concentration is possible when a person is less distracted. The savant brain prefers to focus on a given activity, that is, it directs all attention into one activity. Savants generally have aversion to distractions such as changes in the way that mundane activities are performed. Multitasking in savants may be limited. Savant achievements are, in fact, a form of self-expression. The savant typically loves to focus and concentrate and to practice something well beyond what is normal and to demonstrate their achievements to others.

Many savants seem to have phenomenal memory; minute details can be recalled without effort. This enhanced memory permits savants to have mental images with more detail than ordinary people are able to experience. The savant mind seems to avoid extrapolations to fill in blind spots where facts are missing. They seem uncomfortable with unsolvable problems. It is estimated that 10% of the autistic population and 1% of the nonautistic public have savant abilities. Savants may have difficulties in verbal and nonverbal communication and in social interactions and leisure activities. When it happens that social skills improve and a command of language is achieved, savant skills generally deteriorate, although there are exceptions.

Daniel Tammet

Daniel Tammet (1979–   ) is classified as an autistic savant who can perform mindboggling mathematical calculations at breakneck speed. Unlike most savants, Daniel can communicate what he experiences. Daniel can figure out cube roots quicker than a calculator and has been able to recall pi to 22,514 places. But he cannot drive a car or tell left from right. Daniel describes multiplying 377 by 795. It is a semiconscious calculation that allows him to arrive at an answer very fast. He is able to see numbers as shapes, colors, and textures. "When I multiply numbers together, I see two shapes. The image starts to change and evolve, and a third shape emerges. That's the answer. It's mental imagery. It's like math without having to think."

To Daniel, pi is a particular visual landscape. But he is uncomfortable with too much mental stimulus. In a supermarket "there's too much mental stimulus. I have to look at every shape and texture, every price, and every arrangement of fruit and vegetables; so instead of thinking, 'What cheese do I want this week?' I'm just really uncomfortable." But Daniel says "I do love numbers" and "It isn't only an intellectual or aloof thing that I do. I really feel that there is an emotional attachment, a caring for numbers. I think this is a human thing—in the same way that a poet humanizes a river or a tree through metaphor; my world gives me a sense of numbers as personal. It sounds silly, but numbers are my friends."

To those who doubt that the brain can do arithmetic at lightning speeds, they have been proved wrong by Tammet, who performs multiplication, division, roots, powers, and prime number recognition (refer to the Discovery Channel documentary *Brainman* http://science.discovery.com/convergence/brainman/brainman.html). He calculates without apparent effort, but with great concentration, taking roughly 2 or 3 seconds for a calculation, far less time that it takes for him to verbalize the resulting answer. Daniel obtains correct answers. Many observers agree that Daniel Tammet is not merely reciting memorized answers. He is using his brain in ways that are difficult to explain.

Kim Peek

Another famous gifted savant is Kim Peek (1951–   ). Kim is the inspiration for the character of Raymond played by Dustin Hoffman in the movie *Rain Man*. Kim Peek was born with damage to the cerebellum and agenesis of the corpus callosum. This is a condition in which the nerves connecting the hemispheres are missing. Secondary connections such as the anterior commissure are also missing. From an early age Kim was able to memorize large amounts of information and can recall nearly all the facts in the approximate 12,000 books he has read. Although he has difficulty with ordinary motor skills and is below average on a general IQ test, he is well above average in specialized subtests. Kim recently is developing social skills and is learning new things. For anyone who questions the existence of long-term words of memory as a medium that can quickly be programmed, Kim Peek is an example of a person gifted with photographic memory. He reads a book in about an hour and remembers 98% of everything he has read.

NEURAL MODELS THAT EXPLAIN SAVANTS

Instant Neural State-Machine Learning

Photographic skills require memory; calendar skills require memory. But what does it mean to have a "good" memory? It is usually assumed that a person with a good memory has greater-than-average blank words available in which to place new memories. But memory words are useless if cues are absent for recall. Memory is related to access as much as to volume. Memories of random information are more likely to be recallable if they are connected together somehow by mnemonics, some form of encoding as mentioned in Appendix B, or possibly, interneurons between words in a sequence.

In the context of the memory model given previously, a person who recites phrase after phrase until an entire book is recited may well have a gift for learning in the form of a neural state machine that develops quickly. Neural state machines are logical interconnections that develop between words of long-term memory specifically for executing procedures or reciting narratives, without having to recall and process each word through a short-term memory system. Perhaps synapses within memory-gifted savants are more active than normal. Ignoring comprehension, just seeing the words in a book takes time, possibly enough time to permit synaptic growth for neural state machine learning. For most of us, unfortunately, neural state-machine learning takes more than a few hours.

To counter the argument that state machines will not develop fast enough to explain savant memory in many cases, as when musical scores are memorized after one hearing, for example, one might assume special memory latches in place of the normal synapses. Memory latches may be programmed instantly, giving instant neural state machines. These long-term memory cells for instant neural state machines do not hold any features of memory; they are merely controllers that map a sequence for recall, giving the appearance of great memory. Instant latches in memory savants are more plausible than instant synaptic growth for neural state-machine learning.

Massively Parallel Processing

Especially for savants with skills in arithmetic, subconscious parallel processing provides a better model for activities that are hidden in subconscious memory. Savants routinely demonstrate far more than superficial memorization of given answers, as poor students memorize in order to pass exams for which they are unprepared. Memory capacity is large, probably millions of words, but not infinite. Merely memorizing the products of two arbitrary numbers, each between 1 and 1000, requires a table with roughly 500 million entries, depending on how it is organized. Apparently, there is insufficient memory capacity to support the answers put forth by a gifted savant. They seem to be able to accept any numbers for several categories of operations, multiplications, square roots, and so on. Pure memory would be astronomical even by savant brain standards. Parallel processing must be occurring.

Consider how a person might solve the problem of identifying a prime number using parallel processing. Parallel processing could divide a given number by all candidate integers and thus find all exact divisors in which the remainder is zero. If not prime, a remainder would be zero and we would soon know that a given number is not prime. If all remainders are finite, it must be a prime number. Parallel processing that identifies prime numbers like this is theoretically possible within the savant brain.

Consider next how a person might solve the problem of delineating pi out to hundreds of decimal places. Pi can be expressed as a Leibniz series:

$$\pi = \frac{4}{1} - \frac{4}{3} + \frac{4}{5} - \frac{4}{7} + \frac{4}{9} - \frac{4}{11} \cdots$$

Four is a given number to be divided by odd integers. Each division in the series may be accomplished in parallel. All that remains is a simple accumulation of the remaining terms beginning from the left, spitting out digits verbally as you go, as savants have done. Parallel processing that calculates pi might be available within the savant brain.

Beyond arithmetic, a great many geometric skills are enhanced using parallel processing. For example, if a large "graph" (coordinates in space, many of which are connected with lines) is given, one may find closed circuits or *Hamiltonian cycles* using parallel processing. The shortest Hamiltonian cycle is a solution to the famous *salesman's problem*. In this problem, a salesman must plan a trip to visit a large number of cities exactly once for each city, and then return home, while going the fewest possible number of miles. Exact solutions to problems like this are considered "difficult" because of the large number of possible circuits, but the analysis can be simplified using massively parallel processing, as shown later in the book.

PARALLEL PROCESSING AND THE SAVANT BRAIN

In this section we present a scenario in which words of biological memory are able to accomplish parallel processing in an efficient manner. To do this, interneurons must string laterally through a selection of cells in a word of memory, and selected memory cells in the affected memory words must have conditional toggling capability. *Conditional toggling* is a most elementary and powerful sort of processing in which a cell is moved from true to false or from false to true, according to the truth value of another cell in the subject word.

A toggled cell can easily end up being *logically reversible*, which it is whenever it is toggled by a cell other than itself. Logical reversibility implies that data used in a procedure can always be recovered merely by back-computing. In a sense, it is available even though it is not saved in external memory, which hints at a potential architectural efficiency, the avoidance of external memory. Perhaps more important from the standpoint of physics, logical reversibility implies that no information is lost, which creates the possibility of operations that dissipate no energy. This is consistent with an adiabatic memory system that neither gains nor loses energy.

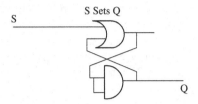

FIGURE 7-1 Long-term memory (read-only) with an AND gate.

Conditional Toggling Neural Models

Toggling means that memory cells can alternate back and forth between true and false. That portion of long-term memory that contains cells that can toggle is defined to be *toggle memory*. Toggle memory can be developed from a basic read-only memory (ROM) cell as in Figure 7-1. As explained in Chapter 4, basic ROM can be set only once, and it stays set indefinitely. The AND gate in the figure provides a necessary propagation delay to ensure efficiency and conveniently allows expansion into a basic set–reset latch as in Figure 7-2. The figure illustrates a circuit capable of toggling with two controls, S and R. The S signal forces Q to latch to true; later, the R signal forces Q to latch to false. The R signal goes through a NOT gate involving inhibitory neurotransmitters in a NOT gate circuit.

Two inputs S and R are easily redesigned into a single input that triggers toggling, as in Figure 7-3. The figure shows a toggle circuit that uses only an input signal T, known as a *toggle signal*, to force the output Q from true to false or false to true, but only if the conditional control is true. The given circuit is termed a *controlled T flip-flop*. When the conditional control signal is true, toggling occurs whenever T is brought true for a specific brief amount of time. In an actual neural circuit, all neural gates, including NOT gates, are properly supported with neurotransmitters, both excitatory and inhibitory. These are not shown for clarity, so the figure does not provide a complete picture of how neurons work. However, it indicates the logic involved.

The toggle circuit may be analyzed as follows: Assume initially that the conditional control is true, that Q is latched to be true (so that Q′ is false), and assume that T is false. When the control T is pulsed to be true briefly, the

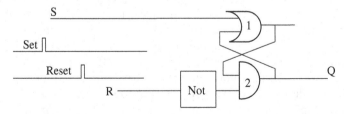

FIGURE 7-2 Rudimentary set–reset interpreted as a toggle cell.

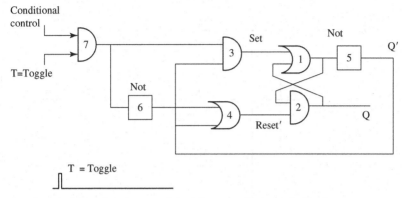

FIGURE 7-3 Conditionally controlled toggle flip-flop.

output of NOT gate 6 goes false; so Reset becomes false briefly; thus, the output Q of AND gate 2 goes false. At this point T is assumed to go back to zero again. Q is held to false by the stray capacitance in the circuit. As the false signal from Q propagates through OR gate 1 and NOT gate 5, Q' becomes true. At this point, Q is false and Q' is true, which is latched by the circuit of gates 1 and 2. Now the system is ready for another toggle. Another toggle is accomplished by pulsing T again.

Toggle memory, radically different from SRAM and DRAM, can be made to support logically reversible computers, important to overall efficiency. Controlled toggling is usually simplified to mean that if certain cells in a word are true, a selected set of disjoint memory cells in that word are made to toggle. The purpose of using disjoint cells is to assure logical reversibility.

Calculations Within a Memory Word

Calculations within a memory word are possible if selected cells are able to send signals to other selected cells to toggle them. Figure 7-4 shows an example of cells A and B sending signals to cell C. In this setup, the horizontal lines represent words and the vertical lines represent control signals that regulate what happens. The AND is taken of the outputs of cells A and B, and the Boolean result is used for a conditional toggle control. In this example, if cells A and B are both true, cell C is toggled. This would be an elementary step in a larger operation.

A word containing cells capable of conditional toggling may be termed a *nanoprocessor* rather than a microprocessor. Nanoprocessors are very much simpler than microprocessors and far more efficient with energy. Also, as technology advances, they are approaching nanometer dimensions, and ideally will someday exist on a scale with atoms.

To accomplish arithmetic in parallel, each nanoprocessor must contain different numbers as a starting point. For example, nanoprocessor 1 may

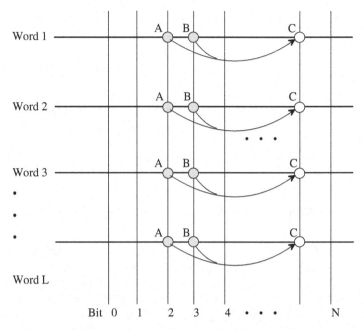

FIGURE 7-4   Parallel operations in L words.

contain a given pair of operands; nanoprocessor 2 may contain another pair of operands; and so on to nanoprocessor L, with a final unique pair of operands. Upon applying a given sequence of controlled toggling, parallel arithmetic is accomplished as demonstrated in the programming examples in later chapters.

What is accomplished could be called *vector arithmetic*, although operations other than arithmetic are readily possible, as shown later. A vector can be defined as a stack of L numbers. The corresponding entries in vectors might be added, accomplishing vector addition, for example. This plan would add corresponding components in parallel, thus speeding vector addition. Another common application is for an *inner product* in which the corresponding elements of two vectors are multiplied. Typical vector operations would be addition, subtraction, multiplication and division, and also roots, powers, and so on. Vector operations are common in many modern application ranging from digital filters to supercomputers.

COMPUTATIONAL POSSIBILITIES USING CONDITIONAL TOGGLE MEMORY

What might be accomplished if conditional toggling and parallel processing were available in brain memory? In a savant brain, parallel processing could speed up arithmetic. Multiplying 345 by 678, for example, can be accomplished by multiplying 678 by 3, while concurrently multiplying 678 by 4, while concurrently multiplying 678 by 5; the product is simply the sum of the partial products.

Identifying a prime number is merely a process of noting when a number cannot be divided by anything other than itself and unity. A parallel processor as above may divide a given number with N binary places by all possible integers simultaneously, up to about half of the given number. If none of the integers go evenly, the given number is a prime number. Mention should be made of locating a desired path that connects a maze of points. This is something that parallel processing in words can help with to a certain extent, as we discuss in Chapter 8.

Operations such as these above are theoretically possible in toggle memory because each toggle operation is not brought to short-term memory for evaluation. Thus, under parallel processing, a savant will not be fully aware of calculations because they are subconscious. There is a need for control signals and they plausibly would enter into short-term memory, as would a sampling of the calculations as they proceed. In the end, interesting outputs of a parallel computation will be flagged and made available to short-term memory. Selected outputs might subsequently be transferred into ordinary long-term memory.

Toggle memory, in so much as it supports parallel processing, might help explain a savant's abilities. It also provides ideas for a new type of hardware processor. Toward this end, the efficiency of hardware processing is a major consideration.

Toggle Memory Energy Efficiency

While a savant is working a difficult problem, he or she can be observed to do so with relative ease, strongly concentrating, but apparently using few calories. This and other considerations suggest the adiabatic model. Given that adiabatic neurons serve well in models of human memory, computer designers are beginning to realize that adiabatic circuits might be useful for man-made computers based on toggle memory. Adiabatic circuits in the world of CMOS require an initial charge, but eventually all charge is returned to its source. Even if the power supply is poorly designed and cannot accept returned charge, at least energy and heat would not be dissipated in the location of the vulnerable microchip, a huge advantage.

Computers and their microchips currently are limited by heat dissipation. Large heat dissipation structures and cooling fans are mandatory to prevent temperature from increasing excessively. From a reliability point of view, any increase in temperature will reduce the life of a chip. Chips run quite hot, as anyone who feels the surfaces of the operating parts within a desktop computer will realize. Unknown to a user, hot spots within a chip would boil water. High temperatures accelerate *electromigration*, in which micrometer-sized connections erode away, causing a chip to wear out.

Cryogenic refrigeration is used in supercomputers, research, and for super-conducting devices, but such low-temperature refrigeration demands vast amounts of extra energy and creates safety problems. Few of us want to sit at a cryogenic cooler noisily leaking liquid nitrogen or helium as we surf the Web. Using human memory as a model, adiabatic logic could revolutionize computers. Computers that avoid energy dissipation might become quite popular: They would minimize dissipation of Earth's resources and thus minimize environmental pollution.

Reversibility

Indirectly related to efficiency is the concept of reversibility. According to Michael P. Frank (1969–   ), a modern advocate of reversibility to reduce energy dissipation, heat problems threaten to end reductions in the physical size of future electronics. Engineers have always been troubled by efficiency, so it is important to investigate this topic.

Mechanical Reversibility   Machines go forward or backward, like a moving picture or an automobile in forward or reverse. The automobile engine itself, of course, is not reversible; the engine runs only one way, so that valves allow gasoline to enter the cylinder and to exhaust the cylinder. The automobile is reversible only in the sense that its transmission gears can be placed in reverse to back up the vehicle. A similar argument may be applied to moving pictures. Mechanical reversibility is unrelated to energy dissipation, but electrical reversibility is important, as described below.

Electrical Reversibility   *Electrical reversibility* means that the energy taken from a power supply by a circuit is returned to the power supply, ideally to recharge the power supply, with none being dissipated in the resistance of the circuit. This may be accomplished with a variable-voltage power supply to charge and discharge stray capacitance gradually, as described in the appendix to chapter 3. Because $i = C \, dv/dt$, a very low rate of voltage change $dv/dt \approx 0$ implies a very low current $i \approx 0$, and thus negligible power dissipation (P) in circuit series resistance (R) because $P = i^2 R$. Energy (E) or calories is the time integration of power dissipation:

$$E = \int_0^t P dt$$

In practice, the power supply might contain inductance, which delivers energy and then accepts it back, as a resonant circuit does; or it might be a special rechargeable battery that is capable of variable voltage. The details of the power supply are not the main focus in this book. The main goal here is that little or no power be dissipated at the location of the circuit so that circuit heating is minimized, thus permitting greater circuit density.

In an electrically reversible circuit, all charging and discharging of stray capacitance must be slow and controlled to avoid heat dissipation; moreover, leakage conductance must be zero. In the limit of very slow charging, such a circuit is termed *asymptotically adiabatic*, meaning that energy dissipation approaches zero as the rate of charge and charging time increase. Instead of asymptotically adiabatic, *approximately adiabatic* is a more accurate term since any real-world circuit is integrated with materials, and thus is expected to have leakage conductance, albeit small. Practical circuit engineers use the term adiabatic for both asymptotically adiabatic and approximately adiabatic, relying on context to clarify academic detail.

Neurons are modeled to be adiabatic and are superior to solid-state devices in terms of flexibility, memory efficiency, and miniaturization, but neurons currently are unavailable for man-made machines. Therefore, our focus will be on CMOS technology. CMOS will be applied to be electrically reversible so as to approach the efficiency of neurons as computing elements in the human cognitive system.

Looking ahead to examples of electrically reversible gates, SCRL (split-level charge recovery logic) is presented in the appendix to this chapter. Like ordinary CMOS logic gates, SCRL operates from input to output such that the inputs cannot be determined from the outputs. That is, an output does not imply a particular input, but rather a range of inputs, as explained using the AND gate below. Yet SCRL in the limit of slow clocking and low leakage conductance is very much electrically reversible and thus is adiabatic. Unfortunately, when SCRL works with external memory such as pipelining as suggested by its inventors, SCRL is no longer adiabatic. The possibility of a sudden change in capacitor voltage crops up, very definitely dissipative, possibly causing a capacitor to explode in extreme cases.

Returning to conventional CMOS logic, the AND gate has two inputs and one output, as shown in Figure 7-5. N- and P-channel metal–oxide semiconductor field-effect transistors (MOSFETs) go into a CMOS gate. CMOS is the dominant technology today partly because it consumes practically no power while standing by with no changes in the input signals. The fact that MOSFETs are submicron sized, cheap to manufacture, and easy to apply are also factors in its overwhelming success. The CMOS gate for AND computes the following Boolean equation (George Boole, 1815–1864):

$$C = A \cdot B$$

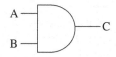

FIGURE 7-5 AND gate symbol.

A and *B* are logical inputs and *C* is an output. The AND gate is not electrically reversible, not so much because it operates only one way from input to output, but mainly because CMOS uses significant power while switching between logic levels. This adds up to undesirable heating.

Reciprocity

Reciprocity is a circuit property that applies to circuits and circuit elements. Many linear components in circuits, such as resistors and capacitors, are bidirectional (or reciprocal); combinational gates like the AND gate above are not. One cannot apply a signal to the output and expect to generate inputs. By forcing an arbitrary voltage to the output of an AND gate, you will only succeed in burning out the gate. If *C* is 0, for example, it is impossible to determine whether *A* is 0, or *B* is 0, or both are 0. *Logical reversibility*, defined below, is a term for state machines and computers, but applies only with difficulty to logic gates, for which reciprocity is inconceivable.

THE COST OF COMPUTATION

CMOS logic gates require several hundred millivolts to operate reliably, and they require current to charge stray capacitance; typically, they are operated as fast as possible, so they dissipate power. To save power while retaining operating speeds, operating voltages are being pushed lower and lower. But signal voltages have to be significantly higher than thermal noise at room temperature to avoid noise errors. Thermal noise averages about 25.8 mV at 300°C, room temperature, expressed as root mean square (rms); noise peaks are much higher than this. To avoid noise problems, the power supply voltages of modern short-channel CMOS logic is close to 1 V. So a certain amount of heat dissipation is expected.

Since heat is a problem, it might be useful to consider some interesting results from the field of thermodynamics. *Thermodynamics* is a field that investigates heat and energy conservation* for averaged systems of particles but does not attempt to analyze these quantities in terms of a combined effect of individual atoms and molecules.

Thermodynamic Reversibility

Consider first the implications of the second law of thermodynamics in a closed system. A closed system means that *free energy*, which usually means kinetic and potential energy, cannot be given or taken by outside sources. In a closed system the change in entropy ΔS is defined to be the change in free energy ΔF divided by absolute temperature T, that is, $\Delta S = -\Delta F/T$. If free energy

---

* Conservation of energy is the first law of thermodynamics.

decreases (because free energy is dissipated by friction in the form of heat) so that $\Delta F < 0$, the negative sign means that entropy increases. The second law can be stated: Entropy remains constant or increases in a closed system.

Because of the omnipresence of friction in mechanical machines, entropy always increases. Because of this, it is sometimes stated that the second law of thermodynamics is equivalent to the impossibility of inventing a perpetual motion machine. However, when friction is low, as when the Earth rotates about the Sun, motion is the same for a long time, trillions of years. Free energy may change forms, perhaps from kinetic energy to potential energy and back again, as in a pendulum, but without friction, free energy is not dissipated and entropy does not increase.

A machine that changes positions very slowly is defined to be in equilibrium at each point of its operation. This is because friction becomes unimportant for very slow motion. If friction is unimportant, the machine is defined to be *thermodynamically reversible*. A thermodynamically reversible machine may run back to where it started, or it may operate in a cycle without having to add energy. Modeling a machine as thermodynamically reversible is equivalent to modeling an electrical circuit as electrically reversible. Thermodynamically reversible and electrically reversible are really the same thing, except that machines run, while circuits are energized. A circuit can be modeled to be electrically reversible if it is charged and discharged very slowly, so that resistive losses are zero. Mechanical engineers use the term *thermodynamically reversible*, while electrical engineers use the term *electrically reversible*; both imply constant entropy.

We note at this point that both reversible machines and circuits appear to be useless since they are too slow to be of practical value. However, circuits can be redeemed, owing to the fact that they can easily be made to be massively parallel, thanks to integrated-circuit technology. Rolf Landauer (1927–1999), working for IBM (International Business Machines), was among the first to call attention to the second law of thermodynamics as it might apply to computers. *Landauer's principle* can be stated as follows: Each bit of lost information will lead to the release of a given amount of heat equal to $kT \ln(2)$, where kT is related to Boltzmann's constant (k) and absolute temperature (T) as described in earlier chapters. On the other hand, if no information is lost, computation, according to Landauer, can be achieved which is thermodynamically reversible and hence results in no release of heat.

Landauer's principle needs some explanation. If no information is lost, it does not mean that no energy is lost. For example, a desktop computer might be designed to conserve information by saving every piece of data in a backup memory. Unfortunately, all of this backup memory would consume vast amounts of energy. On the other hand, if information is definitely lost, energy will definitely be dissipated under this principle. In the SCRL system above, no energy is lost in the gate itself. But the process of changing the inputs, and hence losing all information about the past inputs, could take energy. A previously true input on the input capacitance might suddenly be made to discharge to a different voltage, or a previously false input might suddenly be made to charge to a different voltage. Sudden charge transfers imply high current spikes and energy loss. If the inputs were stored somewhere, the input charges could be modified slowly without energy dissipation. In this case, however, information would not really be lost since the inputs are stored somewhere.

Landauer's energy is, by the way, an extremely small amount of energy, about 18 meV at room temperature, or 2.8×10^{-21} J (2.8×10^{-6} fJ) for each lost bit. It is less than the average thermal energy of a molecule at room temperature. Landauer's energy is not comparable to any logic gates ever envisioned. To see this clearly, compare CMOS and neuron losses to the Landauer energy per lost bit.

Energy dissipation in CMOS can be estimated as CV^2; a short-channel CMOS gate uses 1 V with a 10-fF load for about 10 fJ per bit. This is very small, but CMOS gates typically use gigahertz clocking rates with billions of bits per second; millions of gates are placed on a chip, so power dissipations of a few joules per second are typical. The energy consumed by neural signals does not count conductive losses in the membrane. Energy deposited in a membrane has been lumped with the energy for cellular maintenance, since this loss occurs at all times in every cell of the body. The exact value of this loss depends heavily on the resultant value of the Nernst voltage across the membrane.

Assume half of 70 mV, or 35 mV, on average, across a membrane during continuous spiking. We have been given a membrane conductance of $0.3 \, \text{mS/cm}^2$; although this value might be high, it probably is a worst case. The resulting net conductance in the soma model was 170 MΩ. Using 35 mV, the power loss is 7.2 pW for the soma. This is for a very simple neuron that neglects the axon and the dendritic arbor.

A neural action can last 100 ms (0.1 s), during which time the energy to the membrane is 7.2 pW × 0.1 s = 0.72 pJ for maintenance. Although it is extremely difficult to make comparisons in a meaningful way, the Table 7.1 compares dissipations for a single CMOS gate operating at 1 billion bits per second (1 Gb/s) and 1 billion neurons operating in parallel. Figure 7-6 places this information in a graph; decibels (dB) = 20 $\log_{10}(P/2.8 \times 10^{-12})$. CMOS generally operates at a very high clock rate in a serial fashion, while neurons generally operate at a very low rate in a massively parallel fashion.

TABLE 7-1 Energies Lost per Bit and Power at 1 Gb/s

	Energy/Loss (J/bit)	Power (W)
Landauer	2.8×10^{-21}	2.8×10^{-12}
One CMOS gate	1×10^{-14}	1×10^{-5}
Neural maintenance (billion neurons)	0.72×10^{-12}	0.72×10^{-3}
Neural logic signals (billion neurons)	≈ 0	≈ 0

RELATIVE dB

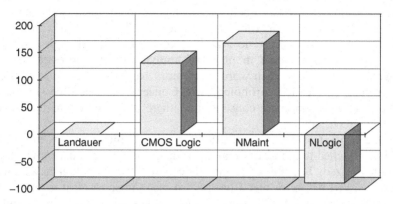

FIGURE 7-6   Estimated energy loss relative to Landauer energy.

Landauer's Energy, Logical Reversibility, and Human Memory

The human memory system has been proposed to be energy efficient. Since lost information is equivalent to dissipated energy, it follows that no information is lost during operations. *Logical reversibility* is a computer term that applies primarily to a computer program. If a computer could run a program in reverse, it would be logically reversible. Logical reversibility suggests that no information is lost, and this opens the possibility of operations without dissipating energy.

Desktop computers are not logically reversible and for a very good reason. They first take input data and then they calculate an output. They cannot take an output and then calculate the input. For example, if the output is the number 16, there are an unlimited number of possibilities for inputs, such as 4×4, $8 + 8$ and so on. A desktop computer does not retain input data values for each of the many steps in a program, so past states are lost forever.

When performing system restoration, however, some computers allow a user to return to a point in the past, such as the beginning of a past day. In this sense a desktop is logically reversible, at least partially. In a desktop computer, logical reversibility for system restoration purposes implies extra memory that is required to reconstruct a past state, and to do this there is an extra cost. Clearly, a logically reversible computer is not necessarily adiabatic, although it has theoretically the potential to be so.

In some ways, brain memory is logically reversible. Normally, a person can recall recent memories in either chronological or reverse chronological order; but of course, one sees only those images that have actually been committed to memory. It is very difficult to recall old images going back in time, mainly because the proper cues are difficult to achieve in short-term memory. Although the recollection process might be extremely slow and difficult, it is still possible to recall a sequence of events going back in time, so in this sense brain memory is logically reversible.

The chronological recall phenomenon has led neuroscientists to speculate that memory words are organized as a linked list. The problem with this idea is that memory words have no addresses to be linked, although associating given features might serve in place of applying given addresses. Another thought is that perhaps each word of memory has a time stamp so that each memory can be recalled chronologically. Concepts such as time stamps and linked lists are engineering concepts and there is no reason to believe that they apply to brains.

In the context of direction of attention in a cognitive system, importance could be attached to a memory search for memories in the order in which they were memorized. The index of importance could be made higher for images memorized just before or just after a given recall in short-term memory. This assumes that there is a way to identify such images, such as the equivalent of a time stamp. Chronologically related images may be presented and accepted into short-term memory, but direction of attention could easily jump to something more exciting from the past, ruining the chronological order. But if all goes well, recall could be logically reversible in a strict sense.

Logical reversibility is not a concept that applies well to memorization. A long-term memory cannot be "un-memorized", so memorization is not logically reversible. Nevertheless, the process of memorization does not lose information. Just the opposite, it keeps it practically forever. This book suggests that neural operations lose no information and that human memory is not subject to the Landauer energy per lost bit. This coupled with adiabatic neurons leads to a model that is energy efficient.

To learn more about adiabatic computers there is a need to design, simulate and build electrically reversible circuits that are also logically reversible, as undertaken in Chapter 8. There are motives for doing this other than neuroscience. One reason is that engineers need to minimize heat dissipation to employ a greater number of processors in parallel using only a small, light power supply. Another reason is that an adiabatic computer, although slow, could very well fit into an extremely small volume. There it could perform many tasks at once, in parallel, solving specialized problems that would be impossible to solve using ordinary sequential computers.

Comments on Information Loss

Clearing means that a bit of memory is reset to false. Clearing is a common way to initialize a man-made computer. Clearing is logically irreversible, because once cleared, the contents of a cleared cell cannot be reconstructed. Clearing typically dissipates energy, since a logic 1 typically is shorted to a logic 0, thus dissipating energy stored in the stray capacitance of the circuit. Even if the bit of memory is backed up so that no information is lost, clearing a register typically dissipates energy, although theoretically it does not have to.

Short-Term Memory   Much of what comes from the senses enters into short-term memory but is not necessarily saved in long-term memory. Short-term biological memory clears itself in a few seconds, suggesting lost information. Information equals energy—so where does the energy go?

Energy is conjectured to be lost at the site of the sensory inputs. Clearly, energy is dissipated irreversibly in order to create sensory information. The eardrum vibrates and vibrations represent energy. Photons are absorbed by the rods and cones of the eyes, and photons represent energy. In this situation, the energy has already been paid for and so is not dissipated again in short-term memory neurons.

Long-Term Memory   When one memorizes something, long-term biological memory becomes written with information. Assuming a read-only circuit model, long-term memory cannot be erased (initialized back to logic 0), so technically, the ideal model never suffers information loss. The information in any given word appears to be backed up with duplications in the hemispheres, and to some extent with refreshed memories that are nearly identical to the original. So a word of long-term memory might be removed without energy loss, suggesting the possibility that old memories might eventually be cleared for reuse. Unfortunately, reuse is neither convenient nor efficient in the given model, so is assumed impossible. More likely, old unused words of memory are dissolved as a matter of routine maintenance even though calories are expended for such maintenance.

Toggle Memory in Savants and Elsewhere   NOT gates are essential to toggle circuits. NOT functions depend on inhibitor neurotransmitters that attach to regions of dendrites. Neurotransmitter ions hold electronic charge and so hold a certain amount of energy, and there may be other energies associated with the construction of inhibitor ions. They are slow to leave, suggesting that NOT gates stay in place longer than other types of gates. It can be argued that eventually, attached neurotransmitters are lost by thermal agitation, by being repelled by internal positive charge, and by attraction from their home bouton. Assuming that inhibitory ions eventually return to their homes to achieve charge neutrality, energy is not lost after all.

To explain how useful operations might be accomplished in a logically reversible computer, the concept of reversible programming is now introduced.

REVERSIBLE PROGRAMMING

Theoretical Model for Logically Reversible Computing

Consider a computer with equal numbers of inputs and outputs, as shown in Figure 7-7. If every input relates to an output, the internal circuits can be such that information is not lost. In particular, no information will be lost if each

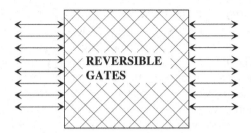

FIGURE 7-7   Equal numbers of bits in and out.

input is transmitted to a designated output via a logically reversible gate. Practical gates have yet to be invented for everyday applications, so the reader need not rush about in an attempt to buy a few. They are called *logically reversible* because they may execute in either of two ways: Operands may flow from input to output or from output to input. Logically reversible computing is not supposed to lose information and thus might open the door to the goal of lossless computing.

Information in neural memory is modeled to be Boolean zeros and ones. For simplicity, imagine that a word of memory has a flag bit (b_0) and N data bits ($b_1 \ldots b_N$). Assume L words up to 2^N words each initialized to a different binary value from zero to $2^N - 1$. It will be shown below how to program logically reversible operations on the contents of each of the L words in parallel. The concept of concurrent reversible operations is novel to many in the field but theoretically, is not difficult. One can perform billions of reversible operations as easily as one, assuming that you have connections to parallel nanoprocessors.

A word of binary information can be expressed as shown in Figure 7-8. This word will be given the ability to test a *selected* set of its own bits; if the bits tested are all true, the word will complement one or more objective bits within itself, but not the bits tested. These have to be disjoint from the objective bits to maintain logical reversibility. Operations like this involve controlled toggling and thus are logically reversible. What we are describing is a state machine that can accomplish steps in a higher-level procedure.

At this point it is helpful to define a *wiring diagram*, diagrams that have been used by reversible computing pioneers such as Charles H. Bennett (1942–   ). A wiring diagram does not involve any wires at all, however; rather, a wiring diagram serves to specify a logically reversible programming system. One may imagine that each line in a wiring diagram is related to a bit position in each of

b_N	$\cdots$					$\cdots$	b_1	b_0

FIGURE 7-8   Word flag bit b_0 and data bits.

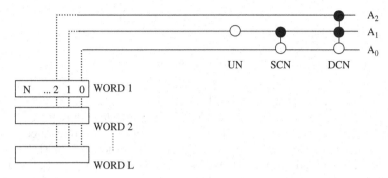

FIGURE 7-9   Relationship between a wiring diagram and bit positions.

the parallel words of memory as suggested in Figure 7-9. There may be any number of words, up to $L = 2^N$, each with different bit patterns. Each word is going to follow the instructions in a wiring diagram.

Shown in Figure 7-9 are the symbols for UN (unconditional NOT), SCN (single-controlled NOT) and DCN (double-controlled NOT); these and a few others such as MCN (multiple-controlled NOT) have been referred to as reversible gates. In the field of digital design the term *gate* suggests something physical that exists, which is a little misleading, because these gates are merely theoretical concepts whose physical implementations continue to be a topic in research. Figure 7-10 illustrates an unconditional NOT (UN). The logically reversible NOT gate is a special gate such that a signal $i_L = i$ on the left is computed on the right as $i_R = i'$, meaning the NOT of i. If i' is applied on the right, i is computed on the left; so this gate is logically reversible. The bubble in a wiring diagram is the symbol for a logically reversible NOT gate.

Figure 7-11 illustrates a single-controlled NOT (SCN). In this case the input $i_L = i$ on the left is simply carried through so that on the right $i_R = i$. The little black dot is a standard symbol for a connection. The $j_L = j$ on the left is complemented only if i is true, or in Boolean terms, if $i = 1$. Another way of expressing what is accomplished is

$$j_R = i \oplus j$$

The symbol $\oplus$ represents the XOR of i with j, that is, XOR(i, j). If i is false, $j_R = j$ and nothing happens. If i is true, $j_R = $ NOT(j), that is j'. Inputs can be applied to the right as readily as to the left, so it is logically reversible. Note that the input i is carried through unchanged. This assures that information is not lost (as it would be in irreversible logic).

$$i_L = i \quad\longrightarrow\!\!\!-\!O\!-\!\!\!\longrightarrow\quad i_R = \text{NOT}(i) = i'$$

FIGURE 7-10   Symbol for an unconditional NOT gate.

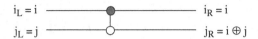

FIGURE 7-11　Symbol for single-controlled NOT.

The idea of controlled NOTs can be extended to any number of controlling lines, creating what may be termed a double-controlled NOT (DCN). The symbol for a double controlled NOT appears in Figure 7-12. A double-controlled NOT computes the AND of i and j, and if the result is true, $k_R = \text{NOT}(k_L)$. The i and j are transmitted without change, so that $i_R = i_L$ and $j_R = j_L$, to ensure reversibility. The double-controlled NOT is also known as the *Toffoli gate* (named for Tommaso Toffoli, Electrical and Computer Engineering Department, Boston University). It is a special case of the multiple-controlled NOT, where effectively the AND is taken of multiple inputs. Multiple-controlled NOTs are useful for detecting a group of inputs that all equal 1.

Simple Applications

As a simple application, imagine many words in a memory system, only one of which contains a code 1, 1 hidden in the x and y positions with x and y known. Along with the code is secret information. Each word can be analyzed concurrently using a DCN. First initialize the flag bit to zero, $b_0 = 0$ in each word. Then apply the DCN. That word that contains the code $x = 1$, $y = 1$, $b_0 = 0$ on the left of the wiring diagram will convert to $x = 1$, $y = 1$, $b_0 = 1$ on the right of the wiring diagram. In other words, the flag is set to 1 to identify the hidden code. The code, along with the hidden information, has been effectively located and may be read.

Using NOT gates and multiple-controlled NOTs, any keyword can be located in one step of the wiring diagram. This simple idea could be extended to an extremely large number of words to identify a code that is well hidden. This results in a solution to the *needle in the haystack problem* if reversible programming can be used. As an example of logically reversible addition, consider $1 + 1$ as shown in Figure 7-13. The binary sum of $1 + 1$ is 10, that is, the modulo-2 sum is zero and the carry is 1. This circuit computes only the modulo-2 sum. Assume that k on the left is initialized to $k_L = 0$. The modulo-2 sum is computed in k_R on the right. For example, if a word had on the left $i_L = 1$, $j_L = 1$, and $k_L = 0$, on the right we have $k_R = i \oplus j = 0$, the correct

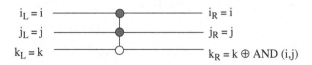

FIGURE 7-12　Symbol for double-controlled NOT.

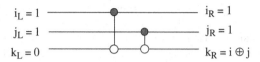

FIGURE 7-13   Reversible modulo 2 addition of $i + j$.

answer. Using wiring diagrams with more sophistication, reversible addition may be extended any number of bits (see Chapter 8) within many words in parallel.

Bits in the foregoing words do not actually move anywhere; they are processed locally. In other words, the processing is data stationary. This avoids delays and the energy loss usually expended for moving data around. In conventional hardware, data-stationary processing is impossible. Data must be moved from mass memory to local memory and then to various registers in a microprocessor; then it must be moved back to local memory and then back to disk memory. This sort of random-access reading and writing is the mainstay of desktop computers and dissipates excessive amounts of power as well as time. Often, a bottleneck occurs on the data bus that drastically slows down a conventional computer. The goal is to eliminate wasted power and bottlenecks, a promising direction.

Irreversible Gates in a Wiring Diagram

Commands such as those above are logically reversible, because the original value of a toggled bit can always be reconstructed: Simply run the commands through the wiring diagram in reverse order. Logically irreversible instructions also are possible theoretically, and occasionally are useful. For example, a bit may test itself, and if true, it toggles itself to false. This is clearing, which is

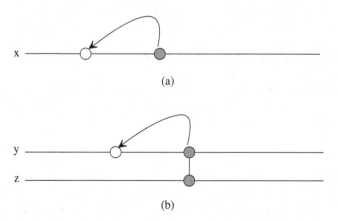

FIGURE 7-14   Logically irreversible gates: (a) reset; (b) conditional reset.

logically irreversible, because there is no history left to compute the bit's original value.

Figure 7-14 illustrates two examples of logically irreversible gates: clearing and conditional reset. *Conditional reset* means that if bits y and z are true, bit y is zeroed. Irreversible gates have no place in reversible computing and are known to dissipate energy, but in practical computing it may be worthwhile to reset a system, particularly at the beginning of a calculation. See the appendix to this chapter for additional information on irreversibility.

CONCLUSIONS

Savant memory systems are modeled for parallel processing by assuming controlled toggling and interneurons for communications within words of memory. Controlled toggling may be applied without loss of information, so Landauer's energy does not apply, creating the possibility of operating without energy dissipation as savants seem to do. Before a system can be adiabatic, however, there is another important requirement. It must be reversible electrically. In practice, this means that all charge used by a circuit must be returned to its source. Conditions for electrical reversibility include slow charging of stray capacitance so that series-resistive losses are negligible, and no trapped unreturned charge.

As a consequence of the Landauer limit, an adiabatic system conserves information, because bits of information are associated with quantities of energy. Not losing information is mistakenly equated with reversibility, although a logically reversible computer could be quite dissipative, depending on its design. More accurately, not losing information permits electrical reversibility. In Chapter 3 we suggested that a system is adiabatic if and only if it is electrically reversible.

In earlier chapters we presented models of electrically reversible neurons and memory system models built up from such neurons. So human memory and memory-based cognition are expected to be adiabatic, as is the logically reversible model for savant memory processing based on controlled toggling. Assuming electrically and logically reversible nanoprocessors, possibly a great many operating in parallel, wiring diagrams were introduced for programming purposes. In Chapter 8 we utilize the adiabatic model of human memory to design electrically and logically reversible nanoprocessors using CMOS as an example technology.

EXERCISES

7-1   Make a graph of the timing diagram for the Boolean variables x, y, and Q for the toggle circuit, shown in Figure E7-1.

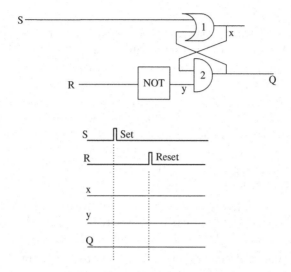

Figure E7-1   Set–reset exercise.

7-2 Consider the friction associated with a coasting bicycle.

(a) What is friction and what does it do?

(b) Is there a way to show that friction is equivalent to lost energy?

7-3 Consider the charging of a capacitor with a power supply that varies from 0 to 100 V dc with a variable-voltage control.

(a) Sketch a circuit diagram.

(b) Exactly how would you increase the voltage to minimize heating in the wires of the circuit? Explain! Provide a graph of the input voltage.

7-4 Wiring diagrams can be programmed to detect a given binary code.

(a) Create a wiring diagram that sets a test bit to be true if a word contains the code 11010011. Use UN or MCN.

(b) What is the decimal value of this byte of code? (It is all right to look up a way to convert binary code to decimal.)

7-5 Assume that DCN or MCN can be used.

(a) Create a wiring diagram using MCN that toggles a test bit to be true if five other bits in the words are true.

(b) Repeat part (a) using only DCN.

7-6 Assuming only UN, SCN, and DCN, it is possible to calculate any Boolean function.

(a) Create a wiring diagram to calculate $A_1 \oplus (A_2 + A_3)$ and place the result in a test bit A_0 that is initialized on the left to be zero.

(b) Test the diagram created in part (a) by using $A_1A_2A_3 = 111$.

7-7   Assuming only UN, SCN, and DCN:

(a) Create a wiring diagram to calculate $A_1 + A_2A_3A_4$ and place the result in a test bit A_0 that is initialized on the left to be zero.

(b) Test the diagram created in part (c) by using $A_1A_2A_3A_4 = 1111$. The result is $A_0 = 1$.

(c) Demonstrate in a wiring diagram that calculation of $A_1 + A_2A_3A_4$ is reversible. In other words, beginning with the output of the wiring diagram diagram on the right, apply $A_0 = 1$ on the right and work to the left to arrive at the original input on the left.

7-8   Show in a wiring diagram how a block of four bits $A_1A_2A_3A_4$ can be moved to positions $A_5A_6A_7A_8$.

7-9   Show in a wiring diagram how a controlled shift is accomplished. In a controlled shift, if a test bit is true, bits $A_1A_2A_3A_4$ are shifted to positions $A_2A_3A_4A_5$; if a test bit is false, no shift is permitted.

7-10   Redraw the SCRL circuit in the appendix to this chapter.

(a) Label the channel resistance 12.5 kΩ in NMOS and 30 kΩ in PMOS; assume that each node has a capacitance of 1.5 fF and that ramp rise and fall times are 1 ms. The system voltage is 1.2 V.

(b) Estimate the energy lost per clock cycle. You may use the loss equations in the appendix to chapter 3.

(c) Estimate the energy lost if P_{DD} and P_{SS} are employed to trap charge to sample gate output. Assume that this charge is never returned.

7-11   Design a three-input NAND gate using SCRL-style circuitry.

7-12   Consider the toggle circuit shown in Figure E7-12. Assume initially that Q is latched to be false (so that Q' is true) and assume that T is false. Trace the operation of briefly pulsing T to be true to cause a toggle.

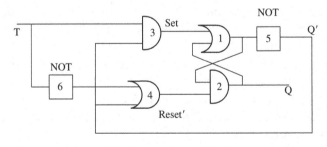

Figure E7-12   Toggle exercise.

7-13 Assume that the delay of each neural gate is 1 ms using the toggle circuit of Figure E7-12.

(a) Determine the maximum allowed width in milliseconds for T.

(b) What will happen if the width of the pulse for T is significantly longer that the maximum width allowed?

(c) What will happen if the width of the pulse for T is too short?

7-14 Provide timing diagrams for two toggle pulses at T using the toggle circuit of Figure E7-12. Show clearly all Boolean variables, including T, Set, Reset', Q', and Q as a function of time.

7-15 Estimate the size of a table that gives the product of two arbitrary numbers, each between 1 and 1 000 000.

7-16 Pi can be expressed as a Leibniz series:

$$\pi = \frac{4}{1} - \frac{4}{3} + \frac{4}{5} - \frac{4}{7} + \frac{4}{9} - \frac{4}{11} \cdots$$

Apply a desktop computer to sum 100 terms.

7-17 Zacharias Dase, a calculational prodigy, calculated pi to 200 decimal places in 1844. He did it mentally using a John Machin-like formula derived in 1706: pi = 4*(4*arctan(.2) − arctan(1/239)). The arctan function may be approximated using arctan$(x) = x − x^3/3 + x^5/5 − x^7/7 + \ldots$.

(a) Test the Machin-like formula to several decimal places using a calculator.

APPENDIX: SPLIT-LEVEL CHARGE RECOVERY LOGIC

Saed Younis and Thomas F. Knight, Jr. devised a style of what has been termed *adiabatic logic*, but more accurately termed *asymptotically adiabatic logic*, published in 1994. The basic idea is to use a variable-voltage power supply, possibly a sine wave of amplitude $V_{DD}/2$ superimposed on a dc voltage of $V_{DD}/2$. It is assumed that the voltage source has a way of storing energy: for example, series inductance. Without dissipating, $V_{DD}(t)$ is supposed to provide power as it approaches a peak, and to recharge with equal power as it approaches a valley. It is significant that power is not dissipated at the locations of the transistors, since the heat released in an integrated-circuit chip is a problem. Example waveforms are shown in Figure A7-1.

Initially, all parts of the circuit are set to $V_{DD}/2$, so that all parts are nonconductive, permitting the inputs to be changed without power consumption. Next, the output gates are slowly turned on by the $P_{DD}(t)$ and $P_{SS}(t)$ signals. Following this, $V_{DD}(t)$ and $V_{SS}(t)$ are applied slowly. The gate

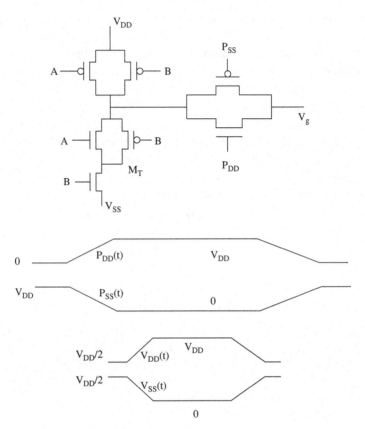

Figure A7-1   SCRL example.

computes the NAND of A and B, that is, the NOT of AND(A,B). Then $V_{DD}(t)$ and $V_{SS}(t)$ are returned to their resting values of $V_{DD}/2$. Finally, $P_{DD}(t)$ and $P_{SS}(t)$ are returned to their initial values.

SCRL is asymptotically adiabatic as clock rise and fall times become longer, and as conductive leakage becomes zero. Note that $P_{DD}(t)$ and $P_{SS}(t)$ must not be returned to their resting values while the gate is active or charge will be trapped at the output V_g. Trapped charge represents energy that can be lost. If a designer wants to depart from an adiabatic system, then $P_{DD}(t)$ and $P_{SS}(t)$ can be manipulated to sample the logic output, and to trap the logic value for use by the next stage.

Note the PMOS labeled M_T. The purpose of this is to prevent trapped charge at the source of M_T. Trapped charge, of course, represents energy that is not returned to the power supply. SCRL logic using more than one stage must be timed so that no energy is dissipated.

In SCRL after the gate operates, all energy at the output of the circuit can be recovered to recharge a power supply. After this is accomplished, the inputs to

SCRL can be changed, assuming that the inputs are generated by another SCRL, whose clocks are appropriately slow in their rise and fall times as well as in their frequency. At some point there are master inputs to SCRL that must be changed. Practical computers constantly change the inputs to blocks of combinational logic such as SCRL. If the master inputs are conventional memory, past inputs are overwritten with new inputs. Thus, information in the old inputs is lost and energy is dissipated. This means that SCRL by itself might be electrically reversible and adiabatic, but SCRL in a computing system is logically irreversible.

For example, P_{DD} and P_{SS} could be deactivated while the gate is active. This would capture a sample of the gate's output. Sampling is a form of memory that might be useful in what is called a *pipelined system*. Pipelining permits the next gate to begin calculations while the present gate is starting a new calculation. Unfortunately, sampling traps charge that usually is dissipated as heat. Thus, sampling is nonadiabatic.

CHAPTER 8

ELECTRICALLY REVERSIBLE NANOPROCESSORS

INTRODUCTION

In this chapter, *reversible* means electrically reversible; this implies a system that does not dissipate energy. Since energy can be related to information, an electrically reversible computer must not lose any information, so it may be designed to be logically reversible. Electrically reversible implies an adiabatic computer. There are plenty of adiabatic gate designs based on charge recovery, such as the SCRL of Chapter 7, but very few adiabatic computer designs.

One fundamental roadblock to the design of adiabatic computers is memory. Memory in the usual sense of RAM generally overwrites old data with new data, thereby losing information; energy is dissipated. The same is true of data registers. But in view of biological memory in the savant, the hypothesis of toggle memory opens new possibilities for hardware design. With care, toggle circuits can be designed to be logically reversible and thus conservative of information; this implies something new, the possibility of an adiabatic computer.

Nanoprocessors based on toggle memory are designed in this chapter, not just functional blocks, but circuits using generic CMOS as an example technology. Translation into other technologies should be easy. Eventually, these designs may be transferred into molecular-sized logic circuits sometimes

Human Memory Modeled with Standard Analog and Digital Circuits:
Inspiration for Man-made Computers, By John Robert Burger
Copyright © 2009 John Wiley & Sons, Inc.

termed *nanobrains*. These devices are experimental, with the goal of vastly reducing the size of computers for gadgets such as microscopic doctors, or factories. They are considered revolutionary. Nanobrains reduce size, but if they lost information, heat will continue to be a problem. Nanobrains are not yet available, so instead, a nanoprocessor is designed herein to be electrically reversible; heat release is minimal, opening the possibility of many nanoprocessors operating in parallel in a small space.

What is presented below is only approximately adiabatic, due to the inevitable leakage that occurs in real-world circuits. Sometimes loss conductance can be neglected, in which case the circuits designed in this chapter are asymptotically adiabatic, meaning that there is arbitrarily low-power dissipation as clock rates are lowered.

Inspired by a variety of biological and physical models, an electrically reversible parallel computer is now designed that is essentially a vector processor. For those unfamiliar with vector processors, we note that a vector processor does more than vector arithmetic. For example, if implemented on a large-enough scale, an electrically reversible parallel computer can help solve NP-complete problems, discussed in Chapter 9. Wiring diagrams are used to guide this logically reversible computer. To begin the process of programming for a logically reversible computer, examples are provided for addition or subtraction, and this applies as well to the parallel addition or subtraction of many operands concurrently.

The necessary power supplies and waveform generators are not included in the following design. Ideally, there would be reversible generators that lend charge and then recover the charge they provided. An example of a reversible generator would be a large high-quality inductance that periodically charges circuit capacitance and then discharges it, as in a resonant high-Q circuit. Reversible power supplies are possible in theory but are beyond the scope of this book. Usually, the power supplies are separate from the nanoprocessors, so even if the power supplies release heat, they can be insulated from the nanoprocessors. Thus they stay cool. The goal is a system that dissipates nearly zero heat at the location of the nanoprocessors, low enough to permit high-density computing in a small package.

A GAUGE FOR CLASSICAL PARALLELISM

A reversible computer that depends on slow charging of stray capacitance is expected to operate at a low clock rate. For example, the simulations below are clocked at about 2 MHz. Depending on how much heat engineers wish to dissipate in the computer, lower clocking frequencies are desirable. They may go down to the kilohertz range as in biological memory to force power dissipation ever closer toward zero. Of course, biological memory is asynchronous and does not require a clock signal, but nevertheless, neurons are slow.

To compensate for slow clocking, massive parallelism is essential. In Chapter 7 we outlined a system in which nanoprocessors operate concurrently. Each nanoprocessor is a word of toggle memory, each capable of working on totally different operands. Assuming technology comparable to what is currently available, a finished product could be similar in size to flash drive memory, but designed to be expanded by adding additional packages. Each package might hold 64 GB (Buslink's USB Hi-Speed 64GB Flash Drive). The approximate volume of each is 2 in^3. Because heat is low in a reversible computer, the packing density may be high. In the spirit of a press release, imagine a large room $40 \times 40 \times 10$ feet densely filled with such packages. The math gives you approximately 10^{18} bytes. A convenient word length might be 10 bytes (80 bits). This gives 10^{17} *memory processor words* operating in parallel, each containing 10 bytes.

A better parameter for size is needed because these numbers are becoming too large to be convenient. A better parameter comes from quantum physics. It is acknowledged that quantum computers do not relate well to classical computers but for a superficial measure, such as the number of parallel processors, consider *qubits*, discussed in Chapter 10. Ideally, a quantum computer holds 2^n numbers that can be related to n qubits.

Qubits are quite mysterious, so they cannot be explained here. All we need to know here is that a quantum computer with about 10^{17} states depends on 56 qubits, since $2^{56} \approx 7.2 \times 10^{16}$. In analogy to this simple statement, a classical computer with about 10^{17} nanoprocessors operating in parallel can be related to 56 *pseudoqubits*. Pseudoqubits do not exist physically and probably will never be confused with qubits, which do exist physically. Pseudoqubits conveniently measure the size of a massively parallel computer of the classical type.

An important consideration is that classical memory technology apparently doubles in density about every two years according to the historically based Moore's law (Gordon E. Moore, 1929–). This is an exponential growth rate. The current number of memory processor words is multiplied by a factor F to predict a future number of memory processor words:

$$F = 2^{\Delta y/2}$$

Note that Δy is number of years into the future. For example, 100 years from now we expect $F = 1.12 \times 10^{15}$, so that the number of nanoprocessors, each with a word of toggle memory, is about $10^{17} \times 10^{15} \approx 10^{32}$. This may be expressed as 106 pseudoqubits. Using assumptions as above, Figure 8-1 predicts numbers of pseudoqubits in a classical computer of the future. We have assumed nanoprocessor toggle memory cells comparable to flash drive memory cells. However, there is likelihood that molecular-sized nanobrains will be available at some point in the near future. This represents revolutionary technology that would greatly increase the slope of the curve in Figure 8-1, implying thousands of classical pseudoqubits.

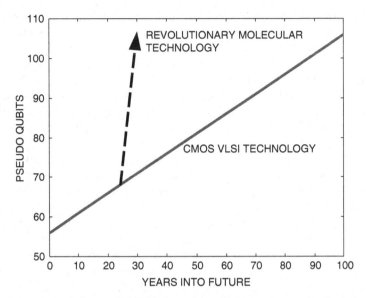

FIGURE 8-1 Massively parallel CMOS trend; revolutionary nanotechnology possibility.

Plans are now presented for an asymptotically adiabatic computer (Burger, U.S. patent 7,242,599, July 10, 2007). The end system has been termed *self-analyzing memory logic* because each word can be directed to test a selected set of bits within itself and subsequently to toggle a disjoint set of destination bits within itself. Computations are data stationary and avoid moving the contents of a word to and from a central processor. At the end of a calculation, memory words with interesting properties are flagged to be shifted out if desired. Initialization and readout circuits are not included.

Both human memory and self-analyzing memory depend on associative processing, but beyond associative processing, the analogy to human memory stops; the building blocks in biological systems are very different from the circuits below, which are expressed using MOSFETs as an example technology. Presented below is the academic version of the patented circuit, presented to show that energy dissipation approaches zero as clock rates approach zero. That is, on paper the system is *asymptotically* adiabatic.

DESIGN RULES FOR ELECTRICAL REVERSIBILITY

To design an adiabatic circuit, there are basic rules:

1. Gate voltages must not change while there is a potential difference between source and drain. The gate voltage must be held fixed at either true or false whenever the channel has a significant potential difference.

2. The potential difference between source and drain must be reduced to zero by appropriate manipulation of the power supply voltages. Only when the potential difference is zero may the gate voltages may be changed.
3. Gate voltages in an adiabatic circuit must change slowly.

These simple rules apply to every transistor in a circuit that is supposed to be adiabatic. We introduce an electrically reversible parallel computer by next considering its architecture. In an attempt to stay on familiar ground in which information cannot be lost, the plan is to implement instructions as given in a wiring diagram. Wiring diagrams were introduced in Chapter 7 as providing programming to a logically reversible computer based on logically reversible gates. In what follows, the computer is logically reversible and follows the usual wiring diagram, which directs a novel implementation of charge recovery logic.

REVERSIBLE SYSTEM ARCHITECTURE

Word layout appears in Figure 8-2 using $N + 1$ bits. Self-analyzing memory words are applied as follows: There will be a global bus 1, known as the *from bus*, which selects a set of bits in each word. There will be a global bus 2, known as the *to bus*, which selects a second set of bits disjoint to the first set, in each word of memory. Circuits targeted by bus 2, the to bus, within each word will be permitted to toggle if and only if all bus 1 bits, those in the from bus, are true. Also, as a trivial subset of the above, the system will be made to execute an unconditional toggle of bits selected in the to bus if there are no bits selected in the from bus.

The word layout uses $N + 1$ bits from 0 to N because bit zero often is reserved as a flag to register the results of testing and toggling on the other N bits. N, by the way, does not have to be a power of 2. Because of nanoprocessor ability to copy bits to new locations within a word, and to implement a Boolean operation on selected word bits within a word, it has Boolean capability. *Boolean capability* means that it is possible to implement a given procedure, such as binary division, within each word of the memory without using a global bus for reading and writing. Millions of such operations, each with differing sets of operands in each word, may occur in parallel.

Self-analyzing memory words may be initialized to a binary count; they have the ability to compute a truth table in parallel for an arbitrary Boolean

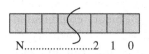

FIGURE 8-2 Word layout.

function. Therefore, by using the flag bit, it is not difficult to locate a particular set of bits that activate a given arbitrary Boolean function. This is essential for those difficult problems in which a really involved Boolean function is known but for which inputs that satisfy the function (to make it true) are not obvious.

Possible Applications

By applying a sequence of from and to operations, a Boolean operation can be implemented on a subset of bits in each word (in parallel) of the memory system. For example, consider a single word with $N = 7$ for the purposes of explaining a self-analyzing memory word. Initialize to $a_7\ a_6\ a_5\ a_4,\ a_3\ a_2\ a_1\ a_0 = 1010,\ 1110$; assume that we want the following Boolean function of six inputs, AND $\{a_7\ (a_6)'a_5\ (a_4)'a_3\ a_2\ a_1\}$; we want to indicate the result by toggling a_0. The procedure is: (1) unconditionally complement a_6 and a_4; (2) toggle a_0 if all bits in positions 1 to 7 are true; and (3) if desired, restore bits 1 to 7 by a second unconditional complement of a_6 and a_4. The result of the operation is $a_0 = 1$ and the register now contains $a_7\ a_6\ a_5\ a_4,\ a_3\ a_2\ a_1\ a_0 = 1010,\ 1111$.

Also of interest is bit-copying. As an example for the purposes of explaining a self-analyzing memory word, assume that a word holds $a_7\ a_6\ a_5\ a_4,\ a_3\ a_2\ a_1\ a_0 = 1010,\ 0000$; the first half of the word, 1010, may be copied into the second half one bit at a time. Since a_7 is 1, toggle a_3 to be 1; since a_6 is 0, a_2 will not toggle; since a_5 is 1, toggle a_1 to 1; since a_4 is 0, a_0 will not toggle. Thus, the result is $a_7\ a_6\ a_5\ a_4,\ a_3\ a_2\ a_1\ a_0 = 1010,\ 1010$, and in effect the first half is copied into the second half.

Self-analyzing memory words might be used in the rapid lookup of data in a table, as in nearly any type of associative memory, but they are intended for much more. Because of their ability to copy bits to new locations, and to implement a Boolean operation on selected word bits, they have Boolean capability. This means that it is possible to implement a given procedure, such as binary division, within each word of the memory without using a global bus for reading and writing. Millions of such operations, each with differing sets of operands in each word, may occur in parallel and may accomplish what has been termed *vector processing*.

Beyond arithmetic, sometimes it happens that the solution to a problem can be expressed as finding an arrangement of bits that satisfies a known Boolean function. To find the solution when N bits are involved, it is possible to use 2^N words, each with $N + 1$ bits. Initialize N registers to binary counts from 0 to $2^N - 1$; initialize bit zero to be 0 in each register. Since the words have Boolean capability, and the Boolean function is known, apply it to each of the N registers; a Boolean function can be calculated as in a truth table. If the function computes to be true, bit zero is toggled from 0 to 1 to serve as a flag. This indicates which of the 2^N binary combinations makes the function true.

The advantage of self-analyzing memory words over prior content-addressable memory (CAM) is that read and write operations using a global bus are unnecessary to change the contents of the words. Prior CAM cannot toggle without reading and writing via a global bus; each toggle operation would require a global bus operation. For an exponentially large number of words, there are going to be an exponentially large number of bus operations. Each bus operation accumulates an increase in time delay and a loss of electrical energy and power. CAM like this cannot handle an exponentially large number of bus operations, and would perform extremely poorly under such conditions.

Self-analyzing memory words need to be initialized to hold binary information. One option for initialization is a system of multiwrite as typically used in historical CAM. This requires the addition of a data-input bus that would be used only for initialization and would not be used during processing, assuming that one needs to avoid inefficiency. Alternatively, build-in transistors (not shown) can be used to set and clear the bits in each word and to initialize each word to a unique binary count.

After a processing procedure, the desired results might need to be read. One option is a system of multiread as in prior CAM. Many applications do not need the entire word, so in such applications only a small subset of a word is brought out. This requires a data-output bus that would be used only to provide the final result and would not be used during processing, to avoid inefficiency. Alternatively, as in prior CAM, the word buses can be employed directly. For example, the locations of true word lines could be the information of interest. This location can be determined by judiciously capturing bus truth values, without attempting readout of memory.

The electronics for each word is specified to be electrically reversible; that is, approximately zero power will be dissipated at the location of the subject circuit. This implies a system in which no information is lost, a situation that has been indicated as a logically reversible computer. Required for electrical reversibility are: slow increases and decreases in power supply voltages, and negligible shunt conductance between nodes that have a finite voltage.

To minimize power dissipation, power-clocking rates are expected to be below a few megahertz, depending on the technology. Thus, to be useful, this logic must be part of a massively parallel system. The goal is a massively parallel computer, electrically reversible and logically reversible, all of which adds up to a system that is asymptotically adiabatic.

ARCHITECTURE FOR SELF-ANALYZING MEMORY WORDS

Figure 8-3 shows computer architecture–based self-analyzing memory words. Words in each row are numbered from 0 to L; cells in each word are numbered from 0 to N. Each word has a local *word bus* that communicates bits within a word but not to any other words. Only in nonstandard applications would the word buses communicate with other parts of the chip or with the outside world. Typically, they are isolated. Not labeled, to avoid clutter in the diagram, are global signals that come from the outside world and go to *each* bit cell of each

CONTROLS

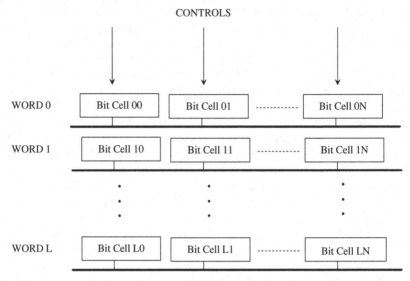

FIGURE 8-3 Architecture using bit cells, also known as self-analyzing memory words.

word. Power supply voltages are V3, V4, V5, V6, V7, and V8. Power supply voltages are variable and move up and down slowly in a rhythmic fashion to provide and collect charge. Certain voltages need complements: V3′, V4′ (the prime meaning "the complement of").

Control lines make contact with each cell in a given column to communicate control signals. The control signals within a given column are **Pre, Fm**, and **To**, all of which conduct signals one way, from the outside world into the memory system. The **Pre** signal is a precharge signal that is global to all blocks. The **Fm** and **To** signals may differ for each of the $N + 1$ columns. The signal **Pre′** may be derived from **Pre**. Signals derived from **To** are **To′, To$_L$, To$_L'$**, and **C**.

Control signals like this ideally turn on and off slowly to minimize heat generation in the CMOS gate circuitry and power usage back where the signals are generated. In this book we are not too concerned about adiabatic operations in the various signal generators and variable-voltage power supplies. These are assumed to be located in locations where we do not care about energy dissipation. In an attempt at clarity and to highlight control signals in the following diagrams, the rise and fall times of control signals shown below are drawn as steps of Boolean logic. Steps imply current surges and energy dissipation of course. In an adiabatic design, these rise and fall times are assumed to be slow (but the slow rise and fall times are not shown to scale below). Slowness is necessary to avoid energy dissipation in the connecting wires because of current surges. Ordinarily, loses in interconnections usually are not significant compared with what is lost in the channels of MOS transistors, but as transistor loses are lowered drastically, wire loses need to be considered.

Bit Cell Overview

A bit cell as used in Figure 8-3 is, in fact, an electrically reversible self-analyzing memory cell. It is educational, especially for beginners in circuit analysis, to go through the circuit step by step. Figure 8-4 shows the plan for a bit cell. The transmission gate (TG) symbols represent CMOS circuits, as shown in Figure 8-5. The NMOSFET is referenced to ground, the lowest potential in the circuit. The gate of the NMOSFET, pin 4, is conducting when the voltage on pin 4 is above the threshold for conduction, which occurs at a higher voltage. The PMOSFET is referenced to a dc voltage labeled V_{DD}, the highest potential in the circuit. The gate of the PMOSFET, pin 3, is conducting when the voltage on pin 3 is below the threshold for conduction, which occurs at a lower voltage. Having back-to-back complementary MOSFETs like this ensures good conduction in both directions.

The timings of the **Pre** and **Fm** signals are shown in Figure 8-6. The **Fm** signal is the first to go true and the last to go false. Both **Fm** and V_{tog} are steady for the AND gate. The adiabatic AND gate may now be activated in each cell of each word of memory. This is accomplished by energizing V1, whose waveform is shown in Figure 8-6. The AND gate is designed to operate transmission gate 2.

At this point the **Pre** signal for transmission gate 1 (TG1) is applied; this will precharge the bus capacitance C_b using charge from source V2. The AND gate now comes into play. If all V_{tog} selected are true, the bus capacitance does not

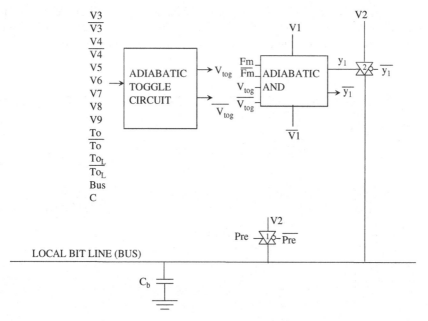

FIGURE 8-4   Self-analyzing memory word cell.

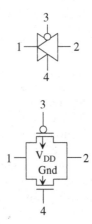

FIGURE 8-5 Transmission gate circuit.

discharge through transmission gate 2 (TG2) as V2 returns to its rest voltage. But if any one of the V_{tog} selected is false, discharge of the bus occurs through TG2. At this point V_{tog} will be either true or false.

If all V_{tog} selected are true, corresponding to source lines in a wiring diagram, the bus stays charged and the bus signal **Bus** stays true. **To** signals are now activated, corresponding to destination lines in a wiring diagram. If the **Bus** is true, an electrically reversible toggle is executed in those bit cells where **To** is true.

Afterward, the **Pre** signal again goes true, to slowly discharge the bus capacitance, completing the execution of a command in the wiring diagram. Not emphasized in this figure is that the control signals **Pre** and **Fm** also

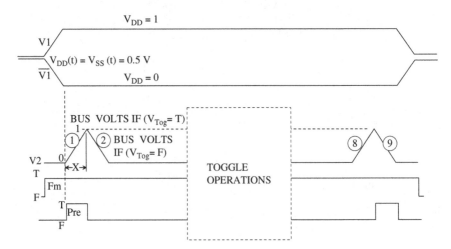

FIGURE 8-6 Pre-and post-toggle operations.

increase and decrease gradually to minimize heating in the interconnecting wires.

Waveforms Needed

The circuit can be understood in detail by referring to the power supply voltages and logic waveforms. The power supply rise and fall times are specified to be t_R, equal to some fraction of a second. Initially, the **Pre** signal goes true for each cell in the system. This permits the bus to be precharged by way of V2. Without loss of generality, a 1-V power supply is assumed. In the region labeled 1 in the timing diagram of Figure 8-6, the bus power supply voltage V2 moves from 0 to 1. Since **Pre** is true, the word bus charges to 1 V through TG1 which occurs in each cell of each word. At the end of region 1, **Pre** goes low.

The goal of the adiabatic AND gate in Figure 8-4 is to implement the following in each cell:

$$y_1 = \mathbf{Fm}\, \mathbf{V}'_{tog}$$

$\mathbf{V}'_{tog}$ is the complement of $\mathbf{V}_{tog}$, properly drawn as $\overline{\mathbf{V}_{tog}}$ in the figure. Consequently, if **Fm** is true and $\mathbf{V}_{tog}$ is false, the desired result is that y_1 is true while y_1' is false. The AND gate is designed as in Figure 8-7. It works using split-level charge recovery, similar to SCRL (discussed in Chapter 7). At rest, while **Fm** is low, the voltage V1 and its complement will be about 0.5 V in this system, so the output will also be 0.5 V. Output-level shifting is necessary to interface to a transmission gate (TG). The voltage sources shown in series with the outputs assure that the N channel (y_1) is cut off and that the P channel (y_1')

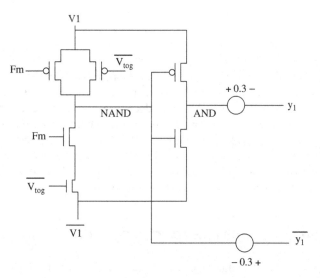

FIGURE 8-7 AND gate with output-level shifting to drive a TG.

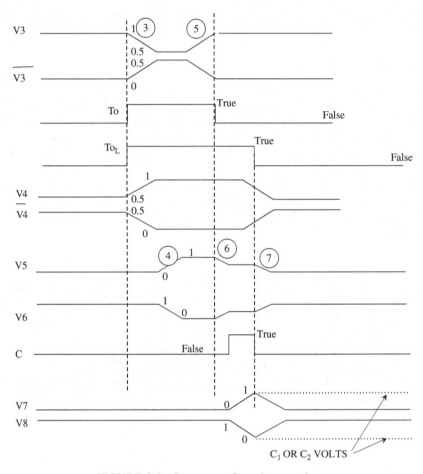

FIGURE 8-8 Summary of toggle operations.

is also cut off. Noise margins suffer a little because the maximum voltages are only 1 V. This is not a fundamental problem; the N channel must turn on with 0.7 V and the P channel with 0.3 V (the ideal threshold will be at 0.5 V).

Return now to region 2 in Figure 8-6. Bus capacitance discharges through TG2 if and only if V_{tog} is false while **Fm** is true. Otherwise, charge is stored in C_b. The **Bus** voltage level is held in C_b for a time until V2 again goes high. In one or more different cells of each word of the memory, **To** and **To$_L$** go high to select candidate cells for toggling as shown in Figure 8-8.

ELECTRICALLY REVERSIBLE TOGGLE CIRCUIT

To and **To$_L$** are control signals from an "outside world" controller unit. V3, V5, and V6 are Power supply voltages that have to be properly sequenced with **To**;

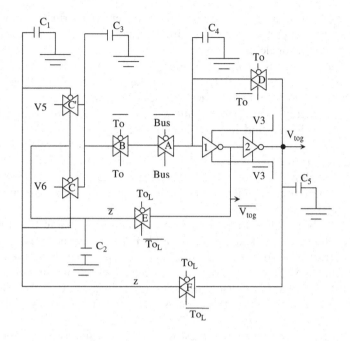

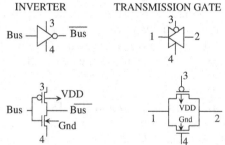

FIGURE 8-9   Toggle circuit.

V3, V5, and V6 move slowly between true and false (and false to true) to maintain an adiabatic toggle circuit. The **BUS** signal is assumed true. V_{tog} will begin a toggle in a controlled way between logic values as soon as **To** goes true. Figure 8-9 shows an electrically reversible toggle circuit.

Operations to Begin an Adiabatic Toggle

Inverters 1 and 2 and transmission gate D (TG-D) constitute a latch. The inverters work using split-level charge recovery similar to SCRL (Chapter 7). In this assumed 1-V maximum system, the latch goes inactive when both V3 and its complement move to 0.5; this is region 3 in the waveform diagram

(Figure 8-8). Prior to a toggle operation the inverters are normally active; V3 is 1V and its complement is zero. They are gradually shut down when **To** goes true, just before a toggle is executed.

To is a control signal from the outside world that goes true when a toggle is needed. **To** going true cuts off the signal through TG-D. When **To** goes true, **To$_L$** also goes true. Prior to this **To$_L$** is false, which enables TG-E and TG-F. The voltages in stray capacitance C_1 and C_2 will follow **V$_{tog}$** or its complement. To begin a toggle, V3 and its complement are reduced to 0.5 V in order to recover the charge in stray capacitance C_5 associated with the inverter outputs. The two inverters are inactivated. **V$_{tog}$** is temporarily 0.5 V. This does not harm the AND gate, however, because the AND gate is not allowed to be active in those cells where toggling might occur (the **Fm** and **To** signals are applied to different cells).

C_3 and C_4 begin by holding a voltage equal to **V$_{tog}$**. These two values of stray capacitance are linked by TG-A and TG-B as soon as **To** goes true and **Bus** is true. The voltage in C_3 and C_4 is now reversed using the external variable voltages V5 and V6. These may be seen slowly changing logic levels in region 4 of Figure 8-8. If **V$_{tog}$** was true, V6 is applied via TG-C; if **V$_{tog}$** was false, V5 is applied via TG-C'. At the conclusion, the voltages of C_3 and C_4 are flipped.

Next, V3 and its complement are restored, as shown in region 5 of Figure 8-8. After this, **To** is returned to false. This latches the new state of **V$_{tog}$** in inverters 1 and 2. Figure 8-10 summarizes the waveforms involved up to this point.

A certain amount of housekeeping is necessary to achieve an electrically reversible circuit. The first goal is to remove the charge that is trapped on C_3.

Judicious Waveform Circuit to Avoid Sudden Discharge of C$_3$ Assuming that **V$_{tog}$** was originally true, the state of C_3 was moved to *false* by V6, which moved from true to false. After **To** goes false again, **V$_{tog}$** equal false is latched. But after **To** goes false, C_3 continues to follow V6, which now reverses and begins to go back to true. Eventually, **To$_L$** will move back to false, so that C_3 is connected to V5. Extreme care is required to avoid a sudden discharge of capacitor C_3 into V5 when **To$_L$** switches back to false.

When **To$_L$** goes false, a **V$_{tog}$** = 0 signal is applied to the transmission gate labeled C'. This will apply V5 directly to C_3 as V5 *is going false*. If **To$_L$** switches at the wrong time, when V5 does not equal V6, energy in C_3 will be dissipated. To avoid this, **To$_L$** is made to switch false at a halfway point where V5 and V6 have equal voltages of 0.5 V. Then C_3 experiences a continuous change of voltage; the final voltage of C_3 goes false, as required. Figure 8-11 indicates the resulting continuous waveform for the voltage on stray capacitance C_3. A little "hill" results, but the rate of change of the voltage is low, so currents are low and electrical reversibility is maintained. Next, some cleanup is required for the charges left in C_1 and C_2.

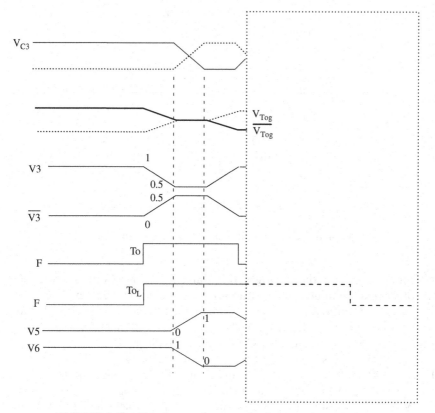

FIGURE 8-10   Toggle waveforms to begin a toggle operation.

Special Circuit to Avoid Sudden C_1 and C_2 Discharge   If To_L is moved to low, the states of C_1 and V_{tog} are opposite and could result in a dissipative discharge. A similar problem could occur in C_2. A special charging circuit can be applied to change the voltage of these capacitors to avoid sudden discharge. This must be accomplished before To_L goes low. While the application is working, the power supply system is going to hold V5 and V6 to be equal until both C_1 and C_2 are corrected.

The special charging circuit is shown in Figure 8-12. Its purpose is to change the voltages of C_1 and C_2 in a controlled manner. This circuit requires the additional control signal **C** and additional power supply voltages V7 and V8 from the outside world. The control signal **C** is used to change the states of C_1 and C_2. If **C** is true and if **Bus** is true, and if V_{tog} is currently true, C_1 can be brought true by switching it to V7; meanwhile C_2 is switched to V8. On the other hand, if V_{tog} is currently false while **C** is true and **Bus** is true, C_1 can be brought false by switching it to V8; meanwhile, C_2 is switched to V7. The

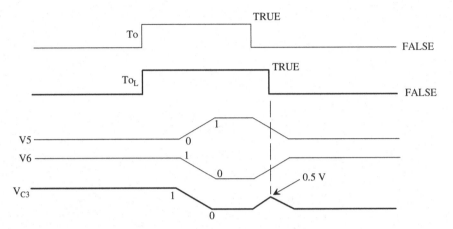

FIGURE 8-11   Continuous voltage waveform in C_3.

sought-after result is that voltages on C_1 and C_2 change from one extreme to the other in a continuous way without current surges and energy dissipation.

The NAND gates are activated before they are needed and deactivated after they are no longer needed using voltage V9 and its complement (not shown). Figure 8-13 shows a typical SCRL gate circuit with three inputs.

The NOT gate is special in that level shifting is used for the output (see Figure 8-14). A dc voltage source is placed in series with the outputs as shown. As with the AND gate above, noise margins suffer a little because there is only a 1-V maximum, but this is not a fundamental problem and short-channel CMOS is expected to work adequately.

This completes the description of the electrically reversible toggle circuit. The use of a NAND gate subcircuit for C_1 and C_2 uses precious floor space to eliminate a loss that is not very significant in practice. However, being able to claim an asymptotically adiabatic circuit is significant academically.

Operations to Conclude an Adiabatic Toggle

The power supply voltage V4 used to provide the complement of the **Bus** signal can now be safely deactivated (returned to 0.5 V), as shown in Figure 8-8. Note that if none of the **Fm** are true, the bus remains charged; in this case, toggling is unconditional in those bit cells where **To** is true.

At the end of a cycle for cell processing, V2 again goes high in region 8, shown in Figure 8-6; if **Fm** is true and the V_{tog} selected are false, the word bus follows V2 up to 1V. If the V_{tog} selected is true, the word bus is already near 1V at the end of region 8. The **Pre** signal again goes true at the beginning of region 9, thus permitting an unconditional controlled discharge of the word bus. V2, the source of charge for the bus, is moved down to zero in region 9, thus leaving the bus with no charge, ready for another operation.

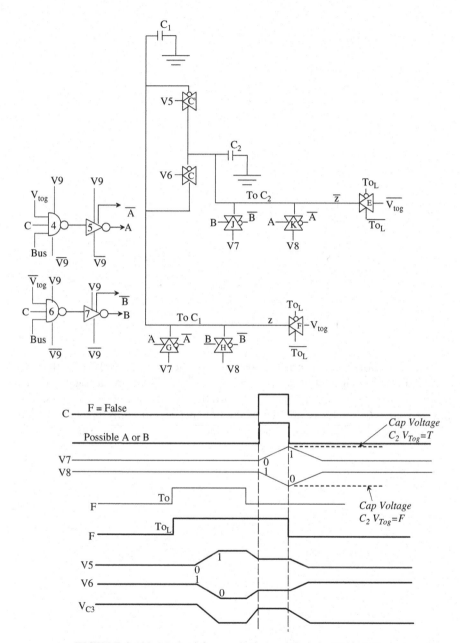

FIGURE 8-12 Method for correcting voltages in C_1 and C_2.

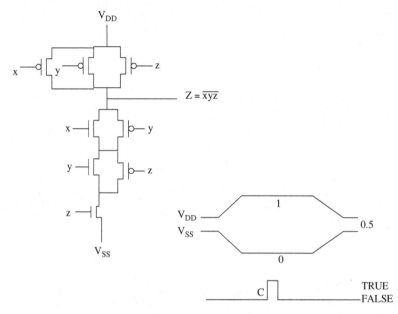

FIGURE 8-13 Three-input NAND gate.

It may be noted that if one attempts to use the same bit cell for both a **Fm** and a **To**, there will be a little problem. When V_{tog} is true and a toggle occurs, there will be a sudden discharge of the word bus, resulting in a release of heat. It has proved difficult to avoid this problem. Theoretical analysis suggests that self-toggling like this is not logically reversible and is in the same class of

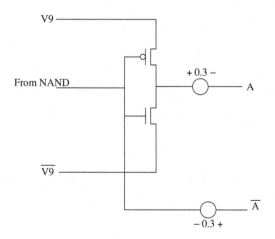

FIGURE 8-14 Level shifting to drive a transmission gate.

operations as clearing a flip-flop. In other words, information is lost, and therefore energy is lost. For this reason the **Fm** bits or cells must be selected to be disjoint with the **To** bits or cells.

Simulation Results

Simulated capacitor voltages are shown in Figure 8-15. Simulations assume short-channel 50-nm CMOS technology. C_1 (Figure 8-9) holds the sampled original value of V_{tog} until operations are completed. In this simulation, C_1 holds logic zero. At some point the voltage on C_1 is moved up to logic true. Simulation shows some drift in the voltage on C_1 prior to the move to logic true. The drift up from zero for the voltage on C_1 is due partly to charge coupling via capacitance in transmission gates C and C' and partly from a small amount of leakage conductance in TG-F, which has voltage across its channels, so may leak a small amount of charge. The effects of leakage could be reduced by increasing capacitance in C_1 and C_2 and by increasing channel resistance in transmission gates E and F. This is a simulation of the extraordinary switching waveforms shown in Figure 8-12. The voltage on C_3 is shown making a smooth uneventful move to logic true, and then down to half voltage, and then back to logic true. This is a simulation of the judicious waveform circuit involving V5, V6, and To_L.

Comments on Power Supplies for C_1, C_2, and C_3

C₁ and C₂ Consider the charge supplied by V7 and V8. During a time while V5 is held to equal V6, capacitors C_1 and C_2 are made to change voltage levels. The energy in C_1 originally came from V7 but is returned to V8; or it could have come from V8 and be returned to V7. For a single toggle, or any odd number of

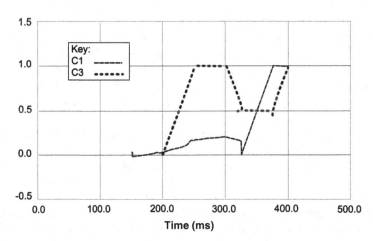

FIGURE 8-15 Simulation result for C_1 and C_3 voltages (all capacitors are 1 fF). © 2006 BGleason Design & Illustration, LLC.

toggles, charge is moved from V7 or V8 and supplied to the capacitance. For two toggles, or any even number of toggles, equal charge is returned to V7 and V8. This may be a consideration when designing power supplies for V7 and V8 for use in the special switching circuit.

C_3 The complementary transmission gates C and C' above accomplish rule 1 for adiabatic design by switching only when V5 equals V6. This permits the voltage on capacitor C_3 to be continuous. For a single toggle, or any odd number of toggles, one half the charges taken from V6 are returned to V5; or one-half the charges taken from V5 are returned to V6. For two toggles, or any even number of toggles, equal charges are returned to V5 and V6. This may be a consideration when designing power supplies for V5 and V6 for use in a judicious waveform circuit.

REVERSIBLE ADDITION PROGRAMMING EXAMPLE

Designed above is a general-purpose programmable computer that is electrically and logically reversible, ready to be constructed. Below we illustrate a basic example of reversible computer programming as educational to those who need to understand computers of the future.

Reversible Modulo 2 Sum for 3 Bits

A reversible adder has two major components: a block that computes the sum and a block that computes the carry. The sum may be computed logically as $a \oplus b \oplus c$, where $\oplus$ means XOR. The sum block receives the binary inputs a, b, and c that are to undergo reversible addition and in a logically reversible step produces the binary outputs a, b, a + b + c, where + in this context means modulo 2 addition, symbolized as in Figure 8-16. This is modulo 2 addition of 3 bits (the carry is ignored). Note the tricky use of c as initialization for toggling based on $a \oplus b$. For example, let a, b, c = 0, 1, 1; then, out of the right side comes 0, 1, 0. Zero is the modulo 2 sum of the 3 bits 0 + 1 + 1. If a, b, c = 1, 1, 1 then, out of the right side comes 1, 1, 1. One is the modulo 2 sum of 1 + 1 + 1.

In reversible programming, as in ordinary sequential machine programming, it is necessary to specify the direction of the programming. The bar in the block symbol indicates the direction of the programming, from left to right. Operations execute in order from left to right. The calculation is logically reversible. Entering 0, 1, 0 on the right, for example, and executing gates in order from right to left results in 0, 1, 1 on the left. The calculation is designed to be reversible for any possible outputs implying that no information is lost. The wiring diagram in Figure 8-16 is reversible because reversible operations are used.

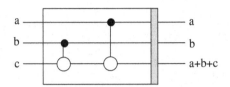

FIGURE 8-16   Reversible sum generation.

Reversible Carry Generator for Two 3-Bit Adders

The carry may be computed as $c_{in0}a + c_{in0}b + ab$, where + in this context means OR. This is known in elementary digital design as the *2-out-of-3 function*, identified in Chapter 5 to be a special case of an indicator that shows a need to learn. The three input bits are c_{in0}, the carry-into operation, and a, b. The carry may be generated using the plan shown in Figure 8-17. If c_{in0} is zero, while a and b are 1 and 1, the inputs on the left are 0, 1, 1, 0. The carry-out is $c_1 = 1$ since $0 + 1 + 1$ equals 0 with $c_1 = 1$. It can be verified by tracing from left to right that the outputs on the right are 0, 1, 1, 1 as required.

Next we show an example of adding two unsigned numbers, each with 3 bits: an addend of 7 added to an augend of 7 (in binary $111 + 111$).

$$
\begin{array}{cccc}
(1 & 1 & 1) & \\
& 1 & 1 & 1 \\
+\,1 & 1 & 1 & \\
\hline
1 & 1 & 1 & 0
\end{array}
$$

The carries are shown in parentheses. These numbers correspond to adding 7 to 7 and arriving at a sum of 14 (1110 in binary). Figure 8-18 shows how this can be done using reversible programming. This wiring diagram is simpler that it looks. Operations are executed one at a time from left to right. First the carries are generated; sums can then be calculated beginning in the most significant place. The zero inputs to each carry block are *scratchpad lines* for the

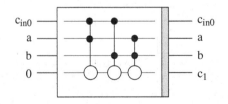

FIGURE 8-17   Reversible carry generation.

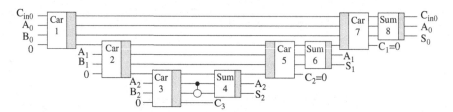

FIGURE 8-18 Reversible 3-bit adder.

calculation. As the sums are computed, the carry programming is reversed to restore the scratchpad lines to zero. Interested readers can trace the result of adding 7 + 7. Let $C_{in0} = 0$; A_0, A_1, A_2 = 1, 1, 1; B_0, B_1, B_2 = 1, 1, 1. The result obtained in this test case is C_3, S_2, S_1, S_0 = 1, 1, 1, 0.

A symbol for 3-bit addition is shown in Figure 8-19, where the input and output lines have been reorganized for convenience. The signals to port A go through unchanged and ensure logical reversibility; the signals to ports A and B are added; the sum appears at port S. The lines into and out of the port labeled "Scratch" are scratchpad lines that provide work space for the various operations. The carry-out (C_3) is also the most significant bit in the case of unsigned addition. The adder symbol works from left to right, as indicated by the bar on the right. It is easy to reverse the addition, to go from right to left merely by applying signals on the right. This approach is extended easily to more bits by using more lines.

There are other ways to accomplish reversible addition, such as computing a sum and a carry one bit at a time as is usually done in manual calculations. This process could be transferred to a wiring diagram, and the result is logically reversible, as long as there are no operations in which a bit zeros itself. The "Scratch" lines in Figure 8-19 were all restored to zero except for the

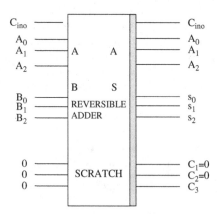

FIGURE 8-19 Reversible 3 bit adder.

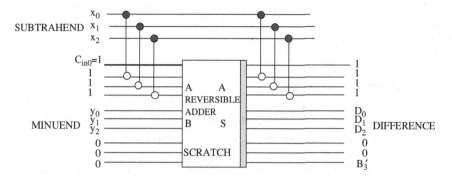

FIGURE 8-20 Reversible 3-bit subtractor.

carry-out C_3 which must be retained to ensure logical reversibility. It is wise to restore scratchpad outputs to their original values so that they are ready for the next stage of programming.

REVERSIBLE SUBTRACTION PROGRAMMING EXAMPLE

In subtraction, a difference can be calculated by taking the *two's complement* of the subtrahend and adding it to the minuend. A two's complement is equivalent to complementing each bit of the subtrahend and then adding 1. Figure 8-20 shows a plan for reversible 3-bit subtraction. The inputs to port A of the adder are initialized to be all 1; the inputs to port A are inverted if a corresponding bit in the subtrahend is 1. This accomplishes a bitwise complement of the subtrahend as applied to port A. The two's complement results by adding 1 ($C_{in0} = 1$). The subtraction of the subtrahend from the minuend appears at the sum (S) port and is, in fact, the difference. The scratch lines are restored to zero except for the complement of the borrow-out, B'_3, whose uses include serving to indicate when a result is negative. This approach to reversible subtraction is easily extended to more bits using more lines. The two's-complement method is not the only approach to reversible subtraction that is available. For example, one could proceed as done for subtraction by hand, calculating differences and borrows one bit at a time.

CONCLUSIONS

This is an original, an electrically reversible machine in which no information is lost and also logically reversible. Circuits as described here may be tedious to those unfamiliar with charge recovery logic, but the design is quite straightforward. Tracing through the circuitry above is an education in how to accomplish electrically reversible circuit design. In keeping with practical technology,

CMOS was chosen as the presentation technology because it is readily available, compact, and inexpensive. To accomplish adiabatic design, each MOSFET must satisfy basic rules:

1. Gate voltages must not change while there is a potential difference between source and drain.
2. The potential difference between source and drain must be reduced to zero by appropriate manipulation of the power supply voltages.
3. Gate voltages in an adiabatic circuit must change slowly.

These simple rules pave the way to electrically reversible nanoprocessors based on toggle memory and to an electrically reversible parallel computer.

Adiabatic computers as designed in this chapter can be programmed with the aid of a wiring diagram, such as those shown for addition and subtraction. Such arithmetic may occur simultaneously in a large number of memory words in parallel, and so accomplishes multidimensional vector addition and subtraction. Words of toggle memory in nanoprocessors may be initialized with differing operands of interest, depending on what is needed. The number of lines $N + 1$ used in a wiring diagram is the same as the number of bits $N + 1$ in each word, N working bits plus a flag bit. Aside from a flag bit, the number of unique initializations of N working bits is 2^N. The number of nanoprocessors L should not exceed this value if one is interested in unique initializations. All steps of a calculation, including the results, are contained within the nanoprocessor itself.

The adiabatic computer awaits practical applications. There is the possibility of exotic calculations involving massive parallelism not possible by any other means. But more fundamentally, it may be possible to have systems that operate for very long durations after an initial charge using minimal outside energy. Longevity is especially helpful in fields such as medical implants and space technology. Low heat releases are absolutely critical to miniaturization.

Beyond such obvious needs, there could develop widespread need for reliable, power-grid independent beacons to guide humans through life, including traffic controls, automated purchasing at supermarkets, and long term security devices. Looking ahead tiny bugbots with artificial intelligence may be the knowledge workers of the world someday. Indeed, they may eventually be packed into a skyscraper by the millions, but only if their design is adiabatic. Slightly more advanced algorithms for adiabatic computing are presented in Chapter 9 as an aid to readers who wish to develop their skills in logically reversible programming using wiring diagrams.

EXERCISES

8-1 List a few possible applications of adiabatic computers as designed in this chapter.

8-2 What do adiabatic computers and human brains have in common?

8-3 Consider a tall stack of words, each with 9 bits; bit zero is initialized to 0 and is a flag bit. In a certain word, a secret code 0011, 1100 exists. This word is buried and lost in a sea of nonordered words. Devise a wiring diagram that will toggle the flag bit to 1 for the occurrence of the secret code. You have just solved a very simple version of the *needle in the haystack problem.*

8-4 Consider adding two unsigned 2-bit numbers by hand. Implement your algorithm in a wiring diagram. Test the design with 10 + 11 to get 101.

8-5 Reversible *signed* addition can be accomplished in a variety of ways. Devise a wiring diagram to accomplish reversible 3-bit signed addition. The leftmost bit of each 3-bit number is assumed to be the sign bit. Test the design with 011 + 111 to get 010 with a carry-out of 1.

8-6 Consider subtracting two unsigned 2-bit numbers by hand. Implement your algorithm in a wiring diagram. Test the design with 11 − 10 to get 01 and no borrow-out.

8-7 Consider words in which a given 4 bits are the first operand, a given 4 bits are the second operand, and one bit is initialized to 0 to be a flag bit. Devise a wiring diagram that can locate operands in a word that add up to an exact power of 2.

8-8 An output bit in a word is initialized to zero while another set of 8 bits hold all possible binary combinations, 255 of them. *A, B, C, D, E, F, G* and *H* are binary variables. Devise a wiring diagram to calculate the

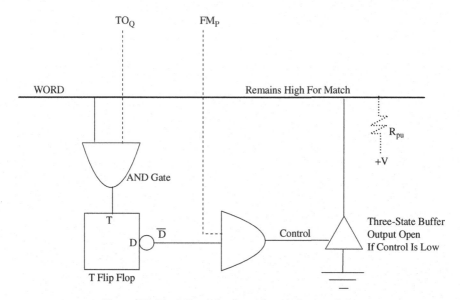

Figure E8-11 Network of small-scale integrations.

following binary function and to place the result in the output bit. Test the diagram for A, B, C, D, E, F, G, $H = 1, 1, 1, 1, 0, 0, 0, 0$ for which $Z = 1$.

$$Z = (A + B)(CD) + (E + F)'(GH)'$$

8-9 If you are a budding electrical engineer, you might have to design adiabatic logic someday.

   (a) State the rules for adiabatic design to arrive at an adiabatic SCRL-NOR gate.

   (b) Design the circuit. Provide a hand-drawn timing diagram that shows how the gate is supposed to operate.

8-10 Simulate your design using practical devices to determine a practical voltage supply waveform that roughly minimizes power dissipation.

8-11 As a budding digital designer, you can implement the logic of self-analyzing memory logic (SAML) using small-scale integrated circuits.

   (a) Apply two AND gates, a T flip-flop, a three-state buffer, and a resistor to implement the logical function of SAML.

   (b) How can unconditional inversion (UN) be accomplished in this implementation?

   (c) Explain UN, SCN, and DCN operations in this implementation.
   (*Hint*: Consider the circuit shown in Figure E8-11.)

CHAPTER 9

MULTIPLICATION, DIVISION, AND HAMILTONIAN CIRCUITS

INTRODUCTION

In this chapter we present example algorithms as expressed in wiring diagrams and intended for a logically reversible computer. Originally inspired by models of human memory and cognition, the programming as expressed in these wiring diagrams applies to a parallel computer in which many nanoprocessors work concurrently. Nanoprocessors are especially small and simple microprocessors based on toggle memory; they were presented in a practical way assuming CMOS technology and VLSI, although the logic may be transferred to better technology as it evolves, such as molecular logic. The end result is assumed to be an electrically and logically reversible system easily programmed using a standard wiring diagram to solve a variety of problems.

By tracing the examples below, an interested reader can learn reversible programming in a wiring diagram. The arithmetic in this chapter differs from the simple addition and subtraction of Chapter 8 in that it employs iteration within a wiring diagram. To accomplish an iterative calculation, a program segment must be designed properly so that is can be replicated adjacent to similar segments as many times as necessary.

Nanoprocessor words must first be loaded with a desired set of operands to be processed in parallel. In an attempt to achieve clarity, in this chapter

Human Memory Modeled with Standard Analog and Digital Circuits:
Inspiration for Man-made Computers, By John Robert Burger
Copyright © 2009 John Wiley & Sons, Inc.

arithmetic is limited to two binary operands in each word of nanoprocessor memory. Binary results for given operands are developed alongside the operands. A flag bit is made true for especially important numerical results, permitting an identification of the nanoprocessor and its operands.

For systematic initializations, such as a unique binary count in each nanoprocessor, a hardware initialization method may be possible for locating inputs that satisfy a given Boolean function. Otherwise, conventional addressing may be assumed for the purposes of initializations. Unfortunately, conventional addressing if used as in conventional RAM or ROM requires a great deal of time and energy in what otherwise is an efficient computation. Conventional addressing uses long-distance buses frequently charged and discharged by bus drivers, releasing much heat. But merely for initialization the extra heat dissipation might be tolerable.

Conventional addressing, with its maze of energy-dissipating, time-consuming wires, is also a way to read out results. Sometimes results are in the form of a simple flag bit within each nanoprocessor. In such cases, conventional addressing can be avoided by serially shifting out flag bits for use by the outside world. Uses of flag bits are:

1. Flag bits can indicate the locations of keywords and associated information in a database.
2. When parallel divisions by integers or prime numbers have zero remainder, a flag bit can indicate the locations of exact factors.
3. When parallel divisions of a given number by each of the possible integers always have a remainder, a flag bit can indicate a prime number.

The systems described in this book are not intended to replace classical computers. Classical high-speed, heat-dissipating computers serve adequately for preprocessing, such as preparing a file of prime numbers. They might also serve for postprocessing, such as doing something interesting with flagged operands.

Consideration is given to an application of wiring diagrams to difficult problems for which the computational time grows geometrically with the number of variables. SAT (satisfiability) problems involving truth tables are easily solved by parallel nanoprocessors as long as the length of the truth table does not exceed the number of available nanoprocessors. In such problems the truth table grows in proportion to 2^n where n represents the number of variables.

As an example of a problem quite different from vector arithmetic, we consider path finding in a graph. Imagine a large graph in which some of the vertices are connected with edges (lines). Beginning at the first vertex, the problem of interest is to follow edges to other vertices, visiting each vertex exactly once, and finally returning home. Such circuits are termed *Hamiltonian circuits*. This problem is difficult because the number of paths available grows in proportion to a factorial of the number of vertices. The question is: How may parallel nanoprocessors assist in locating Hamiltonian circuits? They excel at verifying that a circuit is indeed Hamiltonian, as we shall see below.

An everyday version of the Hamiltonian circuit problem is the *salesman's problem*. Given a list of cities, find the smallest number of miles to visit each city only once, with no backtracking, finally returning home. A solution to the salesman's problem is a closed Hamiltonian circuit with the shortest-possible closed circuit. To solve it, all possible Hamiltonian circuits can be identified and then analyzed to find the shortest path. Algorithms are now presented for standard problems in vector processing: *unsigned multiplication* of operands in parallel and *unsigned division* of operands in parallel.

UNSIGNED MULTIPLICATION

Successive additions could be used to accomplish multiplication, but an add-shift algorithm is far more efficient. To see how the add-shift algorithm works, consider the multiplication of 3-bit numbers diagrammed in Figure 9-1. The *least significant bit* (LSB) of the multiplier is tested, after which the multiplier is shifted right one place. If the LSB is 1, the multiplicand is added into a quantity known as the *partial product* (initially, the partial product is 000). The result is shown at location 1. The partial product is then shifted one place to the right, as at location 2. The process now repeats. The next multiplier bit is also 1, so the multiplicand at location 3 is added to the partial product. The result is at location 4. The partial product is then shifted one place to the right, as at location 5. The process now repeats.

The *most significant bit* (MSB) of the multiplier is 0, so zeros are copied to position 6. The multiplication is now complete: $3 \times 7 = 21$. Add-shift algorithms are easily extended to larger numbers.

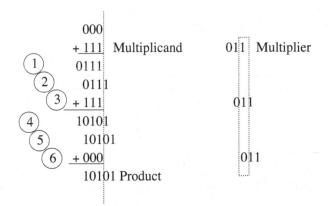

FIGURE 9-1 Add-shift algorithm.

Wiring Diagram for Reversible Parallel Unsigned Multiplication

An add-shift algorithm for 3-bit operands can be transferred to a wiring diagram as in Figure 9-2. This wiring diagram is typical of logically reversible programming. Note that each operation is performed one at a time in an left-to-right sequence. The operations in the lower right are done after all else is done, as suggested by the break (the dashed line). The operations in the lower right are an example of a *logical shift*; they cause the multiplier to shift up. A similar set of operations in the upper right shifts up the partial product. The figure shows one add-shift cycle of the algorithm. In the lower left, the LSB of the multiplier is tested. If the LSB is false, zeros are applied to the A inputs. If the LSB is true, the multiplicand is applied to the A inputs of the reversible adder. The carry-in (C_{in0}) is not used in this case. The new partial product emerging from S is the sum of the inputs to A and the previous partial product, assumed applied at B. After addition, the A inputs are zeroed as shown, in preparation for iteration.

After the addition, a partial product including the carry-out is shifted up in preparation for another cycle of the algorithm. To accomplish iterations of the add-shift algorithm, the Figure 9-2 is replicated as shown in Figure 9-3. Words may be longer than the 21 bits shown; the method is easily extended to larger numbers by using longer words and more lines in the wiring diagram. The result is efficient reversible multiplication, implying that if the resultant product is applied to the output on the left, the original operands can be computed at the input on the right.

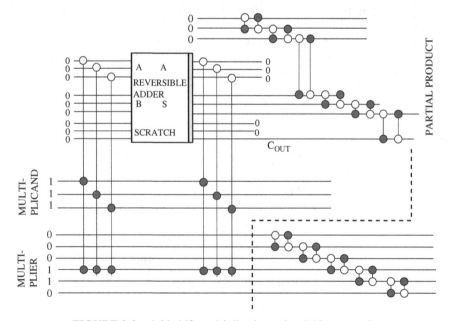

FIGURE 9-2 Add-shift multiplication using 3-bit operands.

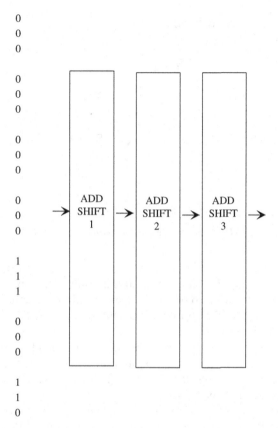

FIGURE 9-3 Iteration of the add-shift algorithm in a wiring diagram.

RESTORING DIVISION

A given integer N represented by n bits may be divided by any integer up to approximately $\sqrt{N}$. If the remainder is zero, the divisor and the resulting quotient are factors of the dividend. Division of a number by another may be accomplished in many ways. The most common method is *restoring division*. It will be seen below that restoring division involves addition and subtraction. Subtraction is accomplished by adding a negative number, so it is convenient to employ sign bits on the left of the binary operands. A 0 indicates a positive number; a 1 indicates a negative number (in two's-complement form).

To demonstrate how restoring division works, Figure 9-4 shows 01111 divided by 011. At step 1 the divisor 011 is to be tried for dividing the first 3 bits of the dividend 011. A computing machine must first negate the divisor and then add it to the first 3 bits of the dividend 011. The negation of the divisor is simply a two's complement, obtained by complementing each bit and then adding 1. The two's complement of the divisor 011 is 101. The two's

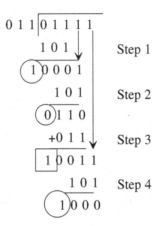

FIGURE 9-4 Restoring division algorithm.

complement is added to the leftmost bits of the dividend as in step 1. If the carry-out of the addition is 1, it means that the result of the operation is zero or positive. Indeed, 011 goes into 011 exactly once with no remainder. The carry-out is equivalent to the first quotient bit and is encircled in Figure 9-4. The process now repeats.

Step 2 is to bring down the next bit of the dividend to form a partial remainder and to add 101 again. In this step the carry-out of the subtraction is 0, which indicates that the result is negative. This carry-out is the next quotient bit and is encircled in Figure 9-4.

Whenever the carry-out is zero, the partial dividend must be *restored*. This involves adding 011 as in step 3. We ignore the carry-out of this addition; it is always 1. The process now repeats.

Step 4 is to bring down the next bit of the dividend. Add 101 again. The remainder is 000 in this case. The entire quotient is built from the circled bits in Figure 9-4 to be 101. The carry within the square is discarded. 15 divided by 3 is 5 with a remainder of zero; in the language of mathematics, Mod(15, 3) = 0.

A small dividend was used for clarity, but the subtract-test algorithm extends in a straightforward way to any number of bits.

Wiring Diagram for Reversible Parallel Restoring Division

Figure 9-5 implements a cycle of calculations for restoring division. Division as in the example above uses 2-bit divisors, but a sign bit is required, so for calculational purposes there are 3 divisor bits. The plan is to compute a two's complement of the divisor and then add the two's complement to the partial dividend as required to accomplish subtraction. The two's complement can be generated as shown in Figure 9-5.

The two's complement of the divisor is obtained by individually complementing each bit of the divisor $(0, x_1, x_0)$ and then adding one. The divisor is assumed

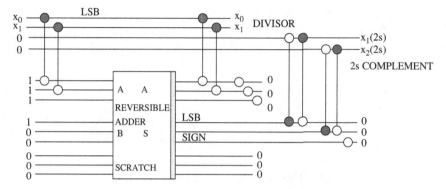

FIGURE 9-5 Two's-complement generator.

to be nonzero and positive. Thus, the negation always has a sign bit of 1. Bitwise complementing is accomplished by the two controlled NOT gates as in the upper left of the figure. This creates the three A-inputs to an adder. On the right of the adder the A-outputs are first restored to 1 and then set to 0 for use in division.

The B-inputs are 0, 0, 1 (with the 1 being in the LSB position). The sum on the right is a two's complement and it always has a negative sign bit since what is being complemented is always a positive number. The S outputs on the right are the sought-after two's complement. This is shifted up for storage in the two's complement lines. In the process, the S outputs are set to zero. The carry-out of the adder is always 0 because the result is always negative; scratch lines remain zero.

The two's complement of the divisor is computed only once, and then is carried through for use as needed. The sign of the two's complement is inferred to be 1 (as it would be for a negative number). All lines are ready for a stage of restoring division.

Example: 4-Bit Dividend and 2-Bit Divisor

A 4-bit dividend and a sign bit: $0y_3y_2y_1y_0$, for example, 0 1 1 1 1, is to be divided by a 2-bit divisor and a sign bit: $0x_1x_0$, for example, 011. Generalization to other numbers is uncomplicated once this simple case is understood. The first partial dividend is on the lines applied to the B-inputs of the adder, the lines denoted by 0, $y(n)$, and $y(n-1)$ in Figure 9-6.

In Figure 9-7, the divisor is denoted by x_1, x_0. The two's complement is labeled $2s(x_1)$, $2s(x_0)$. The two's complement is copied to the A-inputs of adder 1 by the two controlled NOT gates on the left.

Case I: No Restoration (Carry-Out = 1) β_1 is a point where the carry-out emerges. At β_1, a 1 emerges from adder 1 and is copied to the quotient line; then after point β_1, it is converted to zero by an unconditional NOT. The

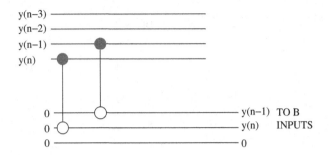

FIGURE 9-6   Initializing the *B* inputs.

double-controlled NOT ensures that at α the *A*-inputs are set to zero. At β₂ the scratch line to the second adder is returned to zero. Zeros are added in adder 2, which is equivalent to no restoration. A zero emerges at β₃ since only 0's are added in adder 2. It remains 0 at β₄.

Case II: Restoration Required (Carry-Out = 0) β_1 is a point where the carry-out emerges. If the result of the subtraction is negative, the carry-out at point β_1 is zero. A zero at β_1 is copied to an output line for the first quotient bit.

Restoring the Partial Dividend   The two's complements at the *A*-output is converted back to 0, 0, 0 at α. Next, the 0 at β_1 is converted to 1 with an unconditional NOT gate. This permits the divisor to be copied to input *A* of the second adder. These lines receive a copy of x_1, x_0 using the double-controlled NOTs shown to the right of α. The scratch lines to the second adder are zeroed. In the second adder the divisor is added back to the partial dividend to restore the partial dividend.

Preparing the Output   The output of the second adder is now prepared for another cycle of the algorithm. The *A*-output is restored to 1, 0, 0 using the double-controlled NOTs shown in the upper right of Figure 9-7.

- *Shifting.* The entire partial dividend is shifted down. At point γ, the next bit of the dividend, the one that has not been used, is shifted down to the line labeled div0, that is, div0 = $y(n-2)$. This is equivalent to bringing down the next bit in the example above. It makes the new partial dividend ready for another stage with $y(n-2)$ as the LSB.
- *Note on $\beta_1, \beta_2, \beta_3, \beta_4$.* If the carry-out is 0 at β_1, it will be 0 at β_2. But the carry-out at β_3 will be 1. This is because a positive number is being added to a negative partial dividend using two's complements. The restored partial dividend is always 0 or positive and the carry-out must be 1. It is inverted to 0 at β_4 with the circuit shown.

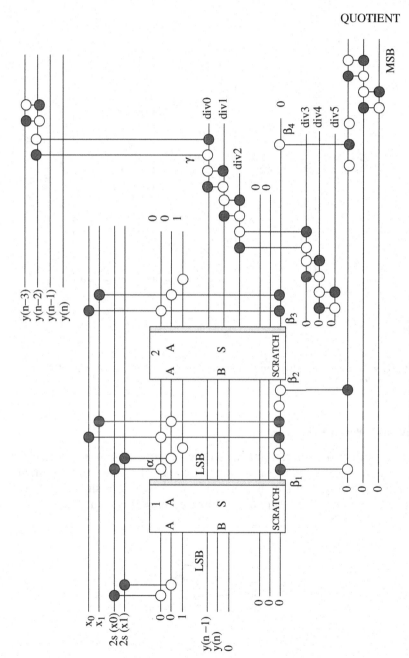

FIGURE 9-7 Reversible subtract-test stage

257

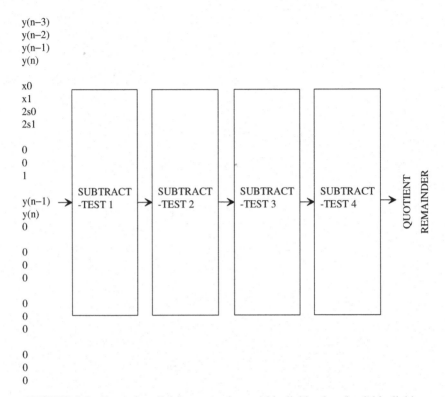

FIGURE 9-8 Restoring division assuming a 4-bit dividend and a 2-bit divider.

Iteration in a Wiring Diagram

The restoring division stage, sometimes called a *subtract-test stage*, may be placed in cascade with similar stages. The same lines of the wiring diagram are run through each stage until all dividend bits are processed as shown in Figure 9-8. As iterations occur, the quotient bits appear in the quotient lines.

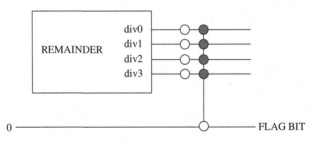

FIGURE 9-9 Flag for zero remainder.

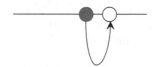

FIGURE 9-10   Irreversible operation.

Detecting Exact Factors

A multiple-controlled NOT can detect zero remainder as in Figure 9-9. This test is performed only after the last stage. If the remainder bits are all zero, the flag bit goes to 1, indicating an exact divisor. Divisors of interest have to be initialized into words that are ready to receive instructions from Figure 9-7. The divisors of interest could be integers or they could be prime numbers, for example.

The Element of Irreversibility   There is a quick and dirty way to reset a line to 0, but resetting a line to zero arbitrarily is an irreversible operation. A symbol for such an operation is suggested in Figure 9-10. An irreversible reset could save two gates, one at β_1, and one at β_2 in Figure 9-10; this is an example of simplifying using an irreversible operation. Of course, extra power is dissipated by such operations, so there is a design trade-off.

SOLVING HARD PROBLEMS

There is a substantial and interesting class of problems, termed *hard problems*, that are really difficult to solve when they are presented on a large scale with many variables. Everyday examples of such problems are games such as jigsaw puzzles, traveling through a maze, finding the most efficient way to pack odd-shaped little boxes into a big box, or most famously, solving the traveling salesman's problem: Given a list of cities, find the least number of miles required to visit each city only once with no backtracking, finally returning home.

When looking for an exact solution to such problems, the possibilities grow prolifically. If there are 11 cities, for example, assume that a trip begins in city 1; there are 10 choices for city 2. From each of these 10, there are nine choices for city 3. Altogether, the number of routes is $10! = 10 \times 9 \times 8 \times 7 \times 6 \times 5 \times 4 \times 3 \times 2 = 3,628,800$. Since any given route could be traveled either way, the actual number of routes is half this, or 1,814,400. Note what happens as cities are added. For 11 cities there are nearly 20 million routes; for 12 cities there are about 240 million routes; for 15 cities there are about 650 billion; for 20 cities there are over 1 quintillion, that is, 1 million trillion, or 10^{18}. As the number of cities increases, the time necessary to find the best route grows dramatically. If all cities were on a circle or on a straight line, the solution would be easy. But in general, an exact solution is not feasible in a sequential computer such as a desktop computer. The system becomes overwhelmed with possibilities.

Problems that are hard can theoretically be solved quickly in a massively parallel computer using as many processors as needed. Whenever a decision must be made that has several different outcomes, several new processors are started up, each chasing a possible solution. Parallel processing for this purpose has never been considered realistic by practical engineers. When parallel processing like this is necessary, theoreticians describe the problem in a rather nebulous way as belonging to *class NP*. This designation is puzzling at first sight, as is its literal meaning, *nondeterministic polynomial*.

Nondeterministic is an academic way of saying that a large number of processors are necessary; *polynomial* means that a solution proceeds quickly only if a large number of processors are used. *Polynomial time* refers to computing time that increases in proportion to some power λ of the number of variables: for example, $K_P n^\lambda$ where K_P is a constant giving an upper bound to computing time. Thus, if a nondeterministic computer is available, the computational time is polynomial. Unfortunately, by merely increasing the numbers of variables slightly, the number of parallel processors required becomes astronomical and impractical, and soon exceeds the number of atoms in the known universe—hence the term *nondeterministic*.

Exponential time is defined to be a computational time that increases as $K_E 2^n$, where K_E is a constant that gives an upper bound to computing time. They really want to emphasize that NP problems cannot be solved in a reasonable way on an ordinary sequential computer. Such computers are feasible only for problems in *class P*, those that compute in polynomial time. Sequential computers are examples of *Turing machines*, named for Alan Turing (1912–1954), who deserves credit for his vision of sequential machines for computing in the 1930s.

When faced with a hard problem with an exponential explosion of work, often there are fairly good approximations to a solution. However, an exact solution is sometimes desired, if only a large enough parallel processor were available. Problems in class NP can be reduced mathematically to an equivalent problem that is also difficult to solve, but whose solution can be verified quickly. That is, given a proposed solution, a yes or no answer can quickly be given as to whether or not the solution is correct. For example, it is easy to see if a jigsaw puzzle is put together correctly. Thus, problems in class NP can be reduced to a problem in what is called *NP-complete*. Problems in class NP whose solutions can be verified quickly are defined to be in class NP-complete. This is another puzzling designation. It suggests problems on the boundary of the NP region in an abstract space of problems (see Figure 9-11). The boundary "completes" the region. That is, the region NP is within the boundary; NP-complete is on the boundary; P is everywhere outside the boundary. The figure suggests that the difference between a problem in P and an NP-complete

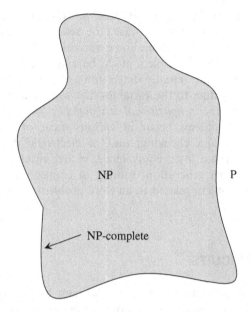

FIGURE 9-11   Abstract concept of *NP-complete*.

problem is small, and in some cases this is correct. There is an ongoing effort to prove (or disprove) that an *NP-complete* problem can be solved in polynomial time.

NP-complete problems are difficult to solve, but when a solution is found, whether by guess or luck, it can quickly be verified to be correct in polynomial time. The hope is that if a solution is easy to verify, perhaps a solution will be easy to obtain. This so far has not proven to be the case. Proving rigorously that any NP problem is solvable in polynomial time is one of the great unsolved mysteries of mathematics.*

SAT Problems

Over the years, mathematicians have proved that all NP problems are in a sense related. By solving one of them, similar methods could be used to solve others. Many problems can be shown to be a form of the *Boolean satisfiability* (SAT) *problem*. This is the problem of determining if the variables of a given Boolean formula can be assigned in a way to make the formula evaluate to true. Or if it can be determined that no such assignment exists, it may be concluded that the function is identically false for all possible variable assignments, or *unsatisfiable*.

---

* It is rumored that the Clay Mathematics Institute is offering a $1 million reward to anyone who has a formal proof that NP = P or that NP≠P.

Boolean satisfiability in a general case is NP-complete as proven by Stephen Cook in 1971. In a worst case, the search for satisfiability could involve all 2^n-entries in a truth table for n variables. The length of the table grows exponentially. A SAT problem might be a little easier if expressed as a decision problem. Without actually determining the variables, is there some assignment of binary values to the variables that will make a given expression true? This is termed the *propositional satisfiability problem*, which is also NP-complete. SAT problems occur in various areas of computer science, including software design checking, and in electronic design automation (EDA) for combinational logic equivalence, model checking, formal design verification, test pattern generation, routing of connections, and so on. An example of a hard problem related to an SAT problem is investigated next in more detail.

HAMILTONIAN CIRCUITS

Hamiltonian circuits were named after Sir William Rowan Hamilton (1805–1865). An example of a simple Hamiltonian circuit appears in Figure 9-12. Hamiltonian circuits occur in *graphs* that are characterized by *vertices* and *edges* (also known as *nodes* and *branches*). The number of vertices, the dots in Figure 9-12, is specified to be n. The number of edges, the lines between the vertices, is specified to be m. If an edge goes only one way with an arrow, the graph is a *directed graph*. If each edge has a specified dimension, the graph is a *weighted graph*.

To have a Hamiltonian circuit, it is required that all nodes be visited at least once and that no node be visited more than once. An example Hamiltonian circuit in Figure 9-12 is 012340. Examples of circuits that are not Hamiltonian are (01240) and (0124340) because the first leaves out node 3 while the second visits node 4 twice. A Hamiltonian circuit can always be "traveled" backward; for example, 043210 is a Hamiltonian circuit.

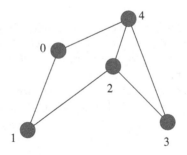

FIGURE 9-12 Hamiltonian circuit.

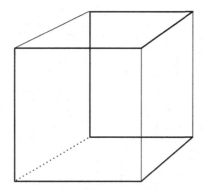

FIGURE 9-13 Hamiltonian circuit on a cube.

Hamilton devised a puzzle in which a path along the edges of the 12-faced dodecahedron was sought (the Icosian game). Figure 9-13 shows a Hamiltonian circuit on a cube.

Strategy for Detecting Hamiltonian Circuits

Testing Many Circuits in Parallel with a Wiring Diagram A plan is now presented for testing whether or not a given path is Hamiltonian. It is unique in that a great many circuits can be tested at once. In an NP-complete problem the verification of a proposed solution is supposed to be the easy part, a class P problem; we now take advantage of this property. Consider the wiring diagram in Figure 9-14, which assumes five vertices. The diagram can be extended to any number of vertices in a straightforward way.

A numerical identifier for each of n nodes in Figure 9-14 can be coded with k bits, where $k = 1 + \text{round}[\log_2(n)]$. Because n is 5, k may be 3, since 3 bits are enough to count to five. This contributes nk lines (15 lines). Inputs to the wiring diagram are labeled with the variables a to e; they are a sort of register that holds codes for vertices. For example, abcde could be vertices 01234, as shown; returning to 0 completes the circuit. Another example is: abcde could be 43120; returning to 4 completes the circuit. The abcde portion (15 bits) in each word of nanoprocessor memory is assumed to be initialized with a code representing some sequence of n nodes, not necessarily a good sequence.

The words of a nanoprocessor or toggle memory might be initialized with permutations of vertices, some of which may be Hamiltonian circuits. If this ideal sort of initialization is not convenient, as it might not be (discussed later), any arrangement of vertices could be used for initialization. For example, we could use convenient arrangements resulting from a binary count that is easy to instill in the technology at hand. In such cases, vertices might repeat, for example, there might occur in the 15-bit count the sequence 01231. If a vertex

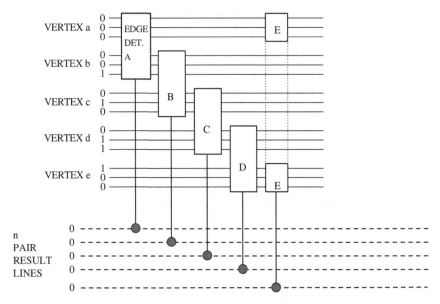

FIGURE 9-14   Framework for a Hamiltonian circuit identifier.

repeats, of course, there is no Hamiltonian circuit for the particular sequence in the particular nanoprocessor holding the tested sequence.

The boxes in the figure are called *edge detectors*. Edges have to be specified between specific vertices in the problem statement. These specifications are going to be coded into the wiring diagram.

A *vertex pair* is defined to be the pair of points defining an edge. A pair result line is where the knowledge of an edge is stored. When there is a unique edge between every pair of vertices in the permutation, a Hamiltonian circuit may exist as defined in a particular nanoprocessor. A flag can be set as in Figure 9-15. There are n pair-result lines. If all pair results are true for a particular input code, it means that enough edges have been found to form a closed circuit. A circuit is flagged using an n-controlled NOT. The flag, by the way, is held in a particular word of nanoprocessor toggle memory.

Edge Detectors   An example of a five vertex detector ($n = 5$) is shown in Figure 9-16. There are m edges ($m = 6$). The figure shows the plan for edge detector A for edges between the top pair of vertices. Other edge detectors have a similar plan. Note that $a_2a_1a_0$ and $b_2b_1b_0$ are identifiers for vertices. In the figure the specified edges are 01, 12, 23, 24, 34, 40. The order of edges is not important.

This is a typical decoding structure. Each vertical line represents a multiple-controlled NOT (MCN). Preceding and following the MCN are unconditional NOTs. Whenever an unconditional NOT is taken for decoding purposes,

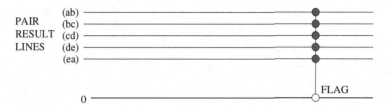

FIGURE 9-15 Hamiltonian circuit flag generation.

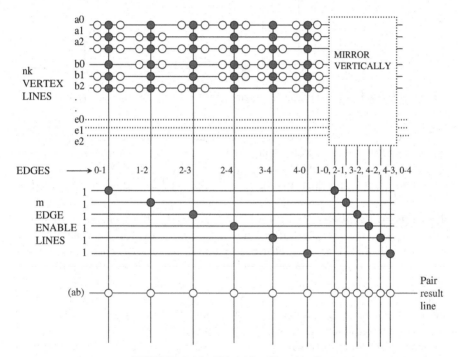

FIGURE 9-16 Edge identifier details.

another NOT restores the original input. For example, in a certain nanoprocessor the vertex sequence is such that vertices 2 and 4 are the first two vertices. They have $a_2a_1a_0$ and $b_2b_1b_0$ equal to 010 and 100. It is specified that there is an edge between vertices 2 and 4. There will be an output from the fourth vertical line from the right, the 2–4 line; all others will be false.

The circuit being considered is undirected; each edge has no particular direction. Therefore, a similar set of multiple-controlled NOTs, but mirrored vertically, serves to decode reverse directions. The reverse edges, diagrammed on the right, are 10, 21, 32, 42, 43, 04. For example, if an edge goes from vertex 4 to vertex 2, the 4–2 line will be activated.

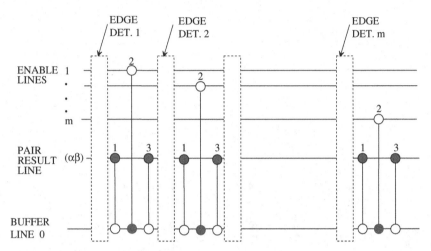

FIGURE 9-17 Disabling an edge (illustrated for the first m edges).

The edge enable lines are initially all true, but once an edge is used, the enable for that edge detector may, if desired, be set to false in that nanoprocessor where that edge is used. This will prevent an edge from being used more than once. Disabling an edge is accomplished as shown in Figure 9-17.

Accounting Vertices If a vertex is used in a trial path specification there will be a toggle in one of the buffer lines in Figure 9-18, for example BUFa_a in response to the vertex 000. However, if the same vertex is encountered again in a trial path specification, a repeat toggle occurs, for example REPa_b in response to another occurance of vertex 000. Ultimately, if each vertex is used at least once, and no vertex is used more than once, the diagram provides an OK signal. A basic DCN (not shown) of this OK signal with a FLAG signal indicates the existence of a Hamiltonian circuit.

The total number of bits B equals the number of wiring diagram lines, about n^2. The calculational time is proportional to the number of steps about $12\,mn$. It is efficient because of the parallel nanoprocessors. Now that the Hamiltonian circuits can easily be verified, let us consider how we might find them—that is, all of them in a general graph. Toward this end, there now ensues a discussion of the initialization of the nanoprocessors.

THE INITIALIZATION OF TOGGLE MEMORY IN NANOPROCESSORS

For a good many difficult problems with an explosion of calculations, specialized algorithms have been developed to provide approximate solutions. Often, rough solutions are considered good enough, as when routing a circuit through a maze of other circuits. In this case, any circuit that does

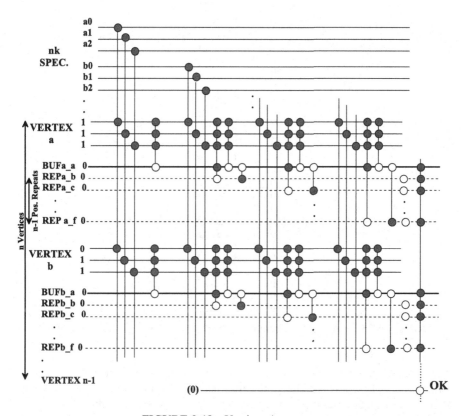

FIGURE 9-18 Vertices Accounter.

not short-circuit is a cause for celebration. Occasionally, however, an exact solution is desired by engineers who want the very best design. In reference to Hamiltonian circuits and the salesman's problem, the best initializations are permutations involving all vertices, obtained as follows.

Beginning at vertex 1, the first choice is limited to $n - 1$, since an edge cannot circle back to its starting point in a Hamiltonian circuit. The second choice can be limited to $n - 2$, since not only can it not return to its own vertex, but it cannot return to a previous vertex. Since no vertex is used twice, the number of possibilities is $(n - 1)(n - 2) \cdots (1)$, or in the language of mathematics, $(n - 1)!$ The last vertex goes to close the circuit. Since each trip can be traveled two ways, the number of choices is $(n - 1)!/2$. For $n = 11$ nodes, there are $(n - 1)!/2 = 1,814,400$ valid choices.

Permutations involving all vertices are ideal initializations since then vertices do not require accounting as is done in Figure 9-18. There are standard interchange algorithms that will compute all permutations of a given set of digits. In time, a great many numbers could be cranked out and applied to program the initial contents of the words of toggle memory automatically in nanoprocessors. Fusible links are considered to be a standard part of

0	4	3	2	1
0	3	4	2	1
0	4	2	3	1
0	2	4	3	1
0	3	2	4	1
0	2	3	4	1
0	4	3	1	2
0	3	4	1	2
0	4	1	3	2
0	1	4	3	2
0	3	1	4	2
0	1	3	4	2
0	4	2	1	3
0	2	4	1	3
0	4	1	2	3
0	1	4	2	3
0	2	1	4	3
0	1	2	4	3
0	3	2	1	4
0	2	3	1	4
0	3	1	2	4
0	1	3	2	4
0	2	1	3	4
0	1	2	3	4

FIGURE 9-19   MATLAB permutations of four vertices beginning at vertex 0.

integrated-circuit technology and are readily available for this purpose. For large values of n, unfortunately, the number of initializations really blows up beyond anything in this world, which is why, basically, these problems are hard.

Consider the example above in a little more detail. There are five nodes, so $4!/2 = 12$ initializations are anticipated. Without loss of generality, any circuit can be assumed to begin at vertex 1. Permutations calculated by MATLAB are shown in Figure 9-19. The underlined numbers are trips going in the opposite direction. Can we somehow determine all permutations in parallel using a wiring diagram? These questions are interesting but are beyond our scope in this book. The simplest thing to do is to process all n^n possibilities:

$$2^{nk} = 2^{n\log(n)}$$
$$= 2^{\log(n^n)}$$
$$= n^n$$

Because it is possible to use programmable links in integrated circuits, memory words are easily initialized to binary counts more or less automatically beginning with zero. This is a standard initialization for nanoprocessors: the firmware approach. It opens the possibility of calculating in parallel a large truth table of a Boolean function, which would enable the solution of small SAT problems, say for 2^{50} initializations, as has been projected to be a possibility today.

For example, if $n = 10$ for a Hamiltonian circuit problem, then $2^{n \log(n)} \approx 10^{10}$: that is, 10 billion words of toggle memory in nanoprocessors. This is a lot. But if we have 2^{50} nanoprocessors available as predicted to be possible in today's technology, such calculations are possible. Even so, it is unlikely that Hamiltonian circuits can be found as above for $n \geq 20$ in the near future—not unless classical computers are brought to bear over a period of time to prepare permutations for future use or if quantum computers can be developed.

LOGICALLY REVERSIBLE PROGRAMMING USING NANOBRAINS

Nanoprocessors may be constructed using current CMOS technology, but CMOS devices are relatively large compared to what is being developed with just a few molecules. We have come to expect logic devices at the molecular level. A recent development in the field of *molecular electronics* is based on a compound known as duroquinone. This molecule is analogous to a hexagonal plate linked with four cones, like a small car. Duroquinone is less than 1 nm wide and is hundreds of times smaller than the wavelength of visible light. When a center molecule is connected logically to adjacent molecules, basic calculations are possible in a laboratory setting. In a demonstrated instance, 17 duroquinone molecules were linked in what was promoted as a nanobrain.

In this book we have developed a model of the biological memory system and artificial intelligence, and have touched on cognition. In view of adiabatic computing, nanoprocessors, and nanobrains, the future seems to promise a revolutionary increase in computing density, and thus the possibility of solving hard problems with thousands of variables.

CONCLUSIONS

Brain models in conjunction with basic physics have led to an electrically reversible (and logically reversible) parallel computer that may be programmed with the aid of a wiring diagram. Three particular examples of programming are provided above for those interested in this type of programming. Wiring diagrams are imagined to be a delineation of parallel events that are occurring in a savant brain in one form or another.

We have shown how standard algorithms can be translated into a wiring diagram for vector processing. Iterative algorithms demand a basic structure such that successive loops are implemented merely by appending a replication of this structure. In this way, add-shift algorithms and subtract-test algorithms for multiplication and division can be planned in a wiring diagram for as many parallel operands as desired. Algorithms like these are far more efficient than primitive successive addition and subtraction for multiplication and division.

The wonders of electrically reversible parallel processing include the possibility of prime number identification and the identification of prime factors by brute-force division. Or one may calculate such constants as π to a fantastic number of places in record time, or multiply really large numbers with little delay. There are many potential applications along the lines of what a savant might demonstrate.

Finding all Hamiltonian circuits in a graph is a typical NP-complete problem that saturates ordinary computers for all but a few nodes. Finding circuits is difficult, but testing a given circuit is easy. A wiring diagram may direct a large-scale testing program for Hamiltonian circuits, testing a great many circuits in parallel. On a small scale of a few tens of vertices, a Hamiltonian circuit tester can sort circuits without difficulty, so all that is necessary is to initialize nanoprocessors with candidate circuits for testing. The ideal candidates are simple permutations of vertices using sequences that list a given vertex only once. Obtaining ideal candidates is the hard part of the problem for larger graphs.

Another approach is to test all permutations, ideal or not, equivalent to testing all binary counts. Although nanoprocessor initialization can be automated for binary counts, the number of nanoprocessors might be large. Here the Hamiltonian circuit problem is essentially translated into a SAT (satisfiability) problem. Solving a SAT problem with parallel nanoprocessors is equivalent to calculating a large truth table and then reading out the entries whose flags are true. Applications to SAT problems demonstrate that parallel nanoprocessors are capable of much more than vector arithmetic. Many tasks big and small, it seems, may be expressed as a SAT problem.

EXERCISES

9-1   Try to identify an application for a vector processor that can multiply a great many numbers in parallel. Consider the rapid multiplication of two very large numbers with perhaps 100 digits each.

9-2   Assume a vector processor that can divide a great many numbers in parallel. Explain how to accomplish a quick calculation of π out to hundreds of places.

9-3   Explain how a vector processor may identify prime numbers. Specify how words in the memory array need to be initialized.

9-4   Assume that all prime numbers up to 83 are given. Explain how a vector processor may be applied to search for prime factors for a given integer: for example, the number 165. Provide prime factors for 165.

9-5   Assuming that Hamiltonian circuits have been flagged, explain how the shortest circuit can be found using a classical computer. Use the simple graph with five vertices as an example.

9-6   Addition may serve to accomplish multiplication. Assume a 2-bit multiplier in the rightmost position of the word; place a 3-bit multiplicand to the left of the multiplier. Devise a wiring diagram to accomplish multiplication by successive addition in each word. One way to do this is to decrement the multiplier until it is zero. For each decrement the multiplicand is added to a partial product that begins with a value of zero. (*Hint*: The wiring diagram must be replicated for up to three additions).

9-7 Subtraction may serve to accomplish division. Assume a 2-bit divisor in the right most position of the word; place a 3-bit dividend to the left of the divisor. Devise a wiring diagram to accomplish division by successive subtraction in each word. One way to do this is to subtract the divisor from the dividend until it is nonpositive. The number of decrements plus one is the quotient. Note that the divisor cannot be zero. [*Hint*: The wiring diagram must be replicated for several subtractions].

9-8 Assuming that all necessary factorials are precalculated and available to initialize nanoprocessors, explain a fast way to calculate a power series representation of e, the constant of calculus using parallel processing.

CHAPTER 10

QUANTUM VERSUS CLASSICAL COMPUTING

INTRODUCTION*

Need for Computational Force Beyond the Brain

In Chapter 9 we examined the topic of NP-complete problems. These problems cannot be solved in a classical computer when there are large numbers of variables, since run times become excessive. Consideration was given to solving such problems in a logically reversible parallel computer, but such computers are limited in practice by the number of nanoprocessors that can be brought to bear on a problem. The number of nanoprocessors must be no less than the length of a truth table for those problems that can be expressed as a SAT problem. Estimates using current technology were about 2^{50} nanoprocessors. This corresponds to about 1 quadrillion (10^{15}), comparable to the quantity of synapses in a human brain, but not enough for the sorts of hard problems being considered.

The future may see *nanobrains*, defined as molecular-sized nanoprocessors. A revolutionary development like this could vastly increase available nano-processors to well beyond current estimates. If this occurs, there may be a

* Thanks to Michael Raymer (University of Oregon) for his helpful suggestions.

practical solution to reasonably sized NP-complete problems. Nanobrains would be great, but lamentably, none are yet available.

The working particles in a quantum computer have sizes comparable to those of molecules and even smaller. Quantum computers come with a host of mysterious advantages and disadvantages along with hope for solving hard problems. In this chapter we attempt a simplified explanation aimed at electrical and computer engineers. By working through this chapter, a reader will benefit from a review of the basic theory of quantum computation, not to mention the enjoyment of reading a systematic formulation. Beyond basics, the reader will discover a concrete connection between quantum computers and classical models that use toggle memory, be they biological or technological.

In a quantum computer one might say that the number of operands is proportional to 2^n, where n refers to a number of particles known as qubits. Later it will be explained that operands are in fact elements of a state vector system. From a certain point of view, one may visualize a giant truth table in one form or another within a quantum computer. In a truth table the number of entries is proportional to 2^N where N refers to the number of binary variables or bits. The truth table metaphor is too obvious to go without mention; and the idea of a truth table is satisfying if not reassuring to electrical and computer engineers.

The promise is hundreds or thousands of qubits and operands nearly uncountable in their vast numbers. This promise is vaguely similar to the promises of nanobrains. These are merely classical logic devices on a nanoscale, whereas quantum computers are special in that they hold in secret a structured pattern. Quantum computer operations go beyond what is possible classically to solve a hard problem. If only we had a quantum computer, but alas none are yet available.

Quantum Computers and Toggle Memory: Biological and Artificial

The paramount reason for presenting this chapter is to show that the transforms for quantum state vectors and the transforms for toggle memory in nanoprocessors have a remarkable similarity. In thinking about this issue, one might expect this similarity, given that T flip-flops and qubits are both capable of alternating between two basic states. Another clue is that both quantum and toggle systems use a wiring diagram for reversible operations. A wiring diagram programs quantum computers as readily as parallel nanoprocessors. Both have particular styles for implementing logic, a fact that may be useful in future computer systems.

A popular speculation is that the human brain incorporates the concept of quantum computation somehow, implying that a brain cannot be constructed artificially with devices of the classical sort. Roger Penrose (1931–) is recognized to be a polymath who enjoys writing books on this topic. In an attempt to summarize what is relevant to us, it is said that the brain is like a quantum computer that operates subconsciously while processing a scramble of information. A given thought initially involves a number of superimposed quantum states, each with a component of information. When the distribution of mass and energy among the states reaches a gravitationally significant level, an event occurs. States collapse into a single observable state. The collapse creates neural signals and the realization of something: a decision to have breakfast, for example.

Penrose's speculation is certainly colorful and certainly has a serious message. The underlying assertion is that brain behavior and cognition cannot be duplicated artificially. This is in contrast to our model of human cognition based on standard analog and digital circuits, a model that points to artificial intelligence. Recall that the model in this book is a complex self-contained machine that selects a direction of attention with pseudorandom recalls and a decoder to permit into short-term memory what is most important at the moment. The end result is the same, a clear message in short-term memory. Indeed, one might conjecture that the message is the result of the collapse of quantum states, the only problem being that quantum states are reserved for particles much smaller than neurons.

Biological memory in savant brains was modeled as having a bank of toggle memory, and this idea was applied subsequently when designing a logically reversible parallel computer. Toggling as controlled by a wiring diagram tangibly connects the transform process in a brain to unitary transforms in a quantum computer. Similar reasoning works for logically reversible parallel computers based on toggle memory. To learn more, we explore the nature of the transforms used in quantum algorithms with an eye toward unifying biological and physical knowledge.

PHYSICAL QUBITS

A quantum computer is based not on bits, but on qubits. A *qubit* may be thought of as a small entity with two physical states, isolated to avoid interference from the environment. A qubit can be constructed using an electron. The two physical states could be the two states of electron spin, for example. Spin is analogous to angular momentum in a spinning top, for example, but quantized to be a given value, either clockwise or anticlockwise (up or down). Up or down is analogous to true or false.

So far, the number of qubits created in the laboratory can be counted on one's fingers, although we still have hope for the many hundreds or thousands that are necessary to make an advance in computer science.

Ideal qubits are physically reversible and do not dissipate energy when they change spin states. Physical reversibility is an important aspect of quantum mechanics, so it is no surprise that qubit operations are logically reversible. In this sense they are similar to logically reversible nanoprocessors designed in past chapters. These nanoprocessors are electrically and logically reversible and used to construct on paper an adiabatic parallel computer. The power supplies, however, might not be electrically reversible, although in theory they could be. In practice, there is always some power dissipation that may be termed *energy baggage* for the technology.

Energy baggage is not unusual. Neural signals have been modeled as adiabatic, but neurons and all human body cells require a steady consumption of calories for maintenance and growth. Heat is released in mammalian cells because of chemical reactions and also because of Nernst voltage, which is generated across membrane conductance. Overall, biological energy is about 50 W minimum for the entire body.

Qubits are physically reversible and ideally dissipate no energy in the process of changing states. In practice, they have an energy baggage like that of any other known computer. Electrons, for example, are extremely mobile and difficult to tame; energy is dissipated in order to isolate them. Researchers are currently attempting to isolate electrons within strong magnetic fields and also to isolate large ions, which are easier to isolate, in what is termed an *ion trap*. The easily manipulated vibrations associated with large ions seem promising for the construction of qubits. But there is a price. Significant energy is required for refrigeration to cool superconducting magnets for magnetic fields to isolate electrons or ion traps. Ion traps also require powerful radio-frequency signals and lasers, both of which dissipate heat. Quantum computers as we know them today require an overall energy. However, this is not a major concern to quantum researchers, who are striving for calculations not possible in any other way.

Quantum computers are delicate. A problem termed *decoherence* refers to the difficulty of isolating a system of small particles from the environment such that they evolve in a predictable way. It is estimated that 50 extra qubits are needed for each operating qubit for error correction because of decoherence. With error correction, it is thought that an ion trap computer can operate up to 10 s at a time, which we are told is long enough for useful computations.

Mathematical Description of Qubits

A qubit is an entity with two observable states, denoted by $|0\rangle$ and $|1\rangle$, corresponding, for example, to spin up and spin down; these may be expressed mathematically as vectors in an abstract vector space:

$$|0\rangle = \begin{bmatrix} 1 \\ 0 \end{bmatrix}$$

$$|1\rangle = \begin{bmatrix} 0 \\ 1 \end{bmatrix}$$

These are the two basis states of a qubit. They form a basis (analogous to a coordinate system) for the linear vector space. A *linear combination* of two basis states results is a state vector:

$$|\psi\rangle = \alpha|0\rangle + \beta|1\rangle$$

The variables α and β are complex numbers such that

$$|\alpha|^2 + |\beta|^2 = 1$$

Another name for linear combination is *superposition*. In a sense, a superposition of basis states represents both $|0\rangle$ and $|1\rangle$ simultaneously. Binary numbers cannot do this; they are either true or false.

Under quantum theory, $|\alpha|^2$ and $|\beta|^2$ are the probabilities of observing either $|0\rangle$ or $|1\rangle$. A novel aspect of quantum theory is the *observation rule*: Attempted observation of a qubit $|\psi\rangle = \alpha|0\rangle + \beta|1\rangle$ forces the qubit into a basis state of either $|0\rangle$ or $|1\rangle$ with probabilities $|\alpha|^2$ for $|0\rangle$ and $|\beta|^2$ for $|1\rangle$. This means that if you attempt to read out the digital information, 0 or 1 held by a qubit, 0 occurs with a probability of $|\alpha|^2$ and 1 occurs with a probability of $|\beta|^2$. Because the coefficients are squared, one cannot read a negative sign in the superposition.

There is another surprise. Observation changes the information you are trying to read. In other words, it is a destructive readout. Thus, it is desirable to arrange for certainty, if possible, by applying procedures that effectively force one of α or β to unity prior to observing a qubit. Another strategy, one that is far less desirable, is to repeat an entire calculation a great many times and then to infer the probabilities of $|0\rangle$ or $|1\rangle$.

When both α and β are finite, a qubit is said to be both $|0\rangle$ and $|1\rangle$. In contrast, a classical bit may be either 0 or 1, but never a mixture. A particular set of n bits can represent one of 2^n binary numbers. But a set of n qubits can represent 2^n binary numbers *simultaneously*, ranging from 0 to $2^n - 1$. Ideally, a simple operation on n qubits is an operation on all 2^n-numbers simultaneously. This is true for any simple operation that can be accomplished in well below 2^n-steps: hence the term *quantum parallelism*, suggesting a new variety of parallel processing.

For example, consider two qubits. Two qubits can be arranged in four ways: $|0\rangle|0\rangle, |0\rangle|1\rangle, |1\rangle|0\rangle, |1\rangle|1\rangle$, corresponding to binary counts 00, 01, 10, 11. These are basis vectors for a state vector resulting from two qubits. Basis vectors such as $|1\rangle|1\rangle$ can be denoted in several other ways: for example, $|11\rangle$ or $|1\rangle \otimes |1\rangle$. The symbol $\otimes$ is termed a *direct product*; basis vectors may be calculated formally as follows:

$$|0\rangle \otimes |0\rangle = \begin{bmatrix} 1 \\ 0 \end{bmatrix} \otimes \begin{bmatrix} 1 \\ 0 \end{bmatrix} = \begin{bmatrix} 1\begin{bmatrix} 1 \\ 0 \end{bmatrix} \\ 0\begin{bmatrix} 1 \\ 0 \end{bmatrix} \end{bmatrix} = \begin{bmatrix} 1 \\ 0 \\ 0 \\ 0 \end{bmatrix}$$

$$|0\rangle \otimes |1\rangle = \begin{bmatrix} 1 \\ 0 \end{bmatrix} \otimes \begin{bmatrix} 0 \\ 1 \end{bmatrix} = \begin{bmatrix} 1\begin{bmatrix} 0 \\ 1 \end{bmatrix} \\ 0\begin{bmatrix} 0 \\ 1 \end{bmatrix} \end{bmatrix} = \begin{bmatrix} 0 \\ 1 \\ 0 \\ 0 \end{bmatrix}$$

$$|1\rangle \otimes |0\rangle = \begin{bmatrix} 0 \\ 1 \end{bmatrix} \otimes \begin{bmatrix} 1 \\ 0 \end{bmatrix} = \begin{bmatrix} 0\begin{bmatrix} 1 \\ 0 \end{bmatrix} \\ 1\begin{bmatrix} 1 \\ 0 \end{bmatrix} \end{bmatrix} = \begin{bmatrix} 0 \\ 0 \\ 1 \\ 0 \end{bmatrix}$$

$$|1\rangle \otimes |1\rangle = \begin{bmatrix} 0 \\ 1 \end{bmatrix} \otimes \begin{bmatrix} 0 \\ 1 \end{bmatrix} = \begin{bmatrix} 0\begin{bmatrix} 0 \\ 1 \end{bmatrix} \\ 1\begin{bmatrix} 0 \\ 1 \end{bmatrix} \end{bmatrix} = \begin{bmatrix} 0 \\ 0 \\ 0 \\ 1 \end{bmatrix}$$

Note that these basis vectors can be written by inspection by placing a 1 in the corresponding binary count position counting from the top. Two qubits produce a general state vector with four elements:

$$|\psi\rangle = \alpha|0\rangle|0\rangle + \beta|0\rangle|1\rangle + \gamma|1\rangle|0\rangle + \delta|1\rangle|1\rangle$$

$$= \alpha\begin{bmatrix} 1 \\ 0 \\ 0 \\ 0 \end{bmatrix} + \beta\begin{bmatrix} 0 \\ 1 \\ 0 \\ 0 \end{bmatrix} + \gamma\begin{bmatrix} 0 \\ 0 \\ 1 \\ 0 \end{bmatrix} + \delta\begin{bmatrix} 0 \\ 0 \\ 0 \\ 1 \end{bmatrix}$$

This combination is a linear superposition of the four basis states $|0\rangle|0\rangle$, $|0\rangle|1\rangle$, $|1\rangle|0\rangle$, $|1\rangle|1\rangle$, where each basic state relates to a corresponding binary number. The number may be identified by counting elements from zero, from the top to the bottom. Expansions like this easily generalize to larger numbers (n) of qubits and state vector elements (2^n).

Taking a direct product as above works even for mathematically complex elements, should they be needed. Unfortunately, it is impossible to say exactly how qubits might be physically implemented in the future, either with electron spins or perhaps something quite different. For the purposes of this chapter, it is assumed that qubits can somehow be implemented in a practical way and, indeed, that they can be manipulated in a manner consistent with quantum theory.

Initialization of State Vectors to Have Equal Probabilities for Each Element

Before beginning a quantum parallel computation, the qubits need to be initialized to represent all integers in parallel from zero up to some positive integer. What we have so far are basis vectors:

$$|0\rangle = \begin{bmatrix} 1 \\ 0 \end{bmatrix}$$

$$|1\rangle = \begin{bmatrix} 0 \\ 1 \end{bmatrix}$$

To distribute the elements of these matrices uniformly, basic state vectors may be multiplied by a matrix $\mathbf{H}$, the basic Hadamard matrix (Jacques Salomon Hadamard, 1865–1963):

$$\mathbf{H} = \frac{1}{\sqrt{2}} \begin{bmatrix} 1 & 1 \\ 1 & -1 \end{bmatrix}$$

Note that $\mathbf{H}$ is its own inverse. In other words, if $\mathbf{H}$ undergoes matrix multiplication by another $\mathbf{H}$, the result is unity matrix $\mathbf{I}$:

$$\mathbf{HH} = \mathbf{I}$$

$$= \begin{bmatrix} 1 & 0 \\ 0 & 1 \end{bmatrix}$$

The unity matrix is a matrix that has 1's on the main diagonal and 0's elsewhere. Applying $\mathbf{H}$ to the basis vectors yields

$$\mathbf{H}|0\rangle = \frac{1}{\sqrt{2}} \begin{bmatrix} 1 & 1 \\ 1 & -1 \end{bmatrix} \begin{bmatrix} 1 \\ 0 \end{bmatrix} = \frac{1}{\sqrt{2}} \begin{bmatrix} 1 \\ 1 \end{bmatrix}$$

$$\mathbf{H}|1\rangle = \frac{1}{\sqrt{2}} \begin{bmatrix} 1 & 1 \\ 1 & -1 \end{bmatrix} \begin{bmatrix} 0 \\ 1 \end{bmatrix} = \frac{1}{\sqrt{2}} \begin{bmatrix} 1 \\ -1 \end{bmatrix}$$

The purpose of multiplying by $\mathbf{H}$ is to evenly distribute the elements of a state vector. Note that the operation of $\mathbf{H}$ on $|0\rangle$ gives two positive equal components, while the operation of $\mathbf{H}$ on $|1\rangle$ contains equal magnitude positive and negative components. A negative sign does not affect the probabilities of observing either $|0\rangle$ or $|1\rangle$.

This method of distributing the elements of the state vector, evenly easily extends to greater numbers of qubits. For example, consider three qubits, which happen to be $|0\rangle|0\rangle|1\rangle$. The Hadamard transform is $\mathbf{H}\,|0\rangle \otimes \mathbf{H}\,|0\rangle \otimes \mathbf{H}\,|1\rangle$. The resulting superposition is a list of 1's with alternating signs:

$$\frac{1}{\sqrt{2}}\begin{bmatrix}1\\1\end{bmatrix} \otimes \frac{1}{\sqrt{2}}\begin{bmatrix}1\\1\end{bmatrix} \otimes \frac{1}{\sqrt{2}}\begin{bmatrix}1\\-1\end{bmatrix} = \frac{1}{\sqrt{8}}\begin{bmatrix}+1\\-1\\+1\\-1\\ \text{---}\\+1\\-1\\+1\\-1\end{bmatrix} \leftarrow \text{center point of the state vector}$$

An identical vector would result by calculating $\{\mathbf{H} \otimes \mathbf{H} \otimes \mathbf{H}\}\{[|0\rangle \otimes |0\rangle \otimes |1\rangle\}$ where $\mathbf{H} \otimes \mathbf{H} \otimes \mathbf{H}$ an 8×8 matrix and is unwieldy. Because $\mathbf{H}$ is its own inverse, $[\mathbf{H} \otimes \mathbf{H} \otimes \mathbf{H}]$ is also its own inverse; to obtain the original state vector, simply multiply the transformed state vector by $[\mathbf{H} \otimes \mathbf{H} \otimes \mathbf{H}]$. Having alternating positive and negative entries as above makes the original state vector uniquely identifiable. Certain other patterns of + and − uniquely identify other state vectors. Negative signs can be seen above but cannot be observed in the lab; physical observation merely results in a probability of $\frac{1}{8}$ of seeing a given state. For example, $\frac{1}{8}$ of the observation would show that

$$|\psi_0\rangle = \frac{1}{\sqrt{8}}\begin{bmatrix}1\\0\\0\\0\\0\\0\\0\\0\end{bmatrix} = |000\rangle$$

and so on for each of the eight state vectors.

Qubit Manipulations

A *unitary transformation* can be used to modify a state vector and hence the probability of having a given combination of qubits. A unitary transform is, by definition, reversible; one can always return to a previous state vector simply by applying an inverse transform. As it turns out, the inverse transform is easy to obtain. It will be seen below that the reversibility of a unitary transform relates to the logical reversibility of a computation that involves state vectors.

Unitary transforms in matrix formulations are accomplished by multiplying the state vector by a unitary matrix. In general, unitary matrices satisfy the relationship

$$U^{*T}U = I$$

where U^{*T} denotes the transpose of the complex conjugate of the matrix U; it can be shown that a unitary matrix of size $n \times n$ has n^2 free parameters; so there are many ways to construct a unitary matrix. We prefer a unitary matrix with real elements, since the inverse matrix U^{-1} is then simply the transpose of the original matrix; that is, $U^{-1} = U^T$. Unitary transforms with real elements can be related to ordinary binary functions such as AND, OR, and XOR, as discussed below.

Consider three qubits. Three qubits can be ordered in eight ways. Each of the eight combinations, upon Hadamard transformation, corresponds to a different unique pattern of $+$ and -1's in the resulting state vector. Symmetry is observed with respect to the center point of the list of elements in a state vector, as illustrated above. Some have *symmetry* (that is, even symmetry with respect to the center point); some have *antisymmetry* (that is, odd symmetry with respect to the center point). The vector above, for example, has antisymmetry about the center of the list, because the lower half of the list is a reflection of the upper half, but with opposite signs.

Generally, a state vector need not be symmetric or antisymmetric. However, if it ends up with either symmetry or antisymmetry, an application of $H \otimes H \otimes H$ will resolve the state vector into three qubits that may be observed with certainty. For example, multiplication by $H \otimes H \otimes H$ of the state vector above results in the following:

$$\frac{1}{\sqrt{8}}\begin{bmatrix} 1 & 1 & 1 & 1 & 1 & 1 & 1 & 1 \\ 1 & -1 & 1 & -1 & 1 & -1 & 1 & -1 \\ 1 & 1 & -1 & -1 & 1 & 1 & -1 & -1 \\ 1 & -1 & -1 & 1 & 1 & -1 & -1 & 1 \\ 1 & 1 & 1 & 1 & -1 & -1 & -1 & -1 \\ 1 & -1 & 1 & -1 & -1 & 1 & -1 & 1 \\ 1 & 1 & -1 & -1 & -1 & -1 & 1 & 1 \\ 1 & -1 & -1 & 1 & -1 & 1 & 1 & -1 \end{bmatrix} \left\{ \frac{1}{\sqrt{8}}\begin{bmatrix} +1 \\ -1 \\ +1 \\ -1 \\ +1 \\ -1 \\ +1 \\ -1 \end{bmatrix} \right\} = \begin{bmatrix} 0 \\ 1 \\ 0 \\ 0 \\ 0 \\ 0 \\ 0 \\ 0 \end{bmatrix} = |0\rangle|0\rangle|1\rangle$$

Amazingly, the matrix is just right to do this. The resulting basis vector may be observed with 100% probability. Opportunities like this for certainty are rare in quantum work.

QUANTUM BOOLEAN FUNCTIONS

Any state vector for three qubits may be expressed as $|i\rangle \otimes |j\rangle \otimes |k\rangle$, where i, j, and k are binary bits; like any three bits, they can count from 0 to 7. Consider a state vector $|001\rangle = |0\rangle \otimes |0\rangle \otimes |1\rangle$. This may be Hadamard-transformed to

$$\psi_1 = \frac{1}{\sqrt{8}} \begin{bmatrix} 1 \\ -1 \\ 1 \\ -1 \\ 1 \\ -1 \\ 1 \\ -1 \end{bmatrix}$$

Note that when there are three qubits, the state vector has eight entries. The elements of this state vector ψ_1 may be numbered top to bottom from 0 to 7. Note the even pattern of alternating plus and minus signs.

Qubit $|k\rangle$ in a three-qubit system is going to be reserved to give an indication of the value of a Boolean function on $|i\rangle$ and $|j\rangle$, assuming that i, j and k are 0 or 1. Consider the truth table for the AND function $ab = c$:

a	b	c
0	0	0
0	1	0
1	0	0
1	1	1

When considering Boolean functions, i and j can be interpreted to be an input, 0 or 1 in $|i\rangle$ or $|j\rangle$; i and j are analogous to a and b; k can be interpreted to be an output. A qubit $|k\rangle$ cannot be set to $|0\rangle$ or to $|1\rangle$ as we did for the output c above. Setting k to 1 or resetting k to 0 is considered irreversible because it overwrites the previous value of k. Qubit $|k\rangle$ may toggle, however. Toggling leaves a way to determine the prior value of $|k\rangle$ and so permits operations to be logically reversible. Therefore, the logic operations of interest are not set and reset, but toggle, and this may go from $|0\rangle$ to $|1\rangle$ or from $|1\rangle$ to $|0\rangle$. For example, if the Boolean function $f(i,j)$ is true for particular i and j, the state of

$|k\rangle$ can be made to toggle from $|0\rangle$ to $|1\rangle$ or from $|1\rangle$ to $|0\rangle$, depending on its initial value.

Toggling of a qubit $|k\rangle$ in a state vector is accomplished symbolically using an exclusive OR operation:

$$|i\rangle \otimes |j\rangle \otimes |k\rangle \rightarrow |i\rangle \otimes |j\rangle \otimes |k \oplus f(i,j)\rangle$$

Note the symbol $\oplus$ for XOR as opposed to the symbol $\otimes$ for direct product. The indices i, j, and k are simple bits, not complex numbers, since only basis qubits are being discussed at this point. The XOR function is accomplishing a controlled toggle of k.

To show how a Boolean function works with a state vector, consider the entries in the state vector above expressed as a superposition of basic components. The normalization factor $1/\sqrt{8}$ is removed to simplify the notation.

$$\sqrt{8}|\psi_1\rangle = \begin{bmatrix} 1 \\ 0 \\ 0 \\ 0 \\ 0 \\ 0 \\ 0 \\ 0 \end{bmatrix} - \begin{bmatrix} 0 \\ 1 \\ 0 \\ 0 \\ 0 \\ 0 \\ 0 \\ 0 \end{bmatrix} + \begin{bmatrix} 0 \\ 0 \\ 1 \\ 0 \\ 0 \\ 0 \\ 0 \\ 0 \end{bmatrix} - \begin{bmatrix} 0 \\ 0 \\ 0 \\ 1 \\ 0 \\ 0 \\ 0 \\ 0 \end{bmatrix} + \begin{bmatrix} 0 \\ 0 \\ 0 \\ 0 \\ 1 \\ 0 \\ 0 \\ 0 \end{bmatrix} - \begin{bmatrix} 0 \\ 0 \\ 0 \\ 0 \\ 0 \\ 1 \\ 0 \\ 0 \end{bmatrix} + \begin{bmatrix} 0 \\ 0 \\ 0 \\ 0 \\ 0 \\ 0 \\ 1 \\ 0 \end{bmatrix} - \begin{bmatrix} 0 \\ 0 \\ 0 \\ 0 \\ 0 \\ 0 \\ 0 \\ 1 \end{bmatrix}$$

Each component is a basis vector with a certain coefficient; coefficient magnitudes are equal, but signs alternate, either $+1$ or -1. The coefficients can be thought of as being generated by a Boolean function $\text{Coef}(i,j,k)/\sqrt{8}$. A truth table for the coefficients in the foregoing expansion is as follows:

i	j	k	$\text{Coef}/\sqrt{8}$
0	0	0	1
0	0	1	-1
0	1	0	1
0	1	1	-1
1	0	0	1
1	0	1	-1
1	1	0	1
1	1	1	-1

Consider now a binary AND function $f(i,j)$ with binary inputs i,j. Note that when $i = j = 1$, the AND function $f(i,j) = 1$. The XOR operation in the equation above is going to toggle the value of k. Where k is 0, it becomes 1 and where k is 1, it becomes 0, as follows. Please note the changes in the listing of k; the last two k-entries change from 01 to 10:

i	j	k	Coef$/\sqrt{8}$
0	0	0	1
0	0	1	-1
0	1	0	1
0	1	1	-1
1	0	0	1
1	0	1	-1
1	**1**	**1**	**1**
1	**1**	**0**	**-1**

Although k toggles, the coefficients do not change. After a toggling operation, the truth table is no longer in ascending order. Usually it is convenient to place the elements of the toggled state vector back into order. Please consider the last two entries for Coef$/\sqrt{8}$ to notice that the pattern has changed. Instead of the regular 1 -1 1 -1 the last four entries for Coef$/\sqrt{8}$ are 1 -1 -1 1.

i	j	k	Coef$/\sqrt{8}$
0	0	0	1
0	0	1	-1
0	1	0	1
0	1	1	-1
1	0	0	1
1	0	1	-1
1	**1**	**0**	**-1**
1	**1**	**1**	**1**

By looking at the pattern of signs, it is clear that the coefficients of basic vectors have interchanged at those locations where $f(i,j) = 1$. For this reason, a logically reversible operation is sometimes considered an interchange operation. At this point it may be recalled that the truth tables above are a representation of state vectors for the purposes of this discussion:

$$|\psi_1\rangle = \frac{1}{\sqrt{8}} \begin{bmatrix} 1 \\ -1 \\ 1 \\ -1 \\ 1 \\ -1 \\ +1 \\ -1 \end{bmatrix} \rightarrow \frac{1}{\sqrt{8}} \begin{bmatrix} 1 \\ -1 \\ 1 \\ -1 \\ 1 \\ -1 \\ -1 \\ +1 \end{bmatrix}$$

Affected entries in the state vector have interchanged by the truth value of the Boolean function being applied. The last two entries have interchanged for the AND function, because only the last two have $i = j = 1$. This is one way to show what a quantum Boolean function does to a state vector under the assumptions above; it interchanges elements, where each element is a coefficient of a basis vector.

Unitary Matrices for Quantum Boolean Functions

A particular unitary matrix may easily be constructed to accomplish an interchange of the last two entries in a state vector:

$$\mathbf{U_f} = \begin{bmatrix} 1 & 0 & 0 & 0 & 0 & 0 & 0 & 0 \\ 0 & 1 & 0 & 0 & 0 & 0 & 0 & 0 \\ 0 & 0 & 1 & 0 & 0 & 0 & 0 & 0 \\ 0 & 0 & 0 & 1 & 0 & 0 & 0 & 0 \\ 0 & 0 & 0 & 0 & 1 & 0 & 0 & 0 \\ 0 & 0 & 0 & 0 & 0 & 1 & 0 & 0 \\ 0 & 0 & 0 & 0 & 0 & 0 & 0 & 1 \\ 0 & 0 & 0 & 0 & 0 & 0 & 1 & 0 \end{bmatrix}$$

The off-diagonal entries in the lower right indicate that the last two entries in the state vector are going to be interchanged after multiplication by $\mathbf{U_f}$:

$$\psi_f = \mathbf{U_f}\psi_1$$

Although this example analyzes the Boolean AND function as applied to a state vector, a unitary matrix may be constructed for any Boolean function. It is merely a question of providing appropriate off-diagonal entries to make appropriate interchanges. A Boolean function applied to a state vector in this way is termed a *quantum Boolean function* because it interchanges state vector elements.

How many Boolean functions are there of n variables? A truth table has a length of $N = 2^n$. N bits can be arranged in 2^N ways; that is, they may count from 0 to $2^N - 1$. So there are 2^{2^n} possible unique arrangements of the bits in a truth table. Each arrangement corresponds to a different Boolean function. Thus, there are 2^{2^n} possible Boolean functions of n variables. This many unitary matrices are available to produce corresponding interchanges. For example, a truth table for a function of the form $c = f(a, b)$ will have 16 arrangements of the four bits in the truth table, where these four bits are determined by a function of two variables. Thus, there are 16 possible functions of two variables.

A significant observation is that basis qubits are toggled by a quantum Boolean function. This suggests that memory elements may be toggled by a classical Boolean function to achieve a logically reversible computer. Indeed, we pursued this idea in earlier chapters.

Entanglement

It is fairly easy to find a state vector that does not convert into a product of basic qubits upon multiplication by the Hadamard matrix. As a simple example, consider the following state:

$$\frac{1}{\sqrt{2}} \begin{bmatrix} 1 \\ 0 \\ 0 \\ 1 \end{bmatrix} = \frac{1}{\sqrt{2}} \begin{bmatrix} 1 \\ 0 \end{bmatrix} \otimes \begin{bmatrix} 1 \\ 0 \end{bmatrix} + \frac{1}{\sqrt{2}} \begin{bmatrix} 0 \\ 1 \end{bmatrix} \otimes \begin{bmatrix} 0 \\ 1 \end{bmatrix}$$

This state will never relate to a simple product of two basic qubits; it relates to the superposition of qubits as shown. If the qubits are observed, there is a 50–50 chance of seeing either $|0\rangle$, $|0\rangle$ or $|1\rangle$, $|1\rangle$; there are no definite output values. Such states are termed *entangled*.

Entangled qubits are linked in a mysterious way. In the example, if a given qubit is observed to be $|1\rangle$, the other must also be $|1\rangle$. Alternatively, if a qubit is observed to be $|0\rangle$, the other must also be $|0\rangle$. This would remain true even if the qubits are separated physically. Under this theory, an entangled qubit could be taken halfway around the world while retaining a probability to be either a 1 or a 0. But if a $|1\rangle$ is observed back home for the first qubit, for example, then a person halfway around the world, upon observing the second qubit, will see a $|1\rangle$. This is an example of a subtle type of communication over a long distance. For example, a 1 might mean "attack" and a 0 might mean "retreat". Both parties could at least coordinate their effort. What is odd about this scenario is that the person back home has equal probability of attacking or retreating. The choice is random.

A substantial elaboration using entangled qubits involves additional qubits and also classical channels of communications as suggested in 1984 by Bennett and Brassard [Charles H. Bennett (1942–) and Gilles Brassard (1955–)]. This gets into a subject called *teleportation*, in which it is theoretically possible for a 1-qubit superposition to materialize at a receiver with the aid of entangled qubits. In practice, unfortunately, qubits entangled or otherwise cannot exist for long because of decoherence, or interference from the environment. Entangled qubits are not easy to maintain, much less separate.

Concerning the AND function no transformation can be found to convert the state $[1, \ -1, \ 1, \ -1, \ 1, \ -1, \ -1, \ 1]'/\sqrt{8}$ into a basis vector. This state vector has neither symmetry nor antisymmetry. So by definition, it is *entangled*.

In contrast, concerning the XOR function the state $[1, -1, -1, 1, -1, 1, 1, -1]'/\sqrt{8}$ has antisymmetry; in fact it can be represented as $[1, -1]'/\sqrt{2} \otimes [1, -1]'/\sqrt{2} \otimes [1, -1]'/\sqrt{2}$, which by inspection can be seen to Hadamard transform to $|1\rangle \otimes |1\rangle \otimes |1\rangle$, a state that clearly is *not entangled.*

State vectors with symmetry or antisymmetry are not entangled and may be observed deterministically. After a final Hadamard transformation, as above, the state vector will have exactly one finite entry, with all others zero. The one finite entry can be identified as a binary identification of qubits, depending on the position of the entry. For example, $[1, -1, -1, 1, -1, 1, 1, -1]'/\sqrt{8}$ after transformation by $H \otimes H \otimes H$ becomes

$$|111\rangle = \begin{bmatrix} 0 \\ 0 \\ 0 \\ 0 \\ 0 \\ 0 \\ 0 \\ 1 \end{bmatrix}$$

The entry is in position seven, 111. This means that the result is $|1\rangle \otimes |1\rangle \otimes |1\rangle$.

Quantum Boolean Function Identification

Readers interested in reversible programming and design might also be interested in knowing ways to identify an unknown quantum Boolean functions. In the field of communications, if someone sends you a physical system described by a state vector that has been acted upon by a Boolean function, the identification of that function might be important. Given functions could point to useful information in a large database.

To study function identification, a test system is illustrated in Figure 10-1. In this setup there are $n + 1$ qubits. The test system provides a standard state vector. First the qubit system is initialized to what may be described as state 1 (box 1). The Hadamard transform then creates alternating positive and

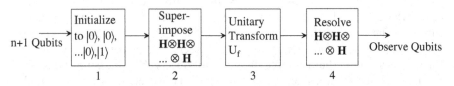

FIGURE 10-1 Boolean function test system.

negative entries (box 2). The state vector is then multiplied by a certain $\mathbf{U_f}$ representing the quantum Boolean function in box 3, essentially mixing up the elements of the state vector. The physical system described by the mixed-up state vector created in box 3 is then sent to another person, who knows nothing about the function. Can the Boolean function be identified? Essentially the receiver is going to implement box 4 in the diagram. The state vector is first multiplied by $\mathbf{H} \otimes \mathbf{H} \otimes \cdots \otimes \mathbf{H}$ and then observed. Once the state vector is observed, it usually is changed permanently by the observation. The state vector cannot be observed again.

When a state vector system is observed, each qubit generally has a certain probability of being 1 or 0. This means that a great many possible state vectors have the ability to scatter a probability in any given observation. One can say that there is a good likelihood of a given function, for example, or that it probably is a function of a given type, but one cannot say for sure what the function is. As with the weather, there is always a chance that a prediction is completely different from reality. To circumvent the uncertainty, it usually is agreed a priori that the function is a member of one of the following classes.

Class 1: Constant Function   The resulting observation of $n + 1$ qubits could have the form $[0 \pm 1\ 0\ 0\ \cdots\ 0]^{\mathrm{T}}$. This is a basis state with one element finite and all others zero. In this case, the underlying function is a constant. A plus sign means a constant function that is 0 for all possible binary inputs in a truth table. A negative sign means a constant function that is 1 for all possible binary inputs in a truth table. A demonstration that all 1's gives $+1$ and all 0's gives -1 is easily accomplished in MATLAB but is beyond the scope of this chapter.

If the qubits in the state vector are being observed in a readout procedure, the negative sign will not be observable. Only probabilities are observable.

Class 2: Test Function   *Test functions* are all functions that create symmetric or antisymmetric state vectors. The $n + 1$ qubits would have a single ± 1 entry in any given place, with 0's elsewhere. This means that the mystery function is a test function. A constant function is a special case of a test function. Using $n + 1$ qubits, it can be shown that there are 2^n test functions corresponding to an entry of a single $+1$ in the state vector. For example, for $n = 2$ the functions are 0, a, b, and $a \oplus b$. For an entry of -1 in the state vector there are 2^n more functions, the complements of the functions above: 1, a', b', $(a \oplus b)'$. Often, test functions contain XOR functions, depending on the size of n and where the ± 1 occurs in the state vector. Test functions are a generalization of the constant function mentioned above. A positive entry refers to a given Boolean function; a negative entry refers to the complement of that function. Assuming that negative signs are not observable, one cannot discern a given Boolean function from its complement. However, to within a complement, a test function may be identified exactly.

Class 3: Balanced Function A function could be *balanced*, meaning that there equal numbers of 1's and 0's in a truth table for the Boolean function. For example, the function with the truth table 01110001 is balanced, although it is neither symmetric nor antisymmetric. A balanced function can be shown to have no finite component in the basic state $|000\cdots01\rangle$; that is, a balanced function will have the form $[x_0 \; 0 \; x_1 \; x_2 \; \cdots \; x_{n+1}]'$. The x-values in this vector may or may not be finite, but since their squares relate to probabilities of observation, x-value magnitudes will be less than unity. If the measured state vector has a 0 in this place, it may or may not be a balanced function. Having a 0 in this place is necessary but not sufficient. All test functions except for a constant function also imply a zero in this place, $[x_0 \; 0 \; x_1 \; x_2 \cdots x_{n+1}]'$.

Returning to the communications issue, it may be agreed that only state vector systems of class 1 or 2 are going to be used. With this a priori knowledge, a single measurement would identify with certainty one of the 2^n quantum Boolean functions (or one of the 2^n complements of these functions). These may be determined with certainty to provide 2^n unique options to a receiver.

Quantum computers were substantially popularized by publication of the Deutsch algorithm (David Deutsch, 1953–). Here we have two quantum Boolean functions, one each from class 1 and class 3. These may be measured to provide with certainty a single bit of information to a receiver. If many copies of the state vector system were available, statistical analysis might be possible as an approach to infer the unknown Boolean function. Statistical analysis to infer a quantum Boolean function is nontrivial and would be an area of future research.

It will be seen clearly in what follows that classical logically reversible parallel computers and quantum computers are intimately related. Their wiring diagrams are practically identical, something that is not generally known.

QUANTUM COMPUTER PROGRAMMING

We now concern ourselves with those Boolean functions used in a wiring diagram. Wiring diagrams, introduced in earlier chapters, denote a sequence of logically reversible operations. Basic practical operations used for both classical and quantum systems are unconditional NOT (UN), single-controlled NOT (SCN), and double-controlled NOT (DCN). Classical reversible computers in this book use wiring diagrams denoting identical bit operations in parallel registers, whereas quantum computers use wiring diagrams denoting qubit operations.

UN Gate

The most basic operation is the quantum unconditional NOT (UN), typically called a *UN gate*. If $|B_1\rangle$ is a basic $|0>$ or $|1\rangle$, the quantum UN can be expressed as $|B_1\rangle \rightarrow |B_2\rangle = |B_1 \oplus 1\rangle$. The symbol for this is shown in Figure 10-2.

$$|B_1\rangle \quad \underline{\qquad\qquad-\!\!\circ\!\!-\qquad\qquad} \quad |B_2\rangle$$

FIGURE 10-2   Quantum unconditional NOT gate.

To investigate the quantum UN gate, we begin with basic states $|01\rangle$ or $[[0 \ 1 \ 0 \ 0]'$. Then we perform a Hadamard transform to give

$$|AB_1\rangle = [1 \quad 1]'/\sqrt{2} \otimes [1-1]'/\sqrt{2}$$
$$= [1-1 \quad 1-1]'/\sqrt{4}$$

Notice the pattern of alternating signs. This state vector can be expressed as a superposition of basic states:

$$|\psi_2\rangle = |AB_1\rangle$$

$$= \frac{1}{\sqrt{4}}\begin{bmatrix}1\\0\\0\\0\end{bmatrix} - \frac{1}{\sqrt{4}}\begin{bmatrix}0\\1\\0\\0\end{bmatrix} + \frac{1}{\sqrt{4}}\begin{bmatrix}0\\0\\1\\0\end{bmatrix} - \frac{1}{\sqrt{4}}\begin{bmatrix}0\\0\\0\\1\end{bmatrix}$$

The superposition may be expressed in a line as $\{|00\rangle - |01\rangle + |10\rangle - |11\rangle\}\sqrt{4}$. The plus and minus signs help differentiate the components of the state vector. We now apply the NOT to each basic state. A new state vector can be constructed one component at a time. Each basic state $|ab\rangle$ will become $|ab'\rangle$. The state vector on the right thus becomes

$$|AB_2\rangle = \{|01\rangle - |00\rangle + |11\rangle - |10\rangle\}/\sqrt{4}$$

Placing the elements in order, the state vector on the right becomes

$$|AB_2\rangle = [-1 \quad 1-1 \quad 1]'/\sqrt{4}$$

Notice, that there is a different pattern in the state vector that will affect future transformations. Imagine four binary numbers 00, 01, 10, 11; the quantum NOT can be thought of as converting them to 01, 00, 11, 10 in parallel.

Physical feasibility is not discussed in this chapter, but it is an issue never the less. If the UN can be accomplished in one operation, these four binary numbers are effectively processed in parallel. Ideally, the UN can be accomplished in a fixed number of physical operations such as laser pulses for any number of qubits in the system. Then the size of the state vector can scale up to a very large size indeed. UN gates as above would ideally scale up to a very large vector while using a fixed number of operations, a definite advantage. But if there are many operations—for example, a need for one or more laser pulses for each of the 2^n elements of a state vector—effective parallelism is eliminated, as would the potential advantage of a quantum computer.

Controlled NOT Gate

Figure 10-3 denotes a quantum-controlled NOT gate. If $|A\rangle$ and $|B_1\rangle$ on the left are basic $|0\rangle$ or $|1\rangle$, the controlled NOT can be expressed as $|A, B_1\rangle \rightarrow |A, B_1 \oplus A\rangle$. That is, if $A = 1$, the state of B_1 undergoes a NOT operation to become $B_3 = B_1'$; otherwise, it is unchanged. As we did for the UN example, we prepare a state vector on the left to be

$$|\psi_3\rangle = |AB_1\rangle$$
$$= [1 - 1 \quad 1 - 1]'/\sqrt{4}$$

This can be delineated as a superposition of basic states:

$$|\psi_3\rangle = \{|00\rangle - |01\rangle + |10\rangle - |11\rangle\}/\sqrt{4}$$

After the controlled NOT operation, the state vector on the right becomes.

$$|AB_3\rangle = \{|00\rangle - |01\rangle + |11\rangle - |10\rangle\}/\sqrt{4}$$

This can be organized to be

$$|AB_3\rangle = [1 - 1 - 1 \quad 1]'/\sqrt{4}$$

The pattern in the state vector changed from $1 \quad -1 \quad 1 \quad -1$ to $1 \quad -1 \quad -1 \quad 1$. This will affect future transformations. In this case, one may imagine that the numbers 00, 01, 10, 11 are changed to 00, 01, 11, 10. If the operation can effectively be accomplished in one operation, these four binary numbers are effectively processed in parallel. Ideally, this will scale up to any sized vector.

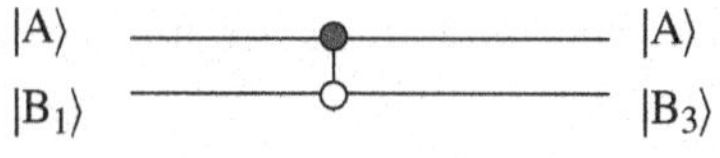

FIGURE 10-3 Quantum-controlled NOT.

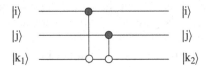

FIGURE 10-4   Addition using qubits.

An application of controlled NOTs would be qubit addition, as shown in Figure 10-4. In this example $|k_2\rangle$ holds the modulo 2 sum of $|i\rangle$ and $|j\rangle$. Think of $|k_1\rangle$ as equal to zero on the left. Then on the right the truth table of interest is

i	j	k_2
0	0	0
0	1	1
1	0	1
1	1	0

This is also the exclusive OR function of i and j. Actually, the wiring diagram uses qubits. The qubits on the left can be prepared as follows using Hadamard transforms:

$$|i\rangle = [\mathbf{1} \quad \mathbf{1}]'/\sqrt{2}$$
$$|j\rangle = [\mathbf{1} \quad \mathbf{1}]'/\sqrt{2}$$
$$|k_1\rangle = [\mathbf{1} - \mathbf{1}]'/\sqrt{2} \ .$$

The state vector on the left is therefore

$$|\psi_4\rangle = |ijk_1\rangle = [\mathbf{1} \ -\mathbf{1} \ \mathbf{1} \ -\mathbf{1} \ \mathbf{1} \ -\mathbf{1} \ \mathbf{1} \ -\mathbf{1}]'/\sqrt{8}$$

This input on the left can be expressed as a superposition to be

$$|\psi_4\rangle = \{|000\rangle - |001\rangle + |010\rangle - |011\rangle + |100\rangle - |101\rangle + |110\rangle - |111\rangle\}/\sqrt{8}$$

The output on the right becomes (changes are highlighted)

$$|ijk_2\rangle = \{|000\rangle - |001\rangle + \mathbf{|011\rangle} - \mathbf{|010\rangle} + \mathbf{|101\rangle} - \mathbf{|100\rangle} + |110\rangle - |111\rangle\}/\sqrt{8}$$

Thus the pattern on the right can be organized to be

$$[1 \quad -1 \quad -1 \quad 1 \quad -1 \quad 1 \quad 1 \quad -1]'/\sqrt{8}$$

The state vector pattern $1 \ -1 \ 1 \ -1 \ 1 \ -1 \ 1 \ -1$ becomes $1 \ -1 \ -1 \ 1$ $-1 \ 1 \ 1 \ -1$ and will affect future transformations. It does not mean much standing alone, being only an intermediate step in a larger quantum algorithm. One may imagine that the numbers 000, 001, 010, 011; 100, 101, 110, 111 are changed to 000, 001, 011, 010; 101, 100, 110, 111 in parallel.

Double-Controlled NOT Gate

This is a quantum gate that performs the NOT operation, depending on two other qubits. The DCN, in conjunction with the SCN and the UN, constitute a *complete* set of gates that can be used to construct an arbitrary Boolean function. The DCN symbol is shown in Figure 10-5. The double-controlled NOT is defined by $|A, B, C_1 > \rightarrow |A, B, C_1 \oplus AB>$, where AB is the AND of A and B. Assume a superposition of states on the left as before:

$$|A\rangle = [1 \quad 1]'/\sqrt{2}, |B\rangle = [1 \quad 1]'/\sqrt{2}, |C_1\rangle = [1 - 1]'/\sqrt{2}$$

The state vector on the left is

$$|\psi_5\rangle = |ABC_1\rangle = [1 \quad -1 \quad 1 \quad -1 \quad 1 \quad -1 \quad 1 \quad -1]'/\sqrt{8}$$

This can be expressed as

$$|\psi_5\rangle = \{|000\rangle - |001\rangle + |010\rangle - |011\rangle + |100\rangle - |101\rangle + |110\rangle - |111\rangle\}/\sqrt{8}$$

Applying $A, B, C_1\rangle \rightarrow A, B, C_1 \oplus AB$ to each basic state gives on the right:

$$|ABC_2\rangle = \{|000\rangle - |001\rangle + |010\rangle - |011\rangle + |100\rangle - |101\rangle + |111\rangle - |110\rangle\}/\sqrt{8}$$

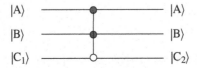

FIGURE 10-5 Double-controlled NOT gate.

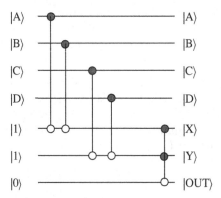

FIGURE 10-6   Locating a keyword.

The state vector on the right becomes

$$|ABC_2\rangle = [1 \;\; -1 \; 1 \;\; -1 \; 1 \;\; -1 \;\; -1 \; 1]/\sqrt{8}$$

Again, this would be an intermediate step in a longer quantum algorithm.

An application of DCN would be setting a flag when a keyword is located. For example, assume that $|A\rangle$ and $|C\rangle$ are known and given as some combination of $|0\rangle$ and $|1\rangle$ as shown in Figure 10-6. The input on the left is a particular state vector system with real elements and is not a superposition of integers. The outputs on the right are defined by the inputs on the left: $|A\rangle$, $|B\rangle$, $|C\rangle$, $|D\rangle$ are unchanged; $|B\rangle$ and $|D\rangle$ are assumed to be a sought-after combination of $|0\rangle$ and $|1\rangle$ to represent the sought-after keyword. The qubit labeled $|OUT\rangle$ serves as a flag when a match is found. For example, if $|B\rangle = |A\rangle$ and $|D\rangle = |C\rangle$, then qubit $|OUT\rangle$ toggles to true. This particular system has 2^7 elements in its state vector system, most of which are used for scratchpad space.

HISTORICAL QUANTUM COMPUTING ALGORITHMS

A quantum computer promises to employ hundreds or thousands of qubits for an extremely large state vector. A major application may be the solution of NP-complete problems. We now present overviews of historical quantum algorithms in a few words per algorithm.

Grover's Algorithm

Grover's search algorithm (Lov Grover) can apply an exhaustive search over the set of possible solutions. The algorithm is usually thought of as applying to an unstructured database. Grover's algorithm is probabilistic, as are most quantum algorithms and provides an answer with high probability. The probability of correctness can be increased by repeating the algorithm.

Suppose that we have an unstructured sea of data in which is hidden some information we want. There are keywords x based on n qubits such that $0 \leq x \leq 2^n - 1$. The number of keywords in the database is $N = 2^n$. We include an additional qubit to tag a keyword of interest. Overall there are at least $n + 1$ qubits in this keyword system, not counting those needed for scratchpad calculations.

A quantum Boolean function $f(x)$ is now constructed that will tag the keyword of interest no matter where it is located in a sea of data. The function is defined on integers x so that $f(x) = 0$ for all x except $x = x_0$. A state vector is prepared for $n + 1$ qubits (associated with 2^n integers y and a tag qubit) as in boxes 1 and 2 in Figure 10-1. This places the n qubits into a standard superposition. In box 3 we apply a unitary transform U_f corresponding to $f(x)$. Box 3 in this application has been termed an oracle because it tags the desired keyword with a negative sign where the function is true. This can be interpreted as tagging x_0 with a negative sign corresponding to the location x_0 of the hidden keyword. We do not know the value of x_0, but once tagged, the oracle knows where it is. Finding it has been compared to finding a needle in a haystack.

The following algorithm ignores any symmetry or special properties resulting from an application of U_f. In special cases, there might be a shortcut to identifying x_0, which is still a topic of ongoing research. The algorithm for the general case is outlined as follows:

Step 1. The qubits are prepared as in boxes 1 and 2 in Figure 10-1. This is assumed equivalent to Hadamard transform on the first n qubits and initializing the last qubit to the quantity $(|0\rangle - |1\rangle)/\sqrt{2}$.

Step 2. Repeat steps (a) and (b) below a number of times equal to m (defined below).

(a) Apply U_f.

(b) Apply to the n qubits the unitary operator $D = -I + 2J/N$, where J is the all-1's matrix.

Step 3. Observe (destructively) the qubits and observe a keyword x.

Step 4. Evaluate $f(x)$. If $f(x) = 1$ then $x = x_0$; quit. Otherwise, go to step 1 to reinitialize and then to repeat the iterative process.

The algorithm above is characterized by the fact that it has an iterative subroutine and that the entire algorithm can be repeated if the destructive readout fails to provide a correct result. The optimum number of iterations can be determined to be $m \approx \sqrt{N}$, by which time there is a very good chance of finding the correct value of x_0 or at least something close to x_0. Refer to the literature for a complete description of the algorithm and an analysis of its performance. Note that Grover's quantum algorithm requires up to $\sqrt{N}$ evaluations of a quantum Boolean function, which seems like a lot of evaluating. However, a classical search might require up to N evaluations. Basically, Grover's algorithm aims to present a value for x_0 using a number of evaluations proportional to $\sqrt{N}$. This is far short of the hoped-for exponential improvement (number of evaluations proportional to n), but for large N the improvement is substantial.

Shor's Algorithm

An example of factoring a number into prime factors is $2,934,331 = 911 \times 3,221$. Shor captured the attention of the world with an algorithm for factoring a large number N into its prime factors: $pq = N$ (Peter Shor, 1959–). The difficulty of factoring a large N into a product of two large prime numbers is crucial to some public key encryption methods. What follows is a brief summary mainly to show the Fourier dimension of a quantum algorithm.

The first step is to evaluate a special function for all integers x up to N: $g(x) = y^x \bmod(N)$, where N is being factored. This function may be evaluated unitarily using a complex of quantum gates. The number of qubits n is chosen such that $N \leq 2^n$. The constant y is chosen so that the greatest common divisor of y and N is 1. For example, if $N = 15$, then y could be 13.

The important bit of knowledge is that $g(x) = y^x \bmod(N)$ plotted as a function of integers x will show that $g(x)$ is a periodic function. A state vector system with n qubits is initialized to all zeros and given a Hadamard transform to create the equivalent of a superposition of integers up to $2^n - 1$. Then U_g, the unitary equivalent of $g(x)$, is applied using a complex of quantum gates that implement $g(x)$. The resulting state vector system will contain entries that are periodic.

Let r be the sought-after period. It is well known that a Fourier transform would display the frequencies in $g(x)$, so clearly, a quantum version is needed. A quantum finite Fourier transform was developed that will display with a high probability the frequency content of $g(x)$, where the reciprocal of frequency is period. After quantum finite Fourier transform, an observation may be taken. There is a good probability of determining a correct value for r. As in practically any quantum algorithm, there is a finite probability of observing an incorrect value. In the end, one of $y^{r/2} \pm 1$ is supposed to be a prime factor; checking for a prime factor is necessary. If a prime factor is found, stop. Otherwise, the entire procedure must be run again. The algorithm is characterized by the fact that multiple runs are permitted.

CONCLUSIONS

It is extremely educational to compare a classical logically reversible computer to a quantum computer. They both employ wiring diagrams, but there are fundamental differences. Nanoprocessors are transparent, and nanoprocessor bits are completely observable. In contrast, quantum computer qubits belong to a physical system that operates in secret; the system cannot be observed without resetting the entire state vector.

Capability for logical reversibility can be related to toggling. We have seen that controlled toggling in systems of qubits can accomplish quantum Boolean logic that is logically reversible. This suggests that controlled toggling in classical nanoprocessors might accomplish classical logic gates. In fact, classical logic based on toggling may be designed to be logically reversible. This permits surprising advantages from an engineering point of view. A parallel computer (or associative processor) designed with toggling can be made to be electrically reversible and thus adiabatic in a limit of slow clocking.

A quantum NOT gate implies toggling of a qubit, which can be viewed as a certain style of toggling (whereas classical T flip-flops represent another certain style). Quantum toggling can be interpreted to be an interchange of elements in a state vector (whereas bit toggling merely flips the bit).

As another similarity, qubit transformations can be adiabatic, the same as CMOS transformations, depending on technology, for example, if electron spin states can be employed. There is undeniable common ground between quantum processing and classical processing. One significant difference is that state vector systems cannot be read out without changing the state vector irreversibly. It must not be forgotten that the potency of a quantum computer has to do with hidden transformations within a state vector system, including the possibility of nonlocal effects because of entangled states. No classical computer has such effects. The fact that a quantum computer might someday process hundreds or thousands of qubits is also a factor that cannot be ignored.

A wiring diagram for a classical computer is supposed to be logically reversible at all times. In contrast, a wiring diagram for a quantum algorithm may involve destructive readout in which the state vector is irreversibly modified. For example, Grover's and Shor's algorithms permit a complete repetition of the algorithm in case the correct answer is not found. This is a significant difference. Readout in a quantum algorithm is an irreversible logical operation in which information is lost; irreversible logic is expected to consume energy.

Number representation in a quantum computer differs significantly from those of classical number theory. In a quantum computer all integers ranging from 0 to $2^n - 1$ are implied in a state vector corresponding to elements of the vector from 0 to $2^n - 1$. Controlled toggling in systems of qubits can accomplish what is called quantum parallelism. This compares to the classical parallel nanoprocessors in the sense that many numbers can be processed concurrently. The coefficients of state vectors may be complex and so may contain phase shifts as necessary for quantum discrete Fourier transforms. This ability is not unique to state vectors, however, since classical systems may also perform complex arithmetic.

Both classical and quantum systems have energy baggage, or energy that is dissipated to maintain isolation from the environment, energy leakage due to nonideal construction materials, and dissipation in power supplies. Everyone understands that computers have air-conditioning and power supply require-ments, although classical adiabatic systems could change this. In theory, classical power supplies might someday be designed to be electrically reversible, although this is going to be difficult. Similarly, quantum computers might someday be designed with environmental protection that does not dissipate external energy.

The most potent computer known is the human brain. But even neurons have an energy baggage in which calories are consumed for maintenance and growth, including simple heating in neural membranes to keep neurons healthy. Quantum computers are important theoretically. For example, Richard Feyn-man used a quantum computer concept to demonstrate the physical possibility of a logically reversible computer. Another application of theory, albeit an extremely humble application, occurs when we used the term *pseudoqubits* to measure the capacity of a classical computer.

The material in this chapter is essential to gain an understanding of the relationship between quantum computer processing and brain memory proces-sing. Particularly in the savant brain, we have hypothesized the capability for controlled toggle memory and parallel processing within subconscious long-term memory, as explained in Chapter 7. Assuming this to be true, operations within the gifted brain are similar to the unitary transformations within a quantum computer. Toggle memory, biological or artificial, may be logically reversible. Logical reversibility, in the sense that no information is lost, is a significant attribute in any computing system and is a prime example of a nonabstract property that man-made and biological computer models hold in common with quantum computers.

EXERCISES

10-1 Calculate the 16 elements of the following direct product in symbolic form:

$$\begin{bmatrix} a \\ b \\ c \\ d \end{bmatrix} \otimes \begin{bmatrix} e \\ f \\ g \\ h \end{bmatrix} = ?$$

10-2 Calculate the four elements of the following matrix combination in symbolic form:

$$\begin{bmatrix} a & b \\ c & d \end{bmatrix} \begin{bmatrix} e & f \\ g & h \end{bmatrix} + \begin{bmatrix} w & x \\ y & z \end{bmatrix} = ?$$

10-3 Prove that the 2×2 Hadamard matrix is its own inverse.

10-4 Provide an example other than the one presented in this chapter to show that a Hadamard matrix $\mathbf{H} \otimes \mathbf{H} \otimes \mathbf{H}$ operating on a symmetric or antisymmetric state vector of dimension eight results in a basis state vector. Why is this called a basis vector?

10-5 Investigate the following quantum computer concepts:
  (a) Quantum teleportation. Are there practical difficulties?
  (b) Grover's quantum search algorithm. What is its significance? Are there practical difficulties?
  (c) Shor's quantum factoring algorithm. What is its significance? Are there practical difficulties?

10-6 List all symmetric and antisymmetric state vectors for a vector of dimension eight. Provide associated Boolean test functions.

10-7 Provide an example of an entangled state vector of dimension eight. Why is it called entangled?

10-8 Assume as many replications of the original state vector system as you need for the following.
  (a) Assume a state vector system whose elements are known to be real and positive, but whose magnitudes are unknown. How might the elements be approximated experimentally using statistics?
  (b) Assume a state vector system whose elements are known to be some distribution of positive and negative. To what extent can the elements be determined experimentally?
  (c) Assume a state vector system whose elements are known to be complex. To what extent can the elements be determined experimentally?

10-9 Explore the possibility of using test functions in a quantum database system.

10-10 Explore the possibility of solving a SAT (Boolean satisfiability) problem in a quantum computer assuming n qubits. Assume that only one set of binary inputs activates the function true and that the function evaluates to be false for all others. Suggest a way to find the activating code.

HUMAN BRAIN ANATOMY

COMPONENTS OF A BRAIN

Fortunately for humankind and perhaps unfortunately for neuroscience, the brain is well protected by the skull; it is difficult to study and it certainly was not the first thing that our ancestors took an interest in, except possibly for bashing out each other's brains. After thousands of years of civilization, it was only in 1649 that René Descartes attempted to explain the brain as a machine. A few years later, Thomas Willis (1621–1675) systematically explored the anatomical parts of the brain. Thomas Willis published an anatomy of the brain and nerves in 1664. His work was quite detailed, with much new information for his day, and presents a dramatic contrast with the vague and poor efforts of previous physicians.

When modeling brain memory, one needs a basic vocabulary. Figure A-1 illustrates the major areas of the brain. The cerebrum is the general volume of the right and left hemisphere regions in the upper forebrain. It contains the *cerebral cortex*, a layer of cells, or *gray matter*, and the underlying connections, or *white matter*. The *frontal lobe* of the cerebral cortex is thought to be where important memories are activated for decisions and actions. It is in front of the ears. The human frontal lobes and the prefrontal cortex directly behind the forehead serve to provide solutions to problems both novel and familiar, possibly generic solutions that have been worked out beforehand and stored in memory. There is

Human Memory Modeled with Standard Analog and Digital Circuits:
Inspiration for Man-made Computers, By John Robert Burger
Copyright © 2009 John Wiley & Sons, Inc.

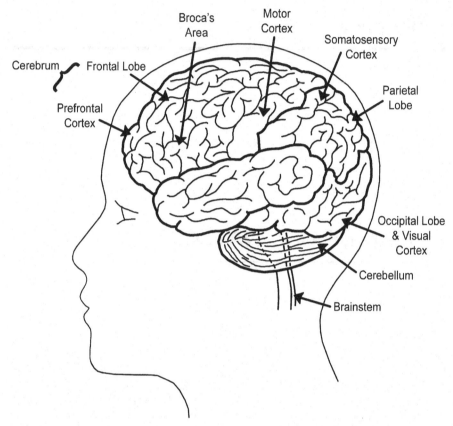

FIGURE A-1   Labeled areas of the brain. © 2006 BGleason Design & Illustration, LLC.

a back-to-front architecture for the cortical areas: The back area contains models of and can recognize danger; the front area stores and enables measured responses. Many mental disorders, such as attention deficits, frontal lobe dementia, and schizophrenia, are caused by problems in the frontal lobes.

Broca's area is located in the lower back part of the left frontal lobe and is associated with the production of spoken and written language. Paul Broca discovered the importance of this region in 1861. Broca's aphasia is a disorder in which a person can understand language but has difficulty in expressing it.

The *motor cortex* is a narrow band in the posterior part of the frontal lobes devoted to the activation of body movements, a band going from ear to ear. The motor cortex works backward and upside down: The left side regulates muscles on the right side of the body, and the right side regulates muscles on the left side of the body. The area at the top regulates our feet, and the area at the bottom, that is, closest to our ears, regulates facial expressions. Most of motor cortex volume in humans is devoted to the complex precise movements of the hands and face.

The *parietal lobes* are in the upper back of the cerebral cortex, behind the ears, and participate in recognition of danger and opportunity. They monitor touch sensations and body positions. Related are the *occipital lobes* (vision) and *temporal lobes* (sound).

The *somatosensory cortex* is a narrow band just behind the motor cortex devoted to touch sensations from the body. The left side receives sensations from the right side of the body, and the right side receives sensations from the left side of the body. Again we are represented upside down, with the top of the brain receiving sensations for our feet, and the bottom, closest to our ears, from our face. The face and hands are highly sensitive to touch and require most of the volume of the somatosensory cortex.

Within the temporal lobes is a left hemispheric bundle, the *angular gyrus*, usually left but not always. It is a connector between the initial written word recognizer and the forward regions of the brain. The *planum temporale* is associated with language comprehension. Typically, it is larger in the left hemisphere within Wernicke's area. Named after the German neurologist, Carl Wernicke, it is a language comprehension region usually located in the upper posterior left temporal lobe. Damage (lesions) in this region results in comprehension problems.

The *cerebellum*, or little brain, is located behind the brain stem, near the little bump at the lower back of the head. It is thought to be a support system for cognitive functions involving sensory input. It has more neurons than those in other parts of the brain.

The *brain stem* is a centimeter or two in diameter and relays information between body and brain. The back of the brain stem is connected to the cerebellum, although there are a number of specialized structures to the hindbrain and the midbrain. Important interior brain systems are shown in Figure A-2.

Hippocampus is a Greek word for Neptune's seahorse, referring to its shape. The hippocampus comprises a pair of curved components under the inside of the temporal lobes. It plays a role in the formation and retrieval of long-term memories. Alzheimer's disease involves the progressive degeneration of hippo-campal neurons and thus of memory functions. It was mentioned earlier how amnesia resulted when a man, called H.M., accidentally had his hippocampus and amygdala removed. This is an example of new knowledge obtained not by funded research, but by pure accident.

The *thalamus* is like a relay station in sorting the senses, except the sense of smell. It has two golf-ball-sized structures deep within the cerebral hemispheres. It is involved in cognitive functions.

The smaller marble-sized *hypothalamus* is below the thalamus and is involved in body regulatory functions such as body temperature, blood circulation, hunger and thirst, sleep, sexual arousal, hormonal secretion, and

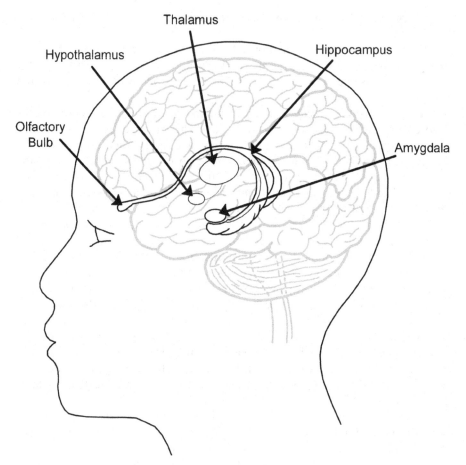

FIGURE A-2   Interior parts of the brain.

defensive responses. Sometimes it is called the brain's brain; it is in the center behind our eyes.

The *olfactory bulb* is the initial odor-processing region. Roughly 30 differing molecules are involved in approximately 10,000 different odors. Seven primary odors in ordinary terms would be peppermint, roses, nail polish, musk, camphor, vinegar, and rotten eggs. Most animals have a more powerful sense of smell than that of humans. The olfactory bulb plays a role in the recall of emotional memories. However, for some reason, we cannot recall the odor of an imagined object as easily as we can recall its shape and color.

The *amygdala* is a pair of complex parts the size of a cherry that activates primal fears and other emotional responses. It has been called the fear button. Each amygdala is about 4 cm into your brain from either temple. When a sudden movement or loud sound is detected, the amygdala will signal the hypothalamus to initiate a standard response: for example, to fight, to take flight, or to freeze.

The amygdala is important to memory because it adds emotional content to an impression. Emotion is an important cue for creating and for retrieving long-term memories. We usually remember details associated with emotional events, such as a first date, or where we were when Kennedy was assassinated, or where we were on September 11, 2001.

If the challenge does not require an immediate response, the *cingulate gyrus* aids in retrieving and analyzing memories of prior situations and developing responses for future use. It helps us to make up our minds about what to do in the presence of ambiguous information. The cingulated gyrus is on top of the corpus callosum that connects the left and right brains. Additionally, it determines the emotional strength of sensory information and presents a result to the cortex.

Brain anatomy details may be found at http://braininfo.rprc.washington.edu and http://www.med.harvard.edu/AANLIB/home.html.

FOREBRAIN STRUCTURE

The verbal description of the general volume of the forebrain is as follows: The cerebrum in the forebrain refers to the combined right and left hemispheres. Each hemisphere is divided into four lobes: three in back to receive and analyze incoming sensory information and a frontal lobe to presents a response. The hemispheres are connected by the corpus callosum and the anterior commissure. Aside from calculational redundancy for reliability, the right brain is geared to novel challenges: for instance, strange faces and new language. The left brain is geared to the familiar: for instance, familiar faces and regular language. It is said that a baby uses the right brain for nonverbal skills but soon develops a language template in the left brain. Overall, the right and left hemispheres are tightly connected. But if ever one half becomes inoperative, the other half takes over.

In the big picture, a large number of neurons and glial cells are organized into the brain stem and the cerebellum for basic body activity. About this are six layers of folded neural tissue known as the cerebrum, constituting most of the neural volume of the brain. The cerebrum has a top cerebral cortex of gray matter and an underlying network of myelinated axons (white matter).

The cerebral cortex is composed of pyramidal and stellate (starlike) neurons. Layer 4 is for input. Layers 5 and 6 are for output. The majority of processing occurs in layers 1, 2, and 3. Through the six layers of gray matter extend hundreds of millions of interconnected hairlike columns, each with about 100 neurons. It is thought that each minicolumn can process a feature of information such as a line or a tone. One hundred minicolumns form a macrocolumn, about the thickness of pencil lead. Thousands of macrocolumns form one of the 50 or more Brodmann areas in each hemisphere.

Korbinian Brodmann was a pioneer in organizing the cerebral cortex into distinct regions based on structural variations. He identified over 50 numbered

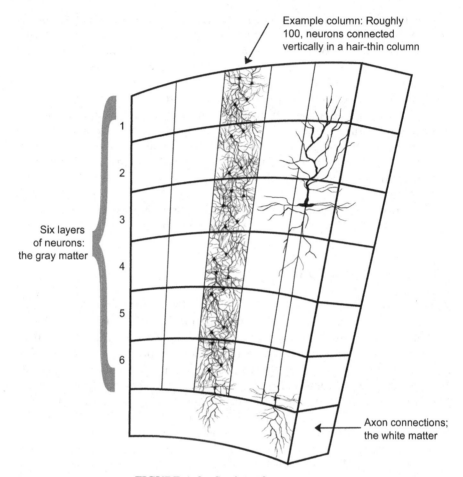

FIGURE A-3   Section of gray matter.

areas in 1909, and the system is still widely used, although others have identified hundreds of additional structural variations. A dense web of axons and myelation (the white matter) goes beneath the gray matter. Figure A-3 illustrates the six layers. Gray matter includes dendritic trees. White matter consists of mylinated axons apparently going to the hippocampus and beyond.

As a point of interest, Alzheimer's and Parkinson's diseases are involved with degeneracy of the hippocampus. Alzheimer's is thought to be caused by a plaque: that is, sticky proteins that fold about neurons and eventually destroy their function. There is also neuronal loss in subcortical areas, including the substantia nigra (black substance). The substantia nigra in the midsection of the brain stem produces dopamine for the basal ganglia and frontal lobes. Extensive cell demise in the substantia nigra results in Parkinson's disease, which usually results in the gradual loss of conscious regulation of movement.

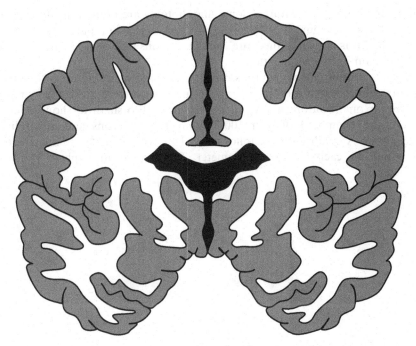

FIGURE A-4 Overview of surface gray matter.

Located beneath the gray matter is white matter, distributed as shown in Figure A-4. Assuming one neuron per feature in each hemisphere, the numbers add as follows. 50 Brodmann areas, each with, say, 10,000 macrocolumns, each with, say, 500 minicolumns, each with about 100 neurons. This represents

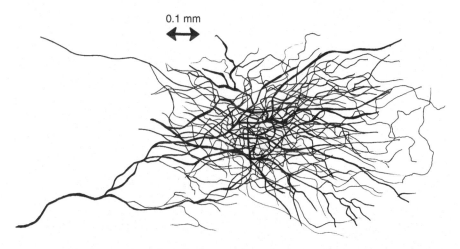

FIGURE A-5 Intersection of two neurons.

25 billion (2.5×10^{10}) features. Some undoubtedly are unused, ready to learn new features, and some may be copies of others for backup purposes. Even so, what remains is immense; there are enough neurons that each feature can have its own axon in its own location.

An intersection of two neurons can be visualized as in Figure A-5. Neural circuits define all that a brain can do. Connections are established in synapses between axonal boutons and dendritic receivers (too small to show). Neural circuits are composed of over 100 billion (10^{11}) neurons and quadrillions of synapses. A quadrillion is 1 followed by 15 zeros (10^{15}). Try to imagine this many marbles each 1/2 inch in diameter. They would fill a sphere 1 mile in diameter.

APPENDIX B

THE PSYCHOLOGICAL SCIENCE OF MEMORY

Fundamental to a memory model is the ability to represent the ways in which information is stored. Human memory can be observed to store for the short term (a few seconds) and for the long term (many decades).

SHORT-TERM MEMORY

Short-term conscious memory is like a puff of smoke that spreads into thin air. As an empirical study of short-term memory, a test was reported by Peterson and Peterson in 1959. Subjects were told a set of three consonants, such as RLZ. After a delay of a few seconds they were asked to recall the consonants. Rehearsal, that is, being allowed to say RLZ over and over again, was discouraged in an attempt to discount long-term memory. The method of discouraging rehearsal was to ask the subject to count backward in steps of three from a given three-digit number, for example, 701, 689, 686,..., immediately after being read the consonants. Under these conditions, it was observed that there was little recall after a few seconds, as shown in Figure B-1.

There is an obvious short-term memory loss in which detail fades away quickly. In this experiment, counting backward was observed to shorten the duration in which detail was remembered. A factor concerning fading may be

Human Memory Modeled with Standard Analog and Digital Circuits: Inspiration for Man-made Computers, By John Robert Burger
Copyright © 2009 John Wiley & Sons, Inc.

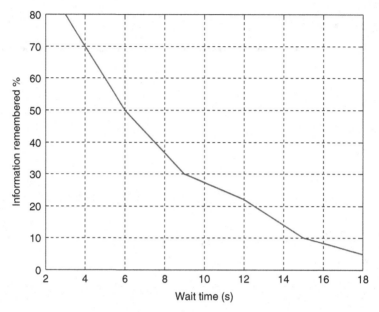

FIGURE B-1   Percentage of information remembered after a given wait time.

that it is accelerated by the imposition of new impressions, that is, by *interference*. This suggests the possibility that interference either sooner or later is the normal way in which a short-term memory impression is terminated. The curve in Figure B-1 suggests that impressions in short-term memory can persist for a few seconds.

LONG-TERM MEMORY

Long-term memory is modeled to be the subconscious storage of information. There is a transfer of information from short-term memory into long-term memory that seems to occur automatically for information that is frequently impressed into short-term memory. In an experiment reported by Murdock in 1962, subjects heard a list of 20 common unrelated words presented at the rate of one word per second in English. Immediately after hearing the list, subjects were asked to write down as many of the words on the list as they could recall, in any order they wanted. The results are shown in Figure B-2.

Subjects remembered relatively more from the very beginning of the list (*primacy effect*), and from the very end (*recency effect*). The recency effect is thought due to short-term memory; the assumption is that words heard most recently are remembered briefly. The primacy effect is thought to be due to long-term memory. One reason for this view is that the subject has had opportunity for rehearsal and transfer into long term memory. For example,

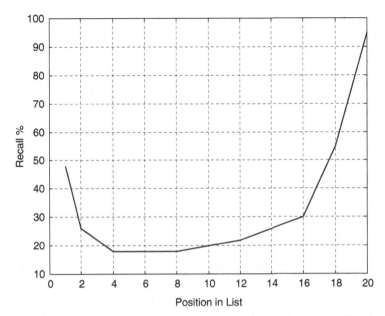

FIGURE B-2 Percentage recall showing primacy and recency effects.

the subject, upon hearing a word near the beginning, could review the sequence word 1, word 2, word 3, and so on, until there are too many words to rehearse this way. Rehearsal apparently facilitates a transfer into long-term memory.

If there is a short wait after the reading of words, the primacy effect is expected to stay about the same, but the recency effect is expected to vanish. Rehearsal during the wait can be discouraged by asking for other mental activities. In 1966, Glanzer and Cunitz reported the data shown in Figure B-3. Long-term memory is unchanged for words at the beginning of the list, while short-term memory no longer exists for words at the end of the list. The speed of the reading of words is expected to affect the amount of rehearsal that is possible, and therefore the number of words committed to long-term memory, as shown in Figure B-4.

Anterograde amnesia is the inability to store or recall recent information, although these amnesiacs can recall information from periods prior to the damage. A striking example of this is a man commonly called H.M., who accidentally had most of his hippocampus and amygdala removed surgically at age 27 (in 1953) in an attempt to control his epileptic seizures. It helped his seizures but left him with anterograde amnesia. Since then H.M. has lived in the world of short-term memory and memories from before the surgery, although it is reported that he can still learn new skills.

In the memory model of this book it is obvious that the operation disrupted the memorization enable circuit. This circuit conveys a signal to unused blocks of long-term memory to accept those current impressions in short-term memory.

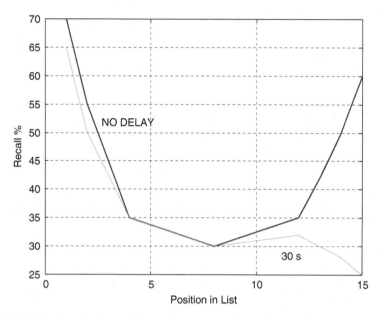

FIGURE B-3   Recall after a 30-second wait, showing a loss of short-term memory.

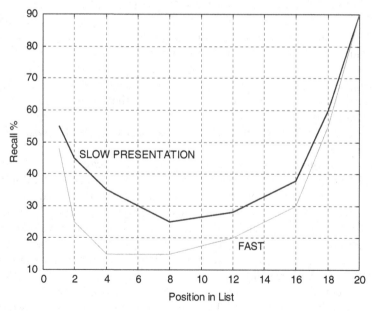

FIGURE B-4   Effect of presentation speed showing reduction in long-term memory.

Most often, amnesia occurs in long-term factual and autobiographical memory. *Retrograde amnesia* is the inability to recall any information that was stored prior to the damage. In the model of this book, it may be concluded that old words of memory have been damaged by an external force, possibly disconnected from the memory system by a disruption of synaptic connections. One can hope that new synapses will form into blocks of long-term memory neurons given enough time. A less hopeful possibility is neural damage, erasing a percentage of old memory impressions. Since recent impressions apparently can be memorized and then recalled without difficulty in those suffering retrograde amnesia, there is little reason to blame the common circuits of the model that convey information between long- and short term-memory.

STUDIES IN LEARNING

An old-style self-disciplined German named Hermann Ebbinghaus (1850–1909) developed an experimental technique that minimized the encoding aspects of long-term memory. He invented *nonsense syllables*, which are two consonants with a vowel in between, such as *zup* and *rif*, but not a word. He constructed about 2300 such syllables. Each was written on a slip of paper. He then randomly drew from 7 to 36 syllables to create a list, and set out to memorize each list serially.

This took considerable time, and in view of our understanding of learning, Ebbinghaus not only memorized, but learned, his sequences of nonsense syllables. Learning in this book implies synaptic growth over time using new neurons developed to identify the next item in a list based on connections to previous items in the list. This is analogous to learning a basic procedure, such as walking, that may be performed automatically without having to recall basic elements into short term-memory. Learning of this sort is termed neural state-machine learning in this book, where states are elements or words of long-term memory. A neural state machine involves interneurons and synapses that establish an automatic procedure between words of long-term memory. As a result, a certain relevant sequence is executed automatically without all the details passing through short-term memory.

Using a method called *serial anticipation*, at clicks from a metronome, Ebbinghaus learned to recall the first item, then the second, and so on, turning the slip of paper face up each time (to verify the correctness of the syllable). He repeated the entire list over and over until the entire list was finally mastered. He recorded the number of times (trials) through the list before it was learned. As an example of mental discipline, he learned thousands of such lists in a few years. The number of trials required to learn a given number of syllables is plotted in Figure B-5. Short lists with 7 syllables are remembered perfectly in a couple of presentations. But a list with 14 syllables took 30 trials, suggesting that much additional effort was necessary to learn longer lists. Overall, the number of trials is proportional to the length

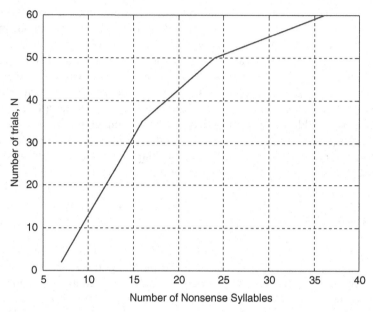

FIGURE B-5 Number of trials N to learn a number M of nonsense syllables

of the list. But for longer lists, the number of trials is less than proportional. This may be an example of a phenomenon in which the brain is *learning how to learn*.

Under the book's model of state machine learning, a new connection involving a new neuron and new synapses is permitted to develop after a *need-to-learn* signal is generated from the circuits of short-term memory. By sending something through short-term memory repeatedly, perhaps using a duration of Δt, the need-to-learn signal is generated by a digital filter and thus activates decoders that pinpoint where new neurons and synapses are to be developed. The total time to learn N quantities of information is thus expected to be $N\Delta t$. Since the number of trials is proportional to time spent, one expects the curve in Figure B-5 to be fairly straight.

The speedup in learning shown in the curve appears to be modest. To explain a speedup in learning, or learning how to learn, it may be conjectured that information is represented more efficiently. Learning involves a packet of information, but there are ways to change what is in a packet. Encoding, for example, discussed below, groups literal alphanumeric characters into meaningful chunks.

Ebbinghaus also noted what he termed a *forgetting curve*. After a few hours he retested himself, finding that he forgot almost everything (or at least could not recall most everything). Figure B-6 illustrates a forgetting curve. The decline is sharpest at first but levels off, indicating that a significant number of syllables are remembered for longer times.

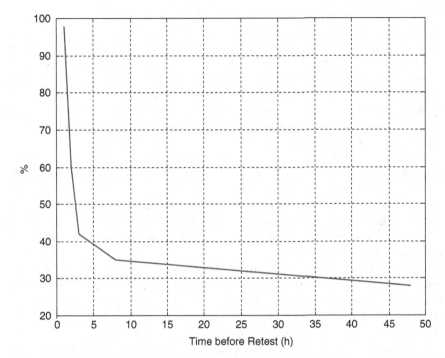

FIGURE B-6   Number still known/number originally known × 100%.

Overlearning

Ebbinghaus also found that rememorizing a list took fewer trials than memorizing it originally. Ebbinghaus discovered that there is much less forgetting when the lists are *overlearned* by further repetition beyond the minimum number of trials.

The all-digital model of learning given in this book depends on connections that are assumed to be secure. The unreliability of connections (resulting in forgetting) is a separate issue. Biologically, it is reasonable to assume that synapses begin small and grow. Size is often confused with strength. Strength does not refer to amplitude but rather, to quantity of excitatory neurotransmitters released. A new and therefore small synapse releasing only a few neurotransmitters is clearly less dependable than a cluster of large well-developed synapses that respond to the same action potential. The forgetting curve suggests that weak synapses are easily undone, possibly the result of the thermal activity of ions. But with additional learning effort, termed *overlearning*, small synapses can be enlarged and strengthened by actions of the learning circuits, possibly by the release of serotonin in the locations where connections are required.

Also vulnerable to thermal activity, but perhaps to a lesser extent, are the neural switches, which dictate the locations of new neurons and synapses.

Even solid-state memories lose information because of thermal activity and hits by outside photons of radiation. To compensate for this in part, error-correcting circuits involving digital parity can be applied in man-made designs. Error correction may be missing biologically, so a forgetting curve is expected.

Also worth considering during memorization are mnemonics. The assumption that nonsense syllables are meaningless can be challenged. Many nonsense syllables, such as *mer* can be thought of as resembling a known word, such as *mare*. Probably there is no verbal material that is completely meaningless, given the creativity of humans.

The *S-R theory of memorization* promotes the idea of stimulus and response. Thus in the series *zup–rif–meb*, *rif* is both a response to *zup*, and a stimulus for *meb*. This is a type of association known as *contiguous association*. Contiguous association is a special case of neural state-machine learning. Under the neural state-machine learning model of this book, the next item in a sequence of states depends not just on the previous item as in contiguous association, but on all previous items.

The encoding part of memorization depends on organizing information into relationships, since organized materials are much more easily remembered than those that are not. We have little trouble remembering long poems that rhyme, for example, but the same hundreds of words arranged in random order are nearly an impossible challenge. Numbers can also be organized. For example, the telephone number 8071625 has great meaning: the 807 and the 1625 are famous types of vacuum tubes used extensively in World War II. Another example is the sequence 149162536481. It can be analyzed as 1, 4, 9, 16, 25, 36, 49, 64, and 81, and each can be recognized as the square of a sequence of integers: $1^2, 2^2, 3^2, ..., 9^2$. These are examples of encoding to facilitate memorization.

An important function of a brain is to encode sensory input into features and relationships. One way to achieve encoding is by practice, so that the mind learns to encode effectively. Recently, a heroic undergraduate devoted many hours to recalling strings of digits in a laboratory environment. In each session he heard random digits at the rate of one per second, a new random sequence in each session. He then tried to recall the sequence. If his recall was correct, the sequence was increased by one digit if incorrect, it was decreased by one digit. After about 20 months of this, the subject's memory of digits after being given a random sequence had increased significantly. This is denoted in Figure B-7 (*length of sequence* indicates the number of digits).

An explanation for the ability to recall random digits presented in a sequence is that the subject encoded the sequences into meaningful parts. For example, he was a long-distance runner. So he thought of digits as running time supplemented by other mnemonics. For example, 3492 became 3 minutes 49.2 seconds; 1944 was near the end of World War II; 893 became 89.3, a very old man. The stated encoding was evidenced by the subject's frequent pause between the recalled groups of digits.

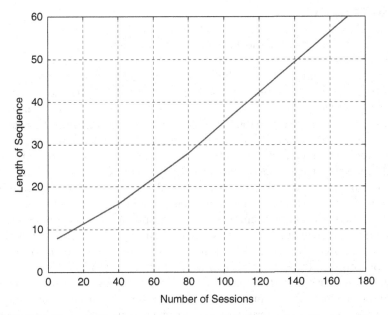

FIGURE B-7 Length of sequence (number of digits) learned vs. Number of sessions.

Figure B-7 shows that the amount of learning is proportional to the time spent, as does the learning curve of Ebbinghaus. In this experiment the apparent speedup in learning might be due to greater cleverness in the encoding.

Encoding of Analog Sensory Information

Encoding has many shades of meaning. A good-sized portion of the brain is dedicated to producing a digital representation of sensory inputs that enter as analog signals; this is a type of *encoding*, also termed *analog-to-digital conversion*. Obviously, we do not store information like pixels in a photograph and bytes in computer memory. Rather, we reconstruct a memory from a large number of reusable features developed from life experiences. A memory of something is encoded into features such as colors, shades, edges, shapes, patterns, locations, emotional impressions, and so on. Because of common features, any one memory naturally associates with a great many others. This is why one is able to visualize someone after hearing the person on the telephone. This type of encoding is automatic, mainly the result of a type of learning identified in this book as *combinational learning*, meaning that neurons and synapses are brought into play to recognize new combinations of existing digital signals.

MEMORY RETRIEVAL

Retrieving a memory that is lost is an everyday problem for most of us. There is a memory search process. An exact set of cues must be presented to retrieve a memory that is buried deep within an associative long-term memory system. Two types of associations are visualized by psychologists: contiguity and similarity. Association by contiguity refers to things that occurred near each other in space and time, like the words of a memorized poem. But this confuses memorizing with learning. Contiguity fits well into the state-machine learning of this book, in which one thing follows another, but it does not fit well into the usual concepts of associative memory. If one chooses to believe that every memory includes a coordinate for space and time, association by contiguity would work fine. Artificial memory systems sometimes do this, but it is difficult to prove that biological memories have stamps. A phenomenon similar to association by contiguity is the logical reversibility of memories, where one can begin at a certain memory and then go forward or backward to recall, or attempt to recall, the next image permitted to long term memory.

Association by similarity refers to common features. In the memory model of this book, memory exists in subconscious long-term memory where memory cells hold features, each represented by a given neuron dedicated to a given feature. A particular set of features constitutes a given image and is defined to be a word of memory. A particular word of memory can be recalled only if exact cues are presented. Inexact cues result in images that are similar: for example, cats and dogs (household pets). They are similar in the sense of two ears, four legs, a tail, furry, friendly, and so on.

The importance of cues was demonstrated in an experiment reported by Tulving and Pearlstone in 1966. Subjects are presented with a list of words in various categories and are asked to memorize them. Then they are asked to recall them. It might turn out that they neglect to recall words from a particular category. But if prompted by the category name, they readily produce several of the associated words.

Memory search and subsequent retrieval is a nontrivial process. Often, a memory appears in a flash after an accurate cue. Sometimes you feel that a name is right on the tip of your tongue, but you cannot remember it. Perhaps the cues you have in short-term memory are incorrect and misleading, giving you a mental block. A person with a mental block must move on to something else for the moment. Later, perhaps in the middle of the night, you will remember the name. The search continued by itself subliminally, producing recall at an unexpected moment.

In ancient times Aristotle discussed retrieval phenomena in his account of memory. He distinguished between remembering and recollecting. In recollecting he noted that ideas succeed each other in a nonrandom fashion. Aristotle claimed that idea A will lead to the recall of idea B, and then to C, and so on. Aristotle, a famous promoter of predicate logic, unwittingly recorded the fact that memory appears to be logically reversible.

SERIAL REPRODUCTION

A phenomenon of interest that many of us have experienced is that things are remembered better than they actually were or worse than they actually were. For example, a teacher who is remembered from childhood might become more idealized; an ex-spouse might be overly vilified. Thus, memories result in new, refreshed memories that are slightly different. A similar experience is *serial reproduction*, in which gossip evolves as it goes from person to person. Each person's memorial becomes a stimulus for the next person, who changes the story slightly. Serial reproduction occurs in memories as well when they are recalled and recommitted as refreshed memories.

MEMORY THEORISTS

We now discuss two people of importance to memory theory, both quite influential, but for different reasons, controversial.

Richard Semon

A memory theorist from the past, Richard Semon (1859–1918), thought that existing vocabulary was inadequate to describe memory and so coined his own terms, as described below. Semon was controversial because of his terms and for other reasons. Semon's background was in biology, not psychology, the bailiwick of memory theory; also, he was divorced. As the worst gaffe of all, Semon claimed that memories can be inherited (the concept of genetic memory and DNA had not yet developed very far). For these reasons he was controversial.

Semon referred to the remembered impression as an *engram*, and proposed that it changes over time. Engrams brought forth to short-term memory depend on what it is important to remember. Important engrams come forth, unimportant ones are ignored. This phenomenon he termed the *direction of attention*.

Another version was the use of the term *stream of consciousness* by the American philosopher William James (1842–1910). The term is colorful and has been used to explain human behavior and literary styles. But using the word *consciousness* refers to something that really needs proof of existence. The existence of consciousness usually means something beyond mere short-term memory, often with religious meanings. It is important to define what is meant by special terms such as *direction of attention* and *stream of consciousness*.

The process of bringing forth engrams was called *ecphory* by Semon. Semon claimed that a memory can change during ecphory. Things are added and subtracted, depending on what is convenient, as in serial reproduction. Subsequently, the augmented memory is then committed as a new, refreshed memory (a new engram). In the recall process, according to Semon, there is interplay between successive recalls. Semon termed interplay between remembered images *homophony*. In *nondifferentiating homophony*, certain image features common to a set of saved images are similar and merge to produce a clear image. Differences in a set of similar recalls tend to fade.

Resonance results in a particularly vivid memory. If something was *rehearsed* over and over, a homophonic process may result in a very vivid recall of nondifferentiating set of images, defined to be a resonance of images.

Differentiating homophony involves few commonalities between successive recalls. These recalls do not form a definite image, but alternate through short-term memory in rapid succession. This occurs when thinking of two completely different things at the same time. Inadequate cues also cause different images to cycle into short-term memory.

Recognition (of a sensory image) was characterized by Semon as resulting from a comparison between information in the environment and information in memory, brought forth under conditions of differentiating homophony. Our model in this book described recognition as possibly a feeling caused by endorphins that are released when a large number of cues are exactly matched, although this has never been proven.

Sigmund Freud

Freud's approach became popular with the middle and upper classes, which strongly supported his work. Sigmund Freud (1856–1939) initiated a realization of the power of the subconscious mind. In his *The Interpretation of Dreams* (1899), Freud proposed ideas that are thought-provoking and controversial. According to Freud, people experience thoughts so painful that they *repress* them, that is, they banish them from short-term memory. Freud argued that the process of repression itself is an unconscious act.

Freud found that he could treat patients by putting them on a couch and gently encouraging them to talk. They were encouraged to talk about dreams, for example. It was important that the analyst not be involved directly, to encourage the patient to project thoughts and feelings onto the analyst. By bringing repressed images into the open, by what Freud called *psychoanalysis*, they can be understood. Through this process, a patient can recall and resolve repressed conflicts.

Psychoanalysis was, and continues, to be controversial. Mental disorders in medical circles are thought to be diseases of the brain, caused either by genetics, disease, or brain damage. The existence of repression is difficult to prove. Philosophically, all proper scientific theories must have the potential to be falsified. As suggested by the philosopher Karl Popper (1902–1994), if a theory cannot be falsified, it is not scientific. Freud's theories involve beliefs that are impossible to falsify: for example, that repressed memories are a cause of neurosis.

DREAMS

Dreams, according to a popular theory, are what we experience as the brain attempts to solve difficult problems as we sleep. Here the brain can test illogical solutions to difficult problems. The catch, of course, is that many difficult problems have no solutions. Unfortunately, the cerebral lobes keep trying (in their own odd way) to solve the problems. On the other hand, every now and then something is solved, as the person realizes upon wakening. The unconscious aspects of human memory are extremely important in this book. Of special interest are circuit models that are synthesized to reproduce the results of subliminal actions, not only for dreams but also for memory searches.

APPENDIX C

BRAIN SCANNING

Brain scanning, also known as *brain imaging*, is potentially a major tool for providing physical insight into how a brain works. This appendix is an introduction to current brain scanning technologies.

ELECTROENCEPHALOGRAPHY

Richard Caton (1842–1926) in Liverpool was first to notice electrical waves in the cerebral hemispheres of rabbits and monkeys in 1875. The first recording of human brain waves, that is, alternating potentials detected by electrodes on the scalp, was made in 1924 by Hans Berger (1873–1941). He named the resulting images *electroencephalograms* (EEGs). EEGs are noninvasive and have proved useful for sleep analysis, coma, and brain death verification. When assessing epilepsy, EEGs can detect seizures and can be accompanied by tests that stimulate a patient in order to study seizure triggers.

After preparing the scalp area by shaving and applying a conductive gel, EEG recordings are obtained by placing electrodes on the scalp. Each electrode feeds a differential amplifier with a voltage gain of 1000 to 100,000, that is, 60 to 100 dB. Scalp voltages are very low, with a maximum of about $100\,\mu V$. If measured invasively on the surface of the brain (by penetrating the skull), this goes up an order of magnitude, to about $1\,mV$. Differential amplifiers are employed because

Human Memory Modeled with Standard Analog and Digital Circuits: Inspiration for Man-made Computers, By John Robert Burger
Copyright © 2009 John Wiley & Sons, Inc.

they resist the pickup of electrical noise. The EEG typically has millisecond resolution, depending on the bandwidth of the differential amplifier.

EEGs are able to detect *evoked potentials* in response to a stimulus, usually electrical, auditory, or visual, but signals are very weak. Signals tend to be buried in the thermal noise that is naturally generated by the electrodes and by the amplifier's input components. Therefore, data have to be taken over time and carefully averaged or filtered to reduce amplifier noise. Technology today would amplify signals and convert them into binary numbers to be stored in hardware memory, typically hard disk. Later, digital filters in a computer can suppress amplifier noise and decipher brain information in the spectrum of the signal desired.

Figure C-1 indicates where the probes are placed: A, auditory or earlobe; N_z, nasion, the delve at the top of the nose, level with the eyes; I_z, inion, the bony lump at the base of the skull at the back of the head. Of interest are the waveforms observed. What are called *gamma waves*, in the approximate frequency range 30 to 80 Hz, appear to be associated with higher mental activity, including problem solving, but also fear. (These gamma waves are unrelated to nuclear gamma waves or gamma rays.) Gamma waves are a simple indication of consciousness. Figure C-2 illustrates typical waveforms.

Gamma waves are highest in average frequency. Next highest are beta waves, in the range 13 to 30 Hz. Beta waves can be associated with active, busy, or anxious thinking. Dominant frequencies can be associated with illnesses and drug effects. Alpha (Berger) waves are in the range 8 to 13 Hz. They are

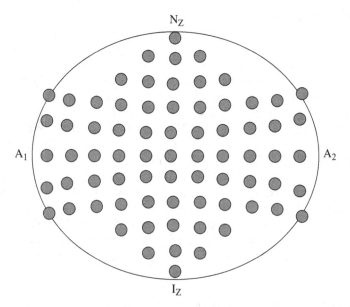

FIGURE C-1   EEG test points.

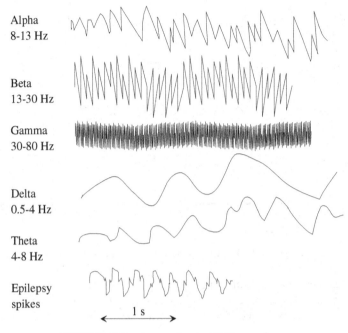

Alpha
8-13 Hz

Beta
13-30 Hz

Gamma
30-80 Hz

Delta
0.5-4 Hz

Theta
4-8 Hz

Epilepsy
spikes

1 s

FIGURE C-2 Approximate EEG waveforms.

characteristic of a relaxed consciousness present by age 2 years. These can be detected with the subject's eyes closed. A variation on alpha waves, termed *mu waves*, might be seen over the motor cortex. Mu waves diminish when a person has an intention to move physically.

Theta waves are in the range 4 to 8 Hz and delta waves are in the range 0.5 to 4 Hz. Delta waves can be associated with children, certain encephalopathies and lesions, and light sleep. An epileptic person may display spikes such as those at the bottom of the figure. It should be noted that most brain waves are low frequency, that is, subaudio. This is consistent with relatively low-frequency neural bursts with periods above 10 ms.

Waves are indicative of the deepness of sleep (see Figure C-3). But EEG has limitations. Actions in individual neurons cannot be seen because the individual signals are too small. Instead, an EEG picks up combined neuron actions, but it is not accurate spatially. Advantages are that the EEG has relatively good time resolution and can observe neural activity directly. Most important, EEGs are generally noninvasive and harmless.

Electromagnetic waves are created by alternating electrical charge from the pulses in neurons. These waves are very weak because the currents involved are very small and very low frequency, and because the detectors at the scalp are relatively far from the sources of the waves, whose intensity decreases roughly as the square of the distance from the source. Electrodes are able to pick up voltages in the microvolt range as these electromagnetic waves pass through the

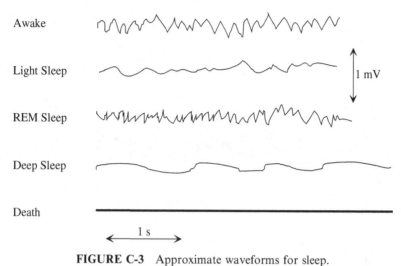

Awake

Light Sleep

1 mV

REM Sleep

Deep Sleep

Death

1 s

FIGURE C-3   Approximate waveforms for sleep.

conducting layers of the scalp, much like a radio antenna picks up a signal. Only a small amount of energy is taken from the wave to be dissipated irreversibly in the resistance of the differential amplifier.

MAGNETIC RESONANCE IMAGING

Magnetic resonance imaging (MRI) generally uses hydrogen nuclei of the type plentiful in ordinary water (H_2O). A strong magnetic field approximately aligns the spin of the nuclei in one of two directions relative to the magnetic field: parallel or antiparallel. The force of the magnetic field causes the axis of the spin to wobble relative to the direction of the magnetic field, much like a spinning top wobbles (or precesses) relative to the direction of gravity. The frequency with which the axis of the spin precesses is called the *Larmor frequency* [Sir Joseph Larmor (1857–1942)]. Pulses of radio frequency (RF) close to the Larmor frequency cause some of the magnetically aligned hydrogen nuclei to change alignment from parallel to antiparallel, and vice versa. As the nuclei realign, they emit radiation at frequencies that can be detected externally. The amplitudes of the radiation detected provide information about the density of the hydrogen nuclei and radio-frequency absorption in nearby materials.

Durations required are about 1 s of strong magnetic field with RF for a significant percentage of tissue nuclei to align. Several trials are required to obtain a good image. Spatial resolution results by observing radiation in three dimensions. Typical resolution is about 1 mm^3. MRI has proved successful in locating pathologic tissue such as brain tumors. MRI uses low-frequency magnetic fields and low-energy radio-frequency fields and so is less harmful to living tissue than x-ray and other high-energy radiation. MRI has better contrast than x-ray, and thus a small tumor is more likely to be noticed.

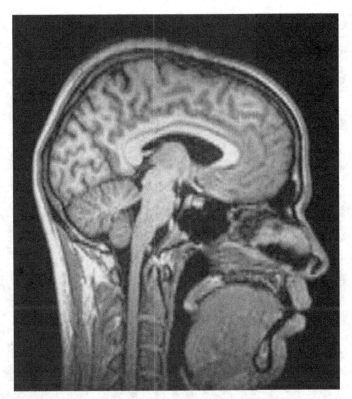

FIGURE C-4   MRI image. (From http://en.wikipedia.org/wiki/Neuroimaging.)

Figure C-4 is an example of the sort of resolution expected using MRI. Figure C-5 illustrates a fabulous image of brain neurons using water diffusion technique with MRI.

MRI has certain dangers:

- *Projectiles.* The magnetic field needed is up to 30,000 times the Earth's magnetic field. There will be tremendous force on magnetic objects. It is important to ensure that a patient has no embedded iron particles, steel pegs, or cardiac pacemakers.
- *Radio-frequency energy.* A powerful radio transmitter is needed for excitation of hydrogen nuclei (proton) spins. This can heat the body and give extra risk to children or elderly patients.
- *Peripheral nerve stimulation* (PNR). The rapid switching of the magnetic field needed for imaging is capable of unintended responses from the patient.
- *Acoustic noise.* Loud noises are produced by rapidly switching the main magnetic field.

FIGURE C-5 MRI of brain neurons. (From http://en.wikipedia.org/wiki/Image: DTI-sagittal-fibers.jpg.)

- *Shut down.* An emergency shutdown of a superconducting electromagnet might occur. This involves the rapid boiling of liquid helium out from the device. Imperfect venting can result in a lethal atmosphere.

Raymond Damadian holds a 1974 patent for the design and use of magnetic resonance (U.S. patent 3,789,832) and is the inverter of MRI. Paul Lauterbur and Peter Mansfield investigated the effects of *magnetic gradients* on imaging and used them to greatly improve the spatial resolution of MRI.

FUNCTIONAL MAGNETIC RESONANCE IMAGING

MRI provides structural information, while fMRI provides functional information in the form of a moving picture. fMRI is a style of MRI in which the brain is activated by actions on the part of the subject, such as looking at something,

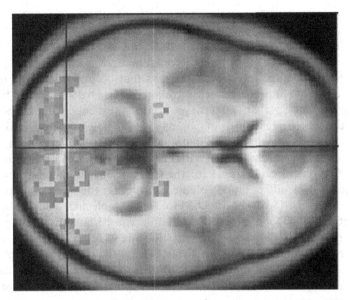

FIGURE C-6 Averaged fMRI overlaid on an x-ray image showing the primary visual cortex. (From http://en.wikipedia.org/wiki/Magnetic_resonance_imaging.)

hearing something, or moving one's fingers. First, an x-ray is taken to create a coordinate system. Next, a series of low-resolution MRI scans are taken: perhaps 150 scans, one every 5 s. These low-resolution brain images are processed into a moving picture in an attempt to observe brain activity. fMRI images take roughly 4 s each; spatial resolution is about 3 mm. Since the intensities of radio frequency from MRI are very slight, individual images are extremely poor. Statistical methods in conjunction with digital filters are essential to reduce noise and artifacts (false features) to produce a moving MRI picture.

fMRI is useful for tracing blood flow; it indicates oxygen use in the brain. The assumption is that neural activity causes a demand for oxygen at the location of the activity. Recall that MRI depends on the detection of radio-frequency (RF) radiations. RF is modulated by oxygen content since oxygenated hemoglobin causes a lower attenuation of radio frequency than does nonoxygenated hemoglobin. The differing attenuations as a function of time are the basis of fMRI. Illustrated in Figure C-6 is a computer-enhanced image overlaid on an x-ray slice of the head.

POSITRON EMISSION TOMOGRAPHY

A positron has the weight of an electron approximately, but with positive charge instead of negative. Positrons are given off during the decay of specific radioisotopes; they soon collide with one of the many electrons available in matter; when a positron meets an electron, they both dissolve, producing two gamma rays (moving in opposite directions). Gamma rays are electromagnetic waves with frequencies higher than those of x-rays, moving in opposite directions. The gamma rays can be detected in a *coincident detector*, that is, a detector that responds only to gamma rays that occur at the same moment, within a couple of nanoseconds. A large number of such detectors can be placed around a patient so that, after appropriate statistical analysis and digital filtering, the source of each pair of gamma rays can be pinpointed. In this way a computer can produce an approximate image of the positron concentrations.

Positron emission tomography (PET) involves the use of differing radio-isotopes. Oxygen-15 can be used for the study of oxygen metabolism; carbon monoxide for the study of blood volume, or water for the study of blood flow in the brain. Fluorine-18 can be attached to a sugar molecule to study the brain's sugar metabolism. Dopa, a neurotransmitter, can be labeled with a positron-emitting chemical to study brain cells that are diseased, as in Parkinson's disease or schizophrenia. Listed in Table C-1 are the half-lives of typical PET radioisotopes or positron emitters. A half-life is the time required for half of the total number of radioactive nuclei to convert spontaneously into nonradioactive elements.

Tens of thousands of coincidence events are analyzed. Data are taken for as long as possible; temporal resolution is on the order of minutes. A patient reclines his or her head inside the large, doughnut-shaped machine. The head must be kept very still. A hypodermic needle injects a minute amount of radioisotope; images may be expected to appear as in Figure C-7.

Cyclotrons are used to produce the short-lived radio nuclides, but this is an expensive process. They decay if stored, so they must be transported immediately to a PET facility. PET (like MRI) is typically employed in conjunction with other imaging technologies. PET is limited by the fact that radioisotopes are dangerous to humans. Short-lived isotopes partly alleviate this issue, as do strict limitations on the number of scans for a given patient. PET scans can locate and monitor rapidly growing malignant tumors.

In one type of application the blood is used to carry radioisotopes to troubled areas of the head. The main assumption is that high-radioactivity deposits are associated with certain problems. For example, a person with Alzheimer's disease can be diagnosed early using a PET image.

TABLE C-1   Standard Half-Lives of Radioisotopes Used in Nuclear Medicine

Labeling Agent	Half-Life (min)
Carbon-11	20.3
Oxygen-15	2.03
Fluorine-18	109.8
Bromine-75	98.0

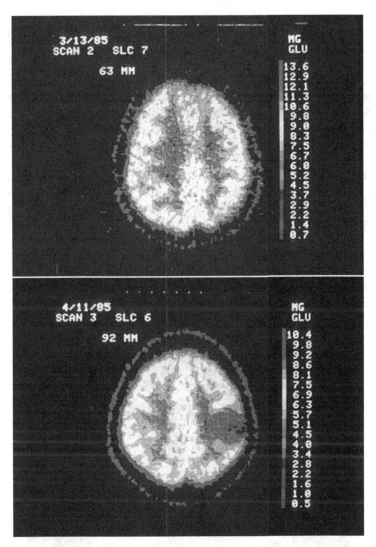

FIGURE C-7 PET slice showing brain disease. (From http://en.wikipedia.org/wiki/Image:Astrocytoma.jpg#file.)

COMPUTERIZED AXIAL TOMOGRAPHY

The CAT was invented in 1972 by Godfrey Newbold Hounsfield at EMI Central Research Laboratories in England. Allan McLeod Cormack of Tufts University independently invented a similar process. The CAT scanner sends focused beams of x-rays from all directions perpendicular to an axis, that is, axially. Originally, the x-ray source and a detector on the opposite side were rotated 180° for each slice of an image, using 1° steps. Currently, fan-shaped beams of x-rays are directed to an array of miniature solid-state detectors that are fixed in position relative to the x-ray source. X-ray sources and miniature detectors on the opposite side can cover 30°. The scan time is about 10 s per slice. Many slices are required for a three dimensional reconstruction of the head.

X-ray transmission data are saved in a hard drive. A computer later processes the acquired data into a three-dimensional image of the brain organized as a stack of slices. The construction of an image in the format of slices of the head is the result of a special algorithm known as a *reconstruction algorithm.*

Scanning may involve intravenous contrast agents. Spatial resolution is at least a millimeter. Newer approaches involve more detectors and slip ring technology that allows for a continuous rotation. The latest technologies allow temporal resolution to be 100 ms or less per slice. Figure C-8 shows what a slice looks like. An important application of CAT is the location of brain disease. Small tumors, for example, are difficult to locate, owing to limited resolution and because of the possibility of artifacts (false indications of tumors). Artifacts occur because of noise in the x-ray detectors and because of round-off errors in the reconstruction algorithm.

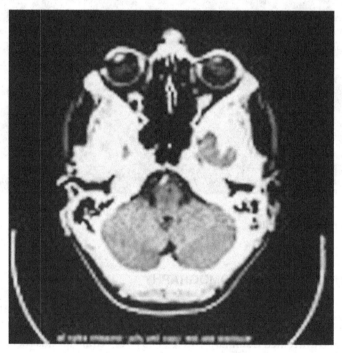

FIGURE C-8   Slice of a head. (From http://en.wikipedia.org/wiki/Computed_tomography.)

TABLE C-2   **Radiation Doses**

Examination	Typical Effective Dose (mSv)[a]
Chest x-ray	0.02
Head CT	1.5
Abdomen CT	5.3
Chest CT	5.8
Chest, abdomen, and pelvis CT	9.9
Cardiac CT angiogram	6.7–13
CT virtual colonoscopy	3.6–8.8

Source: http://en.wikipedia.org/wiki/Computed_tomography.
[a]The sievert (Sv), is the equivalent of joules per kilogram of tissue. Named after Rolf Sievert, a Swedish health physicist, a millisievert is approximately the average background dose that a person accumulates in one year in the United States.

Units

One drawback of CAT is the x-ray dose. Ionizing radiation such as x-rays damages living cells, although neurons have a higher tolerance for radiation then do other types of cells—those involved in human reproduction, for example. CAT is a high radiation event. Table C-2 indicates relative radiation doses for given purposes. Health physicists often think of radiation dose as exposure in units of 1 rad (radiation absorbed dose) assuming x-rays. Any material absorbing energy from nuclear disintegrations at a level of 100 ergs/g is said to absorb 1 rad. The erg is a cgs (centimeter–gram–second) unit of energy: To lift 1 g a distance of 1 cm requires 980 ergs of energy.

One rad of x-ray is defined in human tissue to be 1 rem (roentgen equivalent man). The sievert is a modern measure of rem: $1\,Sv = 100\,rem$; $1\,mSv = 0.1\,rem$. Assuming an exposure of 1 rad, sieverts can vary for non-x-ray radiation such as nuclear radiation. The threshold for serious radiation sickness is 500 mSv. A dose of 5000 mSv is considered the lethal dose for 50% of a population in 30 days.

The doses from CAT procedures are in the range 1 to 10 mSv. This much could result in a small but slightly increased risk for cancer. But it is well to remember that CAT is far less dangerous than some of the diseases being treated.

The curie (Ci) is the unit of radioactivity, defined as $1\,Ci = 3.7 \times 10^{10}$ decays per second. This is roughly the activity of 1 g of the radium-226 isotope as studied by Marie Curie (1867–1934) and Pierre Curie (1859–1906). A modern unit, the becquerel, is equivalent to 1 radioactive decay per second (Antoine-Henri Becquerel, 1852–1908).

APPENDIX D

BIOGRAPHIES OF PERSONS OF SCIENTIFIC INTEREST

Why Read the Biographies of Others?

The names included in this appendix are mainly those of deceased persons whose work has affected this book and its author. Basic facts referred to below were gathered mainly from the World Wide Web, courtesy of Wikipedia, the free encyclopedia. Life summaries of past scientists, often neglected in other texts, are considered important here because student often relate to the trials and tribulations of older generations of scientists, many of whom were financially and socially disadvantaged.

Only a few had material advantages, such as Charles de Coulomb of France and James Clerk Maxwell of Scotland. But most began relatively poor, like William Rowan Hamilton of Ireland and Benjamin Franklin in America. Because of their talent, they became very famous, and in some cases, prospered. The social and financial disadvantages of scientists who you read about in textbooks will be a surprise to young students lacking money, those who see material wealth as essential to a proper career in science. Realizing the difficulties of others makes the reading more interesting.

Competition for credit is intense in the world of science. A major discovery or fundamental contribution often is not enough to secure recognition, since society sometimes gives credit for significant advances to a popular or deserving

Human Memory Modeled with Standard Analog and Digital Circuits: Inspiration for Man-made Computers, By John Robert Burger
Copyright © 2009 John Wiley & Sons, Inc.

person without much regard for the true discoverer. For example, this happened in the case of Robert Brown, the Scottish botanist. Brownian motion was reported by Brown in 1827 but actually was first published by Jan Ingenhousz in both German and French publications in 1784. Also quite commonplace is accepting credit for the work of others. For example, Luigi Galvani published frog leg electricity actually discovered by his assistant. Credit is sometimes received posthumously, as happened with Lorenzo Avogadro, for instance.

Scientific work is supposed to be more than an application of technology. Yet many scientists of the past depended heavily on technology, giving the feeling that "technology" made the discovery, not the person. For example, central to the work of Jan Purkinje was the compound microscope. Galileo Galilei (1564–1642) depended heavily on his telescope. As you read, decide what makes a scientist special.

Scientific personalities vary considerably. Some are driven to apply for every possible award and honor; others strive to please the rich and powerful; self-importance is a common fault. Yet others are able to work without the applause of others, for personal enjoyment. Can you identify such faults and virtues in the subjects below? The biographies in Table D-1 are listed according to date of birth.

René Descartes (1596–1650)

René Descartes was born in La Haye, France, now called Descartes. He was educated at the Jesuit College of La Fleche between 1606 and 1614, and received his doctor of law degree from the University of Poitiers in 1616. He would later claim that his education gave him little of substance, a viewpoint about education shared by other seventeenth-century philosophers. In 1618 he went to Holland and joined the army of Prince Maurice of Nassau, traveling to Germany with them. He returned to France in 1622 and lived there until 1628, when he went back to Holland, where he remained for the rest of his life. Descartes was awarded a pension by the king of France in 1647. Two years later he traveled to Sweden at the invitation of Queen Christina. There he contracted pneumonia, which caused his death on February 11, 1650.

Descartes was famous as a mathematician, scientist, and philosopher. During his early years, he was greatly influenced by the mathematician Isaac Beeckman through their discussions of problems and issues in physics and mathematics. Ancient mathematics, such as the work of Euclid and Archimedes, prompted Descartes' interest in the scientific method, which he believed to be essential to scientific advance. Skepticism was the prevailing view in intellectual circles at the time, as exemplified by Chandoux, who claimed that science could only be based on probabilities. In a famous confrontation in 1628, Descartes attacked this view, claiming that only certainty could serve as a basis for knowledge, and that he himself had a method for attaining such certainty.

TABLE D-1   Dates of Selected Scientists

Birth	Death	Name
1596	1650	Rene Descartes
1621	1675	Thomas Willis
1736	1806	Charles-Augustin de Coulomb
1737	1798	Luigi Galvani
1746	1813	Benjamin Rush
1773	1858	Robert Brown
1775	1836	André-Marie Ampère
1776	1856	Lorenzo Avogadro
1787	1869	Jan E. Purkinje
1791	1867	Michael Faraday
1805	1865	William R. Hamilton
1815	1864	George Boole
1835	1922	Louis-Antoine Ranvier
1844	1906	Ludwig Boltzmann
1852	1934	Santiago Ramon Cajal
1856	1939	Sigmund Freud
1859	1927	Svante A. Arrhenius
1859	1918	Richard Semon
1864	1941	Walther Nernst
1903	1957	John von Neumann
1904	1985	Donald O. Hebb
1912	1954	Alan Turing
1916	2001	Herbert A. Simon
1918	1988	Richard Feynman
1927	1999	Rolf Landauer
1928	1969	Frank Rosenblatt
1929	—	Gordon E. Moore
1933	—	John J. Hopfield
1947	—	John R. Anderson
1951	—	Kim Peek
1979	—	Daniel Tammet

In 1634 Descartes was about to publish a scientific work called *Le Monde* (*The World*), but upon learning that Galileo had been condemned by the Church for teaching a similar methodology, did not proceed. In 1638 he published the *Discourse on Method*, a book containing three essays on mathematical and scientific subjects. Other publications included *Meditationes de Prima Philosophia* (1641) and *The Principles of Philosophy* (1644). Descartes' last work, *Passions of the Soul*, was written as a result of his correspondence with Princess Elisabeth of Bohemia, who had raised the question of how the soul could interact with the body. This work, published in 1649, is composed of a large number of short articles, including a combination of psychology, physiology, and ethics.

Thomas Willis (1621–1675)

Thomas Willis was an English physician, born in Wiltshire, who worked in Westminster, London. From 1660 until his death he was Sedleian Professor of Natural Philosophy at Oxford. He was a cofounder of the Royal Society in 1662, and, through his contributions to the science of anatomy, is often considered the "father of neurology".

Willis was a pioneer in research into the anatomy of the brain, nervous system, and muscles. The circle of Willis, a part of the brain's vascular system, was his discovery. He also developed concepts relating to the functional organization of the brain. For example, he remarked about the arborescent arrangement of the white and gray matter in the cerebellum, and gave a good account of the carotid arteries and the communications which they make with the branches of the basilar artery.

Willis was the first natural philosopher to use the term *reflex action* to describe elemental acts of the nervous system. He was also the first to number the cranial nerves in the order in which they are now enumerated by anatomists, and observed the connection of the eighth pair with the slender nerve that issues from the beginning of the spinal cord. He described the distribution of the cranial nerves in detail and investigated cerebral blood flow.

In 1664 he described the anatomy of the brain and nerves in his *Cerebri anatome*. This important work was the foundation document of the anatomy of the central and autonomic nervous systems, and contained much new and insightful information. He was aided by Sir Christopher Wren, the illustrator of the magnificent figures in the book, as well as by Thomas Millington and his fellow-anatomist Richard Lower.

Charles-Augustin de Coulomb (1736–1806)

Charles-Augustin de Coulomb was born in 1736 in Angouleeme, France to a relatively wealthy family. Coulomb studied at the famous College des Quatre-Nations, where he was inspired to pursue mathematics as a career. In 1757 he joined his father's family in Montpellier and took part in the city academy. Coulomb returned to Paris in 1759 to attend the military school at Mézières, after which he spent time in Martinique to work on the engineering of Fort Bourbon. He returned to Paris in 1781.

In 1785, Coulomb presented three reports on electricity and magnetism. Here we find a presentation of his discovery that the force between static electric charges is inversely proportional to the square of the distance between them: or Coulomb's law. Coulomb explained the laws of attraction and repulsion for electric or magnetic poles, and investigated the quantity of electricity an isolated body loses over time. In his honor the unit of charge is named the coulomb, a fixed large number of electrons.

Upon the outbreak of the French Revolution in 1789 he resigned his appointment and retired to a small estate at Blois. Later he was recalled to

Paris by the revolutionary government to take part in a new set of weights and measures. He was appointed inspector of public instruction in 1802, but his health was poor. Coulomb died in 1806 in Paris, France.

Luigi Galvani (1737–1798)

Luigi Galvani was born in Bologna, Italy. Galvani had intended to study theology and enter a monastery. Dissuaded by his family, he took up the study of natural science as an anatomist and physiologist. In 1760 he married the daughter of one of his teachers. At the age of 25 he was an instructor of anatomy at the Institute of Sciences, University of Bologna. He became especially noted as a surgeon and was chair of obstetrics at the Institute of Sciences, of which he became president in 1772. He kept his chair at the university until 1797, when he resigned rather than take a civil oath demanded by the occupying Napoleonic army. He then took refuge with his brother, having lost his wife, eight years earlier. His friends obtained an exemption from the oath, and his appointment as Professor Emeritus, on account of his scientific fame, but he died before the decree went into effect.

Galvani was one of the first to investigate what came to be turned *bioelectrogenesis*. This began around 1780, when his assistant accidentally touched the bared crural or sciatic nerve of a dissected frog with a steel scalpel while sparks were passing from an electric machine nearby. There was an immediate muscle twitch followed by a kick of the legs. The twitching of the frog's legs led to his theory of animal electricity. Further experiments confirmed this effect. He believed that a nervous electric fluid was secreted by the brain, conducted by the nerves, and stored in the muscles. Thus, he demonstrated the electrical nature of the nerve–muscle function and helped to establish the basis for the biological study of neurophysiology and neurology.

Galvani's colleague at the University of Pavia, Alessandro Volta (1745–1827), was able to reproduce the results but did not agree with the explanation of the phenomenon. Direct proof became available only when technology allowed later scientists to be able to measure the small natural electrical currents which are actually generated in the nervous and muscular cells. Galvani's work was instrumental in leading Volta to the invention of the first electric battery. The term *Galvanometer* today refers to electric meters with an analog scale.

Benjamin Rush (1746–1813)

Benjamin Rush was a signer of the Declaration of Independence as well as an advocate of treatment for the mentally ill. He was born in Pennsylvania in 1746. His father died when Rush was 6. He spent his early life with his uncle, a religious leader who ran an academy. Rush was a Presbyterian but probably had Universalist leanings. The following quote states: "Such is my veneration for every religion that reveals the attributes of the Deity, or a future state of rewards and punishments, that I had rather see the opinions of Confucius or Mohamed inculcated upon our youth, than see them grow up wholly devoid of a system of religious principles."

Rush obtained a bachelor of arts degree at the College of New Jersey and later a medical degree at the University of Edinburgh. He returned to the colonies in 1769 to open a medical practice in Philadelphia and to become professor of chemistry at the College of Philadelphia. In 1783 he was appointed to the staff of Pennsylvania Hospital, where he remained until his death.

Constitutionally, Rush believed that the right to medical freedom should be guaranteed in the Constitution much as the right to freedom of religion. His fear was a class of healers who would be an undercover dictatorship and deny equal privilege to others.

Rush tutored Meriwether Lewis about frontier illnesses for the Lewis and Clark Expedition. He recommended bloodletting for many and he provided the corps with a kit that included opium for nervousness, emetics to induce vomiting, wine, and many of Dr. Rush's Bilious Pills. These pills were laxatives made of more than 50% mercury, called by the corps "thunderclappers". The meat diet and poor water during the expedition gave the men cause to use the pills frequently. Their efficacy might be questionable, but the high mercury content provided an excellent tracer for archaeologists retracing the route to the Pacific.

An interesting story is his favorite method of treatment for certain mental illness was to tie a patient to a board and spin it rapidly until blood went to the head. It is said that he placed his own son in one of his hospitals. He is considered the father of American psychiatry partly because he produced the first text on the subject, *Medical Inquiries and Observations upon the Diseases of the Mind* in 1812. An asylum is constructed in the area of his birthplace and the emblem of the American Psychiatric Association bears his portrait. Rush viewed drunkenness not as sinful but as a disease in which the alcoholic loses control over himself. He developed the idea that abstinence is the only cure for addiction.

The treatments above are consistent with the fact that Rush lived during the age of heroic medicine. He is remembered as a physician, writer, educator, and humanitarian and an early opponent of slavery and capital punishment.

Robert Brown (1773–1858)

Robert Brown was born in Montrose, Scotland and studied medicine at the University of Edinburgh. In 1795 he joined the army as a surgeon. Brown became a naturalist and botanist after joining a historic voyage to chart the coast of Australia in 1801. Returning to England in 1805, he published numerous species descriptions for nearly 1200 species. He was able to transfer to the British Museum in 1827 and was appointed keeper of the Banksian Botanical Collection.

In that year, while examining pollen grains and the spores of mosses suspended in water under a microscope, Brown observed minute pollen particles executing a jittery continuous motion. He then observed the same motion in particles of dust, ruling out that the motion was due to the pollen being alive. Jan Ingenhousz had described such motion using charcoal particles in German and French publications of 1784 and 1785, but the phenomenon is now known as Brownian motion. Brownian motion is a significant clue to the existence of molecules and atoms and the random motion of such particles as a result of thermal energy.

In a paper published in 1833, Brown was the one who named the cell nucleus. It has been observed before, perhaps as early as 1682 by the Dutch microscopist Leeuwenhoek, and certainly by Franz Bauer, who drew pictures of it in 1802, as acknowledged by Brown. Brown was retained as keeper of the botanical department of the British Museum until his death in London in 1858.

André-Marie Ampère (1775–1836)

André-Marie Ampère was born in 1775 near Lyons, France. As an infant he is reported to have played with pebbles to work out arithmetical sums. He clearly had an aptitude for mathematics as a boy, and learned Latin from his father, which he used to enjoy the works of Euler and Bernouilli. When Lyons was taken by the Army of the Convention in 1793, his father, an opponent of the revolution, was executed, throwing young Ampère into deep apathy.

Ampère married in 1799 in Lyons, where he gave private lessons in mathematics, chemistry, and languages. In 1801 he moved to Bourg to be a professor of physics and chemistry. His ailing wife died back home in Lyons in 1804, leaving Ampère permanently saddened.

In 1804 he obtained an appointment in the polytechnic school in Paris and was elected professor of mathematics in 1809. Ampère was reputed to be highly amiable and to have a childlike simplicity of expression that inspired others. Ampère focused on the measurement of voltaic current as it acted upon a magnetic needle, a field that he explored with characteristic industry and care. He developed a mathematical theory to explain electromagnetic phenomena, producing memoirs on the subject between 1820 and 1828. Today the unit of electrical current, the ampere, is named after him. He died at Marseille in 1836.

Lorenzo Avogadro (1776–1856)

Lorenzo Romano Amedeo Carlo Avogadro was born on August 9, 1776, in Turin, Italy. His father was a distinguished lawyer and civil servant who was appointed advocate general to the senate of Vittorio Amedeo III in 1777, and was made president of the senate under the rule of the French in 1799. Avogadro went to school in Turin.

A family background of well-established ecclesiastical lawyers guided Avogadro toward a legal career, and he became a bachelor of jurisprudence in 1792, at the age of 16. Four years later he received his doctorate in ecclesiastical law and began to practice.

In addition to his successful legal career, Avogadro also showed an interest in natural philosophy. In 1800 he began private studies of mathematics and physics. His first scientific research, on electricity, was undertaken jointly with his brother in 1803. In 1809, Avogadro became professor of natural philosophy at the college of Vercelli. The very first chair of mathematical physics in Italy was established at the University of Turin in 1820, and Avogadro was appointed. Political changes suppressed the chair from 1822 to 1832, and he was reappointed to the position in 1834. He remained there until his retirement in 1850.

Chemistry was a relatively new science in the early nineteenth century. In 1811, Avogadro published an article in *Journal de Physique* that drew a clear distinction between the molecule and the atom. He was able to provide an explanation for the way in which one particle of oxygen yields two particles of water: The "atoms" of hydrogen and oxygen are in reality "molecules" containing two atoms each. Thus, two molecules of hydrogen can combine with one molecule of oxygen to produce two molecules of water.

His work was unknown during his lifetime but was presented at a conference shortly after his death. He suggested that equal volumes of all gases at the same temperature and pressure contain the same number of molecules, also known as *Avogadro's principle*. The number of molecules in 1 mole, now called *Avogadro's number*, is named for him but was not actually determined by him.

Avogadro was married and had six children. He died on July 9, 1856.

Jan Evangelista Purkinje (1787–1869)

Jan Evangelista Purkinje was born in Libochovice, Bohemia (now the Czech Republic) on December 17, 1787. In 1819 he graduated from the University of Prague with a degree in medicine. After publishing his doctoral dissertation on vision, he was appointed professor of physiology at the University of Prague. Working at the university, he discovered the phenomenon known as the *Purkinje effect*, whereby as light intensity decreases, red objects are perceived to fade faster than blue objects of the same brightness.

He published two volumes, *Observations and Experiments Investigating the Physiology of Senses* and *New Subjective Reports About Vision*, which contributed to the emergence of experimental psychology. In 1823 he became a professor at the University of Breslau, where he pioneered in establishing laboratory training in German universities. In the same year he also recognized that fingerprints can be used for identification.

Purkinje was the first to use a microtome to make wafer-thin slices of tissue for microscopic examination, and also used glacial acetic acid, potassium bichromate, and Canada balsam in the preparation of tissue samples. In 1829 he described the effects of camphor, opium, belladonna, and turpentine on humans. He also introduced the scientific term *plasma* to describe the component of blood left when the suspended cells have been removed, and the term *protoplasm*, the substance found inside cells.

In addition to expanding our knowledge of the structure and function of the eye, Purkinje was a pioneer in the study of cells. As an early user of the improved compound microscope, he discovered the nucleus in birds' eggs, sweat glands in the skin, and in 1837, large flask-shaped nerve cells with numerous dendrites in the cerebellum (now known as *Purkinje cells*), and in 1839, fibrous tissue in the heart that conducts stimuli from the pacemaker along the inside walls of the ventricles to all parts of the heart (now called *Purkinje fibers*). He also noted the protein-digesting power of pancreatic extracts.

While at the University of Breslau, Prussia, in 1839, Purkinje created the world's first department of physiology; and the world's first official physiology laboratory, in 1842, known as the Physiological Institute. In 1850 he left the University of Breslau to become a professor at Charles University in Prague. He died in Prague in 1869.

Michael Faraday (1791–1867)

Faraday was born in South London in 1791, one of four children. His family was not well off, his father having been a blacksmith prior to moving to London. Faraday received little formal education and had to educate himself. At 14 he became apprenticed to a bookbinder and bookseller, during which he read many books. Faraday developed an interest in electricity.

At 20 in 1812, Faraday was given tickets to lectures by Humphry Davy of the Royal Society. Afterward, Faraday sent Davy a 300-page book based on notes taken during the lectures. Davy's response was very positive and he decided to employ Faraday as a secretary. They found a place for Faraday as a chemical assistant at the Royal Institution. Because of his background, Faraday was not considered a "gentleman". He was asked to fill the role of valet during a European trip of Davy's, and Davy's wife made Faraday travel outside the coach and eat with the servants. The trip gave him access to European scientific elite and many stimulation ideas. Faraday married in 1821.

Faraday established the magnetic field concept in physics and he discovered electromagnetic induction. His inventions of electromagnetic rotary devices are the basis of electric motor technology, a cornerstone in the development of electrical power. As a chemist, Faraday discovered benzene, developed the laws of electrolysis, and invented a system of oxidation numbers and the Bunsen burner. Capacitance is now measured in farads, as is the Faraday constant, the charge on 1 mole of electrons, about 96,485 coulombs. He is remembered for an important law of induction: that voltage generated is proportional to the rate of change of a magnetic field. He was elected to the Royal Society in 1824. Although of humble origins, and not overpowering in calculus, Faraday was one of the most influential scientists in history.

Faraday was a Christian and an environmental activist, warning about explosions in coal dust, for example, and objecting to the use of chemical weapons in the Crimean war. Faraday rejected a knighthood and offers to become president of the Royal Society; he seems to have a modesty seldom seen. In 1848 Faraday was awarded a house free of all expenses or upkeep at No. 37 Hampton Court Road. Faraday retired there in 1858 and died at his house in 1867. He is buried in London's Highgate Cemetery, having rejected burial in Westminster Abbey, but he has a memorial plaque there near Isaac Newton's tomb.

William Rowan Hamilton (1805–1865)

William Rowan Hamilton was born the son of a solicitor in Dublin but was later put up for adoption. Not enough is known about his childhood, but by age 7 he knew much Hebrew and at 13, under the care of his uncle, over 10 languages. He was considered a child prodigy in languages. He enjoyed reading Persian and Arabic throughout his life as a form of relaxation.

Hamilton as a mathematician formulated classical mechanics in such a way that an operator known as the *Hamiltonian* could be derived for quantum mechanics. Hamilton invented the *Icosian game* to investigate closed-edge paths that visit each vertex exactly once on a dodecahedron. In modern terms a Hamiltonian circuit describes such a closed-edge path for any graph.

Hamilton, without assistance, became expert at arithmetical calculations. At age 12 he engaged Zerah Colburn, a famous calculating boy from the United States, and held his own. He soon read Newton's *Arithmetica universalis and principia*, mastering most by age 16. In 1822, his seventeenth year, he began a study of Laplace's *Mécanique céleste*. He gained the Andrews professorship of astronomy at the University of Dublin in 1827.

Established at the Dunsink Observatory near Dublin at age 22, he paid little attention to regular work of practical astronomy. It must be said his time was better employed in original investigations for the advancement of science, for which he was promising. In 1827, he presented a *Theory of Systems of Rays*, dealing with optics and dynamics. He published *On a General Method in Dynamics*, which appeared in the *Philosophical Transactions* in 1834 and 1835. He was knighted in 1835.

Hamilton was a voluminous correspondent. A single letter of his could take up to 100 pages, closely written. He considered every minute feature of a particular problem. He was never satisfied with a general understanding of a question; he pursued the problem until he knew it in all details. Hamilton was always courteous and kind in answering applications for assistance, especially questions about his own work, but he was excessively precise and hard to please with the final polish of his own publications. He published relatively few papers, but each of high quality.

Hamilton retained his faculties to the very last, to within days of his death, as he worked on finishing *Elements of Quaternions*, which he had been working on for the last six years of his life. He is recognized as one of Ireland's leading scientists and is increasingly celebrated.

George Boole (1815–1864)

George Boole was born 1815 in Lincolnshire, England. His father was a tradesman of limited means but with an active mind who was interested in mathematical logic and gave his son his first lessons. Boole's first interest was the classics, and he did not focus significantly on mathematics until after his appointment in 1849 as professor of mathematics in what is now University College, Cork in Ireland. Here he wrote his *Treatise on Differential Equations* in 1859, which contains chapters on earlier investigations into a general symbolic method originally described in 1844. Greater clarity was offered in 1847 in a pamphlet entitled *Mathematical Analysis of Logic*. Boole eventually devised a mature work, *An Investigation of the Laws of Thought, on Which Are Founded the Mathematical Theories of Logic and Probabilities* (1854). Here was a general symbolic method of logical inference in which, by assigning a truth value of 0 or 1 to the elements of a logical statement, a conclusion 0 or 1 could be calculated.

In 1855, Boole married, and his wife who later wrote useful educational notes on her husband's principles. Boole continued to refine his mathematical ideas during the last years of his life. His friends held him in high regard, but the general public knew Boole as the author of abstruse papers with not much practical value. Unconcerned, he was modest and always kept a focus on mathematical truth. He neither sought nor received the attention that would normally be entitled to him by his original works. He died suddenly at age 49 of an attack of fever and possibly pneumonia. As inventor of Boolean algebra, Boole is regarded in hindsight as a founder of digital design and computer science.

Louis-Antoine Ranvier (1835–1922)

Ranvier was born in Lyons, France in 1835. Apparently he had family support to attend medical school, since he studied medicine at Lyons, finishing in 1865. In 1867 he entered the Collège de France and later was appointed to a chair of general anatomy in 1875. He is known as a physician, pathologist, anatomist, and histologist, specializing in the microscopic structure of tissue, and with Victor-André Cornil wrote a textbook on histopathology.

He discovered myelin in 1878, along with the famous nodes that bear his name. There are other anatomical structures named after him, such as Merkel–Ranvier cells in the basal layer of the epidermis, and *Ranvier's tactile disks*, a type of sensory nerve ending. In 1897 he cofounded with Edouard-Gerard Balbiani the scientific journal *Archives d'Anatomie Microscopique*. Ranvier retired in 1900 to his estate in Thelis and died in 1922.

Ludwig Boltzmann (1844–1906)

Boltzmann was born in Vienna. His father was a tax official, his grandfather a clock manufacturer. Boltzmann attended high school in Linz, near Vienna, and studied physics at the University of Vienna, receiving a Ph.D. degree in 1866. He became professor of mathematical physics at the University of Graz in 1869 and in 1873 became professor of mathematics at the University of Vienna.

Ludwig married a mathematics teacher in 1876 and supported her wish to audit lectures long before women were admitted to Austrian universities. She appealed and won. Boltzmann eventually returned to Gras as chair of experimental physics. In 1893, Boltzmann succeeded his teacher, Josef Stefan, with whom he published the *Stefan–Boltzmann law*, and became professor of theoretical physics at the University of Vienna.

Boltzmann's kinetic theory of gasses assumed atoms and molecules, apparently an unpopular assumption in Austria and Germany. There is no indication that he received significant recognition internationally during his lifetime. His most important scientific achievements include a derivation of the distribution for molecular speeds in a gas, the *Maxwell–Boltzmann distribution*, founding of the field in physics known as statistical mechanics, and a remarkable insight into the meaning of temperature. Today he is known in electrical engineering for the fundamental constant of electronics, kT/q, which depends on Boltzmann's constant k, needed to relate temperature to the average energy of a particle.

Boltzmann argued with some of his colleagues in Vienna, particularly Ernst Mach, so in 1900 he went to the University of Leipzig but returned in 1902 when Mach retired. Boltzmann also lectured on philosophy and was enormously successful. Because of these lectures, the emperor invited him for a reception at the palace. In his later years, Boltzmann was subject to undiagnosed bipolar disorder and to suicide attempts, as those close to him were aware. In 1906, Boltzmann took a summer vacation near Trieste, Italy, and hanged himself during an attack of depression.

Santiago Ramón y Cajal (1852–1934)

Santiago Ramón y Cajal was born on May 1, 1852, at Petilla in Aragon, Spain. As a boy, he was apprenticed first to a barber and then to a cobbler. Although he wished to be an artist, his father, who was professor of applied anatomy in the University of Zaragoza, persuaded him to study medicine. In 1873 he took his medical examination at Zaragoza and was drafted into the army as a medical officer. He took part in an expedition to Cuba in 1874–1875, where he contracted malaria.

On his return to Spain in 1875, he became an assistant in the School of Anatomy in the Faculty of Medicine at Zaragoza and then director of the Zaragoza Museum. In 1877 he obtained the degree of doctor of medicine at Madrid, and in 1883 he was appointed professor of descriptive and general anatomy at Valencia. In 1887 he was appointed professor of histology and pathological anatomy at Barcelona, and in 1892 he was appointed to the same chair at Madrid. He was appointed director of the National Institute of Hygiene in 1900. He also founded the *Laboratorio de Investigaciónes Biológicas*, later renamed to the Cajal Institute.

Cajal began to publish scientific works about 1880, covering subjects such as histology and micrographic techniques, general pathological anatomy, and the anatomy of nerve centers and the nervous system. He postulated that the nervous system is made up of billions of separate neurons and that these cells are polarized. He then suggested that neurons communicate with each other via specialized junctions called synapses. This hypothesis became the basis of the neuron doctrine, which states that the individual unit of the nervous system is a single neuron. He shared Nobel prize with Camillo Golgi in 1906 for their work on the structure of the nervous system.

More than 100 scientific articles were also published by Cajal in French, Spanish, and German. These included studies on the structure of the cortex of the brain. He won many distinctions, such as Member of the Royal Academy of Sciences of Madrid, from several Spanish societies. He was also awarded honorary degrees from Cambridge and Würzburg universities and from Clark University in Worcester, Massachusetts. Prizes were awarded to him by many international societies, including the Congress of Moscow.

Cajal married in 1879 and had seven children. He died in Madrid in 1934.

Sigmund Freud (1856–1939)

Sigismund Schlomo Freud was born into an Ashkenazi Jewish family in Freiberg, Moravia (now Pribor, Czech Republic) on May 6, 1856. In 1859 the family settled permanently in Vienna.

An exceptionally good student in his early years, Freud intended to study law; he later decided to pursue a career in medicine and entered Vienna University in 1873, at the age of 17. He began extensive research into the central nervous system in 1876, which, along with a compulsory one-year military service, resulted in his not being awarded a degree in medicine until 1881. At the age of 21 he had his given name abbreviated so that his degree read "Sigmund Freud."

In 1886 he established a private practice in Vienna specializing in nervous disorders and married in the same year. He experimented with hypnotism with his most hysteric and neurotic patients, and published *Studies on Hysteria* (*Cathartic Method*) with Josef Breuer in 1895. His interest gradually moved away from neurological–physiological causes of mental disorders toward more purely psychological causes, and in 1896 he coined the term *psychoanalysis* for his method of investigation. His research and practice were controversial, and his theories continue to be disputed today.

In 1899, *The Interpretation of Dreams* was published; this was the book that Freud regarded as his most important work. He was appointed to a professorship at the University of Vienna in 1902, and by 1910 the International Psychoanalytical Association was founded. Freud was a heavy cigar smoker and was diagnosed with cancer of the jaw in 1923. Yet for the next 16 years he remained productive, publishing many works and receiving many international awards and recognition.

One of Freud's most significant contributions to modern thought is his conception of the subconscious; that people are not entirely aware of what they think, and often act for reasons that have little to do with their conscious thoughts. He also pioneered clinical techniques for treating neurotics. As a neurologist, he was an early researcher on the topic of cerebral palsy.

The rise to power of Hitler and the Nazis caused Freud and his family to flee from Austria to England in 1938. No longer able to tolerate the pain associated with his cancer, Freud died on September 23, 1939, by a physician-assisted morphine overdose.

Svante August Arrhenius (1859–1927)

Svante August Arrhenius was born in Vik, Sweden on February 19, 1859. His ancestors were farmers; his father was a land surveyor employed by the University of Uppsala. The family moved to Uppsala in 1860, and Svante was educated at the cathedral school. The rector was a good physics teacher, and his pupil showed an aptitude for mathematics and physics. In 1876, Arrhenius entered the University of Uppsala, studying mathematics, chemistry, and physics. In 1881 he went to Stockholm to work under Erik Edlund at the Academy of Sciences, assisting with electromotive force measurements in spark discharges.

It was here in 1884 that Arrhenius produced his highly original thesis: Electrolytes, when dissolved in water, yield a solution that conducts electricity, and are separated, or dissociated, into electrically charged particles, or ions, even when there is no current flowing through the solution. The value of his publication was not well understood by the science faculty at Uppsala, where the dissertation took place. However, it did attract the attention of other scientists, including Wilhelm Ostwald in Riga, Latvia and Otto Pettersson, professor of chemistry at Stockholm's Hogskola, a private foundation.

Through Edlund's influence, Arrhenius was awarded a traveling fellowship from the Academy of Sciences, which allowed him to work with various contemporary scientists in other neighboring countries. During these years he proved the influence of electrolytic dissociation on pressure: lowering of freezing point and increase of boiling point; and in later years on biological problems: relationships between toxins and antitoxins and serum therapy.

By 1891, Arrhenius had returned to Stockholm, where he obtained a lectureship in physics at the Stockholm Hogskola and became professor of physics in 1895. He married in 1894 and had one son. He was rector from 1897 to 1905, when he retired from the professorship. He was awarded the Nobel Prize for Chemistry in 1903. When the Academy of Sciences decided to start a Nobel Institute for Physical Chemistry in 1905, they chose Arrhenius to become its chief. In that same year he married his second wife and had three more children.

In addition to his work with electrochemistry, Arrhenius made contributions in other areas of physics, including the importance of CO_2 in the atmosphere for the climate, and additional knowledge of the northern lights. Much of his work after 1900 dealt with the physics and chemistry of cosmic and meteorological phenomena. His achievements received much recognition during his lifetime, with his election as a Foreign Member of the Royal Society in 1911, as well as other medals and numerous honorary degrees from European universities. He died on October 2, 1927, and is buried at Uppsala.

Richard Semon (1859–1918)

Richard Semon was born in Berlin on August 22, 1859 to Jewish parents. His father was a successful stockbroker, at least until the financial crash of 1873; his older brother became a prominent laryngologist in England and was appointed physician to King Edward VII in 1901. Semon was awarded a doctor of philosophy degree at Jena in 1883 for zoological work, and a doctor of medicine degree at Jena in 1886. He led a biological expedition to Australia and eventually was involved in six volumes, entitled *Zoologische Forschungsreisen in Australien und dem Malaiischen Archipel.* As a result, Semon was generally known as a biologist.

Semon fell in love while at Jena: unfortunately, with the wife of his friend and colleague Ludolph Krehl, and she had several children. But love can be blind, and she left her husband and children. As a consequence, Semon had to leave Jena in 1897, after which he chose to become a private scholar in Munich. He wrote monographs, including *Die Mneme* (1904) and *Die Mnenischen Empfindungen* (1923). His memory theory was overlooked in those days, partly because he supported the inheritance of acquired characteristics at a time when the inheritance of acquired characteristics was being massively discredited.

Semon's wife died in 1918, and those sad days also saw the general collapse of his beloved Germany. In the end, Semon believed that he had Alzheimer's disease. On a cold day in December 1918, Semon laid down on a German flag on his wife's bed pointed a gun to his heart, and committed suicide. He left no children.

Because proper terms for the components of memory were nonexistent, Semon coined the word *engram* as "the enduring though primarily latent modification in the irritable substance produced by a stimulus." The term *ecphory* is defined as "the influences which awaken the mnemic trace or engram out of its latent state into one of manifested activity." Another interesting term is *homophony* as existing between two "original sensations," or between "original and mnemic sensations," or between two "mnemic sensations." He proposed a *resonance principle* between engrams to explain the strengthening of a memory.

Although he was not particularly recognized for his efforts, he came to be appreciated after his death. Kurt Koffka, a Gestalt psychologist, refrained from discussing Semon's theory in detail, but noted that "this omission is not due to a lack of appreciation of Semon's great achievement." Quantum physicist Erwin Schrödinger regretted that a physiological model of Semon's theory of memory had not yet been developed "important though it would be for the advancement of our knowledge." Philosopher Bertrand Russell wrote: "The best writer on mnemic phenomena known to me is Richard Semon."

Walther Nernst (1864–1941)

Nernst was born in Briesen in West Prussia, or Pomerania, now Poland. His family was able to send him to the Universities of Zurich, Berlin, and Graz to study physics and mathematics. Nernst became a physicist known for his theories relating to physical chemistry, including osmotic pressure, electrochemistry, including work on electrolytes, and thermodynamics. In 1905 he established his new heat theorem, later known as the third law of thermodynamics, the behavior of matter as temperatures approach at absolute zero. He is known for developing the Nernst equation.

He received the Nobel Prize in Chemistry in 1920 for his work in thermochemistry. In 1924 he became director of the Institute of Physical Chemistry in Berlin. He retired from this position in 1933 and pursued work in electroacoustics and astrophysics. He died in 1941 in Zibelle, Germany.

John Von Neumann (1903–1957)

Born Neumann Janos Lajos in Budapest, John von Neumann adopted the name by which we know him after emigration to the United States in the 1930s. The title *von* was purchased by the Neumann family, who were nonpracticing Jews. His father was a lawyer who worked in a bank. Von Neumann was gifted; at age 6 he could divide two eight-digit numbers in his head, for example. He received his doctorate in mathematics from the University of Budapest at age 23. From 1926 to 1930 he was a private lecturer in Berlin.

Von Neumann was invited to Princeton in 1930, where he was a mathematics professor until his death in 1957. The computer scientist Alan Turing was a visitor at Princeton completing his Ph.D. degree under Alonzo Church. Von Neumann must have taken some interest in the computer theories of these computer pioneers. Years later his name was bestowed on the von Neumann architecture, a serial type of processing used in almost all computers up to now. He was able to publish the concept, although some felt that the name *Neumann architecture* ignored the contributions of John Presper Eckert (1919–1995) and John William Mauchly (1907–1980), who already used the concept during their work on the ENIAC (the electronic numerical integrator and computer), one of the original electronic computers.

Von Neumann was active in many areas, including quantum mechanics, nuclear weapon design, and mathematics, as well as computer theory. He usually dressed in suit a and tie and enjoyed having extravagant parties. He sometimes drove while reading a book, sometimes getting himself arrested as a consequence. He was a hedonist who liked to eat and drink heavily. He liked dirty jokes and would gaze at the legs of young women while at Los Alamos, so much so that the modesty skirts were purchased for office desks. He was married twice, first in 1930 but divorced in 1937, and then again in 1938.

Von Neumann was a character who promoted his personal power as much as possible. He was politically active during the 1940s and 1950s, describing himself as violently anticommunist and much more militaristic than the norm. His efforts at hydrogen bomb design increased his political power. In his active and productive life he contributed valuable theories, including computerized *Monte Carlo analysis* of systems using pseudorandom numbers for inputs, the *minimax theorem* for game theory, *self-replicating automata*, and a formulation of quantum mechanics using linear *Hermitian operators*.

Von Neumann died tragically from bone and pancreatic cancer in 1957, possibly by exposure to radiation from the nuclear tests conducted at Bikini Atoll in 1946. Ironically, he had defended the safety of such testing for many years.

Donald Olding Hebb (1904–1985)

Donald Olding Hebb was born in 1904 in Chester, Nova Scotia. Both of his parents were physicians, as were his two brothers, and his sister became a prominent neurosurgeon. But Hebb wanted to be a writer.

Hebb failed eleventh grade but managed to attend Dalhousie University. Not the best student, he graduated in 1925 to become a teacher. Later he traveled around as a laborer in Quebec. At age 23 he decided to enter the field of psychology. In 1928 he attended McGill University. Shortly afterward Hebb wrote a booklet titled *Scientific Method in Psychology: A Theory of Epistemology Based on Objective Psychology* (unpublished), in which ideas for his later work were developed.

In 1934 Hebb was accepted to study under Karl Lashley at the University of Chicago and followed Lashley to Harvard, where he earned a Ph.D. degree in 1936. Hebb's first wife died following a car accident and he married again in 1937. At the Montreal Neurological Institute he studied the effects of brain surgery. He observed that the brain of a child could recover when a portion of it is removed, but similar damage in an adult might be catastrophic. He deduced the prominent role that external stimulation played in the thought processes of adults, and that a lack of stimulation caused diminished function. Hebb became a professor of psychology at McGill in 1947. He remained there until retirement in 1972.

His book *The Organization of Behavior: A Neuropsychological Theory*, is considered his most important. His theory became known as *Hebbian theory*. To quote from the book: "When an axon of cell A is near enough to excite cell B and repeatedly or persistently takes part in firing it, some growth process or metabolic change takes place in one or both cells such that A's efficiency, as one of the cells firing B, is increased." In other words: *Neurons that fire together wire together*. This concept proved to be influential to psychologists and opened the way for artificial neural networks.

Hebb was successful as a teacher. As a professor, he knew he could not teach motivation, so his goal was only to create the conditions necessary for study. He believed that students should be evaluated on thinking and creating rather than on the ability to recapitulate old ideas. Hebb thought Freud was "not too rigorous." He promoted the objective study of the mind as though it were a biological science. Under his influence McGill University became a prominent center for psychology. Hebb died in 1985, two years after his wife, in Nova Scotia.

Alan Turing (1912–1954)

Alan Turing was born in 1912 in the Maida Vale section of London. His father was a member of the Indian Civil Service and his mother was a daughter of the chief engineer of the Madras Railways. Very early in life Turing showed promise of great abilities. In 1926, at age 14 he attended Sherborne School, an expensive private school in Dorset. Turing was not appreciated by teachers at Sherborne, who emphasized classics and feared that he would be solely a scientific specialist. By 1927, however, he showed unusual ability, solving advanced problems without having taken calculus.

Turing graduated from King's College, Cambridge with a distinguished degree and a dissertation on the central limit theorem in his momentous paper *On Computable Numbers, with an Application to the Entscheidungsproblem* (the halting problem). Here he presented his famous *Turing machine*, a formal and simple device. This was not a practical device, it being much slower than electronic alternatives, but a theoretical computer to solve any problem whose solution can be represented as an algorithm. But according to Turing, it is not possible to decide, algorithmically, whether a given Turing machine will ever halt. Alonzo Church had previously published an equivalent proof using his lambda calculus, but Turing's work was intuitive and accessible.

Most of 1937 and 1938 were spent at Princeton University studying under Alonzo Church, earning a Ph.D. degree in 1938. During the war, Turing was a leader in efforts at Bletchley Park to break German ciphers. He worked on the problem of the German Enigma machine. Within weeks his group had designed an electromechanical machine to help break the Enigma faster than previous attempts. From 1945 to 1947 he presented the first complete design of a stored program computer in the UK. Known as ACE (automatic computing engine), it executed its first program in 1950. Turing conceived of the *Turing test*: A computer could be said to "think" if it could fool an interrogator into thinking keyboard conversation was with a human. In this way he promoted the issue of artificial intelligence.

Turing was homosexual, illegal in the UK in an age of anxiety about Soviet spies who entrapped homosexuals. He was discovered and given a choice between imprisonment or probation with hormonal treatment to reduce libido. He accepted probation but lost his security clearance and his consultancy on cryptographic matters.

A house worker found him dead on June 8, 1954. He apparently died of a cyanide-laced apple, found with a bite taken. But this was never established as technically the cause of death, which was ruled a suicide. His mother insisted that the ingestion was accidental, due to careless storage of chemicals. Others thought that there was a possibility of assassination, due to his knowing much about secret codes and being a security risk.

Turing's main recognition has come posthumously. He is often considered to be the father of modern computer science, with his concept of the algorithm, the Turing machine, the Turing test for artificial intelligence, and practical computer designs such as the ACE and the Manchester Mark I.

Herbert Alexander Simon (1916–2001)

Herbert Alexander Simon was born in 1916 into a Jewish family in Milwaukee, Wisconsin. His father was an electrical engineer from Germany. He attended public school in Milwaukee. The Simon family certainly was not wealthy but was rich in scientific talent. His uncle, Harold Merkel, wrote books on economics and psychology, which Herbert read and enjoyed. Simon received a batchelor of arts degree in 1936 and a Ph.D. degree in 1943 in political science from the University of Chicago.

From 1938 to 1942 Simon directed a research group at the University of California–Berkeley. After that, he taught political science at the Illinois Institute of Technology. Later, Simon was to be associated with various departments at Carnegie Mellon University in Pittsburgh, Pennsylvania, an indication of his multidisciplinary appraoch. Simon concluded that the best way to study problem solving was to simulate it using a computer program.

Simon is considered a pioneer in artificial intelligence, and along with Allen Newell, created the logic theory machine in 1956 and then the general problem solver in 1957. Both programs employed the information processing language with linked list processing invented in part by Simon. Simon was interested in the role of knowledge in expertise. He and colleagues estimated that expertise was the result of learning something like 50,000 pieces of information. A chess master was said to have learned roughly this many patterns. Simon was also interested in how humans learn. He helped develop a theory of learning known as the elementary perceiver and memorizer theory, useful in the field of verbal learning. Later versions were applied to the acquisition of expertise.

He received the Turing Award along with Allen Newell in 1975 for basic contributions to artificial intelligence, the psychology of human cognition, and list processing. Subsequently, he received the Nobel Prize in Economics in 1978, a National Medal of Science in 1986, and the von Neumann Theory Prize in1988. He died in 2001 in Pittsburgh, Pennsylvania.

Richard Feynman (1918–1988)

Richard Phillips Feynman was born on May 11, 1918 in Far Rockaway, Queens, New York. His father encouraged the young Feynman to ask questions to challenge conventional thinking. His mother was his source of a powerful sense of humor. As a child, he delighted in repairing radios and had a talent for engineering. By age 15, he had mastered differential and integral calculus.

In his last year at Far Rockaway High School, Feynman won the New York University Math Championship. He received a bachelor's degree from Massachusetts Institute of Technology in 1939, and was named Putnam Fellow that same year. He obtained a perfect score in mathematics and physics on the entrance exams to Princeton University, an unprecedented achievement. Feynman received a Ph.D. degree from Princeton University in 1942. His thesis applied the principle of stationary action to problems of quantum mechanics.

While researching his Ph.D., Feynman married his first wife. He was persuaded to join the Manhattan Project, the wartime U.S. Army project at Los Alamos developing atomic bombs, because he wanted to make sure that Nazi Germany did not build them first. In addition, his wife had been diagnosed with tuberculosis, a terminal illness at that time, and she resided in a sanatorium in Albuquerque until her death on June 16, 1945.

After the project, he started working as a professor at Cornell University, and it wasn't long before he received other offers. Feynman chose to work at the California Institute of Technology at Pasadena, California, because he enjoyed teaching and wanted to live in a mild climate. He is sometimes called the "Great Explainer" because he took great care to explain topics to his students, producing a series of famous lectures known as the *Feynman Lectures on Physics*. Much of his best work was accomplished at Caltech, where he did research in quantum electrodynamics, for which he was chosen as one of three recipients of the Nobel Prize in Physics for 1965. He developed a way to understand the behavior of subatomic particles using pictorial tools now called *Feynman diagrams*.

He was married twice more, briefly and unsuccessfully. He died of cancer on February 15, 1988.

Rolf Landauer (1927–1999)

Rolf Landauer was born in 1927 in Stuttgart, Germany. He immigrated to the United States in 1938 to escape the Nazi persecution of Jews. He attended Stuyvesant High School in New York City, a science magnet school. After service in the U.S. Navy as an electrician's mate, he advanced to Harvard, where he earned a doctorate in 1950.

He first worked for NASA and then IBM, where he helped manage the Research Division in the 1960s. In 1961 Landauer demonstrated that when information is lost, an associated amount of energy is dissipated as heat. Known today as the *Landauer limit* it applies to computers and communications. Landauer proposed that communications, in theory, can be accomplished without the minimum unavoidable energy use. Dr. Landauer died in 1999 of brain cancer.

Frank Rosenblatt (1928–1969)

Frank Rosenblatt was a computer scientist who devised the perceptron while at Cornell University in 1960. Rosenblatt was a colorful character at Cornell; a good-looking bachelor who drove a classic sports car, he was often seen with his cat Tobermory. He enjoyed mixing with undergraduates. His course on the theory of brain mechanisms drew both engineering and liberal arts students.

Rosenblatt had a professional enemy, Marvin Lee Minsky (1927–☐) of MIT, who crusaded against him and did everything possible to prevent funding for Rosenblatt. Minsky published material arguing that a single layer of perceptrons was not capable of learning to recognize the exclusive OR. Minsky subsequently published material that extended interest in multilayer perceptrons. Not surprisingly, multilayer perceptrons can learn to recognize the exclusive OR. Minsky's argumentative approach delayed the development of artificial neural networks for many years. Rosenblatt died in a boating accident in 1969.

Gordon Earle Moore (1929–   )

Gordon Moore was born in 1929 in San Francisco, California and grew up in nearby Pescadero. He attended San Jose State University, where he met his wife. In 1950 he gained a B.Sc. degree in chemistry from UC Berkeley and then a doctorate in chemistry and physics from Caltech in 1954.

He joined Caltech graduate William Shockley at the Shockley Semiconductor Laboratory division of Beckman Instruments. Sherman Fairchild then attracted Moore to his newly created company, Fairchild Semiconductor Corporation. Moore cofounded Intel Corporation in 1968, serving as executive vice president, president, and then chairman of the board.

Moore was awarded the 2008 IEEE Medal of Honor for "pioneering technical roles in integrated circuit processing, and leadership in the development of MOS memory, the microprocessor computer and the semiconductor industry." He is author of Moore's law, published in 1965 in *Electronics*.

John Joseph Hopfield (1933–   )

Hopfield was born in 1933 to a Polish physicist and his physicist wife. He is one of six children and has three of his own. Hopfield received a B.A. degree from Swarthmore College and in 1958 a Ph.D. degree in physics from Cornell University. He spent two years in the theory group at Bell Laboratories and then taught at UC Berkeley in physics, Princeton University in physics and California Institute of Technology in chemistry and biology. He is now at Princeton, where he is the Howard A. Prior Professor of Molecular Biology.

Hopfield is widely known for his invention of the associative neural network in 1982, now known as the *Hopfield network*.

John R. Anderson (1947–   )

John R. Anderson was born in Vancouver, British Columbia in 1947 in a poor section of the city. His parents encouraged him to attend the University of British Columbia with plans to be a writer, but he became interested in psychology as a quantitative science. Anderson later attended Stanford University, where he worked on programming a computer to simulate human cognition. Here he coauthored a book, *Human Associative Memory*.

Anderson met his wife Stanford and they have two sons. After graduating from Stanford in 1972, Anderson moved to Carnegie Mellon University, attracted there by the work of Allen Newell and Herbert Simon. In 1976, Anderson wrote the book *Language, Memory, and Thought*, in which he presents a theory of higher-level human cognition termed *ACT theory*. The goal was a computer program capable of problem solving and learning: in other words, artificial intelligence. Anderson is the author of many books, including *The Architecture of Cognition* in 1983, in which he defined architecture to include both input–output behavior and physical structure.

Kim Peek (1951–   )

Kim Peek is a savant but is not autistic. He has a photographic memory as well as developmental disabilities. We know him as the inspiration for the character of Raymond Babbit in the movie *Rain Man*. He now lives in Salt Lake City, Utah.

Peek was born with damage to the brain, including damage to the cerebellum, and a missing corpus callosum, the nerve bundle that connects the hemispheres. Also missing are secondary connectors such as the anterior commissure. He did not walk until the age of 4 and still walks in a sidelong way. He cannot button his shirt and has difficulty with ordinary motor skills, presumably due to his damaged cerebellum, which normally coordinates motor activities. Psychologically, Peek scores well below average on general IQ tests.

Since 2004, Peek has demonstrated increasing social skills and likes the attention of being the "real Rain Man." He has started to play the piano, although not a musical prodigy due to limited dexterity, he remembers much and is able to give running spoken commentary on the music as he plays. In listening to recordings, he can distinguish which instruments play which part and can name the composers of music. He also enjoys approaching strangers and showing them his talent for calendar calculations by telling them the day of the week they were born and the news items on the front page of major newspapers that day.

There is speculation that his neurons make other connections in the absence of a corpus callosum resulting in increased memory capacity. According to Peek's father, who acts as his to care given, he was able to memorize things from the age of 16 months. He memorized books and then placed them upside down on the shelf to show that he had done so. He reads a book in about an hour and remembers about 98% of everything. He memorizes vast amounts of information on subjects ranging from history, literature, geography, numbers in sports and music, and dates. He can recall about 12,000 books from memory. Peek has been an object of research at NASA and elsewhere in an attempt to discover how he remembers so much.

Daniel Tammet (1979–)

Daniel Tammet is a British autistic savant with a facility for mathematical problems, sequence memory, and language learning. His mother was a secretary; his father, a steelplate worker. He was born January 31, 1979, one of nine children. As he points out with a smile, 31, 19, 79, and 1979 are prime numbers. Unlike other savants, he has social abilities. But he lives with extraordinary ability and disability, such as the inability to tell right from left or to drive a car. He has to drink his tea at exactly the same time every day. Things have to happen in the same order: brush teeth, take shower, and so on.

As a baby, he banged his head against the wall and cried constantly. His mother would swing him to sleep in a blanket and breastfed him for two years. Doctors thought that he might be understimulated. Then one afternoon in the living room he had an epileptic fit. He was given pills to control his seizures and told to avoid direct sunlight.

In grade school the other children were puzzled by Tammet. At playtime he would rush out, not to play, but to count the leaves in the trees. Later he said: "It sounds silly, but numbers are my friends." As Tammet grew older he developed a need to collect things, such as newspapers. He was shy, but his teachers were always protective. He met his wife, a software engineer, online. They live happily on a quiet cul-de-sac. An aspect of Tammet's autism that causes problems is his lack of empathy. For examples he asked all sorts of questions about faith and death of a friend who had just lost her mother. He says it's his condition—no taboos.

Daniel relates how he experiences numbers as colors or sensations. He claims that in his mind each number, up to 10,000, has its own unique shape and feel. He claims that he can sense whether a number is prime or composite and that he can see the results of calculations as landscapes in his mind. Allan Snyder at the Australian National University said of Tammet: "Savants can't usually tell us how they do what they do. It just comes to them. Daniel can. He describes what he sees in his head. That's why he's exciting. He could be the Rosetta Stone."

He was the subject of a documentary in the UK titled "*The Boy with the Incredible Brain*," broadcast recently under the title *Brain Man*. It showed highlights of his feat of recalling pi and his meeting with Kim Peek, another famous savant. At one moment in the show Peek hugged Tammet and told him, "some day you may be as brilliant as me."

He lives on the Kent coast but never goes near the beach. There are too many pebbles to count. The thought of a mathematical problem with no solution makes him uncomfortable. Trips to the supermarket give too much mental stimulus. He has to look at every shape and texture, every price and arrangement of fruit and vegetables. He cannot work 9 to 5. Instead, he has set up an e-mail business on his own, offering courses in language learning, numeracy, and literacy.

FOR FURTHER STUDY

General Science

John Anderson, *The Architecture of Cognition*, Harvard University Press, Cambridge, MA, 1983.

Daniel C. Dennett, *Consciousness Explained*, Back Bay Books, New York, 1991.

Richard P. Feynman, *Feynman Lectures on Computation* (edited by Tony Hey and Robin W. Allen), Perseus Publishing, Cambridge, MA, 1996.

Ray R. Hassin, James S. Uleman, and John A. Bargh, Editors, *The New Unconscious*, Oxford University Press, New York, 2005.

George Johnson, *A Shortcut Through Time: The Path to the Quantum Computer*, Alfred A. Knopf, New York, 2003.

Eric R. Kandel, *In Search of Memory: The Emergence of a New Science of Mind*, W.W. Norton, New York, 2006.

Anne D. Novitt-Moreno, *How Your Brain Works*, Ziff Davis, San Francisco, 1995.

Matthew M. Radmanesh, *The Gateway to Understanding: Electrons to Waves and Beyond*, AuthorHouse, Bloomington, IN, 2005.

John J. Ratey, *A User's Guide to the Brain*, Pantheon Books, New York, 2001.

Richard Restak, *Naked Brain: How the Emerging Neurosociety Is Changing How We Live, Work, and Love*, Harmony Books, New York, 2006.

Daniel L. Schacter, *Forgotten Ideas, Neglected Pioneers: Richard Semon and the Story of Memory*, Psychology Press, New York, 2001.

H.A. Simon, *Sciences of the Artificial*, 3rd ed., MIT Press, Cambridge, MA, 1996.

Robert Sylwester, *How To Explain a Brain: An Educator's Handbook of Brain Terms and Cognitive Processes*, Corwin Press, Thousand Oaks, CA, 2005.

Daniel M. Wegner, *The Illusion of Conscious Will*, MIT Press, Cambridge, MA, 2002.

Perspectives in Circuits and Systems

Gerd Sommerhoff, *Logic of the Living Brain*, Wiley, New York, 1974.

Leslie G. Valiant, *Circuits of the Mind*, Oxford University Press, New York, 1994.

Textbooks

Henry Gleitman, *Basic Psychology*, W.W. Norton, New York, 1987.

Simon Haykin, *Neural Networks: A Comprehensive Foundation*, Macmillan, New York, 1994.

John G. Nicholls, A. Robert Martin, and Bruce G. Wallace, *From Neuron to Brain*, 3rd ed., Sinauer Associates, Sunderland, MA, 1992.

Milan Paunovic and Mordechay Schlesinger, *Fundamentals of Electrochemical Deposition*, 2nd ed., Wiley, Hoboken, NJ, 2006.

Ben Streetman and Sanjay Banerjee, *Solid State Devices*, 6th ed., Prentice Hall, Upper Saddle River, NJ, 2005.

Research Compendiums

Michael A. Arbib, Editor, *The Handbook of Brain Theory and Neural Networks*, MIT Press, Cambridge, MA, 2003.

Michael A. Arbib and Jeffrey S. Grethe, Editors, *Computing the Brain: A Guide to Neuroinformatics*, Academic Press, San Diego, CA, 2001.

John H. Byrne and James L. Roberts, Editors, *From Molecules to Networks: An Introduction to Cellular and Molecular Neuroscience*, Academic Press, San Diego, CA, 2004.

Christof Koch and Idan Segev, Editors, *Methods in Neuronal Modeling: From Ions to Networks*, MIT Press, Cambridge, MA, 1989.

INDEX

Human Memory Modeled with Standard Analog and Digital Circuits:
Inspiration for Man-made Computers, By John Robert Burger
Copyright © 2009 John Wiley & Sons, Inc.

Printed in the United States
By Bookmasters